Self-Organizing Federalism

Collaborative Mechanisms to Mitigate Institutional Collective Action Dilemmas

This book investigates the self-organizing responses of governments and interests to the institutional collective action (ICA) dilemmas of particular concern to students of federalism, urban governance, and regional management of natural resources. ICA dilemmas arise in fragmented systems whenever decisions made by one independent formal authority do not consider costs or benefits imposed on others.

The ICA framework analyzes networks, joint projects, partnerships, and other mechanisms developed by affected parties to mitigate ICA decision externalities. These mechanisms play a widespread but little understood role in federalist systems by reshaping incentives to encourage coordination/cooperation.

The empirical studies of urban service delivery and regional integration of regional resource management address three questions: How does a given mechanism mitigate costs of uncoordinated decisions? What incentives do potential members have to create the mechanism? How do incentives induced by the mitigating mechanism affect its sustainability in a changing environment and its adaptability to other ICA dilemmas?

Richard C. Feiock's current research on the roles of networks and local institutions in land use governance is supported by the National Science Foundation and the Lincoln Institute of Land Policy. His previous books include *Institutional Constraints and Local Government* (2001), *City-County Consolidation and Its Alternatives* (2004), and *Metropolitan Governance: Conflict, Competition and Cooperation* (2004). His work has appeared in leading journals, including *Public Administration Review*, the *Journal of Public Administration Research and Theory*, *Journal of Politics*, and *American Journal of Political Science*.

John T. Scholz's current research analyzes the problems of developing and maintaining cooperative solutions to collective action problems, emphasizing the role of policy networks, private partnerships, and collaborative government programs in resolving collective problems involved in resource management. His work has been supported by numerous grant awards from the National Science Foundation and has appeared in leading journals, including the *American Journal of Political Science*, *Journal of Politics*, and *American Political Science Review*. He co-edited *Adaptive Governance and Water Conflict* (with Bruce Stiftel, 2005).

Self-Organizing Federalism

Collaborative Mechanisms to Mitigate Institutional Collective Action Dilemmas

Edited by

RICHARD C. FEIOCK

Florida State University

JOHN T. SCHOLZ

Florida State University

CAMBRIDGE
UNIVERSITY PRESS

CAMBRIDGE UNIVERSITY PRESS
Cambridge, New York, Melbourne, Madrid, Cape Town, Singapore,
São Paulo, Delhi, Dubai, Tokyo

Cambridge University Press
32 Avenue of the Americas, New York, NY 10013-2473, USA

www.cambridge.org
Information on this title: www.cambridge.org/9780521764933

First published 2010

Printed in the United States of America

A catalog record for this publication is available from the British Library.

Library of Congress Cataloging in Publication Data

Self-organizing federalism : collaborative mechanisms to mitigate institutional
collective action dilemmas / edited by Richard C. Feiock, John T. Scholz.
  p. cm.
Includes bibliographical references and index.
ISBN 978-0-521-76493-3 (hardback)
1. Public administration – United States. 2. Intergovernmental cooperation – United
States. 3. Public-private sector cooperation – United States. 4. Central-local
government relations – United States. 5. Federal government – United States. I.
Feiock, Richard C. II. Scholz, John T.

JK421.S46 2009
352.3′7–dc22   2008055946

ISBN 978-0-521-76493-3 Hardback

Contents

List of Figures

List of Tables

Contributors

Simon A. Andrew
Department of Public Administration
University of North Texas
Denton, TX 76203

Ramiro Berardo
Department of Political Science
University of Arizona
Tucson, AZ 85721

Kenneth N. Bickers
Department of Political Science
University of Colorado
Boulder, CO 80309

Richard C. Feiock
Askew School of Public Administration and Policy
Florida State University
Tallahassee, FL 32306

Adam Douglas Henry
Division of Public Administration
West Virginia University
Morgantown, WV 26506

Bryan D. Jones
Department of Government
University of Texas
Austin, TX 78712

Mark Lubell
Department of Environmental Science and Policy
University of California, Davis
Davis, CA 95616

Mike McCoy
Department of Environmental Science and Policy
Information Center for the Environment
University of California, Davis
Davis, CA 95616

Megan Mullin
Department of Political Science
Temple University
Philadelphia, PA 19122

Stephanie Post
Center for Civic Research and Design
Rice University
Houston, TX 77251

John T. Scholz
Department of Political Science
Florida State University
Tallahassee, FL 32306

Manoj Shrestha
Political Science and Bureau of Public Affairs Research
University of Idaho
Moscow, ID 83843

Robert M. Stein
Department of Political Science
Rice University
Houston, TX 77251

Annette Steinacker
School of Politics and Economics
Claremont Graduate University
Claremont, CA 91711

Paul W. Thurner
Department of Political Science
LMU Munich
Munich, Germany

Christopher M. Weible
School of Public Affairs
University of Colorado, Denver
Denver, CO 80217

Andrew B. Whitford
Department of Public Administration and Policy
School of Public and International Affairs
University of Georgia
Athens, GA 30602

Preface

Fragmentation of formal authority and the self-organizing activities to resolve the collective problems imposed by fragmentation are enduring traits of governance in the United States (Tocqueville 2003). As policy problems and underlying resource systems become increasingly interconnected, the decisions of one government or independent agency inevitably affect outcomes of concern to the other units. In contemporary societies, the scope and magnitude of unconsidered positive and negative externalities increase as technologies extend the nature and number of public goods while growing economies and populations strain the limits and interconnections of natural systems, particularly in areas where rapid development and growth exceed the capacities of natural systems and therefore dramatically magnify interactions between different policies and authorities (Scholz and Stiftel 2005). This imposes collective action dilemmas on government authorities similar to those much-studied problems for individuals. The costs that these institutional collective action (ICA) problems impose on local actors have generated intensive search for institutions that can coordinate decisions across interdependent policy arenas without threatening the stability and advantages of our decentralized federalist political system.

Recognition of this problem brought the editors together to ask what mechanisms have evolved for dealing with fragmented authority and the resultant collective action problems, and what we know about them. Stated another way, how can local authorities organize themselves to obtain collective benefits of policy coordination when faced with uncertainty and commitment problems associated with collective dilemmas?

Feiock and Scholz have been independently working on issues related to this question for several years. The institutional collective action framework developed in this volume integrates theoretical approaches developed in the editors' studies of urban governance and regional management of common pool resources. Like politics, in many ways "all policy is local." During both policy making and implementation, it is at the local level that abstract policy conflicts become translated into concrete alternatives that demand resolution. It is at this level that the unanticipated interactions across governments and policy arenas are discovered and dealt with by acts of commission or, more normally, by omission. And it is at this level that the inevitable trade-offs required to coordinate policies can potentially optimize the "public value" of collaboration by taking advantage of specific local conditions (Bardach 1998).

Feiock's research focuses on metropolitan areas, analyzing both formal structures and voluntary institutions for resolving public goods and economic development problems. Metropolitan areas provide arguably the best laboratory for studying fragmentation and the resulting policy interactions. Feiock's work on the role of local political institutions in mediating transaction costs in development and service delivery contribute to the framework we develop here (Feiock 2002, 2004). Extensions of his initial work provide a transaction cost explanation of institutional collective action that is applied to investigate how information and agency problems impede the development of joint development ventures (Feiock 2007; Feiock, Steinacker, and Park 2009).

Scholz's work focuses on local policy networks and partnerships in the local integration of natural resource management. Estuaries, the geographic areas where rivers meet oceans, have also provided a productive venue for investigation of institutional collective action. Estuaries are increasingly evolving into important new policy arenas as economic and population growth in them places greater stress on water resources (Scholz and Stiftel 2005). As resource use approaches thresholds in the natural system, decisions by the multiple specialized agencies with formal authority over different aspects of water policies impose growing positive and negative externalities on each other.

Scholz and his associates have found that watershed partnerships emerge where the benefits of coordination are highest and the costs of developing and maintaining the partnership are lowest (Lubell et al. 2002), further developing a transaction cost theory similar to Feiock's. Scholz's work extends this approach to informal local policy networks as well. He finds that regions with well-established local policy networks

and partnerships increase both EPA enforcement and compliance by permit holders with the Clean Water Act (Scholz and Wang 2006), even
though the networks have no formal role in this federal program. Also,
he finds that federal and state policies can affect transaction costs and thus
change the shape of local networks (Schneider et al. 2003). These analyses
introduce many of the research questions and analytic techniques that are
applied in this volume.

We began integrating these research agendas in a joint graduate seminar
and in jointly advising several dissertations. After much discussion we concluded that our two approaches were studying the same basic phenomenon
of government fragmentation, that a growing number of other studies were
addressing this same phenomenon without recognizing the similarity, and
that the collaborative institutions we studied (from policy networks and
joint projects to regional partnerships) were best studied as part of a wider
continuum of self-organizing mechanisms to deal with fragmentation. To
create a common approach for these disparate studies, we then organized a
workshop on self-organizing governance in which the empirical studies
presented by several young scholars from Florida State University (FSU)
and other institutions were discussed by prominent senior scholars. Our
small, intensive workshop ultimately produced the current volume.

This symposium on "Networks and Coordination of Fragmented
Authority" was held in the beautiful and historic Wakulla Springs Florida
Lodge in February 2007 and focused on two tasks that we believe necessary to make progress in this arena. First, we sought to develop a more
integrative theoretical perspective that could pull together theoretical
components and analytical tools used to study these institutions. We
develop the core questions of this perspective in the introduction to this
volume and demonstrate their application in the empirical studies and
conclusion.

Second, because we have been particularly interested in understanding
those institutions that involve self-organizing efforts, we focused our
efforts and attention on the kinds of institutions that have developed
primarily from the efforts of actors directly confronting institutional collective action problems of unconsidered impacts imposed by one actor on
another. To understand any of the various coordinating mechanisms we
considered, we needed to understand how the institution reshaped the
motivations of actors in a way that mitigated the consequences of agency
externalities.

Considerable excitement was generated by connections uncovered
among the problems of institutional development in regional common

pool resource management and urban service delivery. This enthusiasm and desire to speak to larger issues in political science and public policy related to these issues provided the catalyst for the chapters presented in this volume.

This volume begins to fill a gap in the literature and our understanding of the self-organizing aspects of governance that are particularly important in the American federalist system, and the motivations of actors that enable the development and sustainability of self-organizing institutions. Our focus on self-organizing institutional solutions reflects both pragmatic and theoretical concerns. From a pragmatic standpoint, many of the institutional forms we describe are permissive in the sense that central government provides only a basic enabling legislation in which interested actors can themselves determine who can participate and how much authority to cede to the institution. This may be a wise policy strategy to the extent that problems of fragmentation are heterogeneous across geographic units and policy arenas, since the ability to custom design the institution to the specific policy and metropolitan area is likely to enhance performance in comparison to a standardized, restrictively mandated institutional solution. However, understanding and improving the performance of these custom-designed institutions will require an understanding of the forces that shape them and determine their capabilities.

From a theoretical standpoint, we are interested in the innate ability of federal systems to resolve newly emerging institutional collective action dilemmas. Can self-organizing solutions play a major role in enhancing the stability and performance of the formal authority system? We think that the self-organizing institutions of the kind we study in this volume are a vital but understudied aspect of political systems and more than a passing footnote in the U.S. federalist system. Thirty years ago Heclo (1978) observed that informal, self-organized policy networks emerged to coordinate the decisions of federal agencies with overlapping authorities and no formal means of coordination. This volume seeks to make a similar contribution to understanding the problems of fragmented authority in federal systems, particularly at the local and regional levels, by advancing a general perspective on the role of self-organizing governance institutions in mitigating problems arising from fragmented authority.

We analyze the institutions designed to resolve two central dilemmas of governance – the provision of public goods and the governance of common pool resources. The two policy arenas that we have selected present some of the most pressing challenges for self-organizing governance and have provided the venue for considerable institutional innovation. They are also the areas that have generated the most theoretical and empirical innovation in the study of institutional collective action.

Studies of collective action and transaction costs typically assume that institutions are exogenously determined by some statutory authority. Instead, we analyze the dynamics by which the institutional structures emerge, identify the forces that generate institutional solutions, and investigate how resultant changes in motivations and problem definition might induce broader changes in institutions and policy outcomes. This approach allows us to understand the strengths, possibilities, and limitations of self-organizing mechanisms in resolving specific sets of externalities and interdependencies, and to better understand how they fit within existing statutory attempts to resolve problems of fragmentation.

Some initial progress on answering these questions was made 30 years ago when the study of local institutions and fragmented authority was central to the fields of political science and public administration (Ostrom, Tiebout, and Warren 1961; Bish 1971; Ostrom, Bish, and Ostrom 1988). Unfortunately, not much progress has been made on these questions since that time, as the study of local politics has not kept up with theoretical and empirical advancements in other areas of political science. We hope to return the issues of local governance to a central position in political science for the study of American institutions.

This volume is designed for advanced undergraduates and graduate students interested in the broader issues of governance, mechanism design, federalism, and collective action. In particular, we focus on the issues of concern to scholars and practitioners in the subfields of metropolitan governance and collaborative management of natural resources who recognize the importance of expanding both subfields and the need for a common approach to the shared issues. The first and last chapters by the editors together with the Whitford, Steinacker, and Jones chapters provide a common theoretical overview of the full spectrum of mechanisms that have evolved to mitigate collective dilemmas arising from fragmentation of authority in federalist systems. The emphasis is on understanding the role of self-organizing mechanisms that preserve considerable autonomy of local units while enhancing collaboration, coordination, and cooperation on particular policies and projects.

While all chapters address the common concern with self-organizing mechanisms, they approach the common concern in the context of specific issues of metropolitan and regional governance. The chapters by Steinacker, Jones, Andrew, Shrestha, and Bickers et al. specifically focus on issues of metropolitan governance and as a unit explore the important roles of self-organizing mechanisms in the field of urban studies. The chapters by Weible, Berardo, and Lubell et al. provide three different approaches to the study of collaboration and collaborative democracy relating to the governance of natural resources. The chapter by Thurner illustrates the breadth of these common concerns outside the American context, focusing on the problems of organizing collaboration at the central level in the context of the European Union (EU).

This book's unique theoretical approach and analytical synthesis focus on the self-organizing activities of governments and agencies in a federal system to deal with problems of fragmented authority, which makes it a useful classroom text for courses in urban politics, intergovernmental relations, environmental management, and public policy. Our primary concern is with the kinds of mechanisms that can mitigate externalities by coordinating the decisions of all related authorities. In doing so, we bridge the literatures of political science, public administration, urban affairs, and environmental policy. As such, the book provides an excellent text for advanced undergraduates in several disciplines; MPA, MPP, and PhD courses; as well as a resource for empirical scholars.

To understand the evolution of these mechanisms for mitigating ICAs, our inquiry focuses on three key questions about each one: How does it resolve ICAs? What are the incentives of participants to develop and sustain the mechanism? What are its impacts on other ICAs? These questions are woven throughout the book to create a consistent narrative. This pedagogical device makes the volume accessible to students at a range of levels. The target audience reaches beyond the undergraduate political science and policy courses and MPA courses in public administration to PhD curricula in both fields.

One of the major purposes of this volume is to introduce a range of available techniques needed to study self-organizing activities. All the empirical studies in Parts Two and Three illustrate a range of advanced techniques for studying the role of informal networks in the American federalist system, with a focus on developing an intuitive understanding of how the technique can be used to test theoretical propositions. References to more technical sources are included to allow interested scholars to apply these techniques to their own problems. Thus, this volume provides a valuable resource for applied researchers. The chapters in Parts Two and Three include original empirical analyses, but each chapter also synthesizes contemporary literatures that have not before been brought together in a single, generally accessible volume.

The Wakulla Springs symposium was sponsored by the DeVoe Moore Center for the Study of Critical Issues in Economic Policy and Government at Florida State University, whose generous financial and administrative support made the symposium and this volume possible. The contributors to this volume were participants in the symposium, and their discussion played a critical role in the development of the perspective provided in the first and last chapters. A number of colleagues, students, and other scholars participated in the symposium and provided very valuable comments on the work. We particularly wish to thank Charles Barrilleaux, Elizabeth Gerber, Keith Ihlanfeldt, Bruce Stiftel, Carol Weissert, and Kaifeng Yang. We also thank the DeVoe Moore Center staff Judy Kirk, Kathy Makinen, and Susan Ihlanfeldt for assistance with the conference arrangements and preparation of the manuscript. At a more personal level we wish to thank Ruth Feiock and Claudia Scholz for their tolerant support of the project.

PART ONE

SELF-ORGANIZING VERSUS CENTRALIZED SOLUTIONS TO INSTITUTIONAL COLLECTIVE ACTION PROBLEMS

Theoretical Considerations

I

Self-Organizing Governance of Institutional Collective Action Dilemmas

An Overview

Richard C. Feiock and John T. Scholz

Dramatic change has occurred in the last two decades in how governments carry out public policies. In our complex, interconnected, and information-dense world, policy problems increasingly transcend the jurisdictional boundaries of governments and their specialized agencies at all levels (Scholz and Stiftel 2005; Donahue 2006). Examples abound of agencies working across jurisdictions, across levels of government, across agencies, and across sectors (Bardach 1998; Milward and Provan 2000; Linden 2002). Rhodes (2007) argues that in Britain privatization and dispersion of authority have transferred policy coordination functions from the central state to decentralized and informal policy networks. Kettl (2002) describes this as a "transformation of governance" characterized in the United States by the emergence of collaborative institutions in which multiple agencies, governments, and other stakeholders work together to solve problems that affect them.

This volume introduces and develops the institutional collective action (ICA) framework to understand the challenges for governance imposed by the forces of globalization that exacerbate the negative consequences of fragmentation of authority, particularly in federalist systems in which fragmentation is an inevitable aspect of the allocation of formal authority. ICA applies the framework of collective action, initially developed to explain individual behavior, to institutionally defined composite actors such as local governments or government agencies and their constituencies. Fragmented authority produces dilemmas for institutional actors whenever decisions by one authority affect outcomes of other authorities, particularly when independent decisions by each authority lead to poor policy outcomes not favored by anyone: uncoordinated investments by local governments create excessive capacity and expensive service provisions; one authority's regulations undermine the effectiveness of another's; one agency's project competes with that of another agency rather than complementing it.

Our primary goal is to understand the broad range of formal and informal institutions developed to mitigate ICA dilemmas. To do so, we extend the political economy perspective of other recent studies that analyze the critical role of informal institutions in maintaining the stability and viability of the formal, constitutionally defined system of authority in federalist systems. Filippov, Shvetsova, and Ordeshook (2004) argue that the constitution defines the formal rules of governance, but the party structure and social context in a country determine how these rules work in practice. Bednar (2008) demonstrates that formal institutional safeguards need informal institutions that embed them in the social context in order to be effective. While these studies focus on major sources of conflict and disintegration that threaten the stability of the governing system, we focus on the wide range of more common ICA dilemmas that undermine the efficiency of the system.

Our approach recognizes the importance of stability – indeed, the critical separation of powers that provides the fundamental federalist safeguard for stability is a primary source of ICA dilemmas. However, we equally recognize the need of the system to respond effectively to the myriad of ICA dilemmas continuously emerging at all levels of the federalist system, and to do so without relying unduly on centralized coordination mechanisms that might challenge the stability of the system. Consolidation, for example, provides a traditional federalist mechanism for resolving disputes arising from overlapping jurisdictions; consolidate fragmented local government units into a metropolitan government, for example, or consolidate all homeland security functions into a single federal department. Consolidation may mitigate the ICA dilemma by eliminating independent authorities but at the cost of creating great uncertainties about the balance of authority between levels of government (cf. Bednar 2008), disrupting ongoing governance activities, and transforming the ICA dilemma into an intraorganizational dilemma that may be no easier to resolve (see *Whitford* – italics will be used throughout to indicate references to chapters in this volume).

Given the problems associated with consolidation of authority, the perennial concern with fragmentation and resultant government inefficiencies has produced an array of institutional solutions that mitigate ICA dilemmas with fewer disturbances to the existing allocation of authority. These mitigating institutions change over time but utilize surprisingly similar mechanisms across different policy and theoretical subfields.

In the study of urban and metropolitan governance, for example, governmental consolidation was the primary mechanism advanced to address ICA dilemmas in public service provision from the early twentieth century through the 1960s. This was gradually replaced by calls for more multi-tiered regional and overlapping governments and decentralized community control (Bish and Ostrom 1973) and calls for public entrepreneurs and innovative community-based solutions driven by the reinventing government movement in the 1990s (Osborne and Gaebler 1992). The last decade has marked the emergence of a "new regionalist" approach to metropolitan service dilemmas that emphasizes externalities and inequalities in metropolitan areas (Lowery 1998), the economic and environmental interconnectedness of metropolitan regions (Orfield 1997; Barnes and Ledebur 1998), and the role of voluntary cooperation through metropolitan planning organizations, regional planning councils, and regional partnership organizations (Savitch and Vogel 1996; Katz 2000; Stephens and Wikstrom 2000). In the field of natural resource management, the dramatic consolidation of regulatory authority over environmental issues at the federal level in the 1970s eroded slightly during the Reagan years and has been overshadowed more recently by the development of community-based ecosystem management partnerships that emphasize broad participation and consensus-based authority (Rabe 1986).

We focus primarily on this alternative set of institutions in part because centrally imposed solutions have known limitations, in part because the possibilities and limitations of collaborative, self-organizing solutions are less understood, and in part because both centrally imposed and self-organizing solutions can best be understood as part of a single integrated perspective on mechanisms to resolve ICA dilemmas that we see as a central feature of federalist governance.

For us, a critical aspect of these alternative institutions is their reliance on self-organizing actions by affected authorities and stakeholders. We refer to the emergence of these institutions by the title of this volume, *self-organizing federalism*, which we define as the endogenous development and maintenance of institutional mechanisms that mitigate a recognized ICA dilemma by those directly affected by the dilemma. For analytic clarity we distinguish between the actual institutions discussed above and *mechanisms* that, like Weber's "ideal types," refer to the critical abstract properties shared by actual institutions that are relevant to the ICA analysis. We want to understand how self-organizing mechanisms differ in their ability to resolve different ICA dilemmas and how they affect the distribution of the gains of cooperation. Given the limited ability of central actors to impose solutions on even a small fraction of ICA dilemmas, we also need to know how likely each mechanism is to emerge and provide a stable, self-supporting institutional solution based on the self-organizing activities of those affected. Our concern with ICA dilemmas leads to our interest in mitigating mechanisms that range from fully self-organizing to those primarily imposed by central authorities. We want to know when and how they emerge, what they do, and how they affect policy outcomes.

THE INSTITUTIONAL COLLECTIVE ACTION FRAMEWORK

Institutional collective action focuses explicitly on the externalities of choices in fragmented systems in which decisions by one independent formal authority do not consider the costs or benefits that these decisions impose on the constituencies and policy outcomes of concern to other authorities. Thus ICA is concerned with a higher order collective action problem among authorities, some of which were created to govern lower order collective action problems. Although a given ICA dilemma can be very different from the lower order dilemmas that the concerned authorities were created to govern, they also involve the same types of problems associated with public goods, natural monopolies and economies of scale, management of common-pool resources, and so on, as elaborated in *Steinacker*. ICA considers and compares the impact of alternative mechanisms introduced to mitigate the adverse consequences of these decision externalities. Can these mechanisms produce efficient outcomes closer to the Pareto-optimal contract curve, such that no actor affected by the dilemma can be made better off without making others worse off? If so, how are the gains achieved through cooperation divided among the affected parties?

While the efficiency, fairness, and sustainability of outcomes are our primary interest, ICA assumes that these outcomes emerge as a product of individual self-interest as shaped by the structure of formal authority (North 1990). For example, the fragmentation of authority is partly a product of unresolved political disputes in which legislative losers attempt to minimize the effectiveness of agencies authorized to implement the contested legislation, and the continuing political disputes will affect efforts to mitigate such fragmentation (Moe 1991). Furthermore, constituents dominating one political arena are likely to resist efforts from stakeholders in other affected political arenas to constrain their choices (Scholz and Stiftel 2005). Finally, the type of mechanism and specific rules governing its operations will generally impact the relative gains from cooperation and are therefore likely to cause conflict during the development of the mechanism. Thus, in addition to efficiency, ICA is concerned with conflicts that affect the feasibility of developing and institutionalizing any mitigating mechanism, the resilience of alternative coordinating mechanisms under the stress of ongoing conflicts, and the impact of emergent mechanisms on the stability and adaptive capabilities of the full array of formal government institutions.

The approach draws insights from actor-centered (Scharpf 1997) and institutional analysis and development (Ostrom 1990) frameworks. Our concern with alternative institutions is reflected in studies of public sector demand, production and management problems (Bish and Ostrom 1973), and interlocal agreements and grant coalitions in urban governance (Stein 1990; Bickers and Stein 2004; Post 2004). Recent work incorporates concepts from agency and social network theories into the ICA approach to extend it to a broader set of collective decisions relating to urban service provision (Feiock 2004, 2007), economic development (Feiock, Steinacker, and Park 2009), and regional management of natural resources (Lubell et al. 2002; Schneider et al. 2003; Scholz, Berardo, and Kile, 2008).

Institutions as Actors

The theoretical framework of ICA builds directly on the extensive collective action literature concerned with situations in which individual incentives lead to collective outcomes not desired by any of the individuals. In some sense, only individuals are capable of action, yet in both law and practice we know that individuals often act in the name of or in the interest of a group or organization. We investigate collective action as it affects composite or "institutional" actors. The institutional actors can include collective entities dependent on and guided by the preferences of members (i.e., coalitions, clubs, movements, and associations) and more autonomous corporate actors, but our focus is primarily on local, state, and federal governments, their specialized field offices, and organized interests concerned with their activities in a given geographic area.

Composite actors are defined by institutionally determined position, authority, and aggregation rules (Ostrom 2005). Position rules specify the broad capabilities and responsibilities of officials. Authority rules specify the actions those participants may, must, or must not do. Aggregation rules determine how member preferences are aggregated and whether decisions of specific participants are necessary for action at any given node in a decision process. These rules solve the problem of matching empirically observable individual behavior with the institutionally defined unit of reference on whose behalf action is taken. For example, in cities the mayor and council have the ability to conclude legally binding agreements for citizens of the jurisdiction, which is critical to the interlocal agreements studied in this volume by *Andrew* and *Shrestha*. In government agencies, department directors and other officials have specified authority to commit the agency to contracts or agreements, providing a basis for the regional collaboratives studied by *Lubell, Henry, and McCoy* and the joint water projects studied by *Berardo*.

This conception of ICA implies capability for intentional action above the level of individuals. Whether or not one believes that only individuals have intentions, the capability to act at an institutional level is the product of internal interactions within institutional actors. This requires us to pay attention to interactions between and within institutional actors. Principal-agent problems arise from difficulties in aggregating preferences of members of the institutional unit and preference divergence between members and representatives authorized to negotiate collective agreements (Feiock 2007). For example, *Bickers et al.* investigate the impact of electoral incentives on the willingness of local government officials to collaborate with their neighboring counterparts to resolve mutual problems. The capacity for strategic action in collective choice situations depends on the extent of preference integration among members of the composite actor and capacity for conflict resolution when preferences diverge, a point elaborated in *Thurner*'s analysis of the constitutional deliberations of the European Union (EU) and in *Steinacker*'s discussion of agency costs.

Policy Arenas, ICA Dilemmas, and Transaction Costs

The framework described to this point could be applied to any policy arena and any type of conflict, but this volume focuses specifically on ICA *dilemmas* in which institutions acting together can potentially achieve outcomes that are preferred to the best outcomes that institutions could achieve acting individually. The great conflicts that threaten the stability of the system are generally not of this sort, and our analysis has little to say in general about existing zero-sum conflicts in which one side's gain means a loss to the other side. The dilemmas we are interested in can of course degenerate into zero-sum conflicts, particularly when alternative solutions are restricted, and can be drawn in to other zero-sum conflicts involving overlapping policy actors (*Jones*). Given our concern with dilemmas rather than zero-sum conflicts, we focus on the barriers to mutually advantageous coordinated action, which are represented in political economy by the transaction costs required for achieving joint agreements.

The ICA dilemma is shaped by the existing set of statutes and case law – the authoritative, externally imposed rules in a given policy arena. These rules determine the specific authority of each actor in the arena, which, in combination with the underlying interdependencies of the systems being governed, determines the incentives facing each actor. The rules also shape strategies available to the actors in their individual efforts to avoid negative externalities and capitalize on positive externalities. We assume that all actors follow their individual self-interest by selecting the available strategy that most enhances their (generally short-term) interests. In the absence of mitigating institutions, the dilemma by definition leads to outcomes of individual decisions that are collectively inefficient.

This framework can be applied at any level of government; the analyses in this volume alone range from service provision dilemmas among local governments to constitutional development issues facing the European Union. However, the bulk of our empirical studies are drawn from the literatures of metropolitan public service provision and regional natural resource management primarily because these two streams of research have paid considerable attention to problems of fragmentation and collaboration.

In metropolitan service provision and infrastructure development, the history of municipal incorporation and special district formations produced a checkerboard pattern of local governments that encouraged local units to provide customized mixes of public goods to suit the tastes of their constituencies (Burns 1994). One consequence is positive and negative externalities imposed by each city upon its neighbors. For example, a common ICA dilemma among local governments arises if the small size of governments is inefficient for production of the goods each government wishes to provide, and interlocal agreements to share services can provide mutual advantages (*Andrew, Shrestha*). Service production externalities and fragmented authority in metropolitan areas have long been central to fields of political science and public administration (Ostrom et al., 1961; Bish 1971), but they have been neglected in contemporary studies of urban politics, limiting the contribution of the urban subfield to political science (Clingermayer and Feiock 2001; Sapotichne, Jones, and Wolfe 2007).

In regional management of natural resources, the traditional pattern of creating new agencies at different levels of the federal system to oversee each newly discovered use of a resource has fragmented authority over natural systems that do not match the jurisdictional boundaries of these agencies. Scholz and Stiftel (2005) argue that agencies' success in encouraging new uses of the resources they manage, combined with an accelerating pace of development and population growth, has pushed local ecosystems in many regions beyond sustainable thresholds, dramatically magnifying the impacts one agency's decisions have on other agencies and their local clients that share common natural systems. The joint forces of economic development and population growth have exacerbated interdependencies that went unnoticed when population and development stress on natural systems were less of an issue. In response, new collaborative institutions have proliferated along with new studies of these institutions (*Berardo*; Lubell et al. 2002). For example, a city's parks and recreation department project may be combined with a state fish and wildlife commission habitat restoration project to their mutual advantage, while an upstream sewage treatment facility approved by a state environmental agency may impose costs on both agencies if there is no coordinated planning of the two projects.

In both cases, the inevitable fragmentation of authority and consequent externalities do not inevitably lead to inefficiency. Coase (1960) argued that externalities would not result in market inefficiencies as long as property rights were clear and affected parties could costlessly negotiate a joint outcome – that is, as long as coordination among all parties affected by an externality was very easy. For example, as *Andrew* and *Shrestha* note, if city A can easily and securely contract with city B to provide some service that is cheaper to produce in greater volume, then city B can safely invest in the required larger facility to supply both A and B, and both cities can benefit from the resultant lower costs. Externalities only lead to inefficient outcomes when transaction costs prevent affected parties from coming to agreement – the mutually advantageous agreement will not develop without potentially costly reassurances to both A and B that neither will exploit the other – B will not take advantage of its control over city A's service, and A will not seek alternatives that would undermine B's investment.

Transaction cost analysis provides a systematic means to consider the many barriers that prevent authorities from reaching coordinated decisions: information costs limit the range of options being considered by boundedly rational actors, negotiation costs limit actors from reaching agreement on the limited options they know, and enforcement costs limit the willingness to reach risky agreements and the ability to make credible commitments. Higher transaction costs impose greater difficulty in mitigating the ICA dilemma. *Steinacker* analyzes these costs systematically for the major types of ICA dilemmas, and other chapters in this volume evaluate transaction costs for the specific ICA dilemma being analyzed.

Whether analyzing service provision or resource management, the initial step in applying the ICA framework is to identify the relevant actors, the nature of the dilemma they face, and hence the problems of coming to agreement. How many authorities are involved, and how many of their constituencies could potentially gain from coordinated decisions? How large are the impacts of positive or negative externalities both in absolute terms and relative to the resources controlled by the authorities? How homogeneous are the related populations in terms of resources and impacts from existing externalities? Can solutions be developed along a continuum that could equitably divide the potential gains from mutual agreements, or would solutions generally impose unequal costs and benefits on different groups? How variable, how predictable, and how well known are the impacts of the externality over time? Is the cause of the dilemma stable enough to be resolved by one agreement, or does variability over time require a process to continually adjust the terms of agreement?

THE ADVANTAGES AND LIMITS OF SELF-ORGANIZING MECHANISMS

The next step in applying the ICA framework to a given problem is to identify alternative mitigating mechanisms, compare their effectiveness in enhancing joint outcomes, and consider the incentives for developing each mechanism.

The Effectiveness of Self-Organizing Mechanisms

Although Ostrom's *Governing the Commons* (1990) analyzes common-pool resource dilemmas in relatively sparse institutional settings, her approach provides initial criteria that can also be used for evaluating the effectiveness of mitigating mechanisms that have been developed to deal with ICA dilemmas in the complex institutional settings of metropolitan and regional governance in the United States – settings she elsewhere calls "polycentric systems" (Ostrom 2005). Ostrom analyzes locally evolved institutions that are adapted to specific local circumstances and are self-governing by resource users. She argues that these institutions can provide more effective resolution of collective action problems among users than centrally mandated institutions because of the following features: local knowledge, inclusion of trustworthy participants, reliance on disaggregated knowledge, better adapted rules, lower enforcement costs, and parallel autonomous systems (Ostrom 2005: 281ff). Of course, these advantages can only be realized if the design of the institution matches the nature of the users' collective action problem. We argue that self-organizing mechanisms can provide more effective resolution of ICA dilemmas among authorities for similar reasons, but only if the design of the mechanism is suited to the nature of the dilemma. ICA analysis focuses primarily on rules affecting what Ostrom calls the constitutional level – the rules that constrain how independent authorities make rules that, in turn, govern the production decisions of resource users.

Ostrom's design principles include clearly defined membership and institutional boundaries; customized rules designed by those affected for the specific social, economic, and technological features of the dilemma; effective monitoring and enforcement involving members; and low-cost conflict resolution mechanisms. These principles are intended to maximize the potential advantages of self-organizing institutions. By requiring broad consensus of all members, self-organizing institutions enhance the search for mutually advantageous resolution of ICA dilemmas; why would anyone voluntarily join an agreement that would make them worse off? Centrally designated authorities, on the other hand, encourage an escalation of conflict; they provide targets for conflict among advocacy coalitions that seek to impose their preferred policies on weaker, less organized parties.

Self-organization requires negotiation to reach consensus, a process that potentially develops trust and reciprocal arrangements among members that is critical in reducing the costs of reaching and maintaining an agreement. We refer to the patterns of informal relationships as *policy networks*, a more autonomous mitigating mechanism that can provide critical support for monitoring, enforcement, and compliance with the self-developed rules of institutions that impose more constraints on the autonomy of participants. The process of creating and amending the rules governing self-organizing institutions generates greater legitimacy among participants, who can design levels of flexibility and enforcement appropriate for the concerns of participants. And one successful self-organizing effort can increase the likelihood of further efforts to resolve other ICA dilemmas, thus enhancing the institutional equivalent of social capital in the local arena.

In short, self-organizing consensual mechanisms allow authorities and their constituencies to maintain much of their autonomy while potentially mitigating the ICA dilemma. Thus an effective consensual mechanism will in principle be preferred to an equally effective centrally imposed authority that restricts local autonomy. The latter involves a permanent loss of authority and hence diminished ability to influence future decisions of the new authority. Only when the risks and uncertainties of a dilemma are replaced by divisive zero-sum conflicts that threaten the survival of the broader authority system will authorities be inclined to abdicate to a centralized authority capable of resolving the conflict.

Since local actors prefer maintaining as much local autonomy as possible and are willing to fight to preserve it, central actors will also in principle prefer mitigating mechanisms that minimize intrusion on local autonomy. Attempts to reorganize formal authority inevitably meet with resistance from existing authorities and constituency groups concerned that existing services and benefits will be lost in the new order (March and Olsen 1983). Thus mitigating mechanisms that can resolve the dilemma while avoiding these political costs and disruptions would be preferred to a formal reallocation of authority; in the institutionally complex settings of modern federalist systems, self-governing institutions provide an alternative that potentially reduces the inevitable political conflicts involved in revoking existing authority from governments or specialized agencies and reassigning it to a coordinating authority.

The Costs of Self-Organizing Mechanisms

Of course, the gains from mitigating ICA dilemmas come at a considerable cost to participants of self-organizing institutions, which is why successful institutions appear to be the exception rather than the rule in Ostrom's (1990) examples. Ostrom (2005, 282ff) discusses the following limiting factors to local self-organizing efforts: some appropriators will not organize, some self-organized efforts will fail, local tyrannies, stagnation, inappropriate discrimination, limited access to scientific information, conflict among appropriators, and inability to cope with larger-scale common-pool resources.

Particularly in our more complex institutional context, self-organizing activities confront the well-known second-order free-riding dilemma (Bates 1988a) involved in developing mitigating mechanisms; even if everyone would be better off if the mechanism existed, why not let others pay the cost of organizing? The free-rider problem is reduced in part if those who participate initially can shape the rules to claim the greater share of the gains generated through agreements, but the resultant asymmetric outcomes would also reduce the legitimacy and sustainability of the institution.

The second-order dilemma applies to maintenance costs as well as startup costs, both of which reflect the same types of issues associated with transaction costs in the first-order dilemma. Information costs associated with effective participation in the mechanism increase with the complexity and scope of information required to make decisions as well as with the risks involved if the decisions prove to be unwise. Information costs also increase with the potential asymmetry of benefits, since each homogeneous class of participants needs to determine what rules would be in its own interest, what rules would be preferred by others, and what set of feasible compromise rules is achievable. Negotiation costs increase with the number of such groups as well as the potential magnitude of asymmetries, and consensus requirements can further increase the costs of arriving at a decision. Finally, enforcement costs increase as obligations imposed by the mechanism become more costly, particularly when immediate obligations exceed expected long-term benefits of participation.

The design of the mechanism itself can alter maintenance and startup costs for any underlying ICA. Rules determine obligations imposed on members. As obligations increase, so also does the member's exposure to adverse consequences if her interests are not adequately represented in the mechanism's decision process. Buchanan and Tullock (1962) long ago pointed out that constitutional rules and procedures to ensure adequate representation generally increase costs of participation. They argue that optimal rules for governance will balance the costs of participation and the threat from inadequate representation; the greater the obligations affected by the mechanism's decision process, the higher the decision costs required to offset the potential threat of misrepresentation.

Jones refers to the combined set of costs and disincentives associated with self-governing mechanisms as *decision* costs, which include the startup costs and associated free-rider problems, the maintenance costs of participation, and the threat of unfavorable decisions imposing unwanted obligations. These decision costs become increasingly important as mechanisms are vested with government authority to impose their decisions on unwilling members and become prohibitively high when dealing with problems involving nondivisible decisions, conflicts between well-established advocacy coalitions, and agreements that would be difficult to enforce. Since these situations would impose prohibitively high participation costs on self-organizing mechanisms, *Jones* argues that they can be resolved only by the formal authoritative system. This limitation reinforces our earlier caveat that we investigate the role of self-organizing mechanisms as supporting institutions that mitigate dilemmas within the current constitutional system, but do not replace or even radically overhaul the system.

Matching Mechanisms to ICAs: The Cost-Effectiveness Trade-off

Given the difference in transaction costs associated with different ICAs, we would like to know which type of mechanism, with which kinds of rules, would be most appropriate for each type of ICA. Since this critical knowledge has not yet been developed, we offer a rebuttable hypothesis linking mechanisms and ICAs as a starting point for research.

Mechanisms with the lowest decision costs will be most efficient for resolving ICAs with the lowest transaction costs.

The critical assumption behind this hypothesis is that mechanisms must impose greater obligations to effectively mitigate ICAs involving greater risks and hence higher transaction costs. Greater obligations translate into higher decision costs associated with the mechanism. For simple coordination problems among units facing the same payoffs (e.g., all governments in a metropolitan area decide on the same emergency equipment to enhance interchangeability in emergency situations), each unit need not forgo much of its autonomy to ensure coordination. Thus a very low-cost mechanism involving only minor obligations could readily resolve the problem.

For more difficult cooperation problems in which there is considerable incentive to free ride or defect, on the other hand, stronger counter-incentives are needed that will impose greater obligations on members. For example, commitments to large infrastructure projects or to common regulatory policies involve higher transaction costs because of the greater risks of defection. Mechanisms with the credible enforcement power required to support cooperative agreements are also likely to have the power to impose costly adjustments on members. Such mechanisms require more elaborate safeguards and hence greater participation costs to assure members that only legitimate obligations will be enforced.

Incentives will favor voluntary participation in a given mechanism only if the expected benefits from mitigating the ICA exceed the total expected decision costs required to create and maintain the mechanism. To the extent that low-cost mechanisms are effective enough to gain the advantages of cooperation for a given ICA, they provide greater net incentives for participation than higher cost mechanisms. On the other hand, low-cost mechanisms are unlikely to be effective for ICAs involving higher transaction costs, and higher cost mechanisms would then be preferred as long as the expected gains exceed the costs.

For the kinds of difficult issues discussed by *Jones,* the decision costs involved in reaching consensus may be so high that only the authoritative state apparatus may be able to resolve the issue, albeit at the cost of political resistance by those hurt by the authoritative resolution of the dispute. Thus the authoritative decision arenas of the state provide the necessary option when self-organizing mechanisms fail to evolve. The trade-off between more rapid resolution through authority versus more consensual resolution through self-organizing mechanisms depends in part on the costs of delay associated with achieving consensus and in part on the disruption imposed by the ongoing ICA conflict on related issues. Regions with a greater range of available self-organizing mechanisms at least have more options for resolving difficult ICAs, although efficiency concerns are only one of several important forces that determine central authoritative interventions. The mechanisms listed in Figure 1.1 reflect the broad range of trade-offs between effectiveness and decision costs in institutions that have evolved in the United States to mitigate ICA dilemmas. The description of each mechanism is provided in the appendix to this chapter, since we want to emphasize the full spectrum of mechanisms at this point. Our suggested ordering reflects a rough progression from the least intrusive mechanisms that rely on the self-organizing activities of

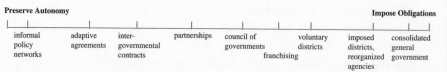

FIGURE 1.1. Mitigating Mechanisms.

fully autonomous participants on the left to the most intrusive that rely on central controls and full loss of autonomy on the right.

Both decision costs and effectiveness tend to increase from left to right. Informal policy networks, adaptive agreements, and intergovernmental contracts on the left impose only a few narrowly defined obligations on participants. Partnerships, councils of government, franchising, and special districts impose increasingly broad obligations that are in part determined by central authorities, and consolidation centralizes authority by fully subordinating or eliminating previously independent authorities. Our starting hypothesis is that mechanisms on the left will tend to emerge for ICAs involving low transaction costs, while those to the right will become increasingly common as transaction costs increase.

These examples of mitigating mechanisms provide only a preliminary classification to help organize the range of actual institutions that have been described in this growing literature. Furthermore, each type of mechanism listed in Figure 1.1 can vary in terms of both costs and effectiveness, depending on how well the design of the mechanism fits with the nature of the ICA dilemma. Understanding these relationships is the primary goal of the ICA research agenda.

Mechanism Dynamics

In addition, the dynamics of mechanism development need to be understood, particularly since different mechanisms and even different rules within each mechanism affect not only the expected costs and gains but also their distribution across different sets of actors. Incentives to participate are likely to be affected by distributive as well as by efficiency consequences of the mechanism, and the particular nature of the ICA dilemma may induce other incentives as well. For example, local and central actors may seek centrally imposed solutions rather than self-governing ones in some plausible scenarios. In some cases, local authorities may prefer to abdicate authority over a troublesome policy dilemma to avoid being blamed or being pressured by powerful interests, as when municipal governments support the shift of hospital and health-care functions to counties and special districts. Similarly, powerful constituencies most affected by a dilemma may oppose a self-organizing institution that would require compromise and may use their influence on central actors to maintain or impose an authority structure they can dominate (Dedekorkut 2005). In other cases, central actors may oppose self-organizing mechanisms that distribute all the gains of cooperation to powerful local

constituencies not favored by central actors. Thus, the anticipated redistributive aspects of these mechanisms are important to understand not
only for normative concerns about the benefits from self-organizing governance but also for understanding the incentives of those involved in
developing them.

In sum, we currently understand too little about mitigating mechanisms to know whether the limitations and alternative scenarios overwhelm the advantages and principles favoring self-governing solutions
to ICA dilemmas. If indeed self-organizing mechanisms prove to be a
large, permanent, and critical component in federalist and other governmental systems, we do not know whether our initial hypothesis will stand
up to rigorous empirical testing.

THE THREE CENTRAL QUESTIONS

To fully develop and test our initial hypothesis, we elaborate on the three
questions we believe need to be addressed in theoretical and empirical
analyses to understand the role of self-organizing mechanisms in mitigating ICA dilemmas.

1. *How does the mechanism reduce transaction costs?* This question
   focuses on the effectiveness of a given mechanism in reducing
   the barriers that prevent coordinated decisions. This phase of analysis resembles the comparative statics approach to evaluating
   institutions by comparing the motivations and hence equilibrium
   outcomes in the presence and absence of the given mechanism. For
   example, ecosystem management partnerships can reduce information costs by subsidizing the planning activities for multiple-actor
   projects that no individual actor would develop alone, reduce
   negotiation costs by creating an impartial public negotiation arena,
   and reduce enforcement costs by providing public means of making
   credible commitments (see, e.g., Schneider et al. 2003).

   Some impacts on transaction costs are less apparent than others.
   For example, state laws to facilitate intergovernmental agreements
   can reduce negotiation and enforcement costs by providing a standardized contractual agreement as a basis of negotiation and access
   to state courts as a relatively low-cost enforcement mechanism. In
   addition to this obvious benefit, *Andrew* and *Shrestha* identify the
   extent to which local governments can themselves further reduce
   transaction costs involved in incomplete contracts by embedding
   individual contracts in overlapping contractual networks that alter

the riskiness of each individual contract. Such informal relationships play a particularly significant role in all the mechanisms we study.

2. ***What incentives do potential members have to create the mechanism?*** This question is central for understanding the self-organizing aspects of each mechanism and hence the likelihood that a given mechanism will emerge in a given situation. In the literature of institutional analysis, this question reflects the "second-order" dilemma involved in the creation of an institution capable of resolving some underlying first-order dilemma (Bates 1998a). Even if all actors would be better off with the institution than they are without it, they all face the temptation to free ride on the effort of others to develop it, leading to an undersupply or failure to develop the institution.

The first question emphasizes the expected gains from creating the mechanism, while this second question balances these gains against the decision costs and risks involved in participation. In particular, this question focuses on what is required to make participants voluntarily submit to the obligations imposed on members. Since these obligations and the rules governing participation are determined as part of the ongoing development of the mechanism, the dynamic processes of development require particular emphasis in understanding how particular mechanisms emerge in specific situations. A careful consideration of incentives is likely to require analysis of the internal rules of the important organizational actors. As noted earlier, *Bickers et al.* analyze how the incentives for local elected officials to collaborate with other local governments can be shaped by the electoral system.

3. ***How do incentives induced by the mitigating mechanism affect its sustainability in a changing environment and its adaptability to other ICA dilemmas?*** Once established, institutions shape incentives in ways that create their own problems and possibilities. To be self-sustaining, an institution must provide incentives that are sufficient to maintain itself in the face of unforeseen shocks from the relevant political, economic, social, and natural systems. The long-term sustainability of self-organizing mechanisms and their long-term effect on the adaptive capability of the formal governing system are perhaps the most important but least-known aspect of self-governing mechanisms.

For example, the altered incentives provided by one mitigating institution may have positive or negative impacts on other ICA

dilemmas and the evolution of other mitigating mechanisms. On
the positive side, an institution established to mitigate one dilemma
may expand its range to mitigate related dilemmas as well. *Lubell
et al.,* for example, analyze the impact of participation in a set of
related venues on the likelihood of more general collaboration, and
Berardo considers how collaboration among partners on one joint
project affects the likelihood of future collaboration. Mechanisms
to resolve one dilemma may generally enhance the ability to resolve
others; networks of reciprocity, for example, provide the basis for
expanding social capital to resolve a range of collective action
problems (Putnam 1993). Policy networks, specific agreements,
and joint projects are likely to coexist with regional partnerships
and councils of governments (COGs), for example, and each may
be most effective in reducing specific types of transaction costs
affecting the same ICA. *Berardo* and *Lubell et al.,* for example,
analyze the reinforcing role of policy networks on project and
regional partnerships, *respectively.*

On the negative side of the same issue, the resources devoted to
developing one institution may not be available for other institutions, creating a competitive rather than complementary relationship between alternative mechanisms and the mitigation of
alternative ICA dilemmas. *Lubell et al.,* analyze how participation
in multiple venues diminishes the marginal impact that participation in collaborative partnerships has on other collaborative
activities. *Mullin* examines the impact of special districts on the
utilization of intergovernmental agreements for the supply of
drinking water. To the extent that mechanisms are found to be
competitive rather than complementary, the emergence of certain
mitigating institutions to resolve one dilemma may actually reduce
the adaptive capacity to resolve newly emerging dilemmas.

Another potential problem involves predictable changes in participation over time that may allow a minority of members to capture excessive benefits at the expense of those without the resources
or abilities to sustain participation. Although widespread attention
may induce broad participation at the time a regulatory agency is
established, the regulated entities most affected by the agency are
likely to remain active, while the broader public moves on to other
issues, leaving the agency increasingly under the influence of the
regulated entities (Downs 1972; Sabatier 1999). Similarly, the long-
term impacts of self-governing mitigating mechanisms need to be

taken into consideration. Selznick (1949), for example, shows how local advisory mechanisms set up to enhance broad participation in Tennessee Valley Authority programs eventually were dominated by local elites with goals quite different from those of the program's initial supporters. Scholz and Wang (2006), on the other hand, suggest that local institutions capable of resolving water-related ICA dilemmas can transform interests in ways that strengthen enforcement of the Clean Water Act, even in conservative communities that generally oppose regulation.

These three questions in part reflect the natural evolution of a given institution; an initial problem is recognized by those affected, the incentive structure induces actions leading to the creation of the institution, and the institution itself restructures incentives that affect both its sustainability and its impact on other potential problems. But these neat categorizations – like the categorization of the policy process into neat stages of problem recognition, formulation, adoption, implementation, and evaluation – tend to underplay the simultaneous interrelationships among these stages. We view the questions primarily as an analytic means of confronting the dynamic interplay between mechanisms and ICAs in federalist systems.

NETWORK ANALYSIS AND SELF-ORGANIZING GOVERNANCE

Previous studies of local collective action problems and institutions have tended to focus either on individual incentives or on institutions; as Granovetter (1985) has argued, both analyses ignore the context of informal relationships that constrains both individual actions and institutional behavior. Network analysis provides a means of bridging the individual and institutional perspectives.

Networks and network analysis are likely to play a central role in the understanding of self-organizing governance. Policy networks are listed as the only mechanism in Figure 1.1 that requires no formal authority from the state – even memos of agreement and contractual relationships require statutory recognition for the authorities involved. The informal policy networks that emerge to coordinate central policies (Heclo 1978) also operate to coordinate action among multiple actors at multiple levels (e.g., Rhodes 1997) and between the local and central authorities (e.g., Schneider et al. 2003).

In addition to this obvious place of networks in the spectrum of self-organizing mechanisms, informal relationships play an important role in complementing and reinforcing the full array of self-organizing mechanisms. Just as "formal" market institutions and contractual arrangements are embedded in social relationships that help reduce the risks and transaction costs of market exchanges (Granovetter 1985), just as any "formal organization" can function despite design flaws because of the embedded "informal organization" (Scott 1995), so also do the formal authority structures in political systems depend on informal, self-organized relationships among authorities and stakeholders for performance and stability to buffer the system from changing demands (cf. Filippov, Shvetsova, and Ordeshook 2004). Formal authority structures are defined in statute while informal network structures emerge unplanned from interactions among formally designated institutional actors and their constituencies. Similarly, formal rules define the critical characteristics of a self-organizing mechanism, while informal networks provide additional structure that can either enhance or weaken the performance of the formally recognized mechanism.

The informal relationships affecting self-organizing mechanisms include a range of possible patterns. The simplest relate to single-purpose dyadic relations between two actors affected by an ICA dilemma. The broader pattern that emerges from such simple relationships can itself become quite complex, reflecting the needs for greater information or for credibility as discussed in *Shrestha* and in *Andrew*. Dyadic relationships can also vary in intensity (Granovetter's [1973] weak versus strong ties) as well as in the multiplexity of exchanges or functions between the two actors. In addition, most informal organizations are likely to include clusters of actors sharing similar needs and beliefs, sometimes organized into opposing advocacy coalitions, and sometimes organized into overlapping pluralistic coalitions linked by constantly evolving issue networks.

Network scholars interested in the study of public policy issues have increasingly combined sophisticated theoretical and analytic tools to explore the motivation of political actors that would explain observed network structures (Provan and Milward 1995; O'Toole 1997; Carpenter, Esterling, and Lazer 2004) and their impact on policies (Scholz and Wang 2006) and collaboration (Scholz et al. 2008). However, even in recent studies that emphasize the critical role of networks for resolving collective action problems (Rydin and Falleth 2006), networks frequently provide a metaphor rather than an analytic tool (Dowding 1995). We believe that theoretical and methodological innovation will be required before the standard individual and institutional-based analyses typical in current political science can help us understand the critical role of these informal relationships in self-organizing ICA mechanisms.

A major obstacle to more systematic analysis is that the standard analytic approaches focus either on individual or institutional components of the political system rather than on the relationships among components that is featured in network analysis. Recent progress in resolving the very complex methodological problems of network analysis holds great promise for expanding this approach beyond its use as a metaphor, although the new techniques are not widely known.

Several chapters in this volume illustrate how available methods can be applied to analyze the critical role played by networks. Although we cannot explain these methods in detail in this volume, each chapter provides references to the critical studies for those interested in applying the techniques. For those with little background in network analysis, social network analysis texts provide an excellent introduction to concepts and analytic techniques (Scott 2000; Knoke and Yang 2008), and more advanced texts catalogue the major concepts and approaches (Wasserman and Faust 1994) and more recent analytic techniques (Carrington, Scott, and Wasserman 2005).

The analytic methods we feature range from reinterpreting critical network measures (*Thurner*) and applying them in familiar regression and correlation analyses (*Berardo, Lubell et al.*), to utilizing Exponential Random Graph models (ERGM) estimated with sophisticated Markov Chain Monte Carlo techniques to detect significant patterns of network structure (*Andrew, Shrestha*). Unlike regression models, the recently developed ERGM approach controls for the potential interdependence of relationships assumed in dynamic theories of network development, a problem that has hindered empirical analyses for several decades. When applied to time series data, these models provide the possibility for analyzing mutual causation of behavior on network structures as well as of structures on behavior (Snijders, Steglich, and Schweinberger 2005; Berardo and Scholz 2009), a critical task for understanding the interrelationships and causal connections between network relationships, other forms of collaborative participation, and collaborative behavior to mitigate ICA dilemmas.

Weible utilizes multidimensional scaling techniques to detect and illustrate patterns among ally and opposition relationships, and then employs a quadratic assignment regression procedure (an older alternative to ERGM modeling) to test the extent to which these patterns are best explained in terms of beliefs or of common participation in related policy arenas. Unlike normal regression procedures, this procedure is not dependent on random sampling and does not assume independence between observations. Sampling procedures to measure network relationships can seldom meet rigorous randomization standards, and network contacts cannot be assumed to be independent of other contacts unless network relationships have no significant effects on each other. Thus quadratic assignment procedures are designed to test for and control potential sources of bias that are common in network analysis.

Thurner applies a more exploratory network approach to determine the most central actors in the policy negotiation process both within one country and across the European Union. He first categorizes the negotiations into multiple tasks and then utilizes sociograms to compare the formal and informal roles played by participants in each of these tasks – an important consideration for understanding the relationship between policy networks and formal authority structures. He then illustrates how centrality scores developed in network analysis can be used to determine the critical members for negotiating teams, suggesting the rich possibilities for applying other concepts developed in network analysis to the problems of institutional design and policy management.

PLAN OF THIS VOLUME

This chapter has provided an overview of our framework for understanding the mitigating mechanisms described above, and the appendix provides an integrated overview of the mechanisms analyzed in this volume. The remaining three chapters in the first section develop critical components of the theoretical dimensions of this framework. *Whitford* focuses on the trade-off between central consolidated control and local autonomy in terms of the vertical and horizontal dilemmas facing consolidation. *Steinacker* extends the transaction cost approach in order to consider relative advantages of the main mitigating mechanisms in four major types of ICA dilemmas. Finally, *Jones* considers several situations and types of ICA dilemmas that self-organizing governance is least likely to resolve.

The next two sections present empirical studies that apply our framework to a range of different ICA dilemmas and different mechanisms, as already discussed. The first of these sections contains studies of service delivery in metropolitan areas. Four chapters analyze the embedded patterns of intergovernmental agreements (*Andrew*) and contracts (*Shrestha*), the interaction of these agreements with other mechanisms involving a greater loss of autonomy (*Mullin*), and the motivations of local officials to develop these agreements (*Bickers et al.*). The subsequent section features studies of regional integration of policies, focusing on the formation of policy networks and position of a collaborative institution (*Weible*), the role of networks in sustaining joint ventures (*Berardo*), the relationship between collaborative partnerships and related policy arenas (*Lubell et al.*), and the broader efforts to integrate national policies through the development of the European Union (*Thurner*).

The final chapter summarizes some of the most important themes each chapter develops toward answering our three questions about self-organizing governance. We reiterate in that chapter that this volume does not offer a theory of federalism or governance but rather attempts to provide a unified perspective for understanding how federalist systems cope with increasingly problematic ICA dilemmas. The ICA framework integrates analysis of the range of innovative new institutions developed over recent decades that tend to be analyzed primarily within isolated policy contexts. The emphasis we place on the self-organizing aspects of governance reflects our belief that they of necessity provide the dominant force for resolving the multitude of constantly evolving fragmentation problems that are particularly pernicious in a federalist system. Direct assumption of authority by the state and the national government can indeed play critical roles, but in relatively limited cases. We believe that their greatest role in mitigating fragmentation problems will come from encouraging and shaping the evolution of self-organizing mechanisms.

We hope that a better understanding of self-organizing mechanisms will have the practical effect of expanding their role in mitigating the ever-expanding range of ICA dilemmas confronting contemporary governments in policy arenas as diverse as metropolitan service delivery, regional management of natural resources, and the integration of the European Union, all of which are included in this volume. How can we better coordinate and integrate services provided by the fragmented collection of local government units that exist in metropolitan areas? How can we prevent one pollution control agency's decisions from imposing unconsidered and unnecessary costs on other agencies and governments operating in the same area? How can we improve the ability of European nations to gain greater benefit from integrated policies?

Solutions to these diverse and seemingly unrelated problems considered in the following chapters have at their core our common concern – how to mitigate ICA dilemmas that arise from the fragmentation of government authority and are exacerbated by expanding trends toward globalization. A better understanding of how these mechanisms work, how they evolve, and what impact they have on related problems as well as on the formal allocation of authority provide a necessary foundation for this process.

Overview of the ICA Mitigating Mechanisms

Since each chapter in this volume focuses on only one or two mitigating mechanisms, this appendix provides a brief overview of the mechanisms studied in the book to illustrate our integrated approach to this class of mechanisms. We begin with those that preserve the most local autonomy, starting at the left in Figure 1.1.

Informal Policy Networks

Informal networks provide a self-organizing structure that preserves full local autonomy and requires no formal authority, although federal and state programs can enhance their development (Schneider et al. 2003). Coordination through local networks has been found to enhance Clean Water Act enforcement (Scholz and Wang 2006) and increase collaborative activities of those most central to the network (Scholz et al. 2008), although cooptation of state and national programs by local networks may divert goals to reflect the preferences of local interests (Selznick 1947). Given the current state of knowledge, we use the term *network* loosely to refer to a broad array of relationships including information or other resource exchanges (*Berardo*), contractual relationships (*Andrew* and *Shrestha*), and alliance relationships that coordinate strategy (*Weible* and *Thurner*).

A critical task in developing the ICA framework is to determine what aspects of networks and types of relationships are most important in different contexts. *Weible,* for example, analyzes the factors that account for the observed structure of networks in the San Francisco Bay-Delta water policy arena, arguably one of the most fragmented and contentious policy arenas available for study. He tests the extent to which informal alliance networks that "act as a hub for coordinating activities to solve common problems" are shaped by common beliefs. *Weible* also develops and tests the alternative functional area hypothesis that in fragmented policy arenas, participation in common subarenas provides an alternative basis for developing network relationships. To the extent that common functional areas are more influential than common beliefs, the resultant networks may provide more effective integration mechanisms across these functional areas.

Several chapters focus on the role of networks within more formal governance mechanisms – *Andrew* and *Shrestha* on how contract networks can reduce the risks of contracting, *Berardo* on how informal networks make joint projects more successful and more likely, *Weible* and *Lubell et al.* on the support (or not) of networks for collaboration, and *Thurner* on the support of informal networks even for consolidation.

Networks are just one of the several mechanisms we examine, and *Steinacker* notes that even in well-functioning policy networks partners may seek more formalized mechanisms for making broader commitments that remain difficult within informal partnerships. However, networks play such a central and underappreciated role in solving institutional collective action problems that we emphasize their role in most of the empirical studies in this volume.

Adaptive Agreements and Intergovernmental Contracts

Federal or state legislation may provide the necessary legal framework for local governments and agencies to develop *adaptive agreements* and more formalized *intergovernmental contracts* with each other, both of which provide means of coordinating specific activities with willing contractual partners. As with informal networks, agreements and contracts require the consent of those involved, so this institutional system preserves the autonomy of local actors while providing a more formalized mechanism for resolving externality issues of concern to the contracting parties. The Coase (1960, 1988) theorem suggests that contracting can resolve many of the diverse externality problems, particularly if enabling legislation minimizes the transaction costs involved in developing, negotiating, and enforcing agreements and contracts between governments or government agencies.

The ability to make binding agreements can be very versatile, involving in some cases two willing governments or agencies and in other cases involving multilateral agreements of all governments in a given area. Agreements can include relatively flexible terms, while contracts generally involve more specific obligations. *Andrew* and *Shrestha* analyze patterns of agreements and contracts between local governments that evolve in response to the risks and problems associated with the production and delivery of different services. Both test the hypothesis that agreements involving greater risk will be more embedded in closed, overlapping relationships associated with greater trust (Coleman 1988; Putnam 1995) since these relationships can reduce the transaction costs of developing, negotiating, and enforcing contracts. *Andrew* tests this hypothesis by comparing riskier adaptive agreements with less risky intergovernmental contracts, while *Shrestha* uses differences in the risks (asset specificity) of contracting for different types of services to expand and test this hypothesis.

Partnerships and Councils of Governments

Broader, more complex problems may involve the creation of formal multifunctional institutions such as regional watershed partnerships (Scholz and Stiftel 2005) and regional economic development partnerships, or regional councils of governments (COGs) (Gerber and Gibson 2005; Park and Feiock 2007). They are voluntary in the sense that members participate at will and must approve activities, and the organization generally has limited authority to force members to comply with its decisions. Decisions by these institutions of necessity constrain choices, or there would be no purpose to their existence; they do, however, generally allow an exit option that limits the ability of the institution to coerce its minority members.

The decision rules for institutional action determine the decision costs of coming to agreement as well as the capacity to mitigate ICA dilemmas. Requirements for unanimity or supermajorities create high decision costs for member governments but ensure that decisions reflect a consensus of all represented interests. Decision rules that entail lower thresholds of agreement, such as majority rule, facilitate cooperative solutions, but operate under the threat of exit by disgruntled members (Gerber and Gibson 2005).

The regional partnerships studied in this volume are primarily concerned with fragmented management of natural resources, but the approach can readily be applied to COGs and other regional institutions as well (Stephens and Wikstrom 2000; Feiock 2007). *Berardo* focuses on multipartner water projects, a form of contractual agreement intended to capture positive externalities of large-scale investments, which fall somewhere between bilateral contracts discussed previously and regional partnerships with broader mandates. Berardo considers the relationship between informal policy networks and formal project partnerships, analyzing the nature of informal relationships that enhance the likelihood of continuing cooperation in future partnership agreements. *Lubell et al.* consider the impact of broader regional partnerships on the level of collaborative activity of participants. They develop and test an important multiple game hypothesis that we will discuss further in the concluding chapter: broad participation in the informal networks centered on multiple uncoordinated decision venues may enhance collaboration and satisfaction with policy outcomes as much as participation in a formal partnership developed specifically to enhance collaboration.

Voluntary Special Districts

Voluntary special districts can provide solutions to ICA dilemmas that involve a more bottom-up process than mandated districts and can provide at least some flexibility for members to determine procedural rules and boundaries. Regional special districts can be created by constituent governments to capture economies of scale to reduce the average cost of service provision to the member jurisdictions. Special districts in some states have the ability to annex surrounding areas. In these cases, enabling legislation specifies the procedure for formation along with some minimal level of power and authority of the district. It is then up to local actors to act collectively to create a district, define its boundaries (see Burns 1994), and create procedural rules beyond predetermined minimal standards if desired. Positive actions or approval by the existing local government units is typically necessary to form these districts, but the enabling legislation limits information, negotiation, and enforcement costs and hence increases the likelihood that agreement can be reached.

These self-organizing mechanisms may or may not be compatible with each other in mitigating a given ICA dilemma. *Mullin*'s study of special water districts focuses specifically on whether special water districts and intergovernmental contracting provide competing or complementary mechanisms for resolving ICA dilemmas of water supply. More specifically, she develops competing hypotheses about whether procedural rules allowing water districts to expand their boundaries will result in lower or higher volumes of intergovernmental agreements for water supply, and tests these hypotheses by comparing intergovernmental agreements in states that do and do not allow flexible boundaries.

Mandated Special Districts

Countywide or multicounty special districts imposed uniformly by a higher authority provide a more limited means of internalizing unconsidered impacts over a broad geographic area by stripping local governments of autonomy in the specified functional area. States use special districts to mitigate the horizontal problem of metropolitan service provision for geographic consolidation of services like schools and fire or police protection. Regional districts can also mitigate mixed problems by absorbing multiple specialized agencies into a new integrated agency, generally under the authority of state governments. For example, the Florida

Legislature created a system of water management districts that consolidated multiple functions within natural watershed boundaries, including authority to enforce national statutes that have been delegated to the states (Hamann 2005).

Although federal and state governments can mandate special districts, the political and administrative costs limit their scope to a narrow range of ICA dilemmas. Statewide mandates for uniform special districts require complicated negotiations to create a single model that can serve differing interests in various regions of the state – in Florida, for example, the five water management districts were given different taxing authorities to appease opposition in some regions. Existing agencies and government units generally resist their loss of authority. The larger units gain efficiencies in production but frequently at the cost of reducing the ability of local units to vary the provision of services to reflect different local preferences. These and other concerns explain why the voluntary special districts discussed above may provide more palatable resolution of ICAs, although the gain in flexibility may also lead to a loss in ability to tackle the most difficult types of questions as highlighted in *Jones*.

Franchising

Franchising provides a little-understood but innovative and promising mitigating mechanism in which a higher level government maintains full authority for a standardized service or regulatory domain, but provides some discretion to lower level authorities, as discussed more fully by *Whitford*. For example, federal or state regulators maintain the authority to establish uniform regulations for air and water pollution, worker safety and health, and many other policy arenas, but then delegate enforcement authority to state or local officials, respectively. This allows the higher level unit to develop universal standards but also allows local units to bring unique local concerns to bear on implementation within the guidelines of the franchise contract.

Consolidated Governments

Similar arguments apply to the creation of consolidated governments. Like special districts, they can vary considerably in their procedures and authority; they can be responsible to local voters, as in the United States, or can be governed directly by appointees of a central authority. Despite arguments that centralization of authority promotes rational and efficient urban policy, efforts at city-county consolidation have been unsuccessful in the vast majority of cases in the United States. Failure of consolidation efforts is attributed to the high political and transaction cost of consolidation and the availability of alternative, less costly coordination mechanisms (Carr and Feiock 2004). Administrative reorganizations to consolidate bureaucratic functions have fared little better (March and Olsen 1984), as illustrated by the difficulties besetting the efforts of the recently created Office of Homeland Security. And the larger the scope, the greater the challenges; for example, *Thurner* describes typical problems the European Union has encountered in its attempt to create a constitution that would consolidate considerable authority in a single European government.

Thurner's study is particularly interesting in pointing out the important role that informal policy networks may play in reducing the transaction costs affecting the development of consolidated institutions. Taking advantage of such design features is particularly important for the EU, where consolidated institutions must be developed without recourse to a preexisting, higher level authority. Under these conditions, the constitution-building effort will succeed only if all nations perceive the constitution as bestowing more benefits than costs, which requires very complex trade-offs across multiple policy areas both within and between countries. *Thurner* notes that the current structure of negotiations reflects the formal authority of prime ministers to coordinate all subordinate ministries within each nation and of foreign affairs ministries to dominate communications between nations. He argues that this structure imposes considerable transaction costs that have caused the observed breakdowns in the adoption of early agreements.

Thurner's provocative thesis is that informal networks of communications across national and functional lines developed because of the inadequacies of formal negotiation channels and that these networks suggest a more efficient way to formally structure negotiations in order to develop a satisfactory resolution for all the complex issues to be negotiated. His proposal to endow the informal network with formal authority reverses the usual perception that informal networks should be shaped to reflect the formal allocation of authority! His analysis serves to remind us that informal networks play important roles in consolidation, which remains true even when imposed by a higher authority. Indeed, consolidation as a solution to fragmentation would seldom be imposed without support from those affected (Carr and Feiock 2004). In many instances, special districts and consolidated governments may arise from self-organizing activities that reach out to external authorities primarily to legitimize the consolidation desired by those being consolidated. Understanding the informal policy networks and other relationships involved in the consolidation process is likely to provide a clearer understanding of the prerequisites of successful consolidation efforts.

2

Can Consolidation Preserve Local Autonomy?

Mitigating Vertical and Horizontal Dilemmas

Andrew B. Whitford

Political scientists have long debated the benefits and costs of federal systems in which authority is fragmented and decision-making units have overlapping jurisdictions (e.g., Riker 1964; Ostrom 1973; Weingast 1995). While federalism is a touchstone for those working on the institutional design of the polity, the problem is really one of optimal delegation when one wants subunits to coordinate their actions in forming and implementing policy. The empirical chapters in this book discuss the ways that relatively independent authorities can craft institutions and agreements that help achieve coordination without having to rely on a hierarchical authority (a coordinator). These chapters offer a range of views on these arrangements – on the role of metropolitan authorities in crafting interorganizational water arrangements, on the role of special districts in forging cooperative agreements for public goods production, and on networks of contractors in emergency management. One way we think about the range of activities these studies describe is that relatively independent authorities "self-organize" in ways that help overcome coordination problems when the overall system of authority is fragmented. This kind of self-organization is probably dynamic and possibly efficient. The focus of this essay is on the delegation relationships that underpin these organizational forms. My central claim is that this kind of self-organization is neither inevitable nor unbounded, since comparable levels of coordination can be obtained under central authorities utilizing the franchising principle.

I focus on the tension between authority that is horizontally fragmented and authority that is vertically fragmented. My starting point is the assumption that nation-states produce and distribute public goods and services,[1] so the designers of political systems want to know what organizational forms of production and distribution help the state attain its goals. Large, complex nation-states (such as the United States) use many different forms of government for producing and distributing public goods; of course, this includes national agencies, geographically contiguous states, and highly decentralized metropolitan authorities, but it also sometimes includes the use of for-profit firms and nonprofit organizations. The organizations that actually "produce and distribute policy" in large nation-states range from highly centralized to atomistic.

A government that delegates authority to its subunits – for example, from a national government to its states, or from a state to its counties – inevitably faces two coordination dilemmas. One is a vertical dilemma that occurs between the delegator and the delegatee. The second is a horizontal dilemma when multiple delegatees want to ensure quality levels among the group. The delegator wants to ensure that the delegatee makes and implements policy within some band of acceptance. At the same time, delegatees want the delegator to guard against other delegatees "cutting" the standard of quality of how policy is made and implemented. An example of this kind of cutting is the kind of "race to the bottom" states may face if companies bid for lower state environmental regulation in return for their capital investments (e.g., Cumberland 1979, 1981). In practice, a central government delegating policy making and implementation to independent jurisdictions wants those jurisdictions to limit to a specific range the policy those jurisdictions deliver. Each jurisdiction wants (for many reasons) the central government to ensure that other jurisdictions maintain minimum levels of policy "quality"; in the case of environmental pollution, they may worry about cutting because policy "spills over" directly if pollution migrates or indirectly if jobs follow capital flows to jurisdictions offering lower quality levels.

I address this question of how to select a form of organization for producing and/or distributing policy in government by considering the analogous situation of a firm that selects a form for producing and/or distributing traditional goods and services (e.g., Williamson 1991). Firms can select from a vast list of forms, but I focus on why firms choose a peculiar hybrid type that lies between using prices in markets and using a pure hierarchy. Two firms often use a *franchise contract* as a way of

---

[1] Services are goods that are produced and consumed at the same time.

balancing between market and hierarchy to construct a specific and contractual symbiotic relationship. These contracts are like markets when two entities trade in capital, labor, or products; the contracts are like firms because they restrict the range of bilateral interactions between the two firms to the point that in some cases it is hard to tell where one firm ends and the other begins (as when firms are fully integrated). Firms pick this form because they think it harnesses the power of markets (where atomistic decision makers respond to local conditions) and of firms (where hierarchy lowers transaction costs). In the United States, almost a trillion dollars of sales were carried out through franchising in 2001 (Blair and Lafontaine 2005, 28).

The theory of franchising is really the theory of how to delegate to multiple independent subunits. Governments do this all the time when local jurisdictions operate within larger jurisdictions. In the United States, the national government delegates – either explicitly or implicitly – to its states; states delegate to the counties. The Constitution delegates – or retains – some powers explicitly for the American states. The problem for a colonizer is to hold together a diverse array of colonies. A confederation like the USSR faced the problem of coordinating the behavior of a diverse array of semiautonomous regions. In each of these cases there is either an explicit or an implicit delegation of power to a grouping of subordinate governmental units. The same holds in the franchising agreement between the franchisor and the franchisee. The franchisor wants to serve diverse local populations but faces constraints to doing so. The franchisee can solve the franchisor's problem, but only if the franchisor gives up a degree of control. The franchisees are willing to limit their own actions (for example, by promising to deliver goods or services of a specified quality level), but only if the franchisor can assure a given franchisee that all the other franchisees will adhere to the limits. Just as in governments, the problems of franchisors and franchisees are problems of delegating power from one level to another and then ensuring that implementers at that other level work with one another to attain the goals of the delegator.

One reason to focus on the co-production of policy as a "franchising problem" is that it illuminates the "double moral hazard" problem that underpins the joint production of policy by central governments and subordinate jurisdictions. On one hand, if it seems that local governments make and implement policy without care for what central governments want, we are really ignoring the central government's role as a "hidden coordinator" to intervene if policy moves too far away from what it wants. On the other hand, a central government that delegates policy-making and implementation authority faces afterward a perverse incentive to undercut its local jurisdictions; central governments often are unable to "credibly commit" to leaving the subunits alone. A state implementing environmental policy may not spend a lot of time worrying about what the national government thinks, but a lack of attention by some states led to national legislation and standard-setting in the environmental policy arena in the first place; the same might also be said of education policy over the last decade in the United States. At the same time, a national commitment to use local jurisdictions to make and implement policy that fits local conditions is not really credible. If some states perform better on that dimension, these lessons from "the policy laboratory" inevitably inform national efforts to create uniform policies that impose better practices on the other states. In the United States, the wide variety of policies implemented by the states to broaden access to health care has led to numerous calls for national implementation of a "Massachusetts-style" system.

In practice, the centralization or consolidation of services at the federal level is only one way of resolving the kinds of institutional collective action problems this book centers on. Other forms of centralized intervention that preserve much autonomy for local authorities may work better at resolving these problems. Yet, full decentralization suffers from its own problems. Local governments face pressure from their citizens and agencies to respond to different task environments. The problem for any "central planner" is to devise institutional frameworks that are flexible but also give subunits reasons to use knowledge of local preferences or task environments to make good decisions. The principal-agency problem that comes out of this puts pressure on central authorities to monitor and evaluate the decisions of the subunits.

This chapter proceeds as follows. I first focus on a theory of these vertical and horizontal dilemmas that centers on franchising contracts between firms that try to resolve two coordination dilemmas – vertical (between franchisor and franchisee) and horizontal (between franchisees) – by using one contract. The third section then turns back to the organization of government and connects the economic theory of franchising to how nation-states select an organizational form for the production and distribution of public goods and services. Last, I offer a few implications that this approach offers for our understanding of horizontal and vertical fragmentation in large, complex polities like the American state.

COORDINATION DILEMMAS IN THE CONTEXT
OF FRANCHISING

Firms, like governments, are governance structures. They are agreements between diverse sets of individuals about how to best achieve goals; represent sets of interests; or distribute power, goods, and resources. We now conceptualize the firm as a nexus of explicit and implicit contracts (Alchian and Demsetz 1972). While many still consider markets as more effective than the coordination of activities through pure central planning (Hayek 1945), firms often work better than markets because they minimize *transaction* costs (Coase 1937); prominent examples of these costs include the difficulty or ease of search, the costliness of information, the time and effort needed in bargaining or making decisions, and the fact that contracts require policing and enforcement.

People putting firms together face the choice between internal production (in other words, using a hierarchical approach to organization) and the use of markets for production. How they respond to this "make or buy" problem comes down to how the different parties to the potential transaction experience asset specificity (whether they experience it together, alone, or not at all) and whether the contracting environment is uncertain and/or complex (whether that uncertainty is low or high). If we take these six combinations as the types of decision environments in which people face this "make or buy" problem (the decision of whether to delegate or not), it turns out that in three of the cases vertical integration (not market-based transaction) is the efficient way to govern. Spot contracts are desirable in one case and long-term contracts are preferred in another; in the sixth case the efficiency of using contracts depends on the frequency of the interaction (e.g., Williamson 1975; Douma and Schreuder 2002).[2] This means that not all problems should be delegated – that having centralized production of goods and services (or in the case of government, policy) makes sense in many situations. In other situations we may see great benefits in delegating production from a central authority to other, decentralized decision makers, although the decision to do so in those cases depends on the motives and incentives of both the delegator and delegatee.

In practice, we cannot easily distinguish between transaction costs and other costs, making it hard to gauge exactly when it makes sense to

---

[2] We might add two more dimensions: the difficulty of measuring performance, and the degree to which the transaction is connected to transactions involving other parties not directly connected to the transaction in question (Milgrom and Roberts 1992, 30).

delegate or use others for production.[3] For example, a recent paper by Crockett, Smith, and Wilson (2006) shows experimentally that in a world made up of generalists and specialists, efficiency comes when people learn and seek out the benefits of trading with specialists; yet the conditions under which that occurs (when the gains from trade with specialists are realized) are fairly difficult to identify. What we know clearly, though, is that not everything is outsourced – that most firms still produce internally, and most firms are fairly hierarchical. These transaction costs, while not always clearly observable, help support a theoretical approach to understanding why firms delegate and contract, even though it may imperfectly predict their architectures.

The reason that governments delegate finds its analogy in the reason that firms "buy" instead of "make." Firms that never buy would become unwieldy, facing serious information and other shortcomings that endanger their ability to accurately and efficiently respond to changing market conditions. Similarly, governments that make and implement policy as a monolith would face shortcomings that would keep them from responding to emerging and complex problems in an efficient way, as well as responding to rich and dynamic public preferences about those policies. These vertical dilemmas are balanced, though, by horizontal dilemmas that emerge if firms only buy instead of make (due to transaction costs) or if governments implement policy only through unattached, atomistic actors with separate jurisdictions. Governments respond to these dilemmas by varying their policy-making architecture across policy areas – some more vertically integrated, others more horizontally disaggregated. Just like governments, not all firms are the same. They select their forms from a long list of alternatives, and in the real world the range includes many hybrid forms that fall in between markets and hierarchies (including long-term contracts, joint ventures, groups/consortia, networks, etc.; see Thompson et al. 1991).

The theory of franchising centers on a hybrid form that is neither purely a hierarchy nor purely a market. To be specific, in a franchise contract, a franchisor imposes on a franchisee a range of conditions (retail quality standards, common hours of business, price controls, nonlinear

---

[3] In any case, organizations may not try to minimize transaction costs. Indeed, the only case in which they would certainly try to minimize transaction costs is when there are no wealth effects (Milgrom and Roberts 1992, 35). This leads us to question the "efficient institutions" basis of a transaction cost theory of how firms select a specific organizational architecture.

payment schedules, etc.) and in turn provides advertising and training, monitors and inspects performance, and holds the power to terminate franchise agreements (Mathewson and Winter 1985, 503). Due to the rapid adoption of franchising starting in the 1960s, scholars turned to it as a unique opportunity for assessing governance in hybrid forms.[4] Franchising's oddities made it a good area for market theorists to use in considering the problems of combining vertical and horizontal concerns in a single contract; for organizational theorists, in turn, the theory of franchising has made it easier for us to understand the dilemmas inherent in organizational forms that combine a role for a central delegator trying to harness the power of delegation to multiple, structurally separate delegatees.

What are the dimensions of this decision environment? Klein claims there are three primary economic questions in franchising studies. First, why do transactors (franchisors and franchisees) use the franchising form? Second, what determines the particular contract terms chosen by the transactors? Third, what determines whether a franchisor owns and operates an outlet or contracts with an independent franchisee for ownership and operation? In the world of business, the key is that franchising permits transactors to achieve the benefits of large scale "while harnessing the profit incentive and retailing effort of local owners" (Klein 1995, 10). In fact, the problem that theorists have identified in the "oddities" of franchising is really common to other areas that students of governance probably find more familiar. Understanding franchising really requires understanding delegation, so the approaches taken usually center in agency theory but often address the role of incomplete contracts and search costs. As a starting point, I summarize how economists explain the firm's initial choice to franchise because it sets the stage for understanding the role of vertical and horizontal dilemmas in the choice to delegate.

We have two basic theories of why firms franchise. In theories of "resource scarcity," franchising helps firms ease financial and managerial limits on their growth (e.g., Oxenfeldt and Kelly 1969). Their evidence for this is mixed, as seen in franchise initiation, the subsequent propensity

---

[4] Franchising is not a global solution to the problems of hierarchies and markets. Its adoption has tracked general growth in the economy, since it is simply one form for use in specific circumstances; franchisees and franchisors bear risk just like other entrepreneurs, both large and small organizations use the form, and franchisees often own many outlets (Blair and Lafontaine 2005, 20–53).

to franchise, and franchise performance (Combs, Michael, and Castro-giovanni 2004). To be clear, if resource scarcity is the reason firms franchise, then they should not be able to find another way around this problem that causes them fewer problems in the long run. For example, franchising is not the only way for capital-constrained investors to raise capital because entrepreneurs could raise capital by offering a portfolio of shares in their distributed outlets at lower cost than obtaining a franchise investment (Rubin 1978). While this seems to question the idea that scarcity underlies the choice to franchise, we do come away with an understanding of the role of geographic dispersion in the calculus.

This gives us a hint of the dimensions of the problem for the franchisor (delegator). How does that dispersion impact the franchisor's monitoring problem? For Rubin, the franchisor solves the monitoring problem by forming a contract that shares profits – a contract that franchisees would be willing to pay a lump sum for. And in fact, franchise contracts normally involve two parts: a lump-sum fee, and a continuing royalty payment that depends on sales (not profits). This is why agency theory (the second main theory of why firms franchise) sees the contract as a way to align firm- and outlet-level incentives, one that is a potentially more efficient governance structure than either markets or hierarchies (Caves and Murphy 1976; Rubin 1978). Franchising solves the hierarchical control problem by giv-ing the franchisee a residual that is gained after expenses, which makes the incentives stronger than those for the managers of outlets the com-pany owns outright: incentives substitute for monitoring.

However, the solution is imperfect because of two problems, one related to vertical and the other to horizontal relations. The first problem, in a form of double moral hazard, is that franchisors can try to cut into franchisee profits, and franchisees can fail to pay royalties or cut quality (Lafontaine 1993; Storholm and Scheuing 1994).[5] The continuing pay-ment is necessary because the franchisor (the delegator) suffers from his own form of moral hazard after writing the contract (Rubin 1978). For instance, a local government that has developed a well-tailored local solution to the problem (as it perceives it) might still have to follow national rules about how and when to treat the problem. National pro-grams, even those with a degree of flexibility, still come with strings attached; a natural example these days is the national No Child Left Behind legislation. In turn, the federal government can claim credit for

---

[5] The franchisor's reputation might give it the power to compensate the franchisee by higher than normal quasi-rents (Klein 1995).

gains even while the local government has taken the risk and paid the cost of developing an innovative solution.

The second problem is when franchisees free ride on one another in situations where investments "spill over" franchises (Caves and Murphy 1976). The franchisor could solve this through greater monitoring, but doing so would cut into his own preferred incentives-based solution to the vertical dilemma, which worries him most.[6] Yet, franchisees worry about a horizontal externality between franchisees; each franchise depends on system quality, which only the franchisor can ensure (Rubin 1978); franchisees are relatively more risk averse, which makes them fear this cutting of quality. There is pretty good empirical evidence for this agency theory explanation of franchising (Combs et al. 2004).

To a degree, the structure of federal systems constrains this problem of opportunism. National intervention and centralization, even with the chance of moral hazard discussed above, constrain how opportunistic local authorities can be. Imagine a system without the possibility of federal intervention. The claim is that local authorities would pose a serious risk of opportunism in problems reflecting institutional collective action. This claim is pretty hard to test (except perhaps using data from international relations), but the claim holds water. In practice, some ICAs are fraught with opportunism and require national solution; for instance, the Taylor Grazing Act "solved" the range wars (Ross 1984). Other ICAs are solved, in part, because of the threat of national involvement, perhaps due to a fear of low-quality intervention; an example is the advent of interstate compacts for the management of low-level radioactive wastes (Kearney and Stucker 1985).

Just as in governance, the problem for franchisees and franchisors is to manage conflict and coordination in a system in which both vertical and horizontal authority are fragmented. In practice, it is pretty clear that franchisors cannot solve all the problems simultaneously. Prices are often higher at franchises than at company-owned outlets, which demonstrates how hard it is to gain full coordination (Lafontaine (1992). Franchises often have lower quality and advertise less (Michael 1999, 2000a). Quality control mechanisms are often not as effective as internal production (Combs et al. 2004).

Just as in a system of fragmented production authority, conflict erupts in public policy when those to whom authority has been delegated

---

[6] This problem is exacerbated when franchisees serve stable client bases (when there is low client mobility across franchises).

(franchisees) pursue objectives with which the delegator (franchisor) disagrees. This is a common problem in American governance, and the examples above show that the same problem haunts the hybrid production of goods and services in the private sector. Yet, conflict also erupts when those who delegate authority (franchisors) pursue objectives with which the delegatees (franchisees) disagree. For example, franchisors may pursue sales over maximizing profits (Dant and Nasr 1998). Franchisors require that franchisees engage in long-term tying (agree to contracts well beyond the length that franchisees are comfortable with; see Spinelli and Birley 1996). Franchisors may emphasize or even enhance competition among franchisees (Zeller et al. 1980). These kinds of conflict are directed at the franchisor by the franchisees, just like the disagreements that erupt when central governments bind the hands of local authorities through unfunded mandates, tying of fund flows to performance metrics or comparisons, or the uneven intervention into local policy making and implementation across different jurisdictions. Franchisors have their own defenses: they can suppress conflict by controlling the brand (Parsa 1999), by writing the contract (Storholm and Scheuing 1994), and by gaining a knowledge advantage by operating their own outlets (Michael 2000b).

All of these problems are trivial if the delegator can easily and cheaply monitor the delegatee – if the franchisor can monitor all the franchisees, or in intergovernmental coordination, if the central government can monitor all the local jurisdictions. We know that firms use franchises in the case of geographic dispersion (e.g., Brickley and Dark 1987; Norton 1988; Thompson 1992; Scott 1995). Of course, geographic dispersion is just a proxy for monitoring costs. With dispersion, the costs of monitoring rise, and the firm is more likely to alter its production to take advantage of effects of residual claimancy by franchisees. Likewise, in the intergovernmental production of policy, central governments face a problem of monitoring policy implementation even if they use their own agents in the field (Fesler 1949; Kaufman 1960); this is a very old problem, discussed widely in the management of the Catholic Church, colonies, and even the Tsarist state. So constitutional architects often see federalism and other forms of decentralized implementation of policy as a solution to the problem of managing a large, spatially distributed state, but in fact the problems of monitoring still persist in an altered form.

Geographic dispersion, however, is not the limit of the problem. Since monitoring can be problematic even in a one-territory firm, an alternative explanation for the nature of franchising contract is that the franchisee holds better local information (Mathewson and Winter 1985; Minkler 1992). The franchisor's problem is then to identify a franchisee who "chisels" on the franchisor's standards in order to mask low output as low demand. How can the franchisor solve this problem? It turns out that the solution reveals a fundamental quandary for the delegator. He could solve this "horizontal externality" problem, which is actually pretty small, by imposing a large penalty, although franchisors would have to rely on royalty payments if franchisees have zero wealth. The solution that emerges is that wealthy franchisees can post the bonds for good performance that are found in many transaction costs studies (Williamson 1983, 1985; Dnes 1996). This is the quandary: the franchisor has an incentive for moral hazard in the case of bonds because contracts are incomplete. The franchisor has to rely on royalty payments for extracting rents, but doing so leaves him with the problem of getting franchisees to reveal effort in a self-enforcing way. The problems of moral hazard on the part of both the franchisor and the franchisee are substantial. As an example, franchisors can engage in dual distribution – having both franchises and firm-owned outlets (LaFontaine 1992). The franchisor can then use franchises to uncover local information that, once uncovered, can be used to target new firm-owned outlets, new franchises, or franchise buy-backs.[7]

Throughout this discussion, the contract remains central to the story of how a franchisor aligns his interests with those of his franchisees. In fact, while in most of organizational economics contracts may be explicit, we often discuss them as being *implicit* (Williamson 1991; Milgrom and Roberts 1992, 132). This question of the explicitness of contracts, which also permeates our understanding of agreements between actors in intergovernmental coordination, raises questions about enforceability and hence weakness in implicit contracts (Laffont and Martimort 2002, 345). Whether contracts are explicit or not, though, does not seem to make much of a huge difference; in fact, relational contracts, which are usually much weaker than even implicit contracts (Levin 2003), actually increase franchisee satisfaction (Spriggs and Nevin 1995). So while contracts, explicit or implicit, help us understand behavior in these hybrid

---

[7] Another reason for dual distribution might be that firms want to signal the profitability of outlets (Gallini and Lutz 1992). Dual distribution signals that demand is favorable. There is little empirical support for this signaling hypothesis (LaFontaine 1993; Thompson 1994).

organizations, their actual performance has more to do with how actors work to maintain a governance structure that balances the incentives of a central actor with the incentives of an array of independent horizontal actors to whom the power to make decisions is delegated. In firms, this "make or buy" problem is a problem in optimal contract design – but in practice the contract is always incomplete and usually implicit. These facts do not deter firms from using this hybrid form because it works better than either markets or pure hierarchies. Similarly, policy is often made and implemented through mixtures of central and local actors even though incentives for self-interested behavior are rife. In many ways, this kind of policy making works "better" than either pure centralization or pure decentralization.

In sum, franchising contracts are hybrid organizational forms that mix hierarchies and markets. They try to solve two problems: the franchisor's requirement that the contract be incentive-compatible for franchisees, and the franchisees' requirement that the contract preserve the quality of their investment by limiting cross-franchise negative externalities. Agency-based perspectives emphasize the double moral hazard–nature of the interaction. On the one hand, franchisees will seek to maximize their gains vis-à-vis one another and the franchisor; on the other, the franchisor can undercut the hierarchical allocation of power and shift gains from franchisees to the franchisor. Incomplete contracts limit the strength of incentives to solve these problems, yet even in the case of incomplete contracts neither franchisors nor franchisees can operate without fully considering how their decisions interact with the others'. In the next section, I sketch three ways we can move from a theory of franchising to a broader understanding of the hierarchical and vertical dilemmas embedded in a federalist system of fragmented authority and overlapping jurisdictions.

CONNECTIONS BETWEEN FRANCHISING AND PUBLIC PRODUCTION

This essay is not the first to try to build a bridge between franchising contracts and American federalism. In 1961, Ostrom, Tiebout, and Warren first tried to connect a "franchise-like" theory of public production for understanding the organization of governments in metropolitan areas, although they did not state the theory in those terms. More recently, in his 1990 article in the *Virginia Law Review*, Jonathon Macey suggested the outlines of a franchise theory of federalism. Essentially Macey argues that federal lawmakers gain by agreeing to allow local regulators to make local laws. In his theory, Congress "franchises" the right to regulate to a local or state government under three conditions. First, Congress franchises when a subgovernmental level has developed a body of law that comprises a "valuable capital asset" and rather than enhancing that asset, federal law would dissipate its value. Second, Congress franchises when the "political-support-maximizing outcome" varies geographically. That variance could have a number of sources: spatial monopolies, local political optima, and spatially distributed preferences. Third, Congress franchises if it can shift responsibility to a subgovernment and thus avoid damaging political opposition from interest groups (Macey 1990, 268). However, for our purposes the most important aspect of this theory is Macey's conclusion: "the point is that the supremacy clause, which permits Congress to trump whenever it sees fit, undermines much of the effect of jurisdictional competition among the states in the provision of law" (Macey 1990, 265).

This chapter emphasizes three ways in which the basic franchising problem helps us better understand governance relations among subgovernment entities in the United States. In general, delegation to the states and delegation to a bureaucracy both involve implicit contracting. Each is the use of a specific organizational form to distribute a policy (an output or an outcome) to a constituency. Nation-states delegate to states, or to bureaucracies, or practice mixed delegation (e.g., regulatory federalism). In the same way, a firm may contract with other independent firms for production as a franchise, retain internal production, or use dual distribution.

First, as Macey suggests, subgovernments have to coordinate their activities because Congress chooses to delegate the authority to produce public goods and services to subgovernmental units. As franchising theory suggests, the interactions between those local or metropolitan governments, or between the states, occur in a governance framework where the federal authority is delegated (or abdicated) through an implicit contract. This serves as a latent source of influence on the shape of intergovernmental production/distribution agreements that can be very difficult to measure. It can be very much like the delegation problem described by Banks and Weingast (1992), in which a bureaucracy "reveals the truth" to a legislature when the legislature has made a monitoring technology available; the implication is that bureaucracies that cannot be controlled are not created. In the case I am addressing in this chapter, the intergovernmental arrangements observed among subgovernments are

framed by a hidden vertical delegation of authority. There is an outer limit
on the range that we observe. Of course, while Macey was interested in
Congress's role, the analysis applies at other levels of the federalist system
as well – in many areas, state constitutions give specific powers to cities or
other regional authorities. Those authorities may then delegate to other,
smaller units (e.g., neighborhood associations). Increasingly, other units
outside government are delegated the authority to design and implement
policies that provide public services (e.g., "contracting out").

Perhaps the most significant example of this American policy is the role
of primacy or partial preemption in the making and implementation of
environmental protection policy. Essentially, federal law preempts the
state-level control of environmental policy for many of the major U.S.
statutes (e.g., the Clean Water Act, the Clean Air Act). Primacy or partial
preemption allows states to take control of some portion of policy implementation – essentially, as the "primary enforcement agent for federal
policies" (Crotty 1987). Primacy hands to the state the power to enforce
but allows the federal government to retain control over the overall shape
of policy (e.g., minimum standards, required control technologies). We
know that primacy shifts a degree of power from the federal government
to the states (e.g., Crotty 1987; Davis 1992; Woods 2006). Yet, it is clearly
the case that primacy exists in a larger institutional context in which the
federal government remains a "hidden coordinator" with significant
power to shape behavior without acting. The fact that the federal government could revoke primacy by resetting floors of enforcement or standards, by changing the statutory framework, or by directly regulating
production processes by means like bans means that the "franchise" of
primacy conveys a degree of contingent power to the states. While the
case of primacy is probably the most notable, other examples show that
the situation is general. The role of local militias, and more recently, the
National Guard, in the overall history of federal military policy shows
that the contingent power of states is limited by the long-term interests of
the state in enforcing uniformity among the states.

Second, franchising theory suggests that vertical coordination problems are solved by an (implicit) contract that recognizes the possibility
of double moral hazard. In governance, the federal government does not
receive royalties from subgovernments per se, but the federal government
does recognize the motivation among some local governments and states
to cut the flow of benefits from the state to the national government (for
example, by not providing public goods at a high enough level to meet
the concerns of those seeking to protect the reputation of federalism as

a governance structure). At the same time, the states recognize that federalization of policy is always possible – even when local governments are producing outcomes at a relatively high level. An opportunistic Congress may see quality outcomes at the state level as evidence for creating a new, specific national legal framework, even if that means a loss of control by the states. This double moral hazard happens because of the monitoring problem that coincides with geographic dispersion. The same dispersion underlies the intergovernmental production of public goods and services. A solution to the problem in franchising is the hybrid form of dual distribution. In American governance, federal law often joins together state and nation in the same hybrid way (e.g., the ten standard federal regions, regulatory federalism, partial preemption/primacy, other organizational forms like the Appalachian Regional Commission; see Derthick 1974). This means that a focus on how local or state governments interact must account for how states react to either action or potential dual distribution. Dual distribution is a credible threat in the implicit contract that reconciles the franchisor's fear of cutting with his hope that franchisees reveal useful local information. In governance, dual distribution can play the same role: keeping local governments from moving too far away from a desired state of public goods production and distribution.

One example of dual distribution that has not received enough treatment in political science is the establishment of a separate Civil Rights Division (CRD) in the U.S. Department of Justice (DOJ) in 1957. The federalization of enforcement of civil rights prosecutions (both from the states and from the DOJ's own U.S. Attorneys) shows clearly how far quality cutting can move a central government toward intervention (Landsberg 1997). In fact, many DOJ prosecutions originate now in the CRD, but states and counties (and, in fact, the U.S. Attorneys) are not per se restricted from handling civil rights cases. But the evidence is compelling that the quality and range of civil rights prosecutions increased dramatically after 1957, even before accompanying legislation. Indeed, one role of the CRD is to bring charges against local law enforcement itself, which is an interesting interpretation of how central governments monitor quality cutting.

Of course, the problem of double moral hazard means that central governments also face incentives to renegotiate the vertical delegation of authority for their own ends. This less positive view of federalization is seen in the example of classical unfunded mandates (e.g., Posner 1998). The normative question of the policy-making value of such mandates aside, there appears to be an extraction logic behind discrepancies between state and national rule making that is rooted in how voters' preferences are expressed at the two levels of representation (Crémer and Palfrey 2000). In Crémer and Palfrey's logic, this equilibrium is probably an "unavoidable feature of federal systems" (2000, 906) – that is, the expression of voters' preferences at multiple hierarchical levels leads to situations in which the national government will impose restrictions on the policy-making and implementation authority delegated to the local level. This restriction is the less-positive analogue to the delegator's incentive to restrict quality cutting.

Third, franchising theory suggests an important role for bonding – which may not be allowed fully in internal production. In regionalization (the use of federal agents in local areas) or dual distribution, Congress is limited in how it can constrain the actions of public bureaucrats (although, of course, there is a wide range of less than fully effective options). Royalties in franchising systems work only if contracts are fully specified and there are no wealth effects; contracts between nation and state are largely implicit (except for a constitutional framework). Bonding and hostages become an alternative (in some franchising, bonds are irrevocable – like franchising fees), but they open up the possibility of franchisor moral hazard. In governance, states never post explicit bonds, but they do offer hostages. Specifically, hostages are required for project-specific capital investments that upon termination could result in a penalty larger than the franchisee can realize by cheating. If imposed top-down, they are accepted because the franchisee has no choice. Yet, the same thing could result if franchisees have to hire an enforcer to ensure that cross-franchise (low) quality externalities do not damage their initial investments (Williamson 1996, 64); this is a straightforward application of the Coase theorem. So if we observe local governments either being required to make great project-specific capital investments (investments perhaps too large), or if we observe those governments investing in cheating detection among themselves, both outcomes are consistent with the rationality of hostaging as a mechanism to deter cutting the quality standard. In fact, they might just "hire" the federal government to play the role of detector.

Two examples illuminate the extent to which bonding is part and parcel of the interplay between federal and local levels in the intergovernmental production of policy. Historically, states receiving federal child care block grants were required to provide a state match of dollars, a requirement that is no longer in force but one that used to lead to states requiring their own local governments to match the state match required by the federal government (e.g., Stoney and Greenberg 1996; Connelly and Kimmel 2003). Perhaps a more cogent example is the requirement of state matches for federal highway funds. In a 2004 report, the U.S. Government Accountability Office argued that because states "substitute federal funds for funds they otherwise would have spent on highways" by about 50 percent, "increasing the required state match, rewarding states that increase their spending, or requiring states to maintain levels of investment over time could all help reduce substitution" (2004, i). Both of these examples are forms of bonds, as predicted by the theory of franchising.

These are three simple ways that the theory of franchising frames the hierarchical and vertical coordination dilemmas inherent in a federal system where authority is fragmented and jurisdictions overlap. In one, the threat of federalization limits the range of options local governments have with regard to how they coordinate. In another, double moral hazard among the federal government and local authorities/states makes dual distribution a credible threat and shapes interactions among local authorities. In the third, local authorities can place bonds or hostages (perhaps reputational) or they might invest in third-party cheating detection – and both are consistent with the joint forcing contract that franchising systems often employ.

SUMMARY

The purpose of this essay is to focus on how authority can be both horizontally and vertically fragmented – and the tension in such distributions. I ask what production and distribution organizational form best attains the goals of the state when it selects from a range of forms including national agencies, geographically contiguous states, and highly decentralized metropolitan authorities. I approach this question by considering the analogue of how firms select a production/distribution form – specifically, a peculiar hybrid organization that lies between the atomistic exchanges of markets and the hierarchical intrafirm production process. Franchise contracts have market-like properties because two types of entities trade in capital, labor, or product markets and firm-like properties because the range of bilateral interactions between the two types of entities is restricted. Franchise contracts are seen as harnessing the power of markets and the power of firms. I offered a glimpse at how the theory of franchising contracts in firms speaks to how they try to simultaneously resolve two coordination dilemmas – vertical (between franchisor and franchisee) and horizontal (between franchisees). I then offered points of connection between the economic theory of franchising and how nation-states select organizational forms for the production and distribution of public goods and services.

There is value in considering horizontal and vertical fragmentation as two sides of the same coin. When political scientists debate the benefits and costs of federal systems in which authority is fragmented and decision-making units have overlapping jurisdictions, and when we discuss the ways relatively independent authorities craft institutions and agreements that enable coordination, the "hidden coordinator" problem looms large. Macey (1990) thinks of this as a consequence of the supremacy clause, which helps provide a formal basis for an implicit contract between hierarchical authority and decentralized local implementation. Even if policy originates at the local level – if organizations "self-organize" methods for maintaining joint production and distribution of public goods and services – that implicit contract reflects concerns about the likelihood of moral hazard–influenced behavior. This essay does not develop a full franchising theory of subgovernments and nations, but instead offers a glimpse into how understanding one is difficult without considering the range of options open to the other.

In sum, the horizontal dilemmas that sometimes seem to plague local governments (or agencies) are connected to the vertical dilemmas that come with federalist intervention (which may come with attempts to solve those same horizontal dilemmas). The "central coordinator" can improve social outcomes by jobbing decision making and implementation to autonomous local agents instead of trying to control everything through a consolidated structure. The theory of franchising shows us some of the institutional features of these kinds of arrangements – mechanisms needed for resolving dual dilemmas that face autonomous local agents trying to coordinate and a central coordinator working to shape the overall outcome. These mechanisms are already part of federalist systems; the theory can help us identify other underreported or underappreciated mechanisms that help solve moral hazard and adverse selection problems within the federalist context.

3

The Institutional Collective Action Perspective on Self-Organizing Mechanisms

Market Failures and Transaction Cost Problems

Annette Steinacker

Studies of local governance structures have a long history in urban politics. The early literature tended to cast the choice as one between a highly fragmented local government system and a centralized, consolidated one (Ostrom, Tiebout, and Warren 1961; Bish and Ostrom 1973). The consolidated system was expected to be efficient and effective in service delivery, capturing economies of scale and scope as well as matching government boundaries to the level needed to address large-scale problems. The relatively infrequent adoption of these centralized government forms, however, highlighted the political obstacles in implementation. Local governments and residents often objected to the reduced local autonomy and voted down consolidation efforts. This left the fragmented government system as the only apparently feasible governance option (Carr and Feiock 2004).

The fragmented arrangement mirrored the private marketplace, with all of its corresponding advantages and limitations. Each local government offered its combination of services for a particular tax price, allowing households to choose their preferred product quality, mix, and price. Competition for a mobile tax base would lead to efficient service provision, resulting in the lowest price for a given quality of service and the highest customer satisfaction. The limitation of this market-based system is its inability to deal with standard market failures. Local governments do not necessarily work together to provide public goods; their actions lead to externalities or spillovers affecting their neighbors; and economies of scale are missed when a monopolistic governance structure is ruled out. Possible cooperation across government units to address these problems was rarely discussed in this formulation, presumably

because the advantages of the system stem from the competitive relationship among governments.

The trade-off in designing local governance systems thus appeared to
be between a more effective consolidated system that was not politically
feasible and a fragmented system that was politically viable but plagued
with market failures.

More recently, attention has focused on the range of governance
options between these two extremes. As *Feiock and Scholz* point out in
Chapter 1, there are many governance mechanisms other than the consolidated system that could reduce the market failures occurring in a
fragmented government system. While other authors have described several of these systems (Hamilton 1999), the conditions under which these
self-organizing mechanisms are likely to develop have not been explored
systematically. To assess the likelihood that these voluntary institutional
arrangements would arise, a better understanding of the political
obstacles to their formation is needed.

The transaction costs literature provides a useful framework for this
task (Feiock 2007). Identifying the nature of the transaction cost can
suggest possible ways to reduce those political barriers, which would
make that self-organizing, cooperative arrangement more likely. With a
better understanding of the political obstacles to different mechanisms,
the relative likelihood of each becomes clearer – a self-organized cooperative structure versus a mandated hierarchical approach versus reliance
on an uncoordinated, fragmented local government system.

The type of service provided will also strongly affect the likelihood of a
voluntary governance structure developing. Service type indicates the
nature of the underlying market failure, the corresponding incentive
structure of potential participants, and the kind of transaction costs that
will exist in creating a new institutional arrangement. In this chapter, I
first identify the set of potential transaction costs associated with forming
any cooperative, self-governing institution. Then for each type of service
problem, or market failure, I analyze the type and extent of transaction
costs involved in addressing the problem and suggest the likelihood that a
voluntary institutional structure will be created.

TRANSACTION COSTS IN SELF-ORGANIZING GOVERNANCE

The necessary condition for any cooperative agreement is an increase in
total benefits available to participants (Libecap 1989; Ostrom 1990).
Reducing a market failure problem will move the outcome closer to the

socially optimal resolution, which implies that sufficient benefits are created to make all participants better off than before. However, transaction
costs also need to be kept low in order for benefits of the new institution
that reduces the market failure to exceed the costs of creating it (Feiock
2007; Feiock, Steinacker, and Park 2009). Transaction costs in creation of
the self-organizing governance arrangements considered here arise from
four primary sources.

The first are the costs of *obtaining information* on the potential
participants and the range of possible institutional solutions. Potential
partners in a cooperative service arrangement will differ in the resources
they can contribute and in their preferences over outcomes. These factors affect which government units are the best candidates for a cooperative venture. The greater the number of potential participants
and the less frequent the contact among them, the higher the information costs in determining which are desirable partners and likely to be
interested in a cooperative venture. High information costs may prevent
participants from identifying the mutually advantageous outcomes that
do exist.

The second are *agency* costs. The public officials who negotiate cooperative agreements are agents of their constituents, leading to costs in
resolving principal-agent issues. Compatibility between actions of the
agent and goals of the principal may be hindered for several reasons.
The public officials' career goals may lead them to prefer different outcomes or different timing of outcomes in order to demonstrate achieve-
ments or avoid mistakes prior to their next election or contract
negotiation. Greater diversity in the constituency can lead to diverse
group preferences, making it harder for the principal to determine which
outcome to pursue. The specific structure and powers of local public
offices, as well as the political security of those who hold them, influence
the level of these agency problems (Park and Feiock 2007).

The third source of transaction costs is *negotiation and division costs*.
While a proposed cooperative structure may lead to joint net gains, disagreement over how those gains are divided among the parties may preclude any agreement. Surplus bargaining gains tend to be divided on the
basis of the relative political strengths of the participants. The greater the
differences across the participants, the more clear-cut it may be that one
party will benefit most and other participants will oppose any proposal.
The other participants gain little and may view the outcome as "unfair"
making it more likely that they will walk away from the proposal.
With incomplete information on the strength of each side's bargaining

position, the negotiation process may be prolonged, eventually eroding any joint gains from the agreement, and the proposed governance structure is abandoned.

Finally, *monitoring and enforcement* costs must be low. If jurisdictions would be tempted to renege on the agreement because they could capture an even larger share of the joint gains from doing so, then the participants must invest in monitoring the contributions of others and punishing those who renege. Monitoring costs increase for services when observation of contribution or use is difficult, such as the level of non-point pollution runoff in a water basin. Situations in which the distinction between an unintentional mistake versus intentional defection are hard to determine, such as release of inadequately treated wastewater during a storm, also raise monitoring costs since only the latter should be punished. Enforcement costs are problematic when the only punishment is one that is very costly to the other participants, encouraging jurisdictions to believe sanctions will never be imposed. For some service conditions, the costs to enforce a voluntary governance agreement may outweigh the benefits from cooperation, precluding formation of a potentially beneficial agreement.

As Williamson (1985) illustrated, when transaction costs are high across multiple administrative units that have conflicting goals, integration into a single hierarchical firm can align many of these goals and result in a more efficient production system. Transaction costs are reduced as incentive compatibility across actors is improved. The local government equivalent to this hierarchical firm structure occurs in two ways. The first is a single consolidated government at the local level, realizing horizontal integration of multiple local government units across multiple services. The second deals with vertical integration across government levels through a single agency for a specific service or policy area. Both structures are typically mandated by a higher level of government rather than created through voluntary organization by the affected parties. Because it is no longer a voluntary decision in which all parties must be made better off, the imposed outcome has lower transaction costs, although the hierarchical approach also results in a greater loss of autonomy for the local residents and sometimes less flexibility to adjust to local service needs. In the local governance arena, when transaction costs for a self-organizing governance structure are high, and efficiency problems from the market failure are severe, a consolidated or hierarchical governance structure imposed by a higher level of government may be the only alternative to address the service issue.

This institutional arrangement is not without its own problems. *Whitford* analyzes how many cooperation issues across individual units are transformed into corresponding principal-agent problems when a single integrated unit is created. His work suggests that hybrid forms of consolidation that can preserve various levels of local autonomy, thereby mitigating some disadvantages of full consolidation, should be given more attention.

LOCAL SERVICE TYPE

The characteristics of a local government service determine the payoffs for cooperation and the level of incentive compatibility across participants, both of which affect the likelihood that cooperation can be achieved. Specifying the problem type also suggests alternative solutions to the problem in the same way that specification of market failures suggests appropriate types of government policies (Weimer and Vining 2004). Cooperation in the form of intergovernmental contracts or local service agreements is only one option in the array of approaches to address the problems created by local government fragmentation. Its effectiveness will depend on the type of problem to be solved, with hierarchical or consolidated mechanisms more effective in different cases.

Several examples of local government services are analyzed in the following chapters. Across the service areas studied, fragmentation creates three types of problems: diseconomies of scale, negative externalities, and common pool resource problems. In all three cases the efficiency of the outcome under a fragmented system of local governments is suboptimal, so cooperation could produce joint gains. Joint gains are only a necessary, not sufficient, condition for possible collaboration. Therefore, the likelihood of a cooperative solution depends on three additional factors. First, the distribution of the increased benefits varies across problem types, in some cases creating incentive compatibility problems and therefore decreasing the ease of finding a cooperative solution. Second, reduction in transaction costs should increase the probability of cooperative agreements, but with the size of the impact depending on the initial difficulty of cooperation. Finally, choice of a cooperative institutional structure will depend on how effective alternative mechanisms would be at resolving the underlying problem. Each of these three problem types will be assessed in terms of the alignment of incentives for cooperation, the potential division problems and reductions in transactions costs that might lower those problems, and the impact of alternative institutional structures. The severity of transaction costs from information, agency, division, and enforcement issues will be considered for different types of service problems. The extent of some of these transaction costs depends on the asset specificity and ease of measurement of the service, so these two characteristics are also used in defining problem types (Williamson 1985). The mechanisms considered range from a consolidated government, similar to vertical integration in a firm, to bilateral voluntary service agreements, similar to a market exchange structure.

ECONOMIES OF SCALE PROBLEMS

Economies of scale are likely in two scenarios for local government services. First, several services such as water supply and distribution or sewer systems have high fixed costs, generally leading to decreasing average costs for all government participants if the scale of operations is increased. These services also tend to have high asset specificity, with a physical plant to be built, and a physical output that is easily measured or monitored.

In the second scenario, there is an occasional need for excess capacity to address extreme situations, such as in police, fire, or emergency medical services. Average service on any given day requires much lower inputs than those necessary for the worst-case scenario. Insurance requirements may push each community to spend more per capita on these services in order to meet these extreme scenarios, but with much of the capacity idle on a regular basis. Again, average costs for each participant would be lowered if they could agree to share services when any member experiences a crisis situation. This differs from the first case in that the services have less asset specificity than for a large physical infrastructure and the outputs are not easily measured. In particular, as *Andrew* notes, each community must still provide services to their own geographic region even in the case of an emergency by one of their partners. The level of response that is appropriate given both local and neighboring demands cannot be easily verified, making defection from an agreement more likely and harder to detect.

In both cases, there is a high potential for incentive compatibility. Everyone may be made better off under cooperation because their service costs decline, so all participants are likely to value coming to some cooperative agreement. There also is a fairly clear rule for division of the gains among participants since their benefit level is strongly related to either jurisdiction size or level of use, with some complications from early entrants as described below. The primary differences between the two cases arise from the diversity of the risks for participants when they play different roles, which alter the transaction costs under different mechanisms.

High Asset Specificity – Large Infrastructure Projects

Consider first the large fixed assets case where there is no current service provider – such as multiple small communities that rely on individual water wells contemplating creation of a centralized water supply, treatment, and distribution system. Cooperation should be easiest to achieve in this case. Collaboration to provide the service on a large scale that crosses jurisdictional boundaries could lower costs for all participants. Everyone potentially benefits, with the amount of the benefit fairly clearly determined by amount of use. Division of the joint gains from the scale economies can be allocated through a cost-sharing arrangement based on that level of use.

Difficulties in allocation typically increase when participants are more heterogeneous – particularly when there are extreme differences in their relative political strengths. When one participant has much greater bargaining strength, perhaps due to its size, it can demand a greater proportion of the benefits. This dominant position, however, is often not considered a "fair" allocation and the other participants may walk away from a deal that leaves them with only very small gains. In metropolitan governance issues, this situation could arise with one large city and multiple smaller suburbs. For a service with scale economies, even though the largest jurisdiction could be in a position to build the facility itself, as long as average costs are declining as the scale increases, that player is still likely to prefer to increase the size of the coalition to provide the service rather than try to extort a better price for himself and possibly lose out on the deal. Transaction costs even in the face of heterogeneity may be low, given that the smaller participants are needed to produce the greatest benefits.

The picture shifts slightly if one large provider of the service already exists, since this position increases that player's bargaining power. Having already provided for the largest fixed costs, the existing provider would face only marginal costs for expansion, while the alternative cost for new communities would include the fixed start-up costs as well as marginal costs. The greatest costs savings for new communities are likely to come from some form of cooperation with the largest service provider, strengthening its bargaining position.

For example, a city may have already constructed a water system to serve its residents, while parcels in the neighboring communities rely on individual property wells. As the smaller communities grow and increase their need for the service, several institutional arrangements could be used to produce the needed service: the existing service provider could expand its boundaries through annexation to include the growing area, the smaller communities could contract for service with the existing supplier, they could build their own service, or they could collaborate with other small communities and create a new service provider. The first two options take advantage of cost savings from the existing provider. However, high asset specificity of the service can create problems for both the existing provider and the new entrants, suggesting neither arrangement may be chosen.

When service provision requires construction of a distribution system, asset specificity and investment requirements are high for the service provider. In a contract arrangement there is a risk to the seller if they invest in the infrastructure and the buyers later renege on the contract – perhaps growth is not as rapid as they expected and the tax base cannot sustain their original negotiated payments. The seller needs to charge a risk premium to cover this likelihood, which may raise the cost to the buyers enough to make other arrangements more competitive. In a contract, there is also a risk to the buyer of opportunistic behavior on the part of the monopoly provider. Arguments that service conditions have changed (an unexpected drought) so that the terms of the original agreement must be modified cannot be distinguished from monopolistic efforts to simply expand their rents once the buyer has committed to the contract. For the buyer, the alternative would be starting over and paying the fixed costs if they provided the service themselves or negotiating a new contract with another provider (assuming one could be found), which would expose them to the same moral hazards as in the first contract, although now in a slightly more competitive setting among providers.

High asset specificity binds both sides. Once the project is built, the seller cannot recover the investment unless payments continue from the single buyer. Correspondingly, once the buyer has begun payments that include the amortized costs of the investment, pulling out of the contract would require absorbing payment for those same fixed costs to reproduce the asset. Both sides are vulnerable to opportunistic behavior by the other partner. The existing provider could minimize this risk by annexation of the new territory, thereby gaining control over the terms of future service provision and capturing the benefits of economies of scale. A contract would be their second choice, where the risk from asset specificity would need to be balanced with the higher monopoly rents they could charge. For the new territories, solo provision provides the greatest control over service quality and level – opportunistic enforcement and bargaining costs would disappear – but the least capture of scale economies. Being annexed comes with lower service costs but also reduced control over service provision as the new territory becomes only one part of the constituency for the existing service provider. Contracts leave the buyers vulnerable to renegotiation demands or termination of the contract. Starting a regional partnership (through a new special district) with other communities that do not currently have the service may be the best alternative for new territories. The larger scale permits capture of scale economies, as would a contract with an existing provider. However, the participants have more equal bargaining power because the infrastructure investment would be made at the same time across all participants, so the asset specificity risk would be shared. Of course, the problem of startup costs reduces the attractiveness of this option.

We should expect that in cases with high costs associated with asset specificity, contracts or intergovernmental agreements would be rare. Vertical integration through a single government provider – county, special district, large city government – reduces transaction costs through alignment of common interests within the same organization. An existing monopolist would prefer annexation of the new service territory when possible – expansion reduces their average costs and there is no risk of renegotiation with partner governments. Potential annexation targets, however, may prefer a partnership with other areas that do not currently provide the service, forming a new special district to capture the vertical integration benefits. This arrangement provides the smaller governments with greater control over the service than being absorbed into an existing government, but it still reduces average costs through capture of scale economies. With no existing provider, the potential coalition partners are more nearly equal, reducing the division and negotiation costs, and thereby raising the likelihood of this choice among new service areas.

Mullin examines this question in terms of the relationship between use of purchase contracts and the ability of existing special districts to absorb new service areas. State laws that restrict boundary changes by special districts constrain the bargaining power of these existing service providers as described above, which should make the contract option more feasible. *Mullin* does find that the state constraints on annexation and consolidation are associated with more contractual relationships, suggesting they act as substitutes. However, the level of contracting is still quite low, possibly reflecting the hazards of opportunistic behavior with monopoly providers. While the boundary constraints protect a district that needs to increase its water supply from a hostile takeover by a district with excess capacity, the alternative of a contractual arrangement is still quite risky. Excess capacity frequently is built into a system in anticipation of future growth. Once that occurs, the service provider has an incentive to terminate, or fail to renew, the contract with the new communities and redirect resources to its own constituents – forcing the new communities to find another supplier.

When economies of scale are gained through large public works projects, the high asset specificity involved suggests that vertical integration would be the most effective form of provision. Contractual arrangements leave both sides vulnerable to opportunistic behavior of the other participants. Transaction costs are high in both the negotiation and enforcement stages. In the negotiation phase, division issues are problematic when the parties differ in bargaining power, which occurs when a viable service provider already exists. Even if an initial agreement can be formed, enforcement costs can be high if each partner then jockeys to use their mutual dependency to extract a better deal. When there are no existing service providers so bargaining power is more equal, a cooperative solution is more likely, but still with a vertical integration arrangement such as a new special district being more probable than a series of contracts.

Monitoring Problems – Excess Service Capacity Agreements

When the nature of the problem is the need to provide excess coverage of an emergency service, the decline in asset specificity reduces the benefits of a hierarchical institutional arrangement, suggesting that interlocal service agreements may be more likely. However, the service outputs also become more difficult to measure precisely or to monitor, which aggravates the ability to create a horizontal, voluntary institutional solution.

Again, incentive compatibility and division of the joint gains are not the barriers to cooperation in this case. Incentives of all participants are aligned, in that each will reduce their service costs if they can rely on the others to provide resources in extreme situations. Jurisdiction size is typically a good indicator of cost savings they would experience and could be used as the primary determinant of the contributions each participant would make, leading to easy determination of a "fair" rule for division of costs and benefits. It is the level of transaction costs across the institutional arrangements that would be the primary issue in determining whether a cooperative solution rather than a hierarchical one could be used. The primary transaction cost obstacles come from information costs regarding the reliability of the other participants and enforcement costs in monitoring responses. If any participant does renege and fail to respond, the principal for the affected jurisdiction would also suffer agency costs in both explaining why the initial contract was a good decision and why punishment might not be undertaken. Network interactions are one mechanism that could reduce these potential costs.

As *Andrew* points out in his analysis of emergency medical services (EMS), cooperative arrangements can take two general forms: restrictive arrangements that are binding contracts or adaptive arrangements that are voluntary, nonbinding, and easily adjusted. The primary enforcement cost for both is to determine whether a participant responded appropriately to a crisis in another community. A service provider may not send adequate resources either because of a legitimate need to serve its own jurisdiction or because it was shirking in order to protect its resources. Members of the coalition should be punished only for the latter case, but objectively distinguishing between the two reasons for the same observed outcome is often difficult. A restrictive contract that always punishes for failure to respond could be too severe, yet failure to punish provides motivation for others to use opportunistic responses in the future. The adaptive voluntary contract does not require punishment because there is no obligation to respond, but it then leaves each participant extremely vulnerable in times of crisis.

Even when it could be clearly determined that a participant had reneged on the agreement, the choice to punish under either arrangement would be difficult. Terminating a contract because a partner failed to abide by the terms has a cost to the terminating government – the need to find a new partner, pay higher insurance rates, or spend more to provide a higher level of service itself. Enforcement of a binding contract is costly as it often involves suing another local government and proving that the contract was abrogated. With the voluntary arrangement, the only enforcement mechanism is failure to provide emergency support to a participant who defaulted on the agreement, but that occurs at some indefinite time in the future. This sets up a situation in which cooperation could unravel easily – the only strategy that imposes adequate costs to prevent shirking may be one of "defect forever" if one of the other players ever does. This also may be the strategy necessary for an agent to meet constituent complaints – why provide support to a jurisdiction that failed to support you in the past?

A structure of network interactions may enable participants to set aside these enforcement issues. A network establishes a set of repeated interactions across issues, which increases information on all sides about the trustworthiness of the government players. If trust or social capital is high due to the network, explicit monitoring to determine the probability of shirking versus legitimate lack of response would decrease. Linkage across issues can establish a quid pro quo on responses – so that no participant wants to renege unless truly necessary because they will face retaliation across a variety of services. Networks identify those participants that do not need to be monitored because they are unlikely to shirk, and they establish a punishment option should it ever be necessary. *Andrew* did find that regardless of whether cities negotiate binding or nonbinding EMS contracts they chose their partners on the basis of a tight, overlapping network structure, which increases the establishment of information and trust over time as well as a credible threat of punishment when necessary.

When the economies of scale in service provision come from substantial fixed investment costs, this high asset specificity favors an institutional structure with vertical integration to reduce the risk of substantial losses from the moral hazard problems. When the service involves an outcome that is not easy to monitor but has lower asset specificity, the transaction costs might be reduced sufficiently through network interactions for voluntary local service agreements to be viable. Strong network connections increase the credibility of service commitments and reduce the need to evaluate all responses for shirking, so these horizontal institutional arrangements become more effective.

POSITIVE AND NEGATIVE EXTERNALITIES

Many metropolitan services produce effects that can spill over to nearby jurisdictions. Of the policies considered in this volume, several water basin activities have this characteristic. Two of the primary goals in watershed management are flood control and preservation of water quality, both of which can have externality impacts. For example, upstream cities make choices about channeling river beds that may increase flood problems downstream, creating a negative externality. Policies on protective buffers near water sources that could decrease pesticide or fertilizer runoff would provide positive externalities to those downstream. In the standard political economy framework, too much of the good that generates negative externalities will be produced when there is no way for those effected to express the value of avoiding the harm and too little of the positive externality will be produced. River beds will be channeled and buffer widths set to reduce erosion for the policy-setting jurisdiction and not to minimize the impacts on downstream communities.

Unlike the economies of scale situations facing new communities, not everyone is made better off by cooperative action to compensate for existing externalities. Those affected by the externality are helped by moving toward the socially optimal outcome, but the producers are harmed by changing their behavior unless there are side payments made to them. Standard solutions to externality problems involve either compensation or coercion. The Coasian framework argues that a voluntary market solution (the cooperative outcome) is possible when property rights to the production of the good are well defined and transaction costs are low.

The primary barriers to this cooperative approach with local government externalities are the division and agency transaction costs. As in the case of existing monopoly suppliers of services discussed above, the bargaining position of the externality producer is extremely strong in these cases, as long as their right to produce the externality cannot readily be challenged. The standard solution to a bilateral bargaining game requires that each participant receive at least the value of his outside option or reservation point – how well he could do if the negotiations fell apart. If after each participant receives these values there is still a surplus, that is divided in favor of the player who feels less time pressure and has greater risk acceptance. The latter are factors in the willingness to extend negotiations rather than immediately accept the minimum reservation value and close the deal. The player with the lower discount factor loses less from the delays created by the negotiation process. The player with the higher value is more willing to accept less of the surplus now rather than losing increments with each iteration or risk losing the deal altogether because the other participant finds someone else to partner with or simply walks away from the deal (Steinacker 2004).

To the extent that the producer of an externality holds the property rights to produce it, the status quo is his reserve point. Even if that point is relatively low and those experiencing the externality value a change quite highly, the producer may still reap the majority of the gains available due to differences in discount factors. The recipients of the externality suffer losses every day that the problem is not resolved, while the producer does not. Getting exactly his reserve price leaves him indifferent between reducing the externality or continuing his behavior, which already provides him with benefits equivalent to the offer price. Holding out for more compensation tends to cost the producer little – the only loss would be the discounted value of getting his payment at an earlier point in the negotiations. Delay generally imposes less harm on the externality producers (sellers) than on the recipients (buyers). Given that the producers have both the status quo as a reservation point and a lower discount rate than the recipients, they are in a very strong bargaining position, enabling them to demand a higher percentage of the joint gains available. Breakdown of negotiations, and therefore the cooperative solution, is more likely when most of the joint gains are being appropriated by the externality producer because there may be too little left to motivate the buyer to continue the negotiations.

This division problem may then combine with some agency costs to preclude striking a Pareto-optimal deal. The buyer must explain the outcome to his constituency (an agent to his principal), who may reject the deal as unfair. The externality producer is engaging in "bad behavior" by creating flood problems or destroying water quality downstream and then they benefit from being paid to stop this bad behavior. A coercive, regulatory solution implemented through appeal to a higher level of government may be more politically acceptable to this agent's constituency. Therefore, with externality problems, even when significant joint gains could be produced, the inequality in bargaining positions may undercut the potential for a cooperative, voluntary solution.

If the producer's right to produce the externality can be challenged, perhaps through judicial action, the situation does become more amenable to negotiated solutions favoring those initially suffering from the externality. The costs of delay created by these challenges can change the cost calculus of the externality producer. For example, cities wanting to grow may face high hold-up costs if those suffering externalities are able to delay permits and hence infrastructural development needed to maintain growth, making the producer more amenable to negotiated resolution.

To increase the likelihood of a voluntary solution, network actions might change the participants' parameters in the negotiation model. If the distance between the bargaining positions could be narrowed, transaction costs would decline. *Weible* points out one way that this could happen. He notes the role that threats can play in inducing cooperation, although his focus is more on promoting agreement within the coalitions on each side of the bargaining game. In the bargaining context, threats suggest that the status quo may not be the outside option for the externality producers, nor may they have unlimited time to come to a negotiated solution that benefits them. If receivers of the externality can make a credible threat that other opponents of the producers, such as the Environmental Protection Agency (EPA) in watershed issues, will take action if the local governments do not resolve the problem, then the outside option shifts to the EPA position. That position may make the externality producer worse off than some of the cooperative solutions that could be reached. In addition, delay now brings costs to the producer. Prolonged negotiations that suggest no progress is being made may spark the third party to intervene. Without knowing at what point this may occur, even the more risk-averse producer may move to a cooperative solution. As the parameters of the two participants in the negotiation move closer, division problems decline. In addition, the reduced payoff to the externality producer lowers the agency costs for the other local government officials in defending the deal to their constituencies.

Network relationships can strengthen the ability of the externality recipients to credibly threaten third-party intervention. The horizontal links among local governments and other actors in the policy arena increases the weight they might have in lobbying for action by the third parties. Vertical links in the network with actors at other government levels – state, federal agencies, metropolitan planning organizations – suggest access to and credibility with the appropriate third parties. While the horizontal dimension of intergovernmental relationships is the focus for many of the other transaction cost issues, the vertical federalism aspect may be critical in addressing externality problems.

This emphasis on an external threat to improve the odds of a cooperative outcome implies that coercion may be central to resolution of externality problems. Coercive power – either threat or use – may be necessary to resolve the inherent incentive incompatibility that is the source of the barriers to cooperation. This suggests that nonvoluntary, regulatory actions by higher levels of government may be an easier, and therefore more common, institutional solution in resolving spillover problems across jurisdictional boundaries than voluntary local agreements. In the next chapter *Jones* argues that the role of coercion needs to be integrated into the theory of self-organizing solutions to institutional collective action problems. The case of externality goods suggests that in situations with incompatible incentives across potential participants the level of decisions costs and the possibility of coercion may play a crucial role in the selection of institutional structures.

Externality problems can be particularly tough cases for cooperative resolution because the incentives of the participants are in conflict. Those affected by the externality want change. The producers have no reason to change unless induced or coerced. Even when joint gains exist, the disparities in bargaining power between the participants lead to high transaction costs from division and agency sources, which can prevent voluntary agreements from being reached. Efforts to change those bargaining positions may improve the odds of cooperation, but unfortunately it appears that those changes may require at least the threat of coercion by an outside party. Networks may enable credible threats of future coercion to be made, especially networks that include links to other levels of government, so that a self-organizing solution may still be possible.

COMMON POOL RESOURCES

A common pool resource (CPR) problem offers a more mixed incentive structure to participants than either the scale economies or externality situations. In the long run, the incentives for all participants would be in alignment. Everyone is made better off if the overconsumption and underinvestment in the resource can be solved. The aggregate output that each gains from the CPR can be higher if the resource is sustained. However, to achieve that long-term improvement participants must consume less in the short run, leading to an immediate decrease in welfare for those who cooperate. In addition, in the short run each participant would benefit most from violating the cooperative agreement while everyone else complies – short-term benefits are even higher than when everyone overconsumes, while the long-term benefits would decrease only a small amount if just one user were not complying. Long term, the incentive of all participants would be to comply with a cooperative agreement. Short term, the incentive would be to defect.

Watershed policies offer the clearest example of the common pool resource problems covered in this volume's empirical chapters. The definition of a CPR is that the good is rivalrous in consumption but exclusion is not possible due to either legal or physical difficulties in establishing and enforcing property rights. Water supply is the quintessential example in which each community's extraction of water from the basin reduces the supply available for others, yet physical exclusion of any government whose geographic location permits them access to the water may be difficult to enforce.

With a CPR, joint gains from solving the overconsumption problem exist, as well as some incentive compatibility. However, the high transaction costs primarily arising from the enforcement costs needed to shift everyone's priority to the long-term goals, plus some from division and agency issues, make this a difficult case for sustained cooperation.

Initial Cooperation Problems

Division costs may be a problem in that the agreement must involve a decrease in current use, or in growth of use, in order to preserve the resource. Several allocation rules that appear fair could achieve this, but each has a different impact on who bears the greater short-term costs. Libecap (1989) outlined several options – first in time or use, proportional allocation based on current or historical level of use, or rotation. Without a clear focal point for the division rule, jockeying among the participants may prevent or delay agreement. Again, severe differences in bargaining position, most often due to differences in size and level of use, may lead the dominant player to push for a division rule that others will not find acceptable.

Agency problems may also be hard for the political officials to avoid since any cooperative agreement imposes immediate costs on their constituencies. Incurring up-front costs to gain long-term benefits runs counter to the short-term political horizon most politicians confront. These agency problems are mitigated in some places by politicians' career ambitions. As *Bickers et al.* point out, local politicians may have career aspirations beyond local office, which reduces their risk aversion and time horizon concerns and can lead to more cooperative local agreements. Claiming credit for having negotiated a potential solution to a serious problem may be enough for the official to move to a different position – before seeing any results from it. However, a reduced agency problem because the politician is planning to move to a different job does not lead to a useful policy mechanism for increasing the chances of collaboration in other places. These agency issues may raise transaction costs sufficiently to require a hierarchical approach to resolving the CPR problems rather than voluntary, negotiated agreements.

Sustained Cooperation Problems

Even if these initial transaction costs can be overcome, ability to sustain the cooperative agreement is tenuous due to the high enforcement costs.

Predictions from Cournot cartel studies (oil, coffee) have found that a coalition is difficult to sustain over time because of the strong incentive to defect for immediate gain (Bates 1998; Koremenos 1998a). Differences in time preferences and risk aversion affect the outcome for this type of good, as they did in the externality case. A low discount rate, so that the value of the continued output in the future is still quite high, suggests that more participants will be willing to forgo excess use today for the sustained benefits in the future. However, if one participant has a much higher discount rate, that player's motive to defect will also be high, and the cartel is more likely to unravel sooner. Once an initial defection occurs, the issue of punishment, as seen with emergency service response, is again problematic. Without punishment, defection of this player and others will occur again. In fact, immediate unraveling with all participants defecting in the next round and continuing to do so is a likely outcome if the first defection is not punished. However, a strong punishment, such as a trigger strategy that does not forgive, lowers the long-term benefits for all participants. If the violator is never brought back into the coalition, the continued drain on the CPR depletes the benefits to everyone. Determination of the appropriate punishment strategy and the corresponding enforcement structure is crucial in establishing a local agreement to resolve the CPR problem.

While a difficult case, not all CPRs have been resistant to cooperative governing arrangements (Ostrom 1990). There are several strands of literature that suggest potential resolutions of the CPR problem. Evolutionary equilibrium studies have focused on the mix of players who might defect versus cooperate in the population and the impact this will have on cooperation (Axelrod 1984; Bender and Swistak 1997). While in actual CPR settings it is not possible to alter the set of participants, this approach does suggest that greater information on the distribution of types of participants in the metropolitan area will help determine whether a self-organized voluntary approach to the problem might occur or if a more hierarchical institution will be needed. Working from an Iterated Prisoners' Dilemma (IPD) model, studies of international treaties and business cartels have considered what strategies would sustain cooperation over time – from trigger strategies with different levels of forgiveness, to phased negotiations (Langlois and Langlois 2001), to limited duration of contracts and renegotiations in response to external changes (Koremenos 2002).

Ostrom and colleagues have combined elements from several perspectives in their extensive field and experimental studies to identify conditions that are more likely to lead to cooperation (Ostrom 1990; Ostrom,

Gardner and Walker 1994). Their suggestions have focused on better communication, repeated interaction among participants, and an endogenously adopted sanctioning system, even if third-party enforcers must be hired to implement it. All three of these factors can be easier to establish with a tightly linked network structure in the region. Communication among CPR participants increases the speed of the learning process about the needs of the potential collaborators and the set of strategies the players may use. This shortens the negotiation phase by highlighting the outcomes that lie in the feasible set. Without the strong communication element, learning about other government units happens only following actions of the other players, which occur less often and provide less information. Repeated interactions can update the relevant information and assess compliance with current agreements. When the enforcement mechanism is chosen by the participants, the legitimacy of the system is established and norms of compliance are higher. This reduces the monitoring costs and increases the likelihood that sanctions will be imposed if violations are found. Information costs and enforcement costs may drop when local governments interact in a strong network structure, which increases the chances that CPR problems may be resolved with voluntary agreements.

Berardo also considers the question of how collaboration among government units is sustained over time. He examines whether working together successfully in the past increases the likelihood of collaboration on current water basin projects. He also tests for the impact of both strong and weak tie network connections on collaboration. Previous experiences of working together, especially when the relationship involved the participants exchanging critical resources that could not be obtained independently, did lead to future collaboration, as did network ties of either kind. All of these factors are mechanisms that would provide credible information about the involved participants and build trust for future relationships. Enforcement mechanisms were not explicitly needed in this case, since each project had a defined life span. If a participant did not contribute to the project as expected, that government unit could simply not be chosen for future partnerships. This builds in the limited duration mechanism that Koremenos (2002) found effective in creating contractual relationships. No single long-term contract with all contingencies must be negotiated at the beginning of the cooperative relationship, so initial cooperation is easier. But there is also a clear potential for an unknown number of future beneficial projects, so the "shadow of the future" will still affect compliance in the current stage.

In common pool resource cases, the strong incentives to default in the short term work against the long-term incentive to comply and reap greater benefits. Overcoming this time-dependent incentive incompatibility, first by negotiating acceptable allocation schemes and then enforcing them, requires overcoming high transaction costs. Vertical integration avoids many of those costs. In a fragmented metropolitan region, creation of a special district that covers the relevant area could resolve the CPR overconsumption and underinvestment issues by bringing all decisions into a single organization. For services with a well-defined and moderate geographic scale, this may be an easier institutional arrangement to create than a series of voluntary agreements to control resource use. However, for many services such as watershed protection it may be difficult to get complete coverage of the relevant area in a single organization – in part because the boundaries are uncertain and permeable and in part because the geographic scope would be very large. These same physical features lower the ability to enforce exclusion of those outside the special district from use of the resource. In this case, voluntary agreements among some subset of participants in the watershed may be a more effective and feasible solution, even with the transaction cost barriers. Recent work on CPR problems or more general Iterated Prisoners' Dilemma cases have identified mechanisms that may have led to voluntary resolution of these issues. Intergovernmental networks can be helpful in laying the conditions for the self-organizing solutions through development of communication, repeated interactions, and more effective monitoring and enforcement techniques.

SUMMARY

By considering different sources of transaction costs and classifying the type of service problem that communities are attempting to solve, the nature of the difficulties and the odds of achieving a self-organizing cooperative solution become clearer. When economies of scale are the motivation, everyone could benefit from cooperation. But the high risk from fixed asset specificity when a large infrastructure investment is needed is often enough to preclude cooperative agreements and force a hierarchical approach where risk is internalized. If the economies of scale do not require infrastructure investment but rather pooling of capacities to respond to emergency situations, there are still transaction costs from determining compliance with the agreement and punishment strategies if there is defection. Network interactions may help identify partners where defection is less likely and build an enforcement structure by tying responses in one area to actions in other policy areas as well as responses over time in the same area. This may be sufficient to reduce the transaction costs and allow voluntary service agreements to develop.

When the service involves negative externalities the odds of cooperation decrease because the incentives of the participants are in conflict. The recipients of the externality benefit from solving the problem, but frequently the creators must pay the cost by changing their behavior. This suggests compensation or coercion will be necessary to see a change. Compensation reached through bilateral bargaining, the traditional Coasian answer to externalities, is hindered by division and agency costs. The externality producers are the dominant bargaining partner because the current outcome is already quite good for them. The status quo is their reservation point and they do not suffer many costs from prolonged negotiations to achieve a better outcome. The result is that they can expropriate much of the benefits from resolving the externality problem by forcing those who are suffering to pay their maximum value to change the outcome. This disproportionate result may encourage the recipients of the externality to walk away from the negotiations because they will benefit so little. It is also a difficult outcome for a political agent to sell to his constituency, as it appears that the other government is extorting them and reaping benefits from its initial bad behavior. Coercion in the form of mandated change from higher levels of government may be more likely in this case because that can generate a more "fair" outcome as perceived by most of the participants.

Networks may help in this case, but their effectiveness depends in part on the threat of coercion by those higher level governments. The threat of an imposed solution may change the externality producers' expectations about the likely alternative outcome and the amount of time available to achieve a deal so that they accept a more equitable division of the benefits from cooperation. Strong ties to the third-party enforcers through a network increase the credibility of this threat, and strong ties among local governments can increase their lobbying force when appealing to these enforcement agents.

Common property resources can also be a difficult case for local cooperation. The incentive structure for all participants resembles that of an Iterated Prisoners' Dilemma game. In the long run, everyone could gain more from cooperation in reducing use of the CPR. But in the short run, everyone prefers to defect while others cooperate, which would give them the highest benefits in that round. If it is difficult to monitor use of the

CPR, enforcement costs are high. If it is difficult to determine the reasons for overuse so that defection from the agreement could be either intentional or a mistake, then establishing an appropriate punishment strategy is difficult. Extensive work in this area, including the more general approaches to IPD problems, has identified several factors that can increase the likelihood of sustained cooperation over time. Networks again can help establish or reinforce some of these – such as the importance of communication and learning about the other participants, opportunities for repeated interactions, and norms of compliance that are most likely when the sanctioning structure was created by the participants themselves. Use of a hierarchical structure so that all areas who use the CPR are part of one organization could resolve some of the difficulties in moving from a short- to a long-term perspective and thereby establish compatible incentives for resource sustainability. However, given the scale and sometimes ambiguous boundaries of many of these CPRs, even vertical integration may not completely internalize the problems. This highlights that even an imperfect horizontal service agreement can have value in reducing the problem. For these self-organized local arrangements, overcoming the enforcement transaction costs will the biggest design issue.

Local government fragmentation does contribute to problems with service delivery in many fields. Movement to vertical integration through consolidation of government units or a strong hierarchical structure is one approach to address these problems, but it is not always necessary or the best option. Cooperative local service agreements and contracts can resolve a number of these issues. However, the likelihood that these agreements can be formed and will be effective depends on the nature of the service and the corresponding transaction costs. Just as the argument that consolidation provides the only solution has proved to be too sweeping, so too is the argument too sweeping that horizontal local service agreements can always provide a solution. The characteristics of the service will affect whether the incentives to cooperation are consistent across participants and over time, the type and level of transaction costs, and the chances that these costs can be reduced sufficiently so that a feasible and sustainable distribution of the joint gains will be possible. For some service types, hierarchical structures will be the more effective institutional structures and for others it will be cooperative agreements. With careful analysis, more situations in which local service agreements or other cooperative institutional structures are feasible solutions to problems arising from government fragmentation could be identified and effective mechanisms crafted.

4

Conflict, Power, and Irreconcilable Preferences

Some Limits to Self-Organizing Mechanisms

Bryan D. Jones

What are the effects of fragmented authority in metropolitan areas? This book focuses on one of these: how local governments and agencies can self-organize to obtain collective benefits of policy coordination when faced with uncertainty and commitment problems (*Feiock and Scholz*). It is claimed that the self-organizing development of institutions can reduce the "transaction costs" that prevent the resolution of institutional collective action (ICA) problems, but that the evolution of these institutions is dependent on the motivations of those involved to help develop and maintain the formal arrangements. Analysts in the past have indicated that transaction costs can be mitigated in the design stage, when authority is granted to governmental units. What is new about the approach articulated in this book is that costs also may be mitigated during a second, evolutionary phase in which networks of actors can operate to alter and overcome the transaction costs they have been given exogenously when the set of institutions operative in the metropolis were constructed formally.

Most important, the framework explicitly points toward the motivations of actors that basically cause evolutionary pressures on a decentralized governmental system. To understand emerging patterns of cooperation in what they call "self-organizing" institutions, *Scholz and Feiock* (Chapter 1) argue that instead of assuming that the shape of the institution is exogenously determined by some statutory authority and analyzing only the effects of that institution, we need to analyze the forces that generate institutional solutions to the ever-changing problems of fragmentation in the US federalist system. The tasks facing statutory or constitutional authority they refer to as "first-order collective action problems"; the second, motivational aspects of creating institutions are "second-order problems." This is exactly the right direction in which the study of metropolitan organization and regional governance should move. It refuses to allow the study of governmental arrangements to remain in the comfortable analytic world of comparative statics, demanding instead that researchers examine the emergence, evolution, and even disappearance of formal institutions and informal networks of policy actors.

The *Feiock and Scholz* framework is inherently dynamic and as a consequence it immediately becomes more complex but more central for understanding patterns of multijurisdictional cooperation. As firmly as I support the general thrust of this enterprise, I nevertheless want to suggest here that a model of metropolitan and regional organization that rests on transaction costs is incomplete, and incomplete in a manner that can lead to misleading models and poor policy advice. It focuses on situations that might be improved through cooperation, pushing the conflict focus of most classic studies of multijurisdictional arrangements. In particular, the ICA framework does not fully incorporate three elements that are crucial to address if we are to move toward a stronger theory of governmental organization in metropolitan regions:

1. The necessity of incorporating elements of conflict theory in which zero-sum elements in the network can be more critical than incompletely incorporated positive sum elements in deterring policy action.
2. The need to incorporate boundedly rational actors in the model, actors capable of misunderstanding the problem space and engaging in incomplete, localized search for solutions that they subsequently become emotionally attached to, creating the perception of zero-sum games even when the underlying ICA is actually a positive-sum game.
3. The necessity of appreciating spillovers among the various networks and other mitigating mechanisms in the metropolitan system, since mechanisms to resolve positive sum gains cooperatively in one policy subsystem may impose losses on other systems.

These elements imply a multijurisdictional, multilevel system of games in which bargaining plays a central role. It is not clear that the analytical capacity to engage in such an analysis exists, especially if we accept the key implicit premise of the *Feiock and Scholz* framework that the evolution of process implies there may be no stable policy equilibrium. Nevertheless, I want to suggest a potential strategy for analysis that does address both the conflict theory and the evolutionary elements of inter-jurisdictional politics. This is a recent bargaining/game-theoretic model developed in international relations to study bilateral interchanges in which a complex issue space is involved. This is not at all farfetched; forty years ago Matthew Holden (1964) suggested that political scientists study cities using the same tools as international affairs, and Norton Long's 1958 essay on metropolitan organization suggests the game meta-phor to describe patterns of conflict among governments. In a very prom-ising empirical essay in this volume, *Lubell, Henry, and McCoy* apply Long's basic notion to patterns of interaction among governments engaged in watershed management.

TRANSACTION AND INTERDEPENDENCE COSTS IN THE METROPOLIS

Steinacker discusses four kinds of transaction costs that are critical to the ICA framework: information costs, agency costs (ensuring that agencies represent constituencies), negotiation costs, and enforcement costs. Yet these costs underestimate the cost structure actually faced by participants in metropolitan governance.

It is important to distinguish between *transaction* costs and *interde-pendence* costs in policy-making processes. The starting point is Buchanan and Tullock's *The Calculus of Consent*, published in 1962. They conceive of any governmental decision-making arrangement as involving a fundamental trade-off between the *decision (or participation) costs* of coming to a decision, on the one hand, and the imposition of unwanted *external (or externally imposed) costs* by the decision-making structure, on the other. Decision costs are high when many actors are involved in a decision, such as would be the case in a New England town meeting. But the *decision rule* for coming to a decision is also critical. A New England town meeting where everyone gets a say but the majority rules in the end is a model of efficiency compared to a Quaker assembly in which unanimity and legitimate agreement among all is required; it is not acceptable for some to go along simply to bring the meeting to a close.

In such a setup, decision costs are high, but imposing unwanted external costs on even a single actor is impossible. When a single "dic-tator" is empowered to make a decision for all, decision costs are much lower, but the potential for imposing external costs on the rest of the group is very large. The sum of these two costs is the *interdependence cost*; in an ideal world this sum would be minimized or at least reduced

in making institutional and constitutional changes (Buchanan and Tullock 1962, 46). But, of course, actors may erroneously focus on a single
set of costs and because of uncertainty may set up a constitutional or
decision-making structure that doesn't work very well because the resultant interdependence costs are higher than the expected gain from the
governance structure. Thus Buchanan and Tulloch formulate the old
"democracy-action" trade-off in an elegant fashion: too much democracy leads to inaction; too much concentrated power leads to abusive
government.

This analysis of governance, involving a political struggle over who
sets the constitutional rules and hence who bears the decision and external costs of governmental action, is quite distinct from the usual transaction cost analysis. The use of transaction costs has become quite loose
in political science. It is drawn from economics, where parties want to
engage in an exchange that is fully voluntary between the parties. So the
question is to determine what costs they must overcome in order to consume the bargain. If the costs are high enough, they will not be able to
consume the bargain (in the language of pubic choice economists, the
arrangements will impose "deadweight costs" on the economic activity
that could emerge from the bargain). So lowering transaction costs will
lead toward a Pareto optimum, ceteris paribus.

By definition, ICA problems assume that mutually preferred outcomes
exist, so the primary question about interdependence costs addressed in
the *Feiock and Scholz* overview is whether the gains from achieving the
preferred outcome offset the combined decision-making and external
costs for a given mechanism. When interdependence costs exceed the
potential gains from cooperation, no self-organizing mechanism will gain
voluntary support.

The relevance of transaction cost analysis is particularly questionable
when conflicts involve zero sum games in the sense that all recognized
alternatives create winners who cannot directly compensate the losers. If
actors have incompatible preferences over the limited set of available
alternatives, for example, or if the costs of delayed decisions (e.g.,
increase in expected costs of all alternatives, ongoing costs of the status
quo, and holdup effects on all other decisions that are postponed) are
higher than the potential gains from eventual coordination, then we do
not have an ICA coordination problem; rather we face an *institutional
conflict resolution* (ICR) problem. This has been the traditional focus of
metropolitan government studies, since the majority of conflicts that are
generally studied appear to resemble ICR rather than ICA problems.

For ICR problems with high interdependency costs, abdication of decision authority to a central decision maker may be justified to the extent that the savings from an expedited decision process outweigh the potential external costs. The key issue here is the extent to which majorities are allowed to coerce minorities into taking action (or failing to take action) that they do not want to take. In the separation of power arrangement of American government, decision costs are very high because concern with external costs has led to the requirement to produce supermajorities to get major policy action. To the extent that ICR is the dominant type of problem facing governance institutions, a bargaining framework and conflict theory is more appropriate than a collective action approach for understanding and mitigating the costs of conflict. The major activities contributing to participation costs in these settings include lobbying, coalition-building activities, venue shopping, and confrontation among advocacy coalitions seeking to influence the authority's decision, which can be quite distinct from the activities contributing to institution building and maintenance studies in ICA settings.

In vertical or hierarchic authority systems, networks are critical in part because policy professionals share preferences. Actually it is better to conceive of policy professionals as sharing *outlooks*; that is, policy professionals at different levels of government share professional training and in general define the policy problem facing them in similar ways. Surely one reason for the emergence of vertical networks is the coordination of the definition of problems and the search for solutions. So the *Feiock and Scholz* perspective is also relevant to such vertical networks. But political leaders at different levels of government may not share perspectives (e.g., *Whitford*), and there is a robust literature on the inherent conflict in the roles of grantor and grantee, both in the American intergovernmental relations literature and in the international relations literature. So once again analysts need both models of cooperation and conflict.

Finally, no conception of the metropolis is complete without a full appreciation of the role of state governments. No subunit in states is independent in any sense comparable to state governments that are constitutionally protected in the U.S. Constitution. States are intimately involved in not just the creation of municipal governmental units; they are important funding sources and sources of legal constraints and mandates. That makes the state bargaining actors as well as the final arbiters in specifying statutory authority. That is, the state must be considered a unique actor in both the ICA problem and the development and maintenance of any mitigating mechanism.

Problem-Space Specification, Solution Search, and Discovering Preferences

A second cost relevant for metropolitan governance is what Frank Baumgartner and I termed "cognitive costs" (Jones and Baumgartner 2005). Cognitive costs represent constraints imposed on the problem-solving abilities of political actors due to the cognitive architectures of the participants. Constraints on the allocation of attention to an issue, causing actors to juggle among the various issues without devoting sufficient time to resolve any of them, provide a key example. This constraint can be severe in many decision-making situations because attention allocation, human or organizational, is a bottleneck through which the most important issues must be filtered. A second example is Herbert Simon's classic "identification with the means" in which people become cognitively and emotionally attached to a particular solution to a problem, pursuing it well beyond its comparative utility. This tends to narrow the search and lead to suboptimal choices. It is feasible only because of the extreme uncertainty concerning ends-means relationships in many policy problems.

Conflict can exacerbate the problems of cognitive costs in authoritative systems. In particular, cognitive responses to conflict can transform an emerging ICA dilemma into a zero-sum problem in which participants fail to recognize mutually advantageous solutions. For example, Sabatier's advocacy coalition framework provides numerous studies in which identification with the means becomes embedded in a coalition-building strategy that is particularly essential when the authority can impose a single decision on everyone. Advocacy coalitions continue to battle each other for years in a given regulatory arena and have little incentive to search for mutually satisfactory solutions while conflicts continue. Cognitive costs can become more important in federal systems when higher level government intervention transforms a self-organizing setting into an authoritative setting.

Both the ICA and ICR perspectives often treat the policy space (both the problem space and the solution space) as well defined and known or readily discovered by the participants. Because of cognitive costs, this is often not the case. Part of the process of bargaining invariably involves mutual specification of the problem-space, even when protagonists have fixed preferences for solutions.

The bargaining process can incorporate the "shadow of the future" in repeated games, but it can also involve seemingly "irrelevant" alternatives.

Facilitators in conflict situations invariably introduce alternate dimensions to transform the situation from a one-dimensional situation to one with more parameters, and that tends to encourage productive solutions. Policy learning is important here. Learning does not concern just finding out how a policy works but also the context within which policy is delivered. This implies that any policy network may overcome transaction costs, in the sense of reducing barriers to a policy settlement, but it also may aid in policy learning and reducing real decision costs by modifying the preferences of participants. But, as I show later in the chapter, communication often leads to hardening of positions and increased "identification with the means."

WHAT KIND OF COLLABORATION?

In some kinds of policy-making systems, collaboration has been studied, but such collaboration does not always lead to collective goods. When does collaboration become oligarchy? When collaboration occurs in the classic regulatory subsystem, it often deteriorates into capture by those with resources and capacities required to participate. Interestingly, this can happen when groups with substantially different resources attempt to collaborate in seemingly open, cooperative systems. So it is essential that we keep in mind that some forms of collaboration are conspiracy, or indications of disproportionate power relations. In a metropolis, cooperation can involve severe power differentials if it is required by statute or if collaboration provides the only way to achieve a collective good. To view such arrangements as "voluntary" often misses the crucial coercive aspects of the decision-making arrangements.

Collaboration among one set of metropolitan actors can impose disproportionate costs on other actors. For example, *Lubell et al.* present data showing that environmentalists in collaborative arrangements are less satisfied than other actors and feel that the arrangements are less fair. It is likely that these participants view themselves as losing to business interests in collaborative arrangements. Again, these are supposedly voluntary arrangements in which disproportionate power should not be in evidence.

The pro-collaboration arguments are particularly troubling when one views the nature of cumulative disadvantages experienced by residents of some governmental jurisdictions. Indeed, the spatial concentration of such disadvantages has traditionally been a core concern of urban analysis. This does not mean that such resource-poor jurisdictions are helpless in pluralist, collaborative systems. But it does mean that resource differentials can transform a purely collaborative arrangement into one fraught with bargaining and classic strategic action (see Jones and Bachelor 1986).

It may be easier to collaborate when subsystem participants agree to impose costs on the broader public through taxation, user fees, or externalities such as displaced congestion in a transit system. These conditions can be manipulated by subsystem participants when the general burden is low on a per-citizen basis and where the "fiscal illusion" allows citizens to be fooled concerning the real cost of a service (Buchanan 1967). In any case, we cannot be fooled into thinking that successful collaboration in a policy subsystem invariably produces collective goods for the community, even if it does so for the participants in the subsystem. Thus, collaboration within authoritative structures can amount to collusion.

IS A MORE COMPLETE THEORY OF COLLECTIVE ACTION POSSIBLE?

My final question is this: can a more satisfactory theory be developed of collective action in formally decentralized policy-making systems? The essays in this volume that incorporate transaction costs and informal networks of actors are proof enough of the theoretical and empirical breakthrough that this conception offers. I have little to criticize about this approach, except that it is incomplete, and as such it cannot provide a full theory of metropolitan organization. Such a theory would need to incorporate the *Feiock and Scholz* approach as well as the multi-issue conflict-management perspective inherent in Norton Long's (1958) ecology of games. Institutions in the metropolis can be forums for building trust and overcoming transaction cost barriers to collective action, but they also can be arenas for the interplay of interest politics and stalled action. The reason may be the failure of the system to provide enough trust to overcome transaction costs, but it may also fail to produce action because of external and decision-making costs. Any institutional arrangement results in considerable institutional friction that inhibits action. And I mean friction and *not* veto points – it is a dynamic process, not a static one – that need to be studied. But veto groups can be overcome by sustained attention to a matter, since cognitive/emotional dynamics in policy making can overcome the built-in friction of formal institutions (Jones and Baumgartner 2005).

Such a model should incorporate a bargaining approach, in which three components are realized:

- A distinction between transaction and interdependence costs.
- Bargaining among governmental units of disproportionate power (where that power may vary by issue-area).
- Issue multidimensionality and attention allocation.

Liu's Spatial Supergame Model

In what ought to be recognized as a critical theoretical breakthrough, Liu (2006) has developed a spatial supergame bargaining model for bilateral international relations that involves issue complexity, attention allocation, and a multitude of bargaining agents. It is of course no simple matter to extend this to a multiple actor situation, but conceptually it is straightforward. At least some ICA problems in the metropolis involve bilateral bargaining relations, and the model may be directly applied to them.

Liu's approach is capable of addressing the major problem of "issue juggling" among unitary actors in which the intensity of attention to issues varies across time, and thus addresses the limitations imposed by the cognitive architectures of actors. He describes his model thus: "Two players interact with each other over *multiple issues* concurrently across time, and they are playing *multiple issue games* simultaneously and continuously" (Liu 2006, 43). Liu's model differs from the two-level game approach used by Tsebelis and others; whereas the two-level game approach assumes that a government "plays multiple games with *different* players (i.e., domestic and international players), the spatial supergame model suggests that a national government simultaneously plays multiple games with the *same* international opponent" (Liu 2006, 44).

Figure 4.1 shows the representation of the game at one point in time. The game structure moves through time, with varying weights on the dimensions. In the case that the issue structure collapses into a single issue, as is the case in an "attention vortex" discussed below, any solution at that time will take on the characteristic of a one-shot game, and hence would have a Nash solution. Liu's formulation thus may be seen as a generalization from which both the single-issue supergame and the one-shot simple game can be easily derived.

Liu sees the juggling of issue weights as a function both of the exogenous world and the cognitive architectures of the players. Cognition works through attention allocation and the processing of real-world

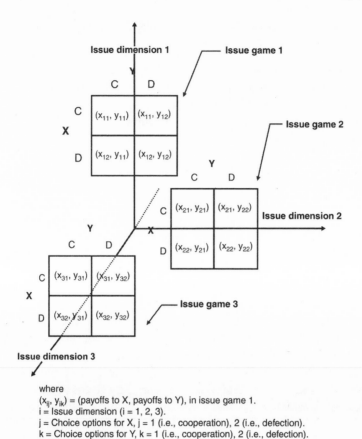

where
(x_{ij}, y_{ik}) = (payoffs to X, payoffs to Y), in issue game 1.
i = Issue dimension (i = 1, 2, 3).
j = Choice options for X, j = 1 (i.e., cooperation), 2 (i.e., defection).
k = Choice options for Y, k = 1 (i.e., cooperation), 2 (i.e., defection).
C = cooperation option.
D = defection option.

FIGURE 4.1. Liu Spatial Supergame Bargaining Model for Bilateral International Relations.

information. That is, information serves as signals but the attention allocation process interprets the signals – by adding weights to the issues in the bargaining process.

The Alaska Way Viaduct as an Attention Vortex

An interesting case in point has emerged in Seattle with the reconstruction plans for the Alaska Way Viaduct that was damaged in the 2001 Nisqually earthquake. The case illustrates the necessity of using both the self-organizing approach advocated by *Feiock and Scholz* and a multilevel bargaining model along the general lines of Liu's model. In this case, as the issue took shape, the preferences of actors unfolded. Three central players emerged: the State of Washington, represented by Governor Chris Gregoire; Seattle Mayor Greg Nichols and his strong allies in the business community; and King County Executive Ron Sims, who mobilized environmental interests. Three basic solutions to the problem were placed on the table: rebuild the viaduct, replace it with a tunnel, and replace it with surface boulevards.

Feiock and Scholz view self-organization in terms of creating a single decision mechanism to link choices across multiple games to ensure that these externalities are taken into consideration within each independent authority. Nevertheless, some situations, such as the Alaska Way Viaduct described here, make voluntary solutions extraordinarily difficult.

The City of Seattle experienced internal divisions centering on differences in conceptions of the problem-space and the best solutions. The City of Seattle government and civic elites focused on traffic flow and restoring the waterfront, since the viaduct currently divides the waterfront from the rest of the city. The tunnel option emerged as the City's preferred option for addressing both issues. The State of Washington was primarily interested in traffic flow and costs, with the replacement viaduct being the preferred solution. The King County Council and Executive Ron Sims weighed in with a preference for the surface street plus additional mass transit.

One of the most important aspects of the issue has been the increased attention it has received in the current legislative session. One blogger said "both Iraq and the Viaduct have created an attention vortex in Olympia and D.C., preventing anything else from getting done."

A major consequence of an attention vortex is that it makes difficult any system of side payments or variations in issue emphasis that Liu has shown can lead to better policy outcomes. In effect, his supergame structure that initially has varying weights on the issue dimensions now collapses into a single game. Because attention is focused, basically this winds up as a one-shot game in which neither the "shadow of the future," nor variability in issue emphasis, nor side payments can prevent what may be a suboptimal solution. The result is a zero-sum structure in which decision-making costs are high because external costs are imposed on the losing party.

Figure 4.2 depicts the decision structure for this critical transportation project. The City prefers a combination of city enhancement and maintenance of traffic flow; the State prefers to address traffic issues within a reasonable cost ("The tunnel is a luxury the taxpayers of Washington

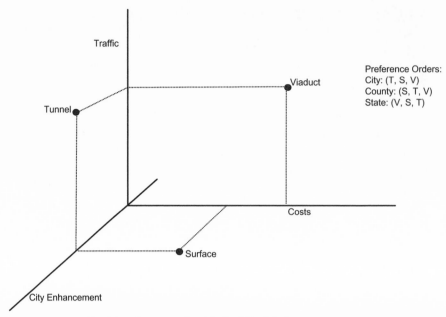

FIGURE 4.2. Decision Structure for Alaska Way Viaduct.

cannot afford," Speaker of the House of Representatives Frank Chopp and 29 members of the House Democratic Caucus wrote to Governor Chris Gregoire); the County wants city enhancement (along with enhanced mass transit) with a reasonable cost.

Once the supergame structure of three two-way games (traffic vs. costs, costs vs. city environmental enhancement, enhancement vs. traffic) has degenerated into a single-shot game, the self-organizing governance approach is not really relevant. Straightforward analysis of preference orders suggests that the surface street option (the first priority of one actor and second for the other two) would win in most voting schemes. Yet it was preferred by the least powerful set of actors, and most reasonably objective observers viewed it as practically untenable (partly because of its effects on traffic into and out of the Port of Seattle, which would cross the surface streets or involve significant viaduct rebuild, causing the cost of the option to escalate).

The disproportionate power of the state is indicated by a listing of funding sources for the project:

- 2005 Gas Tax (Partnership Funding) – $2 billion (State)
- Transportation 2003 Account (Nickel Funding) – $177 million (State)

- 2005 Federal Earmark Funds – $207.5 million (Federal Government)
- Other Funds – $19 million

  ○ City of Seattle ($15.8 million)
  ○ Puget Sound Regional Council ($1.2 million)
  ○ Corps of Engineers ($100,000 for the seawall)
  ○ Federal 2003 budget ($2 million)

It is clear that the state was the elephant in the room because it was the source of most of the funding. The mayor was supported by the business community of Seattle and the "civic power structure," which proved less important than urban "regime theory" would suggest. King County would have been a minor player in the system even with "Green" support for the surface street option, but the fast-paced evolution of the politics of the situation played into Sims's hands.

When Washington Governor Chris Gregoire threatened to take the State's funding off the table, Seattle's Mayor Greg Nichols quickly arranged for a citywide referendum. Gregoire objected but fell silent because it meant opposing a public say on the project. In the subsequent referendum, Seattle citizens decisively voted down the option of a tunnel *and* a replacement of the elevated highway. (It was scant consolation to the governor that the tunnel was defeated by a greater majority than the viaduct.) The ballot wording made it difficult to interpret exactly what this meant, but it certainly gave new life to the surface street option (although this option was not on the ballot, and its cost is not likely to be a lot cheaper than the viaduct option).

Both Gregoire and Nichols agreed to a "cooling off" period during which other options could be considered. Nevertheless the State is proceeding with the destruction of the viaduct. The Washington Department of Transportation's statement is one of political impasse: "The end result for this project will be the replacement of the viaduct and seawall. The final design will be developed through a collaborative process." It is quite clear that such collaboration will not lead to a policy settlement because transaction costs are reduced but rather because some sort of intergovernmental bargaining has resulted in the necessary side payments that can be interjected into the process once the attention vortex dissipates.

In sum, the project development had four phases:

- Inattention, followed by
- Serious attempts to consider design and funding simultaneously, then
- The attention vortex
- Political deadlock

During the funding and design phase, the actors' identification with specific means firmed, so that by the time of the attention vortex, conflict had become fully zero-sum. It is not inconceivable that new solutions will be proposed basically modifying the viaduct design to mitigate its downtown impact, but that remains to be seen and will in any case be difficult, given the manner in which the "food fight" among major actors has proceeded.

Here we have a case in which networks of actors, including the major political officials and transportation bureaucrats at the state, county, and city level, are well developed into advocacy coalitions and a clear case of where the status quo is suboptimal. All actors saw some benefit in moving from the status quo, and in that sense there was a collective action problem. But no amount of discussion could resolve the impasse because major actors differed in their rankings of the solutions. Neither could power resolve the impasse. The mayor and his allies, the Seattle business community, strongly favored the tunnel option, but Governor Gregoire and the Democratic caucus in the legislature insisted on the viaduct rebuild. Neither set of strong players could impose its preferred solution, offering an opening to the weaker player (King County Executive Ron Sims and his allies in the environmental community).

Liu's supergame model, based in divergent interests among participants, fits this policy scenario better than the self-organizing approach does. Attention activates the game played among competing issues. Dropping the Alaska Way Viaduct from the active political agenda allowed the major participants to agree on the construction of a transportation package that included funding for the removal of the viaduct but no money for the (as yet undetermined) replacement. The deliberate intermediate solution was to create a future situation in which participants would have to forge a final solution. In effect, the intermediate solution, tearing down the viaduct, would create an untenable situation while guaranteeing Seattle a piece of the future transportation pie.

SUMMARY

The self-organizing approach to metropolitan organization advanced by the editors of this volume represents a major breakthrough in understanding policy making in decentralized systems with overlapping jurisdictions. It has great virtues, because it offers a theoretical underpinning that is associated with a new methodology. It is in addition fundamentally dynamic and evolutionary, because linkages are not static but evolve in response to the problem-space faced by participants. These are very important contributions, and as a consequence they add considerably to our toolbox for analyzing public policy in the metropolis.

Nevertheless, the self-governance approach is incomplete because it may not adequately incorporate the more conflictual elements of metropolitan organization. Incompleteness in this case risks consequential problems. In particular, communication can reduce transaction costs, but it may or may not resolve external interdependence costs. Transaction cost barriers to intergovernmental collaboration may be overcome if new solutions are developed that can achieve a policy settlement, but it is just as likely that communication will increase the vigor with which participants defend their preferred solutions.

It is likely that a single theory of metropolitan organization will elude us for the present. If so, then it is critically important that we carry forward both theories of collaboration, based in an analysis of transaction costs and collective goods, and conflict theories, based in divergent preferences and zero-sum outcomes. Surely in this sense the study of the metropolis evokes the study of international relations, in which cooperative arrangements overlie a complex system of bargaining among and between nations (and other nonstate actors).

The pluralist tradition of metropolitan organization emphasized conflict, but conflict that did not cumulate across issues. The public choice approach emphasizes that at least some urban issues involve conflict that can be resolved through the reduction of transaction costs. Neither approach incorporates the notion of cumulative disadvantages plaguing some urban residents that many urban analysts have demonstrated. A full theory of metropolitan organization would appreciate all of these, yet we live in an imperfect theoretical world. At present, all we can do is to remind ourselves that our favored theories are almost certainly wrong but just as certainly incorporate important elements of the metropolitan world.

PART TWO

INTEGRATING METROPOLITAN SERVICE PROVISION

Networks, Contracts, Agreements, and Special Districts

5

Adaptive versus Restrictive Contracts

Can They Resolve Different Risk Problems?

Simon A. Andrew

Studies of interjurisdictional activities often define contractual arrangements as simply a means to protect local government transactions and procedural rights. Instead, we argue that interlocal agreements constitute a set of special relations, which we refer to as "contractual ties" among governments. Depending on the types of agreements adopted, a network of contractual ties provides local governments with a means of mitigating mutual institutional collective action (ICA) problems by creating potential access to an array of tangible and intangible resources that exist outside each government's organizational boundaries (Gulati 1998). When local officials enter into short- or long-term contracts, their interactions can lead to regular and sophisticated systems of communication (Thurmaier and Wood 2002). It is through repeated interactions that local officials can judge the trustworthiness and legitimacy of their contracting partners, qualities that are crucial for the creation of self-organizing institutions. Contractual ties are embedded in a rich social context in which information and opportunities are exchanged, the risk of opportunistic behavior can be reduced, a cohesive set of preferences can be aligned, and a common interest can be coordinated and mobilized (Maccaulay 1963; Shapiro, Sheppard, and Chraski 1992; Jones, Hesterly, and Borgatti 1997).

The substantive focus of this study is on the emergence of contractual ties among local government law enforcement departments, emergency medical services, and fire departments within a polycentric governance system (McGinnis 1999). Planning for emergency quick response and recovery efforts often requires local entities to enter into strings of formal and informal agreements. Public safety activities generally produce positive externalities, but they are highly diverse, ranging from recurring public safety activities (e.g., standard police patrol, crime and fire suppression) to episodic events such as emergencies and disaster events (e.g., evacuation planning, mutual aid responses). These transactions present different types of risks that may affect the willingness of local governments to enter into one form of agreement over another. The willingness to participate in these agreements also depends on the local governments' abilities to overcome the transaction costs of contracting that can result from certain community characteristics and political institutions (Feiock 2007).

This chapter differentiates two broad categories of contracts: restrictive and adaptive. Adaptive arrangements provide local governments with the flexibility to adapt to changing circumstances, but they increase the potential risk of opportunistic behaviors. In this situation, local governments may seek to enter into adaptive agreements with a closely bonded or overlapping set of partners in which trust and potential for mutual sanctions can reduce the risk of opportunism.

In contrast, a restrictive arrangement can minimize the risk of opportunistic behavior, but it presents a special dilemma because parties to an agreement may be locked in or lose control over the provision of services. Thus the agreement cannot easily adapt to changed conditions. Local governments are expected to select partners in restrictive agreements whose recurring services are less likely to be in demand by others when some emergency strikes, creating an emergent pattern of sparsely connected exchange partners.

These arguments have relevance to ICA problems for explaining the emergence as well as the expected structure of self-organizing governance mechanisms that local governments adopt in response to local circumstances. Legally independent but functionally interdependent units of government can customize their interactions to reap the advantage of associational benefits and buffer the effects of a changing environment better than a central hierarchical structure (Ostrom and Ostrom 1999, 113). The set of rules and procedures they develop reflects quasi-market arrangements among fragmented localities that arise as local governments attempt to sustain self-organizing governance in the provisions of public services (McGinnis 1999).

Patterns of contractual ties emerging over a period of 17 years in Florida's four largest metropolitan areas are analyzed using the SIENA network analysis program. The results reported here suggest that risks of opportunism are a predominant concern for both types of contractual arrangements. In both cases, local governments tend to seek the partners of their contract partners. Multilateral agreements also influence the formation of adaptive contractual ties, but substitution effects are also observed, suggesting that local governments entering into multilateral agreements are less likely to establish bilateral agreements. There is also evidence to support the influence of political institutions and the preference for partners with similar characteristics on the formation of bilateral contractual ties.

RESTRICTIVE AND ADAPTIVE CONTRACTS

State statutes provide the legal framework within which local governments negotiate agreements and determine the scope, stringency, and degree to which any contractual arrangements can be enforced. While some state statutes authorizing negotiated agreements are broadly defined, others are more specific and impose stringent procedural requirements (ACIR 1985). Depending on the definitions and scope of state statutes authorizing their usage, interlocal contractual arrangements can be classified into two broad categories, restrictive and adaptive, with the former reflecting complete and the latter reflecting incomplete contracts. An arrangement is restrictive if the specific rules governing that transaction are specified clearly and the outcomes of the transactions are predictable and included in the contract. To be effective, the arrangement must be backed by specific state statutes or local ordinances that can feasibly be defended (in an economic and legal sense) in the legal system. Restrictive contracts, such as interlocal service agreements and contract or lease agreements, are often observed in transactions involving financial or tangible resource exchanges, especially for recurring public safety activities (Atkins 1997; FLCIR 2001).

On the other hand, alternative sets of contractual rules exhibiting adaptive or flexible features may be necessary to accommodate unanticipated changes in future conditions (Heckathorn and Maser 1987; Baird 1990; Maser 1998; Gillette 2001). Such adaptive arrangements can greatly reduce the transaction costs of writing and implementing a contract, especially activities related to episodic events such as emergencies and disaster events for which outcomes are difficult to determine in advance. In the local government context, an agreement about a set of contractual rules that allows local governments to perform services that are nonobligatory, reciprocal, and yet easily terminated without legal consequences is regarded as adaptive. Examples of adaptive arrangements include memoranda of agreement, memoranda of understanding, and mutual aid agreements.

However, we know very little about the different types of adaptive arrangements and how they might affect the decisions of local governments. Take a mutual aid agreement as an example. When local governments cannot respond to an emergency situation, they typically rely on mutual aid agreements with neighboring communities for quick reinforcements (Lynn 2005). But the neighboring communities are under no obligation to furnish aid when requested if such aid will endanger their own personnel or overwhelm their capacities to cope with an emergency. In some instances, efforts to enter into such an agreement face difficulties because local governments cannot evaluate effectively whether the agreement can be honored or implemented fully. Cities can go it alone but may not be able to build the capacity to cope with a large-scale emergency.

Alternatively, local governments could enter into more binding arrangements such as interlocal service agreements, contracts, or lease agreements. Although the specific set of rules can be specified clearly and the outcomes are predictable, they also present a dilemma because once the agreement is adopted, it becomes legally binding. Parties to the agreement may not be able to respond to changed conditions, leading to suboptimal contracts and preventing exploration of better arrangements.

The different types of agreements have implications on the formation of contractual ties. Depending on the types of agreements adopted, they affect interlocal relations because they signal interjurisdictional activities that can be carried out jointly or independently by another jurisdiction via monetary or nonmonetary exchanges. They have a direct effect on the flow of communication and availability of shared resources (personnel and equipment). For instance, local governments are motivated to craft mutual aid agreements in order to request reimbursement for providing the mutual aid and benefit from pooling of resources, especially when the capacity to respond to a large-scale regional event is questionable. This does not mean that all forms of formal agreements are important for pooling resources, since local governments have different capacities subject to institutional constraints. There are also indirect effects from interlocal agreements. Local governments not directly involved in an agreement may feel some effects in a joint coordination effort as the effectiveness of emergency response and strategies adopted may change the region's standard procedures and alter expectations about the likely alternative outcomes.[1]

---

[1] For example, with the recent recognition of the National Fire Protection Association (NFPA) 1600 standards by the 9/11 Commission and the emergency management community's acknowledgment of the Emergency Management Accreditation Program (EMAP) standards, local officials may be held accountable if they fail to address known risks and prepare for disasters reasonably (Bea 2004; Waugh and Streib 2006).

Interdependent-Risk-Spreading Hypothesis

According to the interdependent-risk-spreading hypothesis, the threat of shirking on contractual obligations imposes great costs on local governments that have already invested their resources, efforts, and time in negotiating, implementing, and maintaining their contracts. Within the context of public safety activities, risks of nonassistance impose costs on localities during an emergency, and these costs can be minimized when localities can share their tangible resources. This is common in nonbinding adaptive contracts found in areas related to emergency preparedness, mitigation planning, and mutual aid. However, the inherent difficulty in determining the outcomes of such activities and in knowing other actors' true intentions creates risk. It is uncertain whether a nonbinding contract, with its flexible terms and conditions, can actually constrain opportunism.

The top half of Figure 5.1 illustrates the interdependent risk-spreading-hypothesis and the preference of local governments to be part of a cohesive subgroup. In this illustration, solid lines represent existing contractual arrangements, and dotted lines indicate the choice of a contracting party facing City A. For example, when deciding whether to enter into an agreement with either City B or City D, City A would rather establish a contractual tie with City D because a highly clustered network provides extensive monitoring mechanisms, facilitates mutual reciprocity, and ensures that members in the network play by the rules of the contractual game. The triangular relationship between cities A, B, and D is a classical representation of network closure (Coleman 1988, 1990). In a highly clustered network, each government has the ability to impose constraints on those that attempt to shirk or act opportunistically, ensuring the stability and standards of provision of those services.

In the case of episodic events such as emergencies and disasters, some forms of assistance can be expected from other jurisdictions even if such assistance might entail considerable costs to the helper. To ensure that the terms of the agreement are followed and the benefits of cooperation are realized, the parties to the agreements may prefer to form agreements with other localities that have established contractual ties with each other. A dense network structure adds greatly to the incentive for members to maintain commitments to assist others when emergency strikes.

A similar argument can also apply to restrictive contracting for routine activities. Such agreements generally have a high startup cost, so defaulting from the contract is costly in terms of the financial investment

A. Interdependent-Risk-Spreading Hypothesis

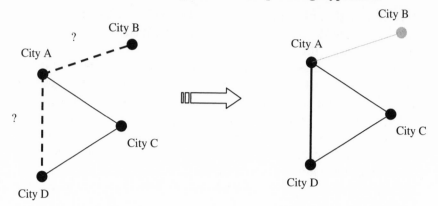

City A considering whether to
form a tie either with City B
or City D at t_1.

City A decided to establish a tie
with City D rather than City B
at t_2.

B. Independent Risk-Spreading Hypothesis

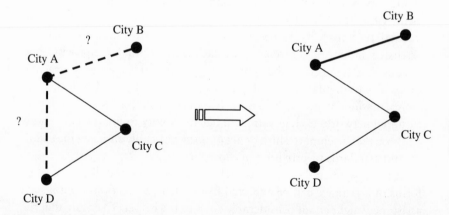

City A considering whether to
form a tie either with City B
or City D at t_1.

City A decided to establish a tie
with City B rather than City D
at t_2.

FIGURE 5.1. Interdependent-Risk-Spreading and Independent-Risk-Spreading
Hypotheses.

already committed for rendering the services. From the transaction cost perspective, a clustered network provides the advantage of reduced cost of monitoring and enforcing the obligations. The reputational costs may also prevent defections, as other localities sharing common contractual partners can provide threats of collective sanction. At the dyadic level, a contractual tie implies expectations that another local government (alter) will avoid a strategy option that is attractive to itself and seriously hurt its collaborative partner's (ego) interests. A costly investment to rebuild credibility is anticipated if a local government breaches a contractual arrangement in such settings.

Independent-Risk-Spreading Hypothesis

Alternatively, the formation of contractual ties can be explained by the independent-risk-spreading hypothesis. According to this hypothesis, local governments seek to maintain a limited number of contractual ties because such arrangements involve costly investments. In adaptive contracting, local governments may prefer what Richard Emerson (1962) referred to as exclusive exchange partners. In public safety, for example, local governments may be better off if they enter into exclusive agreement with governments whose services are less likely to be in demand by others when some emergency strikes.

The bottom of Figure 5.1 illustrates the independent-risk-spreading hypothesis for a set of adaptive contracts. For instance, when deciding whether to enter into a contractual tie with either City B or City D, City A would rather establish an agreement with B because B has no obligations to A's current partner. Thus, A would have exclusive access to B in a situation when an emergency affected A and C. City D, on the other hand, would have commitments to both A and C and would therefore be less likely than B to provide the contracted assistance to A without overloading its available resources.

Of course, differences in capacity will also affect partner choice, and this explains the dependency between larger and smaller cities. Unless the state should intervene via a statewide mutual aid agreement, a larger city having a better capacity to cope with an emergency tends to attract those smaller cities that require mutual assistance during emergencies or major disasters. In most instances, smaller cities would enter into an agreement with their county government. From the independence of risk perspective, smaller cities would prefer to enter into agreements with a larger or distant locality that has the capacity to host and maintain emergency support, but they would be more reluctant to enter into nonexclusive agreements with similar smaller cities for fear that the others might not be able to provide the adequate assistance (or even default on their agreements) when requested.

Clarifying the independence in risk hypothesis for a set of restrictive contractual ties takes a bit more explaining. For instance, given the high sunk costs of routine emergency management activities (e.g., first response medical services, special assistance for law and order, vehicle maintenance, or fire suppression) and the potential threat of opportunistic behavior and default, local governments may well prefer to establish a restrictive or binding set of legal agreements to govern their transactions (e.g., interlocal service agreements, contracts, or lease agreements). But a locality would enter into a binding contract with specific cities to minimize the risk of opportunistic behavior only if there is a lack of alternative sources for the provision of the services. Although the monitoring and enforcement costs would be higher if City A were to contract with City B rather than City D, it can take advantage of its privileged exclusivity with City B. Diversification can induce competition among possible partners in the provision of routine activities. That is, nonexistence or existence of a contractual tie creates opportunity for localities to act entrepreneurially and negotiate their contracts successfully. Hence, in restrictive contractual arrangement when actors are faced with potential threat of opportunistic behaviors, a sparse network structure will emerge.

RESEARCH DESIGN AND DATA

In Florida, the expansion of interlocal contractual arrangements has occurred since the passage of the Interlocal Cooperation Act of 1969. The statute provides a broad legal framework within which local governments can address state-authorized programs such as county and municipal planning, land development regulations, and community redevelopment standards (ACIR 1985). The statute has been used extensively by law enforcement agencies, sheriffs' offices, fire departments, and emergency medical service units for arranging the provision of routine services such as police patrol, fire suppression and first response services, and communication systems. Other state statutes related to public safety include Florida's 1985 Local Government Comprehensive Planning and Land Development Regulation Act (i.e., on joint planning agreements to manage local growth) and Florida's Mutual Aid Act. They determine the types of contractual arrangements used to govern interlocal transactions and provide expectations about the likely outcomes and the amount of resources needed to achieve those outcomes.

To explore the motivation for local governments to enter into an agreement, I first classified agreements into two general categories: restrictive and adaptive. These broad classifications reflect the degree of incompleteness of different types of arrangements. We identify the different type of agreements using information provided by various counties to the Florida Department of Community Affairs (DCA).[2] The *Interlocal Service Delivery Reports* contain information about (1) the types of agreements, (2) the effective date and expiration dates of the agreements, (3) the number and composition of actors involved, and (4) the nature of goods and services being rendered.

I limit the research site to Florida's four largest metropolitan areas: Miami-Fort Lauderdale-West Palm Beach Metropolitan Statistical Area (MSA), Tampa-St. Petersburg-Clearwater MSA, Orlando-Kissimmee MSA, and Duval-Jacksonville MSA. Given their geographical locations, these metropolitan areas are vulnerable to a wide range of natural disasters. They are also the largest and the most densely populated metropolitan areas in Florida. Almost half of Florida's cities are found in these metropolitan areas and their political structures are also highly diverse.[3]

I then identify the municipal and county governments involved in providing public safety in the study area. Although Florida's statutes encourage local governments to coordinate their activities, they do not mandate nor specify with whom these governments should establish contractual arrangements. Thus, there is considerable discretion as to the number of parties that can be involved in any of the contractual arrangements.[4] A total of 223 city and county governments in the metropolitan areas have established interlocal agreements within the period of our study. Local governments that have not engaged in any form of contractual

---

[2] In 2002, the Florida Legislature established a requirement for all counties with populations of more than 100,000 and the municipalities and special districts within those counties to submit an inventory of their existing and proposed interlocal service delivery agreements. The *Interlocal Service Delivery Report* was to be submitted to the Florida Department of Community Affairs by January 2004.

[3] Duval-Jacksonville is a consolidated government, Miami-Dade is a unique two-tier local system, and the other MSAs are highly fragmented.

[4] Local governments can also establish contractual ties with nonprofit organizations (i.e., hospital and churches), special districts, regional, and state and federal governments. For the purpose of this study, we only analyze agreements between local governments – that is, municipal and county governments.

TABLE 5.1. *Contractual Tie Changes between Subsequent Observations*

	No Tie	New Tie	Broken Tie	Maintained Tie
	$0 \rightarrow 0$	$0 \rightarrow 1$	$1 \rightarrow 0$	$1 \rightarrow 1$
Restrictive Contractual Arrangements				
t_1-t_2	24,657	45	32	19
t_2-t_3	24,633	56	37	27
t_3-t_4	24,594	76	19	64
Adaptive Contractual Arrangements				
t_1-t_2	24,641	52	42	18
t_2-t_3	24,586	97	44	26
t_3-t_4	24,546	84	24	99

arrangements are included to control for the propensity of cities to establish contractual ties with each other conditioned upon the presence of nonparticipating localities in the metropolitan areas.

Next, I specify the time periods to determine the dynamic process of contractual ties. The selected time periods provide reasonable changes in the number of ties over time: $t_1 = 1988-1992$, $t_2 = 1993-1997$, $t_3 = 1998-2000$, and $t_4 = 2001-2003$.[5] Information on contractual ties was transformed into a sociomatrix at four points in time that allows for three observations of change between these time points.

The changes in contractual ties for the pooled data set are summarized in Table 5.1. In particular, the data show that local governments generally establish new ties (os$\rightarrow$1s) as time progresses and are also likely to maintain their existing ties (1s$\rightarrow$1s) over the same periods. Note that the contractual ties in Table 5.1 are for nondirected matrices. One reason for using nondirected matrices is to establish whether a contractual tie exists rather than showing the direction of resource flows. Note also that the contractual ties are for bilateral agreements rather than multilateral agreements. A separate analysis will determine whether multilateral ties influence the formation of bilateral ties.

---

[5] SIENA does not require constant length for time units. Because there are several ways local governments can extend their contractual ties to the next periods, we have coded the length of a contractual tie using the following criteria: (a) the moment they entered into an agreement, (b) the moment they dissolved or terminated an agreement, and (c) the moment they maintained their joint agreement.

Dynamic Processes of Contractual Ties

The explanation of the observed network dynamics (a change in network structure from one network space at t_1 to another network space at t_2 and so on) is formulated in terms of transition probabilities between the observed networks, with the first observed network space being conditioned upon the previous one (taken as starting value of the stochastic process). A test of the relative value and significance level for the two main structures in Figure 5.1 requires a model that is conditioned on the original network and takes into account the relative dependence of all ties. This is conducted using the SIENA software that estimates models of network evolution based on what Snijders (2001, 2005) calls the "actor-oriented model." The model estimates factors that explain the changes in contractual ties as well as the frequency by which an actor has the opportunity to make a decision over a period of time (Steglich, Snijders, and West 2006, 17). A data pooling technique that uses "structural zero" to represent nonexistent ties between different areas offers the possibility of analyzing all four metropolitan areas simultaneously as one big structure without assuming that the actors from different metropolitan areas could establish a contractual link.

Formulating Network Effects

Following the basic network analysis approach, the observed network for the selected metropolitan areas can be represented as an $N \times N$ matrix reporting all contractual arrangements among all N actors. The entry i, j equals 0 if actor i has no contractual ties with actor j, and can equal 1 to indicate the presence of contractual relationships. According to the "actor-oriented" model proposed by Snijders (2005), "the objective function of actor i is the value attached by this actor to the network configuration x" (Snijders 2005, 15).

To determine whether the interdependent-risk-spreading and independent-risk-spreading hypotheses can explain the formation of contractual ties, we use the "transitivity triad effect" and the "betweenness effect" (Snijders et al. 2007). The transitive triad effect refers to the number of triplets in the network. In a nondirected matrix, it is defined formally as $= \sum_{j<h} x_{ij} x_{jh} x_{hi}$. The equation captures the preference for being part of cohesive subgroups. The effect measures the total number of triadic relationships in a metropolitan area in which actor i is involved, which reflects a local government's preference to enter into agreements with the partners

of their partners. According to the interdependent-risk-spreading hypothesis, the transitive triad effect will be positive for both restrictive and adaptive forms of interlocal contractual arrangements. A large and positive coefficient parameter for the number of transitive triads in relation to the other structural effects would suggest that local governments establish closely knit contractual ties with each other, and therefore they share similar behavioral expectations to resolve risks of opportunistic behavior.

The betweenness effect captures the preference of local governments for being in an intermediary position between unrelated others, as indicated in the bottom panel of Figure 5.1. The network measure is denoted by $s_{i2}(x) \sum_{j,h} x_{hi} x_{ij} (1 - x_{hj})$. The dominant presence of the betweenness effect suggests that the formation of contractual ties in a metropolitan area emphasizes the importance of establishing contractual ties with other localities that have no contractual tie with each other. A positive betweenness effect suggests that local governments prefer to avoid risk associated with a densely connected group of localities. The independent risk hypothesis predicts that the betweenness effect will be positive for the restrictive and adaptive forms of contractual arrangements. This measure emphasizes nonredundancy in that actors h and j will not be linked. According to the interdependent risk spreading hypothesis they will be linked in order to pool resources and spread risks.

Other Influences on the Formation of Contractual Ties

Council-manager form of government. Scholars have argued that professional administrators in the council-manager form of government are motivated to enter interlocal agreements as a means of promoting minimum service standards in metropolitan areas; these administrators generally have longer tenure and a long-range outlook, and they are more progressive or innovative in the contracting process. Stein (1990) argues that professional administrators may be motivated to engage in intergovernmental contracting in order to produce efficiency gains that help to establish their track record and pave the way for upward mobility. In a situation when there is a rapid political change or technical difficulties, professional administrators regularly dominate interjurisdictional activities (Raab 2002). The role of professional administrators has also been highlighted in Thurmaier and Wood's (2002) account of interlocal agreements among governments in the Kansas City metro area. I hypothesize that the council-manager form of local government has a positive impact on the dynamic process of contractual ties. To operationalize the political institutions of local jurisdiction, I created a dummy variable – that is, if a local government is operating under a council-manager form of government, it is coded 1; otherwise 0.

County government. Previous studies argue that county government should take on a larger role in the provision of public safety for a region, based on the benefits of economies of scope and the importance of resource accumulation (Rubin and Barbee 1985; Waugh 1994). County governments are politically and administratively closer to state and federal governments in terms of receiving resources and technical assistance. They are better able to act as mediators of intermunicipality policy goals and policy preferences because they generally have a larger geographical base and a broader perspective on regional needs. Smaller and isolated municipalities lack the incentive to cooperate with each other in the provision of public safety, and thus the county can fill the role as central coordinator (Waugh 1994). Furthermore, in Florida, most emergency management activities are conducted at the county level. We thus hypothesize that the county government is more likely to be involved in contractual ties. The influence of county government is operationalized using a dummy variable – that is, if a local government is a county government, it is coded 1; otherwise 0.

Community characteristics. Characteristics of communities such as their economic base and demographic composition are salient to local governments' interest in and ability to negotiate interlocal contractual arrangements (Feiock 2007). For instance, compared with less-affluent governments, wealthy governments generally possess a greater tax base and access to capital markets as well as a larger population of service recipients. Although they are able to take on risks associated with the costs of contracting, they are less inclined to enter into interlocal agreements simply because they have the capacity to produce or provide the needed services themselves rather than relying on others for assistance. In addition, the transaction costs of interlocal contracting are often lower in homogeneous than heterogeneous communities because these communities generally share a wider set of core values, the intensity of conflict is more muted, and local officials face less internal opposition than in more heterogeneous communities. As a result, agreements on services are more easily achieved with similar communities.

To test whether the characteristics of local communities influence the formation of contractual ties, I rely on the 2000 U.S. Census data. Median household income is used as a proxy for community wealth and to capture the importance of a local government's capacity to provide services in-house. The proportion of the population that is non-Hispanic white is used as a proxy to reflect the importance of homogenous preferences. Both variables are converted to natural logs. The median household income and racial compositions are analyzed as a constant covariate. This is because my main interest is on differences in economic and sociodemographic characteristics across jurisdictions rather than across time. Changes in a jurisdiction's community economic and sociodemographic composition across time are held constant; thus the variables of interest are differences across jurisdictions and their effect on changes in contractual ties.

Homophily effects. The homophily hypothesis argues that local governments will form contractual ties with similar others. The theoretical and empirical evidence regarding homophily has been inconclusive or mixed. For example, Wood (2004) argues that city managers tend to align with each other because of established norms of professionalism developed through their training and association meetings. This is contrary to work in the new public management (NPM) tradition that views city managers as free agents driven by efficiency. This perspective argues that managers are willing to enter into restrictive agreements with *any entities* that can generate potential savings or better value for the taxpayers even if their contracting partners are dissimilar to themselves. With regard to county government, most public safety activities are conducted with cities located within their boundaries rather than with other counties, suggesting little intercounty contracting.

Another argument related to similarity addresses the composition and economic characteristics of localities. Wealthy suburbs may be more inclined to enter into interlocal contractual arrangements with communities of higher rather than lower socioeconomic status (SES) because services like public safety make up a small proportion of suburban governments' expenditures. They enter into agreements among themselves because of similar preferences for standards of services. Dye et al. (1963) found that interlocal agreements were more common among communities in semirural than urban areas because of lesser social distance than among those cities located in urban areas. Foster (1998) found that central cities and suburbs having similar social characteristics are more likely to forge interlocal alliances than are central cities and suburbs with dissimilar attributes. Based on the homophily hypothesis, we test whether contractual ties are more likely to be formed (1) by local governments with similar political institutions such as forms of government, and (2) similar population characteristics in terms of income and racial composition.

SIENA can test the homophily hypothesis by creating a "covariate-related similarity" measure, which has a higher values when the similarity of the attribute between actor i and its counterparts grows: $x_{ij}(\text{sim}^v_{ij} - \text{sim}^v)$, where v is the variable in question, x_{ij} represents the existence or not of the link between i and j, sim^v_{ij} is the similarity in the value of the variable between i and j on a 0–1 scale, and sim^v is the mean of all similarity scores. In this case, a positive value of the coefficient translates into growing utility for actors creating links with other actors with similar positions. A positive parameter implies that actors prefer ties to others with similar preferences (on the variable in question) thus contributing to the network-autocorrelation of that variable. A negative parameter suggests that the actors' preferences for dissimilar others drive the dynamics of contractual ties.

Multilateral agreements. The total number of multilateral agreements (i.e., arrangements that involve three or more parties to one agreement) might also influence a local government's decision to enter into bilateral ties. The number of collaborators entering into a multilateral agreement is related to Olson's (1965) notion of group size in that it dictates the relative distributional gains and the monitoring and enforcement costs of behavior. The smaller the group, the easier it is to form a contractual arrangement because there are fewer problems determining how benefits will be distributed; the monitoring cost will be lower and thus there will be fewer shirking problems. A large number of collaborators in a multilateral agreement decreases the relative benefits to individual collaborators. Furthermore, inability to renegotiate terms of a contract can turn into a joint-decision trap unless those mostly benefiting from the contract are willing to renegotiate and adjust to an unanticipated change of conditions (Scharpf 1997).

However, multilateral agreements have an advantage over bilateral agreements. For instance, most local governments would enter into multilateral agreements in an attempt to develop regionwide coordination efforts such as providing for operational assistance, emergency mutual aid responses, regional mitigation or preparedness, or developing a specific task force agreement. These agreements bring together key decision makers who share information and physical assets. It is "through this sharing from multiple agencies that line officers, investigators and analysts are most likely to make the essential connection that can prevent terrorist attacks" (Lynn 2005, vii). Although the initial organizational costs might be substantially higher than for a bilateral agreement, the more frequently a local government enters into multilateral agreements, the less will be the organizational costs incurred by the locality, and thus the easier it is to pool resources from others without having to enter into separate and more costly bilateral agreements.

TABLE 5.2. *Descriptive Statistics*

	Mean	S.D	Min	Max
Political Institutions				
County Government	0.10	0.31	0	1
Council-Manager Form of Government	0.52	0.50	0	1
Communities' Characteristics				
Proportion White (log)	5.97	0.95	2.78	8.20
Median Household Income (log)	4.62	0.16	4.17	5.30
Restrictive Interlocal Contractual Arrangement				
Multilateral Agreement $(t_{1,2})$	2.67	2.25	0	6
Multilateral Agreement $(t_{2,3})$	3.08	3.39	0	15
Multilateral Agreement $(t_{3,4})$	2.86	1.82	0	6
Adaptive Interlocal Contractual Arrangement				
Multilateral Agreement $(t_{1,2})$	0.13	0.34	0	1
Multilateral Agreement $(t_{2,3})$	0.63	2.09	0	18
Multilateral Agreement $(t_{3,4})$	0.29	0.62	0	2
No. of Observations = 223				

We hypothesize that multilateral agreements are a substitute rather than a complement to bilateral agreements. If the multilateral agreement variable has a negative effect, it means that those local governments with a higher number of multilateral agreements attach less value to the formation of bilateral ties. That is, the greater the extent to which a local units relies on multilateral agreements, the less likely it is to also enter into bilateral agreements. This variable is operationalized using what Snijders et al. (2005) call the "actor's changing covariates" that indicates total number of multilateral agreements shared by each actor pair for the first three time periods: $t_1 = 1988–1992$, $t_2 = 1993–1997$, and $t_3 = 1998–2000$. Descriptive statistics of these variables expected to influence contractual ties are presented in Table 5.2.

RESULTS AND ANALYSIS

The final estimation results for the two types of contractual arrangements are presented in Table 5.3. SIENA estimates the Exponential Random Graph model based on the method of moments, implemented as a continuous-time Markov Chain Monte Carlo simulation. The unilateral

TABLE 5.3. *Parameter Estimates (β) and Standard Errors in Restrictive vs. Adaptive Interlocal Contractual Arrangements*

	Restrictive Contractual Arrangement	Adaptive Contractual Arrangement
Rate Parameter (rho) $t_{1,2}$	2.43*** (0.37)	3.39*** (0.52)
Rate Parameter (rho) $t_{2,3}$	2.57*** (0.35)	7.38*** (1.53)
Rate Parameter (rho) $t_{3,4}$	2.36*** (0.31)	2.60*** (0.34)
Network Structure Effects		
Degree (Density)	-1.80*** (0.06)	-1.78*** (0.05)
Transitive Triads	1.11*** (0.14)	0.97*** (0.09)
Betweenness Status	0.15*** (0.02)	0.08*** (0.01)
Political Institutions Effects		
County Government	0.07 (0.24)	-0.01 (0.24)
Council-Manager	0.26* (0.15)	0.13 (0.14)
Communities' Characteristics Effects		
Proportion White (log)	0.38*** (0.11)	0.49*** (0.08)
Median Household Income (log)	-0.15* (0.09)	-0.23*** (0.07)
Homophily Effects		
County Government Similarity	-0.42*** (0.16)	-0.27** (0.14)
Council-Manager Similarity	-0.01 (0.09)	0.08 (0.07)
Proportion White (log) Similarity	-0.46 (0.42)	-1.04*** (0.36)
Median Household Income (log) Similarity	0.45 (0.32)	0.88*** (0.22)
Multilateral Agreement (Restrictive)	-0.01 (0.03)	–
Multilateral Agreement (Adaptive)	–	-0.05*** (0.02)

Note: Standard errors within parentheses level of significance: *** $p<0.01$, ** $p<0.05$, * $p<0.10$.

initiative and reciprocal confirmation (UIRC) model for nondirected matrices is used for the nondirected relationships (Snijders 2005). The UIRC model assumes that mutual agreement between two actors is required for a contractual tie to exit; one actor proposes a link that max-imizes the actor's expected payoffs, as in the directed model, but the UIRC model allows the other actor to refuse the link if it is too costly. The convergence diagnosis produced t-statistics <.0, indicating no conver-gence problems, and the rate parameters (rho) in Table 5.3 are all positive and significant. This indicates that local governments' contractual ties undergo a reasonable amount of small changes to come up with a global dynamic that resembles the observed network under the current model specification. The remainder of this section first interprets the effects of network structures then discusses the other independent variables.

In the left column of Table 5.3, the formation of restrictive contractual ties has a higher parameter estimate for the transitive triad effect ($\beta = 1.11$, $p<0.01$) compared to the betweenness effect ($\beta = 0.15$, $p<0.01$). Both parameter estimates are positive and statistically significant. The fact that the transitive triad effect is positive and greater than the be-tweenness effect suggests that contract selection is driven by the extra attraction for a locality to establish ties with other local governments that have already established ties with each other. These results support the interdependent-risk-spreading hypothesis, which predicts the importance of the effect of transitive triads on the formation of restrictive contractual ties. The interpretation of the parameter estimates for restrictive contrac-tual ties requires that both coefficients must be adjusted to account for the costs of contracting – that is, degree or the number of ties established by local governments (Snijders et al. 2007). For example, the coefficient for the degree effect is negative and significant, as expected, which reflects the costs of establishing and maintaining a contractual tie ($\beta = -1.80$, $p<0.01$). Simply entering into an agreement with another locality does not necessarily produce benefits; other positive structural effects are necessary to justify the costs of contracting. The calculations presented by Snijders (2001), the objective function for the restrictive contractual ties, is illus-trated below for network effects.

$$f_i(x) = \sum_j \left(-1.80x_{ij} + 1.11x_{ij}x_{ij}x_{ij} + 0.15x_{ij}x_{ij}(1 - x_{ij}) \right)$$

The objective function can be substantively interpreted using Figure 5.1 as the example. Taking into account the baseline cost of -1.80, City A obtains $1.11-1.80 = -.69$ in utility if it establishes a contractual tie with City D (on the condition that City D also agrees to the proposed new tie). If City A were to consider a new contract with an isolated city like City B and City B agrees, then City A will only receive benefits of $0.15-1.80 = -1.65$. Creating a tie that establishes a transitive triad or a betweenness structure would not be sufficient to offset the contracting cost, but the transitive triad provides considerably more utility than the betweenness structure. A tie with a city already connected with two of City A's partners would provide double the utility and would therefore provide a positive $2.22-1.80 = .42$ units of utility. What the analysis shows is that the dynamics of contractual ties, in the presence of contracting costs, continue to favor a configuration of transitive triads or densely connected ties in order to minimize the initial costs of contracting.

In the right column of Table 5.3, the objective function for the adaptive contractual ties is illustrated as follows:

$$f_i(x) = \sum_j \left(-1.78x_{ij} + 0.97x_{jh}x_{jh}x_{hi} + 0.08x_{hi}x_{ij}(1 - x_{hj}) \right)$$

Again, the dynamic process of adaptive contractual ties emphasizes the importance of the transitive triad. The results show a higher parameter estimate for the transitive triad ($\beta = 0.97$, $p<0.01$) compared to the betweenness effect ($\beta = 0.08$, $p<0.01$) with both parameter estimates again being positive and statistically significant. The benefit from a single addition of either network structure is again not sufficient to offset the contracting costs in this case of -1.78, but contracts with a new partner sharing at least two common contracting partners again provides a positive incentive. For both types of contracts, the upper configuration in Figure 5.1 is strongly preferred over the lower configuration.

Table 5.3 also reports the influence of political institutions on the formation of contractual ties. Council-manager forms of government show a positive and significant effect on the formation of restrictive contractual ties ($\beta = 0.25$, $p<0.10$). This effect is also positive for adaptive contracts, but not significant. The results suggest that local governments with professional administrators tend to develop a clear set of contractual rules, presumably to secure and safeguard their constituents' transactions. County governments, on the other hand, had no significant effect in either model, so they appear no more likely than other governments to be a part of either type of contract.

The advantages of interlocal contractual arrangements also depend on the extent to which existing political institutions can bring about consensual interactions among public officials charged with coordinating regionwide activities. Despite the theoretical argument that professional administrators will prefer to form contractual ties with similar others, there is little empirical evidence to support this proposition. Our analysis reports mixed findings with no statistically significant estimates. As for county governments, the similarity effects are both negative and significant for both restrictive ($\beta = -0.42$, $p<0.01$) and adaptive contractual arrangements ($\beta = -0.27$, $p<0.01$). These findings support our earlier hypothesis that county governments tend to contract with municipalities rather than with other county governments. From the transaction cost perspective, the results also suggest that cities establish contractual ties with county governments to reduce the administrative costs of having to deal directly with state and federal government requirements and to avoid investing their own resources in the provision of certain public safety activities.

In the center rows of Table 5.3, we test whether community characteristics have an effect on the formation of contractual ties. We anticipate that the transaction costs of interlocal contracting are often lower in racially homogeneous than heterogeneous communities because local officials face less internal opposition when homogenous communities share wider core values. Our empirical results support the greater propensity for predominantly white localities to form contracts for both restrictive ($\beta = 0.38$, $p<0.01$) and adaptive agreements ($\beta = 0.49$, $p<0.01$). On the other hand, communities that are predominantly white generally prefer to enter into adaptive contractual ties with nonwhite communities, as indicated by the homophily effect ($\beta = -1.04$, $p<0.01$).

Communities that have a higher median household income with greater tax base and access to capital markets are less inclined to enter into agreements with other localities for both restrictive ($\beta = -0.15$, $p<0.10$) and adaptive agreements ($\beta = -0.23$, $p<0.01$). This finding suggests that wealthy communities have the capacity to produce or provide the services themselves rather than relying on others for assistance. Although some scholars argue that wealthy suburbs are more inclined to enter into interlocal arrangements with higher units of governments than less affluent communities (Dye et al. 1963; Foster 1998), the homophily result for income suggests that wealthy communities are more likely to enter into adaptive arrangements among themselves than with poorer localities ($\beta = 0.88$, $p<0.01$). This presumably is motivated by similar preferences for standards of services, suggesting similarity in preferences can support the creation of self-governing institutions.

In the bottom rows of Table 5.3, we compare the effect of multilateral agreements on the formation of contractual ties. The advantage of a multilateral agreement is the ability of its members to pool resources and exchange information in functional areas such as operational assistance, emergency mutual aid responses, regional mitigation planning, or preparedness strategies. Local governments can utilize a multilateral agreement for these purposes without having to sign multiple bilateral agreements with other localities separately. Our results demonstrate that as local governments increased their usage of multilateral agreements, they were less likely to enter into bilateral adaptive agreements ($\beta = -0.05$, $p<0.01$). It appears that a multilateral approach is a substitute rather than a complement for a bilateral approach for adaptive agreements. On the other hand, multilateral activities seem to have no effect on restrictive agreements. The substitution effect for multilateral activities thus appears limited to more nonbinding contracts such as mutual aid agreement, memoranda of understanding, or memoranda of agreement.

SUMMARY

Our study has analyzed the relative prevalence of risks associated with interlocal contracting in a metropolitan area. Local governments appear to favor overlapping contractual ties for the provision and production of public safety for recurring activities as well as for episodic events. Despite the costs associated with interlocal contracting, we find that the overlapping network structures associated more generally with social capital emerge in the context of interlocal agreements to mitigate the problems of coordinating both kinds of services studied in this chapter.

The emergent pattern of voluntary contractual ties supports the ICA argument that self-organizing action by local government actors can produce institutional mechanisms to minimize service externalities in polycentric systems. A closed, connected configuration of contractual ties not only integrates specialized agencies in the deliberation of policy objectives but also provides the foundation for collaborative agreements and other forms of cooperation. The empirical analysis specifically focuses on how two distinctive types of contractual arrangements can encourage cooperative solutions involving recurring and episodic public safety activities. Local governments forming contractual ties within the context of public safety activities gain associational benefits by sharing information and enhancing the scope of contractual agreements. For both types of service, a closely knit structure reduces the enforcement and monitoring costs of cooperative agreements better than a central hierarchical structure can.

The results also clarify that local governments act upon their preferences based on the political and demographic characteristics of the other local jurisdictions. Although many scholars have argued that institutional contexts such as community characteristics, political institutions, and the nature of goods and services influence local collaboration, systematic empirical investigation of these relationships is rare. This chapter provides some of the first evidence to assess how similar community characteristics and political institutions influence the formation of contract network ties in a diverse metropolitan area. It is also the first to show that multilateral agreements – a different set of institutional arrangements – adversely affect the formation of bilateral contractual ties for adaptive but not for restrictive contractual agreements. The next step is to assess the specific evolutionary process that can explain the factors influencing the formation of ties and the impact of network structures on the behavior of local governments and the performance of their interactions.

Investigating the dynamics processes of contractual ties can test our predictions about the different types of contractual arrangements and how these arrangements are being employed by local governments to mitigate the transaction costs of contracting. The different types of arrangements – that is, restrictive or adaptive contracts – impose different kinds of opportunities and institutional constraints on local governments and thus alter the expectations and motivations for entering into interjurisdictional activities. A sparse network structure which implies that a few links might provide benefits for diversified contracting partners can also encourage entrepreneurial activities and competitive behavior (Granovetter 1973; Burt 1992; Feiock 2007). But the evolution of contractual ties in the area of public safety did not exhibit this pattern. A high and positive value of transitive triad relative to the betweenness score in both forms of contractual arrangements suggests a general tendency for local units to form overlapping contractual ties.

The ICA framework can enhance understanding of the formation of contractual ties and the roles contracting networks can play in those arenas. The argument is that local governments facing collective action problems should be able to address their dilemmas through self-organized action to enter into networks of contractual ties to achieve some common purposes. Although local governments still rely on the existing governance structure (i.e., state-level rules) to facilitate the problem-solving process, they are also motivated to develop complex networks of contractual ties in order to mitigate deficiency of hierarchical governance. Our empirical results suggest that local governments have the tendency to develop and maintain overlapping contractual ties as mechanisms to monitor and enforce individual partners' contributions to collective efforts.

6

Do Risk Profiles of Services Alter Contractual Patterns?

A Comparison across Multiple Metropolitan Services

Manoj Shrestha

One of the dilemmas local governments confront in metropolitan service provision is how to ensure efficient supply of public services in a horizontally fragmented system of governments. A multiplicity of local jurisdictions enhances allocation efficiency by providing customized mixes of public services to suit local preferences. However, acting independently, local units can produce externalities and diseconomies of scale constraining Pareto-efficient supply. Externalities, positive or negative, occur when benefits or costs of a service spill over the boundaries of a jurisdiction. Likewise, diseconomies of scale arise when greater fragmentation limits the ability of local jurisdictions to reduce the average cost of production. These problems increase when decisions by one local government impact other local governments in ways that are not considered by the deciding government. This creates institutional collective action (ICA) problems in public goods supply (Feiock 2004, 2007).

How do local governments resolve such systemic problems in metropolitan service provision? The ICA framework outlined in Chapter 1 suggests that fragmented governments are often capable of solving interdependent problems endogenously so they are better off individually and collectively than they would be acting alone (Lubell et al. 2002). It is increasingly recognized that the key issues in service provision are less about whether a function should be public or private, and more about what configuration of formal and/or informal organizations is needed to perform that function (Wise 1990) and what the structural properties are of such configurations (Agranoff and McGuire 1998). Unfortunately, we know very little about the patterns of service contracts between local governments and whether these patterns vary by service. This chapter addresses this gap in the literature by analyzing the patterns of interlocal service networks in the provision of municipal services.

Local governments can utilize various institutional mechanisms to organize service delivery in fragmented settings, as described in Chapter 1. As local governments move from independent action to cooperative resolution of decision externalities, they face a range of governance options. These choices range from informal policy networks at one extreme to voluntary consolidation of local governments at the other extreme with a variety of intermediate arrangements such as interlocal service contracts (agreements), regional partnerships, and voluntary special districts in between.[1] Informal networks emerge without central intervention from interactions between institutional actors, although higher level authorities can facilitate the development of such networks (Schneider et al. 2003). Voluntary consolidation occurs when two or more local governments form a unified government over a larger geographic area. Although voluntary consolidation can address externalities and diseconomies of scale in service provision, it rarely occurs in practice because of total loss of political autonomy and the availability of less costly choices (Carr and Feiock 2004). While regional partnerships and voluntary special districts offer such alternatives, they require consensus or majority decisions of the constituent governments that demand surrender of autonomy in decision making.

Another option that local governments utilize for public service provision is interlocal service agreements. These agreements are voluntary because entry into and exit from such agreements depend on the will of the participating local governments, even if such agreements may be aided and shaped by federal or state statutes. Voluntary interlocal agreements provide an important but little understood aspect of the fragmented political system in solving ICA problems in municipal service provision.

Local governments commonly practice interlocal service agreements (Friesema 1971; ACIR 1985; ICMA 1997; Thurmaier and Wood 2002; Andrew 2006). Municipal service delivery studies show that almost

---

[1] There are also mandated or imposed solutions. Geographic or functional consolidation and countywide or multicounty special districts imposed by the state are two such alternatives. The market can also address some of these problems. For example, it can account for externalities to some degree through price mechanisms such as the polluter pay principle. Similarly, it can aggregate service demand for multiple jurisdictions and can produce a service at lower average cost. However, many pure public goods such as police or fire protection and merit goods like water supply or health services are typically not produced in the private market.

one-third of local jurisdictions use service agreements to deliver about one-sixth of all public services (Warner and Hefetz 2001). Pay-for-service, joint service, and mutual aid agreements are widely utilized forms of service agreements. In *pay-for-service agreements*, a buyer jurisdiction pays an agreed price to the supplier jurisdiction in exchange for a service. *Joint service agreements* occur when local governments invest in the co-production of a service. *Mutual aid agreements* are service quid pro quo standby arrangements in which two or more local governments agree to mutually lend services to one another on request at their own cost. Like private contracts, these service agreements are incomplete because parties are boundedly rational and are unable to fully account for the behavioral opportunism and environmental uncertainties surrounding the agreement. These transaction uncertainties increase contractual hazards and hence transaction costs for the transacting jurisdictions.

While the whole spectrum of service agreements is a subject of interesting theoretical and substantive investigation, this chapter focuses on analyzing pay-for-service agreements for multiple services. These agreements involve much strategic behavior on the part of both the buyer and supplier governments to mitigate transaction risks involved in service provision. It examines this phenomenon from the perspective of the "buyer government" that is purchasing a service from another government, and relates transaction risk profiles of services to specific patterns of service contracts that they seek in response.

The chapter proceeds as follows. First, it outlines the study setting. The next section builds upon the framework advanced in Chapter 1 to develop an explanation for self-organizing patterns of service contracts and derives testable hypotheses. Subsequent sections present the research design and the results. A final section summarizes the main conclusions and outlines the issues for future research.

THE STUDY SETTING

This study analyzes the patterns of pay-for-service agreements among general purpose local governments in Pinellas County, Florida. Comprised of one county government and 24 cities, Pinellas County is one of the most highly fragmented counties in the State of Florida. These governments differ in their size and other socioeconomic attributes, suggesting that the externalities and diseconomies of scale problems that these units face also differ. By implication, the expected benefits from collective action (Sandler 1992; Feiock, 2004) will also be different across jurisdictions. Although pay-for-service agreements are somewhat similar to private contracts in terms of the self-interested behavior of actors, the process involved in service agreements is unlike bidding methods utilized in private contracts. Service agreements typically follow bargaining and negotiation among a limited set of parties to arrive at mutually agreed terms and conditions. These agreements then shape the "rules of the game" as well as the payoff structure for the transacting jurisdictions (North 1990).

The transacting governments, however, face exchange risks in forming and executing service agreements. The exchange risks result from transaction-specific investments involved in the production of an agreed-upon service. Such customized investments are "asset specific" (Williamson 1981) because alternative uses for these investments are absent or minimal. Asset-specific investments may take many forms.[2] The lower the alternative use value of such investments, the greater the level of asset specificity becomes. The level of asset specificity involved in such transactions matters because a higher level of asset specificity leads to greater dependency between the transacting jurisdictions (Williamson 1991). It is not just the supplier government, which typically makes transaction-specific investments, that becomes tied into the transaction. The buyer government also gets locked into it. This is especially true when an "outside option" for the asset-specific exchange is limited or an alternative mode of exchange (for example, a market) for the service is expensive.

THEORY AND HYPOTHESES: TRANSACTION RISKS AND CONTRACTUAL PATTERNS

The theoretical premise is that the potential benefits from cooperative problem solving motivate local governments to engage in pay-for-service exchanges. However, as the Coase theorem (1960) suggests, the formation and maintenance of service contracts suffer from transaction costs

---

[2] Williamson's discussion (1991) of asset specificity includes (1) *physical asset specificity* when local units make investment in equipment and machinery specific to a transaction such as water treatment and supply, (2) *human asset specificity* such as knowledge and experience of building officials (human capital), (3) *dedicated assets* that are general investment made to meet the demand of the transacting party, (4) *site specificity* when investments in assets are made to minimize inventory and transportation costs such as fire stations close to communities, and (5) *temporal specificity* when investments are made for quick service delivery such as distribution/location of emergency medical vehicles for timely response.

that need to be minimized in order to achieve efficiency. As a result, the transacting jurisdictions develop specific patterns of service relationships to offset the transaction costs. This premise is based on the exchange embeddedness idea, which postulates that the transacting actors develop structures of relationships to facilitate economic exchange (Granovetter 1985). Two main transaction risks that buyer governments face in pay-for-service contracts are associated with behavioral and environmental uncertainties (Williamson 1991).

Behavioral uncertainty in service contracts arises when a provider government is tempted to capture a larger share of the aggregate gains. The supplier can use various means to accomplish this, including an increase in price, reduction in quality, interruption in supply, or simply backing out of the agreement. The incompleteness of the contract and the limited ability of buyers to detect providers' actions increase the buyers' concerns regarding supplier opportunism. The buyers' vulnerability escalates when their dependency on the supplier increases because of either their limited outside options or their disadvantageous situation owing to information asymmetry, fiscal stress, or small size.

Buyer governments can also face environmental uncertainties due to unexpected breakdown in technology or sudden occurrence of natural incidents affecting the supply. Asset-specific investments involve specific technologies or processes that are subject to the risks of failure (Williamson 1996). Random acts of nature such as a medical or fire emergency may also lead to unexpected breakdown in supply. Such acts of nature can occur in multiple places simultaneously, which creates the risk of concurrent occurrence. In this situation, a buyer may be unable to receive the service because the provider may not have surplus capacity to serve others when it faces emergency in its own jurisdiction. Since the scale of such uncertainties and their spatial distribution are difficult to predict, providers may underinvest in the capacity to deal with unpredictable future emergencies. Buyer governments become particularly vulnerable when frequency and variance of such environmental uncertainties increase (Williamson 1996).

These transaction risks can differ by types of services involved in inter-local contracts. Consider, for example, water or sewer service. These services typically require large dedicated investments because of their capital-intensive nature. Alternative providers for these services are also generally limited. As a result, buyers are more likely to be concerned about supplier opportunism due to their greater dependency on the supplier. Likewise, police or building inspection services are human asset-specific in nature. Here, buyers are more likely to be concerned with the quality of supply requiring a credible supplier. Police or building inspection officials may engage in "job action"[3] creating a sudden crisis in the law enforcement or building inspection services. Demand for fire and emergency medical services, on the other hand, can occur simultaneously in multiple places, increasing the vulnerability to environmental uncertainties. On-site quick response is critical for efficient delivery of these services.

Transaction risks make contracting costly. Since buyer jurisdictions face different transaction risks, they develop specific networks of contracts to mitigate those risks. Networks are the result of the purposive actions of actors seeking to resolve cooperation or coordination problems in exchange (Scholz, Berardo, and Kile 2008). Networks facilitate the flow of information about actors' behavior and reduce the cost of screening and finding potential partners. Networks also serve as a basis for evaluating the credibility and competency of the potential partners (Granovetter 1985; Gulati 1998). Studies of cooperative exchange in different settings such as mental service delivery (Provan and Milward 1995), public agency management (Agranoff and McGuire 2003), natural resource management (Lubell et al. 2002), economic development (Feiock, Steinacker, and Park 2009), and infrastructure provision (LeRoux and Carr 2007) show the importance of networked relationships in facilitating service delivery improvements.

Based on the premises discussed here, Table 6.1 summarizes the transaction risks to be considered, the hypothesized patterns of service contracts associated with each risk, a diagram that illustrates each pattern, and the parameter statistic that will be used to test the hypotheses.

Supplier Opportunism and Reciprocity, Transitivity, and Popularity

When a buyer government is primarily concerned with supplier opportunism, it may develop reciprocal or closed relationships or it may seek a popular provider that already has service contracts with many buyers. Gulati and Gargiulo (1999) argue that timely and relevant information on competencies and reliability of potential providers is critical for forming relationships and that this information comes from direct alliances with a

---

[3] One such form in the case of police is so-called blue flu; this occurs when substantial numbers of police officers pretend to be ill at the same time and stay at home rather than report for duty.

TABLE 6.1. *Transaction Risks, Hypothesized Patterns of Service Agreements, Graphic Configurations, and Parameter Statistics*

Transaction Risks	Expected Pattern of Relations (network measures)	Hypothesis	Diagram	Parameter Statistic
Supplier opportunism	Reciprocal relations (Reciprocity)	H1	6.1a	$\sum_{i \neq j} x_{ij} x_{ji}$
	Closed relations (Transitivity)	H2	6.1b	$\sum_{i,j,b} x_{ij} x_{ib} x_{jb}$
	Popularity pattern of relations (Alternating in-k-star)	H3	6.1c	$\lambda^2 \sum_{i=1}^{n} \left\{ \left(1 - \frac{1}{\lambda}\right)^{x+i} + \frac{x_{+i}}{\lambda} - 1 \right\}$

for some value λ.

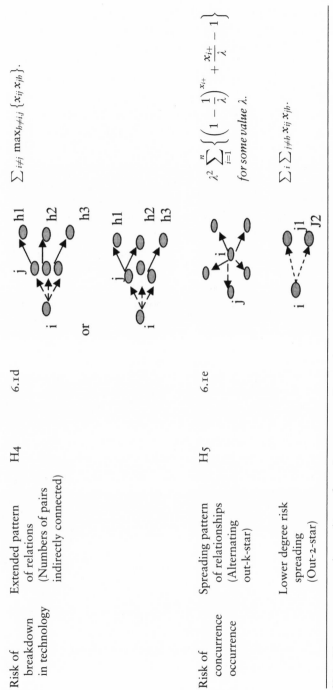

Risk of breakdown in technology	Extended pattern of relations (Numbers of pairs indirectly connected)	H4	6.1d	$\displaystyle\sum_{i\neq j}\max_{h\neq i,j}\{x_{ij}\,x_{jh}\}.$
Risk of concurrence occurrence	Spreading pattern of relationships (Alternating out-k-star)	H5	6.1e	$\displaystyle\lambda^2\sum_{i=1}^{n}\left\{\left(1-\frac{1}{\lambda}\right)^{x_{i+}}+\frac{x_{i+}}{\lambda}-1\right\}$ _for some value λ._
	Lower degree risk spreading (Out-2-star)			$\displaystyle\sum_{i}\sum_{j\neq h}x_{ij}\,x_{jh}.$

Note: Diagrams represent the graphic configurations corresponding to the network measures.

partner, from indirect alliances with third parties, and from a partner's position in the contract environment.

Reciprocity. Forming a reciprocal contractual relationship with a supplier jurisdiction is one way to control the likely risk of supplier opportunism. In a simplex contractual relationship, reciprocity occurs when two governments buy and sell each other the same service. As shown in Diagram a in Table 6.1, the buyer government i forms a reciprocal agreement with the supplier jurisdiction j (indicated by a dashed arrow from buyer to supplier) which has an existing relationship with buyer i (indicated by a solid arrow). For this, both parties make asset-specific investment in the production of a service. While this is atypical in a normal buyer-seller exchange, it is plausible once the geographic and temporal dimensions of the exchange are considered. When jurisdictions are contiguous, a buyer that purchases a service from a supplier for one portion of its territory can become the supplier of the same service to a specific subarea in the supplier's jurisdiction. For example, when the sewer pipes are placed in adjacent jurisdictions, both jurisdictions can utilize spatial advantage to get benefit from the reciprocal sewer service contracts. Similarly, reciprocity can occur at different times. For most building inspection agreements, for example, both contracting parties use each other's building inspectors when they face temporary service gaps or when their own inspectors are unavailable.

Reciprocity can control supplier opportunism in at least two ways. Reciprocal contracts develop mutual dependency and can in effect hold each other hostage to prevent defection by either party (Williamson 1996). It can also develop a basis for more cohesive relationships leading to mutual solidarity and trust (Coleman 1988). Mutuality offers prospects to gain firsthand experience about the partners and for repeated interaction because of the fixed boundaries of jurisdictions (Feiock 2007). This strengthens existing relationships and builds trust that helps mitigate supplier opportunism (Granovetter 1985). Thus,

H1: When faced with supplier opportunism, a buyer government forms reciprocal contracts with a supplier government.

Transitivity. Forming a closed set of relationships is another strategy a buyer government may use to control potential supplier opportunism, as shown in Diagram b in Table 6.1. When a buyer jurisdiction i is purchasing a service from jurisdiction j, and when jurisdiction j is buying from jurisdiction h, then buyer i can prevent supplier j's opportunistic behavior by entering into a service contract with jurisdiction h. For jurisdiction i, any defection by jurisdiction *j* (*i*'s provider) is checked in such a transitive relationship because information of any wrong behavior by *j* can be easily spread within the closed group. Partners watch each others' likely opportunistic behavior, and a wrongdoer may face group sanctions. These factors could be strong enough to curb *j*'s temptation for opportunistic behavior toward *i*.

Moreover, since the supplier *j* is the source of information for the buyer *i* about the jurisdiction *h*, the likelihood that the buyer *i* would enter into service relations with *h* will depend on the credible information supplied by the provider *j* (Carpenter, Esterling, and Lazer 2004). The supplier *j* may thus be sensitive about its local reputation, which may self-restrain its temptation for opportunism (Gulati and Gargiulo 1999). Thus, the threat of detection of wrong behavior, group sanction, and the concern for local reputation may prevent supplier opportunism in the closed pattern of contractual relationships, particularly as the number of overlapping relationships involving *i* and *j* increase. Thus,

H2: When faced with supplier opportunism, a buyer government develops a closed pattern of relationships with a third partner.

Popularity. A buyer jurisdiction can also seek contractual relationships with a popular supplier to prevent supplier opportunism. A supplier is "popular" when many buyers seek service contracts with this supplier. Such a popular supplier is more credible than a supplier having a few buyers. As shown in Diagram c in Table 6.1, supplier *j* is popular because it attracts many buyers. In this situation, buyer jurisdiction *i*, concerned with potential supplier opportunism, will enter into a contract with the jurisdiction *j* because buyer *i* observes differences in potential reputation effects across potential suppliers in the existing exchange setting and finds that the supplier *j* is the most credible.[4] Thus, buyer *i*'s preference for a service agreement with jurisdiction *j* reflects a preference for a popularity pattern of service contracts.

Poppo and Zenger (2002) argue that a credible supplier restrains itself from opportunistic temptation out of fear of losing its reputation for trustworthiness. A popular jurisdiction may find it extremely costly to put at risk its hard-earned reputation among the larger set of constituents for short-term opportunistic gains. This creates a "self-enforcing range"

---

[4] In the absence of information, buyer *i*'s preference for a contract with provider *j* may be perceived as emulating or mimicking the behavior of other buyers (DiMaggio and Powell 1983; Watts 2003).

(Klein 1991) for the supplier that is determined by the relative loss of credibility over the gains due to opportunistic behavior. Besides, any wrong behavior by the supplier may signal its wrong intent and trigger buyers to forge an alliance. This will be disadvantageous for the supplier, who would certainly prefer to avoid mass defections. Thus,

H3: When faced with supplier opportunism, a buyer government forms a popularity pattern of contractual relationship.

Technological Risk and Extended Patterns of Relationships

When a buyer jurisdiction faces environmental uncertainties such as sudden breakdown in technology leading to failure in supply, it seeks service contracts with a supplier that has fewer supply obligations and possibly possesses multiple sources for its supply. This relationship pattern provides the buyer a safety net in times of crisis or abrupt change in supply. In Diagram d in Table 6.1, buyer i partners with provider j because j has more than one source of supply. This extended pattern of contractual relations provides i greater reliability of receiving the service from j. Even if provider j's own plant breaks down, other supply options for buyer i via provider j are open to fill the gaps in the supply. Hence,

H4: When faced with the risk of technological failure, a buyer government forms an extended pattern of contractual relationship with a supplier government that has fewer supply obligations and possesses multiple sources of supply.

Risk of Concurrent Needs and Spreading Patterns of Relationships

When a buyer government encounters the risk of concurrent service needs in multiple communities, the buyer is more likely to spread the risk by forming agreements with as many providers as possible. Emergency services such as fire protection, disaster management, or emergency medical services suffer from such risks. As depicted in Diagram e in Table 6.1, buyer i spreads its risk by forming a service contract with supplier j (represented by a dashed arrow) even if it already has existing contracts with other suppliers. Contracting with only one provider is likely to lead to a crisis in supply when, for example, fire occurs in multiple communities simultaneously. Spreading the contract out to many providers increases the chances for the buyer to receive fire protection service from at least one or more providers since it is unlikely that all providers would face the fire emergency at the same time or at the same scale. Thus,

TABLE 6.2. *Frequency of Pay-for-Service Agreements by Service Type in Pinellas County, Florida*

Service Category and Type	Pay-for-Service Agreements
Water-related	
Water	39
Sewer	59
Conservation	24
Utility billing	19
Public safety	
Police	55
Protective inspection	24
Fire protection	40
Emergency medical service	34
Emergency disaster	8
Jail	4
Transportation	
Road/street	8
Traffic installation & maintenance	29
Mass transit	6
Landscaping	2
Culture/Recreation	
Library	1
Parks	3
Special facilities	2

H5: When faced with the risk of concurrent service need, the buyer government seeks to form a spread pattern of contracts with multiple provider governments.

DATA, MEASURES, AND ESTIMATION

Relational data on pay-for-service contracts were gathered from the official records of the local units in Pinellas County, Florida. The city clerks, responsible for maintaining the official records, were the main contacts for the data. Frequent office visits were made to document the information that included the name and type of agreement, beginning and expiration dates, brief accounts of the agreements, and their amendments or renewals, if any. The motivation for a single-county focus was to collect in-depth information on multiple services for comparison. While this design raises concern about generalizability to other counties, variations across the units and the services included in the analysis provide for greater generalizability across different service areas for different types of governments.

The collected data were verified and supplemented with the inventory of service agreements prepared by Pinellas County for the Florida Department of Community Affairs[5] and with the online records of the Pinellas County Clerk of the Circuit Court.[6] In addition, since the agreements involve at least two parties, this built-in cross-check minimized the risk of missing important information.[7] Data on community attributes were gathered from multiple sources including the Pinellas County publications and the Web sites of the local governments and the Florida Legislative Committee on Intergovernmental Relations.

Pinellas County has a long history of service contracts dating back to the mid-1950s, long before the Florida Interlocal Cooperation Act (Florida Statutes, 163.01) was enacted by the state legislature in 1969 (Shrestha 2008). While service contracts grew over time, termination of contracts was infrequent. This implies that the local units, once they enter into a contract, prefer to retain the relationship. Hence, this analysis focuses on all pay-for-service contracts that existed in 2005. Table 6.2 reports that the frequency of these contracts varies by service and ranges from 1 for the library to 59 for the sewer service. Out of 17 services that had pay-for-service contracts, only water, sewer, conservation, utility billing, police, protective inspection, fire, emergency medical, and traffic signal installation and maintenance services are included in the study. The remaining services had too few contracts for any meaningful stochastic analysis and thus were not included.

Network Measures

The network measures listed and illustrated in Table 6.1 are used to analyze the pattern of service relations hypothesized above. Each measure

---

[5] Florida's statute required all counties and cities above 100,000 residents to submit the inventory of interlocal agreements to the Department of Community Affairs (DCA). My discussions with DCA, county, and city officials indicated that the inventory underreported the intercity agreements in particular.

[6] The online record Web site of the Pinellas County Clerk of the Circuit Court records service agreements made since January 1, 1990. The database is incomplete because city clerks do not submit many routine interlocal agreements to the circuit court for official recording. An anonymous city clerk confirmed that the clerk's office is selective about which agreements to submit for record because doing so costs money. The online records Web site is https://pubtitles.co.pinellas.fl.us/login/clerkloginx.jsp.

[7] The difficulties in accessing interlocal agreements are not unusual. In this regard, Friesema (1971, 40) noted that "these officials did not even recall or have any records on agreements the interviewers already knew about from recent reports in the press."

calculates the number of the specified structure associated with each observed contract, and the estimation process then determines which structures appear most frequently for each type of service.

Reciprocity measures whether the pay-for-service relationships extends from a buyer government, i, to the provider government, j, when j already has service relations with buyer i. A positive value for the parameter would mean the presence of reciprocal relationships in the observed agreements, with the expectation that buyer i increases utility by entering into a service agreement with provider j, when j also has such an agreement with buyer i.

Transitivity measures closed relationships between actors when the buyer government i attempts to minimize the supplier j's opportunism by forming closed ties with the third provider h, which supplies to provider j. The statistical measure in Table 6.1 calculates the number of transitive triplets in the observed networks of contracts. A positive parameter indicates the presence of transitivity effect in the pattern of relationships.

The alternating in-k-star parameter captures the idea that a buyer government, i, seeks to collaborate with a popular provider, j, to reduce risks of supplier opportunism. A popular provider attracts many buyers and therefore has highest incoming service agreements.[8] The parameter gives the value of the alternating in-k-star statistic by counting the in-degrees distribution of service agreements observed in the data with geometrically decreasing weight for increasing popularity (Snijders et al. 2006)[9]; this reflects the increasing transaction costs the buyer experiences when forming a relationship with a crowded supplier that has many buyers to pay attention to. A positive parameter value indicates the prevalence of a popular provider in the observed relationship.

The number of ordered pairs indirectly connected statistic measures the preference of a buyer, i, to contract with a supplier government, j,

---

[8] In simple terms, in a directed relationship (diagraph), the outward link is "out-degrees" and the inward link is "in-degrees." In a pure "in-star" network, the actor in the center (star) has positive in-degrees but zero out-degrees whereas actors in the periphery have positive out-degrees but zero in-degrees.

[9] In the alternating in-k-star statistic, λ is some constant weight (usually $\lambda = 2$) whereby the impact of higher order popular actors is reduced. This means that once a provider government (node) attracts a certain number of contracts (buyers), attracting additional buyers adds progressively little to its "popularity." For example, for $\lambda = 2$, there is little difference between a node of 5, 6, or higher in popularity. The same is true for λ in the case of the "alternating out-k-star" statistic. For details, see Snijders et al. 2006.

which has multiple sources of supply. As depicted in Table 6.1, contracting with a provider having multiple sources of supply ensures greater reliability in supply because even if one source is in trouble, other sources will still be available to fill the gap. The value of the statistics for this relationship is estimated by counting the frequency of such relationships a buyer has in the observed network.

The alternating out-k-star statistic measures the tendency of the buyer government, *i*, to seek service contracts with multiple provider governments, *js*. By forming a wider network of contracts, the buyer ensures adequate supply even if there is concurrent need for the service in multiple places. The statistic, illustrated in Diagram d in Table 6.1, calculates the value of the spreading pattern by counting the out-degrees distribution of the service agreements that buyer *i* has with the providers in the observed data, with geometrically decreasing weight for additional contracts (Snijders et al. 2006). A positive alternating out-k-star parameter indicates the presence of a centralized buyer purchasing a service from many provider jurisdictions.

The out-2-star parameter was also included in the model to capture buyers' tendency to spread risks with two providers. Inclusion of lower degree parameters in the higher degree model is also considered to improve the convergence or to find a model that better fits the data (Snijders et al. 2006; Robins et al. 2007). The graphic configuration of the out-2-star pattern and the corresponding statistics are shown in Diagram e in Table 6.1.

Controls

Attributes of transacting jurisdictions and covariate conditions such as economies of scale, principal jurisdiction, geographic proximity, attribute similarity, and existing service relations can also influence interlocal service agreements. These are included as control variables in the models.

Economies of scale effect. The economic principle suggests that greater horizontal fragmentation, which makes jurisdictions smaller in size, prevents local units from realizing economies of scale in self-production. Hence, the desire for efficiency can encourage smaller governments to enter into service contracts with other local governments, possibly with the larger ones. Service contracting enlarges the consumption base. An increase in production to cater to a larger population reduces the average cost of production for each contracting partner. Capital-intensive services such as water and sewer are generally more prone to economies of scale than labor-intensive services like police or fire protection. The population size of the governments, operationalized as the natural log of population in thousands, measures the potential for economies of scale. The effect of this size variable is captured by the *size alter effect*,[10] which reflects the tendency to contract with larger sellers.

Principal jurisdiction effect. The Pinellas County government and the cities of Clearwater, Largo, and St. Petersburg are considered the principal supplier jurisdictions in the area because they are bigger in size and possess greater capacity to invest, produce, and manage public services. Hojman and Szeidl (2006) argue that actors that provide more critical resources become central in the network because they can acquire relatively greater capacity to create large aggregate gains. Buyer governments are, therefore, likely to be attracted to these principal jurisdictions. A binary variable reflecting principal governments is included to capture this effect.

Geographic proximity effect. Contiguous jurisdictions may find service contracts more economical than jurisdictions that are separated by greater distance. Geographically proximate governments typically experience greater spillover effects that can motivate them to cooperate. Thus, proximity can condition buyer governments to contract with the contiguous providers resulting in a regional pattern of central providers (Hojman and Szeidl 2006). This effect is captured by creating a geographic proximity (dyadic) matrix that is coded 1 if the local governments share one or more borders and 0 otherwise.

Similarity effect. Similarity based on geography or other attributes can also induce local jurisdictions to form service relationships with one another. Location within the same service area and having the same form of government are two such similarity factors that can influence service contracts.

Generally, it is easier for a local government to work with peers belonging to the same service area than with those that are outside the service area. In Pinellas County, the water and sewer service areas are defined for coordinated planning and delivery of these services. The constituent jurisdictions share similarity of purpose and increased possibility of interaction. Hence, the likelihood of a contract is greater between the governments belonging to the same service area than between the governments in

---

[10] In network terminology, an "alter" is an actor to whom a relationship is extended (in this case, the supplier government) and a "node" is an actor who initiates the relationship (in this case, the buyer government).

TABLE 6.3. *Network Descriptive of Pay-for-Service Contracts in Pinellas County, Florida*

Service Type	Density	Average Degree	In-degrees Range	Out-degrees Range
Water	0.04	1.04	0–21	0–2
Sewer	0.05	1.24	0–15	0–4
Conservation	0.02	0.40	0–5	0–4
Utility billing	0.013	0.32	0–7	0–1
Police	0.035	0.84	0–19	0–2
Inspection	0.035	0.84	0–13	0–3
Traffic signal installation & maintenance	0.033	0.80	0–18	0–2
Fire protection	0.026	0.64	0–2	0–11
Emergency medical service	0.031	0.76	0–4	0–15

different service areas. This effect is captured by the *same service area* binary variable that is coded 1 for the local governments located within the same service area and 0 otherwise.

Likewise, similar professional orientation and training help develop common values and norms of behavior. Professional local government managers serving in a council-manager form of government are often drawn from similar professional backgrounds and training and are more likely to communicate and share information among themselves than with managers serving in communities with a mayor-council form of government. A common form of government reduces the transaction cost of negotiating service agreements among professional managers (Zhang 2007). A binary variable representing the *council-manager form of government* captures this effect.

Existing relations effect. Local governments engage in multiple agreements involving one or many services. Existing service relations can facilitate formation of new service agreements due to familiarity and trust arising out of their interactions and experiences in dealing with each other. Likewise, for technically or functionally related services, agreements on one service may affect the agreements on another service. For example, the sewer service agreements may be influenced by the water service agreements as the size of the sewer pipe depends on the amount of water use. Hence, both joint service agreements and pay-for-service agreements for technically or functionally related services are included in the model. These variables are represented by their respective binary matrices.

Description of Observed Pattern of Service Relationships

Service agreements were transformed into separate binary matrices for each service of directed buyer-supplier relationships among all 25 governments in the study. Rows represent buyer governments and columns represent seller governments. A buyer government entering pay-for-service agreements with a supplier government is represented by 1 in the matrix, and 0 indicates an absence of such an agreement. The descriptive statistics of the observed network characteristics for each service are reported in Table 6.3, and networks graphs drawn using the UCINET program for visual examination of the pattern of service relationships are shown in the appendix at the end of the chapter.

Both visual and descriptive measures reveal important characteristics of the patterns of contracts. The contractual relations are sparse as indicated by their low density – the actual number of contracts divided by all possible contracts. The density is less than 0.05 for most services, so less than 5 percent of all potential contractual relationships are actualized. The average number of contracts per buying government is also low, as indicated by an average degree of 1 or less. Strikingly, there is greater variation in the outgoing contracts from a buyer (out-degree) and incoming contracts toward a provider (in degree), by service type. The incoming contracts have a greater range for the water, sewer, police, inspection, and traffic installation and maintenance services. The graphs in the appendix indicate that other suppliers are also important for these services, but their buyer base looks small. For the building inspection service, some reciprocity can be observed in the appendix graphs. The conservation and utility billing graphs indicate the tendency toward a central supplier, but the pattern is very sparse. In contrast, for the fire and emergency medical services, the outgoing contracts have a greater range, indicating that some buyers are contracting with multiple providers for these services. The network graphs for fire and emergency medical services imply that the buyer is central in buyer-supplier contractual relations for these services.

Estimation Technique

The ERGM (p^*) model in the Simulation Investigation for Empirical Network Analysis (SIENA) program is utilized to test the likelihood that the hypothesized network structures will be observed in the cross-section network data for individual services.[11] The p^* model is considered to be the most promising class of statistical models for evaluating structural properties of social networks observed cross-sectionally (Snijders et al. 2006). The model is actor-oriented, which means that actors are assumed to form relationships taking into account the expected utility and costs involved in forming and maintaining such relationships. The p^* model in SIENA uses the Metropolis-Hastings algorithm for generating random draws from the observed graph distribution and employs the stochastic approximation algorithm to estimate the parameters reflecting the structural patterns (Snijders et al. 2006).[12] It estimates the probability that the network structures included in the model appear at greater frequency than would be explained by a random graph with the same number of local government actors and contracts. In this model, the prevalence of local structure is considered a predictor of the global structure (Steglich 2006).

The model is conditioned on the observed networks and considers the potential random contracts, the relative dependence of all contracts, and the effect of actor attributes and covariates on such contracts for the robust test of the structural features of the observed networks. It simulates the distribution of random graphs from a starting set of parameter values and refines these estimated values by comparing the distribution of random graphs with the observed graphs (Wasserman and Robins 2005). The estimated parameters provide the likelihood of the structural effects observed in the network data (Robins et al. 2007).

The SIENA program implements a Markov Chain Monte Carlo (MCMC) estimation for the p^* model (Snijders et al. 2006). This algorithm computes the Monte Carlo approximation of the maximum likelihood estimates. The program does a convergence check by verifying how close the average statistics calculated for the generated graphs are to the observed values of the statistics. If the convergence diagnostic statistic (t-statistic) for the algorithm is less than 0.1 in absolute value, the parameter is considered to be converged well. The default conditional

---

[11] SIENA is a statistical program included in Stocnet, a software package for the study of network analysis. A free copy of the software can be downloaded at http://stat.gamma. rug.nl/stocnet/.

[12] The specification provided by Snijders et al. (2006) is based on a higher order dependence structure of a social phenomenon and is capable of modeling higher order graph structures (k-stars, k-triangles, and independent 2-paths), controlling for actor attributes and dyadic covariates (for details, see Robins and Pattison 2005; Snijders et al. 2006; and Robins et al. 2007).

TABLE 6.4. *p** *Parameter Estimates for the Structural Patterns of Pay-for-Service Contracts in Pinellas County, Florida*

1	Water	Sewer	Conservation[a]	Utility Billing[b]	Police	Inspection	Traffic Installation
	2	3	4	5	6	7	8
Reciprocity	−3.57 (2.02)	0.60 (1.08)	1.09 (1.93)	0.00 (fixed)	−4.03 (fixed)	6.67*** (1.25)	−8.88 (12.79)
Closed relationship (transitivity)	−1.91 (fixed)	−0.05 (0.29)	0.20 (1.27)	0.00 (fixed)	−0.43 (0.68)	n/e	n/e
Popularity (alternating in-k-stars)	2.86* (1.34)	−1.99 (2.10)	−3.35 (3.89)	−6.07 (14.70)	3.60*** (0.70)	1.48* (0.81)	2.52* (1.28)
Extended pattern (number of pairs indirectly connected)	0.67** (0.24)	0.20* (0.11)	1.87* (1.10)	−3.66 (12.07)	n/e	−0.62* (0.28)	0.41** (0.17)
Connecting to 2 partners (out-2-stars)	−3.89 (1.69)	−0.07 (0.47)	−0.34 (1.38)	−4.88 (fixed)	n/e	0.42 (0.47)	−2.17 (1.35)
Geographic proximity	2.52** (1.19)	0.18 (0.62)	0.02 (1.02)	0.77 (1.01)	1.92* (0.68)	0.79 (0.57)	0.97 (0.77)
Service area similarity[c]	1.69 (1.07)	1.13 (0.64)	n/a	n/a	n/a	n/a	n/a
Manager govt. similarity	−3.37* (1.66)	−0.30 (0.58)	0.31 (0.88)	−1.57 (1.25)	−0.84 (0.69)	0.20 (0.47)	−0.02 (1.04)
Economies of scale	1.57 (1.13)	1.41* (0.66)	0.32 (0.40)	99.62 (135.36)	−0.05 (0.24)	0.15 (0.26)	1.54 (1.93)
Principal jurisdictions	0.14 (1.71)	3.02 (3.19)	7.35 (6.23)	0.00 (fixed)	0.21 (1.07)	−0.58 (1.23)	1.38 (fixed)
Bilateral joint contracts[d]	n/e	1.67* (0.67)	0.72 (0.90)	n/a	0.00 (fixed)	n/a	5.17 (7.87)
Sewer pay-for-service contracts	0.84 (0.85)	n/a	n/a	5.50 (7.16)	n/a	n/a	n/a
Water pay-for-service contracts	n/a	1.86* (0.84)	0.12 (1.15)	−5.13 (7.20)	n/a	n/a	n/a
Road pay-for-service contracts	n/a	n/a	n/a	n/a	n/a	n/a	1.94 (1.75)

All models have good convergence with $t \leq .1$; * $p < 0.05$, ** $p < 0.01$, *** $p < 0.001$.
Figures in parentheses are standard errors. Convergence diagnostics, covariance, and derivative matrices are based on 1,000 iterations in phase 3 of the SIENA program.
n/e = parameter dropped because of nonconvergence.
n/a = not applicable.

[a] The model without principal jurisdictions showed a size effect close to statistical significance.
[b] The model did not converge well.
[c] Applicable for water and sewer services only.
[d] Joint agreements for the respective services in the column.

TABLE 6.5. *p* Estimates for the Structural Patterns of Fire and Emergency Medical Pay-for-Service Contracts in Pinellas County, Florida*

Parameters	Fire[a]	Emergency Medical
1	2	3
Reciprocity (mutuality)	n/e	2.88 (2.18)
Transitivity (closed relationship)	0.28 (1.19)	n/e
Number of pairs indirectly connected (extended pattern)	−0.66 (0.61)	n/e
In-2-stars (lower degree popularity)	0.19 (0.61)	0.19 (0.99)
Alternating out-k-stars (spreading pattern)	1.68** (0.47)	3.72** (1.31)
Geographic proximity	2.51** (0.80)	1.99* (1.10)
Manager govt. similarity	−0.62 (0.69)	0.09 (0.99)
Economies of scale	0.57 (0.37)	1.11* (0.65)
Principal jurisdictions	−1.19 (1.24)	−1.88 (1.98)
Bilateral joint agreement[b]	1.09 (0.76)	3.04* (1.63)
Fire pay-for-service contracts relations	n/a	1.94 (fixed)

All models have good convergence with $t \leqslant .1$; * $p<0.05$, ** $p<0.01$, *** $p<0.001$.
Figures in parentheses are standard errors. Convergence diagnostics, covariance, and derivative matrices are based on 1,000 iterations in phase 3 of the SIENA program.
n/e = parameter dropped because of no convergence.
n/a = not applicable.
[a] Inclusion of emergency medical service pay-for-service contracts did not converge the model and therefore was dropped from the model.
[b] Joint service agreements for the respective service in the column.

simulation option was used for the model estimation.[13] A forward selection procedure was followed for the estimation of the parameters; that is, the structural parameters were modeled first, followed by the additional actor attributes in the model. The convergence diagnostics, covariance, and derivative matrices were based on 1000 iterations. The standard t-values test the significance of the estimated parameters.

RESULTS AND DISCUSSION

The findings for the services that are subject to supplier opportunism and risk of technological breakdown are reported in Table 6.4, and the results

---

[13] The SIENA manual advises using the conditional (default) option for better convergence of the algorithm. It keeps the total number of ties (in this case, service contracts) fixed at the observed value, implying that there is no separate parameter for the density statistics (Snijders et al. 2005).

for the services that are more vulnerable to spatially distributed uncertainties are presented in Table 6.5. The program was not able to estimate all the hypothesized structural effects for all services. This is more likely because some observed networks did not have enough service relations to estimate the particular structures in the model. All reported results satisfy the convergence limits. These results are discussed next in relation to the transacting governments' motivations to seek specific contractual patterns to offset the transaction risks involved in forming and safeguarding service contracts.

Mitigating Supplier Opportunism

The results show that buyer governments seek to form contractual relationships with a popular, and hence credible, provider to control supplier opportunism for most services (hypothesis H3). This is evident for the water, police, inspection, and traffic installation/maintenance services. The alternating in-k-star parameter reflecting this tendency is significant and positive for these services, controlling for the attributes and other structural features in Table 6.4. This suggests that for a buyer government, a service agreement with an established popular provider is important to mitigate its concerns for potential supplier opportunism. A service agreement with a popular supplier offers the buyer a sense of reliability because other jurisdictions are also purchasing from the same supplier. The supplier's reputation may also restrain its temptation for opportunistic behavior. This provides additional assurance to the buyer. Note though, that no support for this tendency was found for the sewer, conservation, and utility billing services.

The buyer government's preference for a reciprocal contract pattern (hypothesis H1) was not found to be the norm in service relationships. As can be seen from Tables 6.4 and 6.5, the reciprocity effect is not significant for eight of the nine services in the analysis, suggesting that mutuality is either not a preferred option for the buyer, or it is not feasible with the same service. The direction of the parameter is also not consistent enough to determine any likely tendency. However, for building inspection services, the reciprocity parameter is significant and positive (Table 6.4, Column 7), indicating the prevalence of reciprocity. This result is consistent with the situation in the study area. Most jurisdictions have their own building inspection official. However, they face temporary service gaps created by the increase in short-term demand or by temporary absence of the staff due to illness or vacation. The reciprocal pay-for-service agreements in building inspection allow the contracting local units to cover these short-term service gaps. Reciprocity also controls potential defection by the other partner because of their mutual dependency for the service.

As shown in Tables 6.4 and 6.5, the closed pattern of service relationships (hypothesis H2) was also not found to be significant for any of these services. The direction of the transitivity parameter is negative, suggesting that buyer jurisdictions do not prefer closed sets of contracts for these service transactions. Since measurement difficulty is absent or negligible for the pay-for-service agreements, it may be that buyers do not encounter significant credibility of commitment problems from the supplier government that would require buyers to form closed service contracts. The reputational effects associated with popular suppliers (H3) apparently provide sufficient credibility for most service areas.

Mitigating Uncertainties from Breakdown in Technology

Mixed evidence was found regarding the expectation that buyers prefer to contract with a provider that has multiple sources of supply when faced with the risk of breakdown in technology (hypothesis H4). The "number of pairs indirectly connected" parameter, capturing the extending pattern of contractual relations, is positive and significant for three out of seven services in Table 6.4. These are water, sewer, and traffic services. For the building inspection service, the parameter is negative and significant, suggesting that the buyer government prefers to avoid an extended pattern of relations. For water, sewer, and traffic services the buyers' dependency on the provider is high because they generally require a highly asset-specific investment. This may induce buyers to form extended patterns of contractual relations to assure supply in the event of technological failure. This may not be the case with the building inspection service because of the presence of reciprocity, which is not present in the water or sewer services.

Mitigating Spatially Distributed Uncertainties

When faced with the risk of concurrent occurrence in multiple communities, buyer governments prefer the spreading pattern of contracting with multiple suppliers (H5). The "alternating out-k-star" statistic captures the prevalence of a spreading pattern. It is significant and positive for the fire and emergency medical services, the two services most prone to spatially

TABLE 6.6. *Comparison of the Patterns of Pay-for-Service Contractual Relationships across Services, Pinellas County, Florida*

Patterns of Contractual Relationships	Water	Sewer	Conservation	Utility Billing	Police	Inspections	Traffic Installation	Fire	EMS
Reciprocity						+			
Closed pattern									
Popularity pattern	+				+	+	+		
Spreading pattern								+	+
Extended pattern	+	+	+			+	+		

Note: + indicates presence of the pattern.

distributed uncertainties. Here, a broader network of contracts increases the probability for the buyer to obtain this service because not all providers are likely to face the problem at the same time or to the same degree. Since the buyer is not critically dependent on one provider in a spreading network, it can access other providers in case one provider behaves opportunistically because of simultaneous emergencies. Defection from a provider is less damaging in this structure because other providers are available in the network.

Other Effects

The economies of scale variable was found significant in forming service contracts for the sewer, emergency medical, and fire services, controlling for the attributes and other structural effects. For other services except police, the direction of the estimated parameters is positive, suggesting at least some attractiveness of supplier size in forming service agreements. For sewer service, the presence of four providers in the study area (Pinellas County, St. Petersburgh, Largo, and Clearwater) offer the potential for economies of scale compared to the availability of only one or two large providers that might have exhausted the technological limit beyond which constant or diseconomies of scale might occur. For fire and emergency medical services, fixed investments vary little by the size of the area served. Here, an increase in the population served reduces the average cost. The principal jurisdiction variable was not found significant, suggesting that buyer governments are not attracted to the principal jurisdictions in forming service contracts.[14]

Geographic proximity effects were significant only for the water, police, fire, and emergency medical services. Proximate providers have a direct cost advantage over more distant providers. For example, the length of the water distribution line is less, police patrolling distance is shorter, and fire and emergency response is quicker. For fire and emergency medical services, this is especially evident because they are also characterized by temporal specificity (requiring quick response to save lives or property) and site specificity (delivery units close to property or

---

[14] Although there is high correlation between the size and binary principal jurisdiction variables ($r = 0.7$), the inclusion of principal jurisdiction in the models did not significantly affect the parameter estimates. However, for the conservation service, the model without principal jurisdiction makes the size parameter close to statistical significance. The utility billing and traffic installation services faced convergence problems.

to people for quick response). Proximity also increases the chances of repeated exchange between the partner governments. This increases the likelihood of service agreements and reduces transaction barriers by increasing trust and the symmetry of information.

Belonging to the water and sewer areas and institutional similarity measured by the council-manager form of government did not significantly influence the formation of service contracts. There is no consistent direction of the parameters across services to indicate any tendency. Likewise, for most services, the existing pay-for-service or joint service agreements were not influential in forming new agreements. Nevertheless, the positive direction of the coefficients for most services implies that the existing service relations can facilitate formation of service agreements.

SUMMARY

This chapter investigated the link between local governments' response to transaction risks and the consequent networks of service agreements in a public service exchange setting where the general-purpose local governments of Pinellas County, Florida, engaged in pay-for-service agreements to resolve ICA problems in municipal service provision. It was hypothesized that buyer jurisdictions develop a network of service contracts to mitigate supplier opportunism and environmental uncertainties in service exchange, which then lead to the emergence of specific patterns of service contracts.

As summarized in Table 6.6, the overall findings indicate the prevalence of mixed patterns of contractual relationships suggesting that the transacting jurisdictions form networks of service contracts that differ depending on the risk profiles of the service. For asset-specific services such as water, police, inspection, and traffic services that are prone to supplier opportunism, buyer jurisdictions prefer the popularity pattern that seeks contractual relationships with a credible provider. On the other hand, for fire and emergency medical services that can be demanded concurrently in multiple communities, buyers prefer the spreading pattern that seeks to develop service relationships with multiple provider jurisdictions to minimize the risk of not getting the service when needed. Finally, for water, sewer, conservation, building inspection, and traffic services that exhibit the risk of breakdown in technology, buyers prefer the extended pattern that seeks service relationships with provider jurisdictions that have multiple sources of supply. Notice that buyer governments seek multiple structural assurances for water, inspections, and traffic installation services where dependency concerns appear to be particularly troublesome. In these service areas, buyers seek both popular providers to ensure credibility as well as extended patterns of contractual relationships to mitigate technological and supply uncertainties.

The results support the conjecture that local governments systematically self-organize contractual service relationships to resolve collective action problems in public service provision. Significant coefficients were observed in eight out of nine services despite variations in self-organizing patterns across services. The emergent pattern of these service contract networks is a voluntary response of local governments to the need to mitigate the transaction risks they face in service exchange. The presence of the structural patterns of service contracts, controlling for the attributes of transacting jurisdictions and covariate conditions, supports this proposition. The results suggest that local governments not only rely on bilateral interlocal service contracts and formal institutions, but also develop self-organizing patterns of contractual networks to resolve the public goods supply problems in horizontal federalism.

Some limitations to this study should be noted. Individual services are assumed to present unique technical and functional problems leading to specific transaction problems and associated self-organizing network patterns. However, local governments may consider service relations in their entirety, so overall trust and credibility of commitment may be more important than the service-specific technical or functional characteristics of individual services. Then the patterns observed for individual services would be interdependent. For example, reciprocity across rather than within service areas can be especially important if a local unit is in an advantaged position regarding one service but is in a disadvantaged position in another service (Feiock 2007). Future inquiries should address this important governance question of interdependence, which might even suggest an integrated, informal mechanism for regional governance.

In addition, cross-sectional network analysis assumes that the networks are stable or at equilibrium. This assumption is justified in our analysis because contracts are seldom terminated in Pinellas, but it does not allow us to analyze how service networks develop and what service networks prevail over time. These would require longitudinal analyses. Finally, since local governments also practice joint and mutual aid agreements in addition to pay-for-service agreements, future inquiry needs to investigate what network structures local governments develop in adopting and safeguarding multiple forms of contracts.

APPENDIX. SOCIOGRAMS OF OBSERVED NETWORKS OF
PAY-FOR-SERVICE AGREEMENTS IN PINELLAS COUNTY, FLORIDA

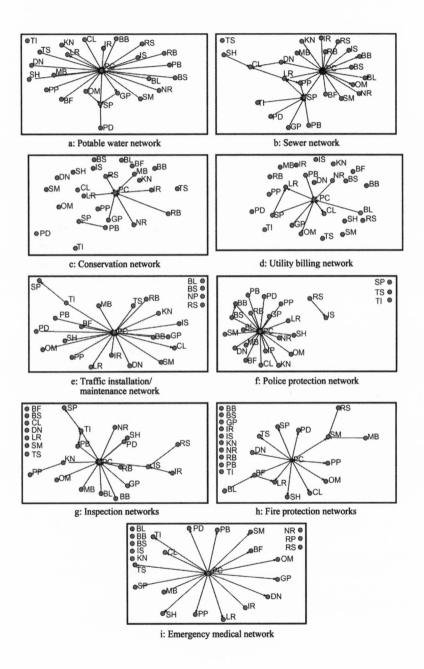

a: Potable water network

b: Sewer network

c: Conservation network

d: Utility billing network

e: Traffic installation/
maintenance network

f: Police protection network

g: Inspection networks

h: Fire protection networks

i: Emergency medical network

7

Special Districts versus Contracts

Complements or Substitutes?

Megan Mullin

Local infrastructure development gives rise to important collective action dilemmas, including scale economies that may not coincide with the scale of existing local governments and negative effects from promoting growth that spill over into neighboring jurisdictions.[1] These dilemmas are amplified in the case of infrastructure for drinking water provision. Securing water supply to meet a community's demands involves competing for access to an increasingly scarce common pool resource. Once a supply source has been identified, the provision of drinking water is capital intensive, with high fixed costs for the construction of storage, treatment, and distribution facilities. These assets are highly specific and cannot be deployed for other local government functions. Thus, local governments can impose substantial costs on their neighbors when making decisions regarding water infrastructure expansion. They also can help their neighbors to achieve growth goals or resolve water scarcity issues by cooperating for drinking water provision.

This chapter focuses on the role of special districts in resolving local coordination problems. Special districts often have been seen as a formalized institution for promoting regional cooperation. They allow boundary design to the scale of public problems and may produce greater efficiency in the marketplace for local public goods. Where fragmentation of local authority has interfered with policy coordination and created gaps in local service provision, a common response has been the creation

---

[1] Portions of this chapter are adapted, by permission, from Megan Mullin, *Governing the Tap: Special District Governance and the New Local Politics of Water*, Cambridge, MA: MIT Press (2009).

of a new special district to consolidate authority and promote efficient production of public goods. If state law, local interests, or specific problem conditions rule out special district formation, then existing governments must organize themselves to satisfy service demands and address impacts of water provision on natural resources and neighboring communities. One possible solution is the extension of an existing special district's boundaries to regionalize service delivery and take advantage of economies of scale. Many scholars have highlighted the flexibility of special district boundaries once established, arguing that this flexibility allows for governance that is more adaptable to changing resource constraints and patterns of demand. Another alternative is for special districts and local general purpose governments to coordinate their efforts through intergovernmental contracts for the production and delivery of services.

Both of these strategies for mitigating institutional collective action (ICA) problems offer potential benefits for regions suffering negative consequences from fragmented authority. Boundary extension provides a formal and permanent commitment by a government to provide services in an area, but it might spark conflict by altering political constituencies and extending the authority of a single agency – perhaps encroaching on a neighboring jurisdiction's expansion plans. Because they require ongoing consent by their signatories, contracts and agreements are less stable but may be more likely to produce a solution that is advantageous for multiple governments. The analysis that follows examines whether the strategies are complements or substitutes to one another. By allowing special districts to bypass negotiating with their neighbors, boundary flexibility may reduce the incidence of cooperative agreements that could help achieve policy efficiencies. Alternatively, it might promote cooperation by offering more creative solutions to regional conflict.

The following section discusses in greater detail how special district boundary flexibility and intergovernmental contracts each serve as an institutional mechanism to mitigate interlocal collective action dilemmas. I then offer hypotheses about the relationship between these mechanisms. The empirical analysis focuses on local water policy. I find that for a special district with surplus capacity for production or provision of drinking water, flexible boundary change rules that allow expansion of the district's customer base reduce the likelihood that the district will establish contracting relationships to share its surplus capacity with neighboring governments. The results demonstrate the importance of considering the entire package of coordinating institutions that are available in a region when we examine how local governments develop solutions to collective action dilemmas.

BOUNDARY FLEXIBILITY AND INTERGOVERNMENTAL AGREEMENTS

As autonomous local governments with much of the power and stability of cities and counties, special districts diversify local public economies by providing goods and services that other local governments cannot or will not take on. They may supplement the efforts of general purpose governments, or they may replace the city or county in providing an essential local function. Special district boundaries frequently crosscut the boundaries of other local governments, creating layers of local authority that vary in their geographic and functional breadth.

Many scholars have expressed optimism about the potential for special districts to help overcome interlocal collective action problems and improve efficiency in local service delivery. Specialization allows the scope of each governmental unit to be designed appropriately for the policy area it oversees, allowing economies of scale to be captured and the consequences of policy actions to be internalized (Ostrom, Tiebout, and Warren 1961; Hawkins 1976; Ostrom, Bish, and Ostrom 1988). Advocates of regional governance as a means to improve policy coordination view functionally specialized metropolitan bodies as a politically palatable first step toward a broader regionalism (Downs 1994; Altshuler et al. 1999; Pagano 1999).

Although many of the perceived benefits of special district governance stem from policy specialization, some analysts argue that it is the flexibility of special district boundaries that helps reduce spillover effects and heighten responsiveness to changing public preferences (Foster 1997; Hooghe and Marks 2003). These treatments suggest that special districts produce efficiencies not only at the formation stage, when their geographic territory can be designed to capture economies of scale and minimize negative externalities, but throughout their life span, as boundaries get adjusted to address new spillovers or accommodate changing populations or preferences. Changing special district boundaries can provide a stable service commitment that addresses the immediate policy demand. However, it may reduce the decision-making autonomy of neighboring governments and cause conflict that contributes to new interlocal problems.

Empirical evidence on special district boundary changes is scant. The literature on city boundary changes has identified cost savings in service provision as one motivation for municipal efforts to annex neighboring unincorporated territory, along with other rationales including expansion of the tax base and local preferences to change the racial balance of the city (Liner 1990; Liner and McGregor 1996; Austin 1999; Feiock and Carr 2001). Efficiency and service considerations are likely to predominate in the case of special district boundary changes. Special district boundaries do not shape perceptions of local political community as city boundaries do, and special districts lack the land use authority that would allow them to practice exclusionary politics (Danielson 1972). Moreover, it is uncommon for special districts to manage redistributive functions that create the strongest justification for a large tax base. Some special districts do have the authority to impose property taxes, thus creating an incentive to widen their jurisdiction. But in general, expansion of special district boundaries is likely a response to changing service demands or opportunities to achieve policy efficiencies.

Boundary changes can help to solve a local policy dilemma by shaping a single jurisdiction to the scale of the problem or service demand. Another strategy is the development of cooperative agreements between governments. Intergovernmental agreements may consist of contracts for the purchase of goods or services by one government from another, or arrangements for a government to provide a good or service outside its jurisdictional boundaries. Cooperative agreements between localities are solutions to ICA dilemmas, and they can help reduce damage from spillovers and otherwise overcome the negative impacts of fragmented governance (Post 2004). Pursuit of cost savings is a dominant reason for contracting by local governments (Stein 1990; Morgan and Hirlinger 1991). Contracts may increase efficiency by taking advantage of slack in existing infrastructure and capturing economies of scale. They allow separation of the production and the provision of public goods and the development of competitive markets for each (Ostrom et al. 1961).

Contracts and interlocal agreements are among the most adaptable strategies for self-organization. With fixed terms, they require ongoing approval from participant governments. Although legally binding while in force, they allow decision makers periodically to reevaluate community needs and introduce alternative solutions in response to new externalities or changing public preferences. In light of these potential benefits even boundary review commissions – state and county institutions established to guide local government creation and boundary change – have begun over time to promote intergovernmental agreements as an efficient and less controversial alternative to annexation (ACIR 1992, 33).

THE RELATIONSHIP BETWEEN COORDINATING MECHANISMS

The formation of a new special district may itself represent an effort to resolve local ICA problems (Feiock and Carr 2001; Carr 2004; LeRoux and Carr 2007). Once created, however, special districts contribute to the fragmentation of authority that can give rise to further policy conflicts. Specialized governments are able to employ the same strategies that cities use to address these challenges – they can change boundaries and develop cooperative agreements with their neighbors.

The empirical analysis presented here tests whether a relationship exists between these mechanisms. In the case of cities, efficiency goals have been shown to be a primary motivation for both municipal annexation and the establishment of interlocal agreements. Cities rarely have the opportunity to choose between these tools, however, because city boundaries cannot overlap. Annexation therefore requires a supply of annexable land. Indeed, Stein's (1990) analysis of municipal service arrangements showed no consistent relationship between a city's annexation authority and its decision to contract for services. Special district boundaries have been perceived as more flexible and able to adapt to changing problem conditions and public demands than cities. If it is more feasible for special districts to change their boundaries, does this affect their incentives for developing interlocal agreements with other governments?

I focus here on districts with slack resources. A district with excess capacity in its infrastructure might have choices between providing services to new customers on its own or forming an agreement to sell that capacity to a nearby jurisdiction. The effect of boundary flexibility on that decision might operate in either direction. One hypothesis is that boundary change and intergovernmental cooperation are substitute strategies, meaning that boundary flexibility reduces the likelihood of engaging in interlocal agreements. If the decision between expansion and contracting is a simple trade-off between the transaction costs of building support for annexation and those of developing an agreement with another government, then lowering the costs associated with boundary change should lead to a decline in cooperative agreements. Special districts producing negative externalities could seek to internalize spillovers through expansion rather than negotiate an agreement with neighboring communities that suffer costs from the district's operations. With less boundary flexibility, interlocal cooperation may seem a more attractive strategy.

Alternatively, boundary flexibility and intergovernmental cooperation might complement one another by increasing the range of possible solutions to policy dilemmas created by local fragmentation. Post (2002) has shown that a larger supply of potential partners increases the incidence of interlocal expenditure agreements. Boundary flexibility does not increase the density of governments in a region, but it does allow territorial change by those governments that may cause them to become more likely partners for an agreement – for example, by creating overlap or a common boundary that facilitates labor sharing or infrastructure extension. The possibility of boundary change may create opportunities rather than hurdles for creative intergovernmental problem solving.

EMPIRICAL ANALYSIS OF LOCAL WATER POLICY

The empirical analysis tests the relationship between boundary flexibility and interlocal cooperation in the domain of local water policy. The provision of drinking water is one of the most important services that American local governments oversee, and the nature of the good makes it particularly vulnerable to coordination problems and policy inefficiencies.[2] The typical policy challenge begins with new demand for water service. This new demand might result from residential or commercial development in a growing community, but it also arises in aging communities where declining productivity of individual wells brings about demand for connection to a community water system. Whether or not the new demand is located within the existing service area of a public water utility, delivering drinking water to satisfy the increased demand may pose a difficult policy challenge. A utility with a monopoly on service to the territory may need to acquire new supplies in order to avoid jeopardizing water service to its existing customers.[3] As common pool resources, groundwater aquifers and clean rivers are vulnerable to over-exploitation; utilities have more incentive to secure a plentiful water supply for their own customers than to protect the source for other communities or for ecosystem health. Moreover, the capital-intensive nature

---

[2] The Environmental Protection Agency (EPA) estimates that 57 percent of community water systems are privately owned, but they serve only 14 percent of the population (U.S. EPA 1997, 7–8).

[3] Approval of new development by general purpose governments without assurance of adequate water supply is itself an important coordination problem. See Hanak (2005) for a discussion of this issue in the California context.

of water storage and treatment facilities creates scale economies that can make it particularly costly for small utilities to expand service.

Intergovernmental coordination is even more difficult if the new demand falls outside the existing service area of any utility. On top of the supply questions described above, local governments must coordinate in order to ensure water provision without duplicating effort. Frequently, the policy solution in these situations is for a nearby utility to expand its service area to include the territory where the new demand is located. If a city or county operates the utility, this typically involves extending the utility's service area outside the jurisdiction of the responsible government. Many states permit extralocal service provision, especially by utilities. A city's decision to annex new territory typically would involve more considerations than water service alone. For water districts, extending service would more likely entail a boundary change. Changing the district's boundaries includes residents of the new territory as constituents of the district, subject to fees and taxes imposed by the district and able to vote for district officials and bond measures. Special district boundary change does not affect citizens' definitions of their local political community, so it is not likely to encounter any more resistance than would be the case for a simple extension of service. Indeed, existing residents of the water district might insist on boundary change in order to extend the district's revenue base.

An alternative solution to this policy challenge would be the establishment of interlocal cooperative agreements. Cooperative agreements allow separation of responsibility for water supply and water service. The utility with the most proximate water mains usually will be the most cost-effective service provider, but in some cases it will not have sufficient water supply for new customers. Neighboring utilities may have slack resources for water production after building in excess capacity in anticipation of future demand.[4] In other cases, the best solution might involve utilizing infrastructure owned by multiple utilities. Boundary change creates a permanent commitment for a utility to serve the new territory, while interlocal agreements promote ad hoc policy solutions that may supplement or replace that commitment.

Two cases demonstrate the possibility of special district boundary change and interlocal cooperation to serve as either complements or substitutes to one another. The first case involves a nearly decade-long

---

[4] Seasonal variation in demand for water is another important source of slack resources. In climates susceptible to drought, seasonal variation also is an important source of uncertainty about water demand.

dispute over a proposal to build 11,000 new homes in Dougherty Valley, on the outer edge of the San Francisco Bay area. County officials approved the development, but the project remained on hold for years while its backers sought to secure a source for water and agreement by a utility to deliver it. Many of the proposed strategies for supplying water to Dougherty Valley drew opposition from neighboring governments and their constituents based on projected impacts on reliability of service to existing customers and the possibility of stimulating further population growth in the region. The agreement that finally resolved the dispute entailed a neighboring water district annexing Dougherty Valley in order to deliver water purchased from another district located hundreds of miles away and transported through the pipes of a third water district – a creative solution that combined contracting and boundary change.[5]

Water district boundary change is much more difficult in Pennsylvania, where state law ties the boundaries of municipal water authorities to the boundaries of municipal governments. Thus independent authorities are not able to expand their boundaries to close service gaps. In the south central part of the state, a developer building a subdivision on the border between Menallen Township and Bendersville Borough sought to annex the entire project area into Bendersville in order to obtain service from the borough's water authority. Townships and boroughs are general purpose authorities in Pennsylvania's local governance system, and the annexation required majority support from voters in both municipalities. Bendersville voters approved the referendum, but Menallen residents voted overwhelmingly against annexation on the guidance of township officials, who cited expected losses in tax revenues. Lacking authority to expand its boundaries to cover the project area, the Bendersville Water Authority entered into an intergovernmental agreement to serve the new subdivision (Guo 2007). Agreements like this allow water distribution to adapt to changing patterns of demand in suburban Pennsylvania, but the cost may be accountability of water systems to their customers. Whether contracting or expansion is the better solution will depend on the nature and extent of the policy dilemma, and there may be trade-offs between efficiency and accountability. The focus here is on whether the availability of boundary change as an alternative strategy affects the decisions that special districts make about entering into interlocal agreements.

---

[5] See Mullin (2009) for a detailed discussion of the Dougherty Valley case.

Data

The analysis estimates the effect of water district boundary flexibility on incidence of revenue-generating intergovernmental agreements.[6] Data on intergovernmental agreements come from the finance phase of the 2002 Census of Governments. The dependent variable is dichotomous; an intergovernmental agreement is seen to exist when a water district reports any local intergovernmental revenue.[7] Across all functions, special districts are less likely than their general-purpose counterparts to establish intergovernmental agreements: 32 percent of special districts report some local intergovernmental spending or revenue, compared to 54 percent of cities and towns. As Stein (1990) has shown, the nature of a good can influence the likelihood of alternative service provision. Interlocal cooperation is rarer for water, with only 12 percent of water districts participating in interlocal agreements and half of those obtaining revenue from their contracts.

The key independent variable, boundary flexibility, refers to the stringency of state rules guiding the process of special district boundary change. When crafting legislation that enables formation of new special districts, states define the process for boundary expansion and change. These rules then become part of the package of constraints and opportunities that district officials face when considering strategies for addressing policy challenges related to water service. Previous research demonstrates the importance of state policy for stimulating special district formation and reliance (MacManus 1981; Bollens 1986; Burns 1994; Foster 1997; Austin 1998; McCabe 2000; but see Carr 2006). States may also exercise influence over ongoing special district operations by determining the package of institutional mechanisms available to help local governments solve policy problems.

Studies of the relationship between municipal boundary rules and annexation activity have produced mixed results (Dye 1964; MacManus and Thomas 1979; Galloway and Landis 1986; Liner 1990; Liner and McGregor 1996; Carr and Feiock 2001). Data are not available for special district boundary changes as they are for city annexations, so we cannot measure the direct effect of rules on district expansions. But for the current purpose, it is rules rather than actual boundary changes that are of interest. Regardless of the frequency with which special districts alter their

---

[6] For analysis of expenditure contracts, see Mullin (2009).

[7] Included in the analysis are independent special districts that report water supply as their primary function. The dependent variable measures only intergovernmental agreements related to water functions.

territorial reach, it is the obstacles they face in doing so that define the flexibility of their boundaries. State rules make it more or less difficult for special districts to absorb new territory.[8] If a relationship exists between boundary flexibility and intergovernmental cooperation, district officials will consider the relative ease of both strategies in deciding what mechanisms to employ. Rules grant or withhold voice for residents of the district and the new territory, and they set procedural requirements for hearings and county review of a boundary change proposal. Restrictive rules will make boundary change a less attractive option for district officials. If cooperation is a complementary strategy, restrictive rules also should suppress interlocal agreements. If the strategies are substitutes, agreements should replace boundary changes where rules are stringent.

The source for data on boundary change rules is state enabling legislation. Starting with a sample of 21 states that are most reliant on special districts for retail water provision, I compiled a list of all water district types in each state using information from the Individual State Descriptions volume of the 2002 Census of Governments (U.S. Census Bureau 2005). I then consulted state statutes enabling each special district type to code procedural rules for changing district boundaries subsequent to district establishment. The procedural rules parallel requirements for municipal annexation identified and coded by the Advisory Commission on Intergovernmental Relations (ACIR): majority approval of the boundary change by residents of the district, majority approval by residents and/or landowners of the territory to be added to the district, organization of a public hearing, and approval of a county governing authority (ACIR 1992).[9] These rules are combined into an index scored 1 to 4 measuring the stringency of rules for special district boundary change.[10] In addition, I measured whether a requirement exists for new territory to be

---

[8] Carr and Feiock (2001) report the surprising finding that more restrictive annexation rules actually increase the frequency of municipal annexation. In estimating the relationship between rules and actual annexations, this and other studies in effect are measuring the degree to which annexation opponents are able to exploit those rules. Carr and Feiock suggest that their result may be attributable to annexation supporters pursuing smaller proposals that encounter less resistance. Because special district boundary changes do not directly affect residents' perceptions of their political community, they are not as likely to spark controversy and attract opposition. Therefore I assume that a larger number of procedural hurdles serves as a disincentive for district officials to pursue boundary change.

[9] In some cases, referendum or majority approval is required only upon request. Because local actors must consider the possibility that someone will request the referendum, these cases are coded as requiring majority approval.

[10] Scale reliability as measured by Cronbach's alpha is .64.

contiguous with a special district's existing jurisdiction: the rule is scored
1 if there is a contiguity requirement, and 0 if not. After coding boundary
change rules, I assigned values to individual water districts. Some states
have common boundary change rules that apply to all special districts. In
other states, I scored each district's type using information contained in
district names and state and individual district Web sites. The analysis
omits districts formed under specific enabling legislation and districts
with boundaries that must be contiguous with a city or county. These
omissions removed four states from the sample, producing a dataset con-
taining 1,383 water districts in 17 states. The 17 states included in this
analysis contain two-thirds of the water supply special districts in the
United States. Summary statistics for this and other variables are provided
in the appendix.

Measuring boundary flexibility by the number of rules restricting
boundary change, a more flexible special district is one with a lower score
on the boundary rules index. If boundary flexibility is a substitute for
intergovernmental cooperation, then we should expect a positive relationship between boundary rules and incidence of a revenue-generating
interlocal agreement. A negative effect would suggest a complementary
relationship in which restrictions on boundary change reduce agreements
by suppressing opportunities for creative interlocal collaboration.

Other variables in the models control for fiscal, intergovernmental,
institutional, and problem severity conditions that also could affect the
likelihood of water districts engaging in interlocal cooperation. Missing
from the model are demographic characteristics of special districts that
might influence local preferences for cooperative agreements. Very few
states make available geographic data on special district boundaries that
would allow calculation of the size, wealth, or homogeneity of a district's
population. Consequently, the analysis focuses on economic factors, the
supply of potential cooperative partners, district governing structure, and
the local policy context. Except where noted otherwise, the data source is
the 2002 Census of Governments.

Fiscal Variables: Fiscal variables measure the capacity of a special district to fund its own water supply functions and offer production resources to its neighbors, as well as the tax burden on area residents. Larger
districts should have more opportunity to build and operate their own
water storage and treatment facilities, while small districts may be more
reliant on contracting with neighbors. *Current expenditures (log)* is an
indicator of district size; it measures logged general expenditures for current water operations. *Debt finance* is a dichotomous variable indicating

whether the water district reported to the Census of Governments that its operations include financing public facilities or services by issuing public debt. A positive response suggests that the district perceives the construction of capital facilities as one of its primary functions, suggesting that it may have extra capacity to share with neighboring jurisdictions. The model also includes a variable for *Property taxes per capita* imposed by the state and all local governments located within the district's home county. A heavy tax burden on the local population will make boundary change less attractive to special districts, and they may be more likely to cooperate rather than build and operate their own expensive facilities.

Intergovernmental Variables: Post (2002) finds that interlocal expenditures are more likely to occur where local governments have access to a larger number of potential partners. *County local governments* measures the number of local governments located within the special district's home county. *Multicounty* districts reach across county lines and therefore should be more likely to find opportunities for collaboration. Districts with *Common boundaries* have boundaries that correspond to a single city or county, possibly encouraging a long-term cooperative relationship between these governments with a shared jurisdiction. The degree to which a special district focuses on a single function also might influence its opportunities for collaboration. *Proportion spending on water* indicates the proportion of the district's current general expenditures that are dedicated to water. Finally, I included two variables to control for the use of other coordinating mechanisms in the face of interlocal policy challenges. *City annexation rules* is a four-point index measuring the stringency of procedural requirements for municipal annexation, compiled by the ACIR (ACIR 1992). As with special districts, municipal boundary change may be a complement or a substitute to intergovernmental cooperation. This variable captures the impact of city boundary flexibility. Local actors also might choose to address service gaps or policy inefficiencies by creating a new special district. *District formations* is the change in the number of special districts located in the county between 1992 and 2002, per 10,000 county residents.

Institutional Variable: Drawing on analyses demonstrating the importance of local government structure as a factor influencing interlocal cooperation (Morgan and Hirlinger 1991) and other local policies (Clingermayer and Feiock 2001), the model includes a variable measuring the proportion of the special district's governing board that is elected rather than appointed to office. Data for *Proportion elected* come from the 1992 Census of Governments, the last time the Census collected data on popularly elected officials. Elected boards should have a stronger incentive to seek out policy efficiencies in order to lower the tax and fee burden on district constituents. However, appointed boards could have a broader geographic scope and may even include representatives from other local governments that could be potential partners.

Problem Severity Variables: The final set of control variables addresses the seriousness of local water policy problems. Lubell et al. (2002) show that cooperation is more likely to emerge where objective conditions related to a public problem are more severe. For this analysis, communities are most likely to confront water supply challenges where the local climate is hot and dry and where population growth has strained existing infrastructure and supply sources. These conditions may give rise to the kind of collective action problems described earlier and the need for a coordinated policy response. Climate variables come from maps produced by the National Climatic Data Center (NCDC) showing annual data on mean total precipitation and mean daily maximum temperature, computed for the period 1961–1990. The NCDC integrates point measurements collected at thousands of weather stations nationwide with other spatial datasets to generate these climate maps. To assign values to the water districts, I plotted each district as point data in the center of the district's home county. Merging the point data with the climate maps produced values for the utilities on *Precipitation* and daily maximum *Temperature,* each variable scored as an index. *Population growth* indicates the percentage change in population of the water district's home county between 1990 and 2000.

The analysis uses a complementary log-log model to estimate the effects of these variables on the likelihood that a water district engages in interlocal cooperation. The functional form accounts for the rare occurrence of intergovernmental contracts: among the sampled water districts, just 6 percent participated in revenue contracts. The asymmetric complementary log-log link is appropriate for this type of binary distribution in which positive responses are rare.[11] The models cluster observations according to the state laws that set rules for boundary change. In some cases, the cluster is defined by the statute enabling the specific type of water district; in other cases, all of a state's water districts belong to the same cluster because a single law governs boundary change for all district types. The dataset includes 23 clusters of water districts in 17 states.

---

[11] Results are robust to use of other functional forms, including probit and the linear probability model.

RESULTS

Results from the analysis of revenue agreements appear in Table 7.1. The analysis reveals a positive and significant relationship between the stringency of boundary change rules and a special district's likelihood of receiving interlocal revenue. Figure 7.1 shows the form of that relationship. Increasing the number of procedural hurdles for district boundary change from one to four boosts the likelihood that a district will participate in a revenue-generating contract by 7.5 percentage points. This finding supports the hypothesis that boundary flexibility and intergovernmental cooperation are substitute strategies for addressing local coordination problems. When a water district has surplus supply or other resources, it could put those resources to use by expanding its own boundaries to enlarge its customer base, or it could establish a cooperative agreement that allows other local governments to take advantage of the district's excess capacity. Depending on the nature of the specific policy problem, either of these strategies might be the more efficient and durable policy solution. But the analysis suggests that the two are in fact alternative solutions – where boundary change is a more feasible strategy, the incidence of interlocal cooperation declines.

Requirements that additional territory be contiguous to a water district's existing jurisdiction have the opposite effect: they reduce the probability that a district will enter into a revenue agreement. Special districts that are able to expand into areas noncontiguous to their existing boundaries are 3.7 percentage points more likely to enter into revenue-generating water contracts. This result may signify diversity in the types of coordination challenges facing local governments. It is possible that special districts view annexation and contracting as substitutes in the typical case of service extension beyond district boundaries, but when faced with more complex and far-reaching collective action problems, creative boundary manipulation helps promote cooperative policy solutions.

Among control variables, fiscal measures of a district's capacity have an important influence on the likelihood that a district will contract out water supply or services. Districts with larger budgets and those reporting debt financing as a primary function are more likely to engage in interlocal cooperation. Contracting behavior does not seem to respond to existing demands on the local tax base. Just two of the variables that account for a district's intergovernmental context operate as predicted: boundaries that correspond to those of a city or county increase the likelihood of revenue contracting, and recent special district formations in the

TABLE 7.1. *Establishment of Interlocal Revenue Agreements on Water*

Boundary change rule index	.64 *** (.20)	
Contiguity requirement	-1.07 ** (.39)	
Fiscal Variables		
Current expenditures (log)	.28 *** (.07)	
Debt finance	.49 ** (.19)	
Property taxes per capita	.10 (.36)	
Problem Severity Variables		
Precipitation	.07 (.12)	
Temperature	-.05 (.06)	
Population growth	-1.09 (.82)	
Constant	-5.88 *** (1.08)	
Intergovernmental Variables:		
County local governments	-.00 (.00)	
Multicounty	.22 (.19)	
Common boundaries	.70 *** (.20)	
Proportion spending on water	.68 (.48)	
City annexation rules	-.22 (.15)	
District formations	-.27 ** (.09)	
Institutional Variable		
Proportion elected	-.54 (.35)	
N	1393	
Pseudo R²	.11	
Log pseudolikelihood	-291.06	

Coefficients are from complementary log-log estimation with observations clustered by special district types sharing the same boundary rules. Estimates are significant at * $p<.05$, ** $p<.01$, *** $p<.001$.

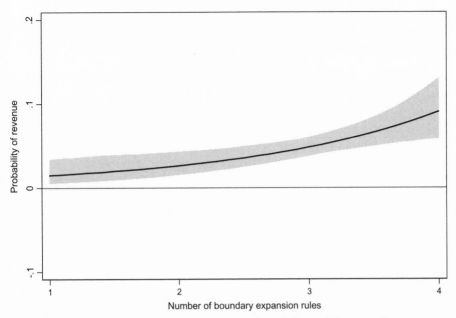

FIGURE 7.1. The Relationship between Boundary Rules and Revenue Contracts. (Gray band indicates 95% confidence interval.)

county have a large negative effect on cooperation. The latter result supports treating contracting, special district formation, and district boundary expansion as three substitute strategies for the provision of local services. Neither election of district officials nor the severity of water problems in the region appears to influence cooperative behavior.

Table 7.2 unpacks the boundary change index to show the effect of specific boundary rules.[12] Results indicate that it is the referendum requirement within a district's existing service area that is the biggest hurdle to boundary change and therefore the most important stimulus for adoption of interlocal agreements. With other boundary rules and control variables held constant, requiring majority approval within the district for a boundary change increases the likelihood of a revenue-generating interlocal agreement by 4.2 percentage points. None of the other requirements have a significant effect on revenue agreements when measured independently, including contiguity rules.

---

[12] The requirement for a public hearing is sufficiently widespread that its inclusion in a multivariate model perfectly predicts the absence of an interlocal agreement. Hearing requirements therefore have been dropped from the model reported in Table 7.2.

TABLE 7.2. *The Effect of Specific Boundary Change Rules on Interlocal Agreements*

Boundary Change Rules		*Intergovernmental Variables*	
Majority approval within district	.96 *(.41)	County local governments	–.00 (.00)
Majority approval in new area	.19 (.41)	Multicounty	.24 (.21)
Public hearing	–	Common boundaries	.69 ***(.20)
County approval	.73 (.61)	Proportion spending on water	.66 (.47)
Contiguity requirement	–1.16 (.75)	City annexation rules	–.21 (.16)
Fiscal Variables		District formations	–.28 **(.10)
Current expenditures (log)	.27 ***(.06)	*Institutional Variable*	
Debt finance	.51 **(.19)	Proportion elected	–.39 (.37)
Property taxes per capita	.16 (.36)	N	1393
Problem Severity Variables		Pseudo R²	.11
Precipitation	.04 (.12)	Log pseudolikelihood	–222.64
Temperature	–.10 (.08)		
Population growth	–.96 (.84)		
Constant	–4.91 ***(1.10)		

Coefficients are from complementary log-log estimation with observations clustered by special district types sharing the same boundary rules. Estimates are significant at * $p<.05$, ** $p<.01$, *** $p<.001$.

SUMMARY

The analysis presented here sheds light on the complex institutional environment within which local actors select strategies for addressing policy challenges that cross jurisdictional lines. Other chapters in this volume describe how problem characteristics and existing intergovernmental relationships affect the response of local authorities to an ICA problem. These factors influence the transaction and decision costs involved in creating and sustaining a mechanism to address the problem. But governments must decide not only whether to address an externalities problem; they also must decide how. My findings indicate that the choice of a self-organizing mechanism depends on its relative cost compared to alternative solutions, which in the study presented here is shaped by state laws.

A government with slack resources can boost regional efficiency in service delivery either by expanding its jurisdiction to secure a permanent market for its services or by establishing interlocal agreements that allow neighboring jurisdictions to make use of the surplus capacity. Interlocal agreements are a flexible policy tool that can help close service gaps and overcome a mismatch between the distribution of resources and resource demand. At the same time, the transaction costs for developing an agreement may be high, and the possibility of renegotiation or exit heightens uncertainty for participants and creates challenges for long-term planning. This chapter has explored whether the attractiveness of intergovernmental policy coordination is contingent on the ease with which local governments can act alone. The findings indicate that a relationship does exist between solo and joint policy strategies. Special districts that face few obstacles to changing their boundaries are less likely to engage in interlocal partnerships in order to solve regional problems.

Although boundary change and interlocal contracting appear to be substitute strategies for water districts with excess capacity, it is important to note that one district's boundary change might represent a cooperative outcome. Faced with a policy challenge related to water supply, localities in a region might agree that expanding the boundaries of an existing water district is the best mechanism for internalizing spillovers or achieving efficiency gains. Acting alone does not necessarily mean acting without consultation. The data analyzed here do not allow inferences about the process of policy choice in these scenarios of fragmented authority.

If water districts are acting unilaterally, however, they may be contributing to the development of further collective action problems down the road. Nationwide, water supply is becoming a more important consideration in planning and zoning for growth. Coordinated planning for water and land use is necessary to ensure adequate water supply for all essential uses while protecting the environment and economic productivity. Understanding boundary change as a substitute strategy to cooperative agreements has important implications for the possibility that coordinated planning will emerge. Flexible boundaries may create an incentive for water districts to preserve slack resources in order to expand into new territory. This could drive land use policy, as city and county planners increasingly respond to availability of water supply. The end result may be the creation of new spillover effects in other policy areas, if growth gets misplaced due to water districts' management of their surplus capacity. If boundary flexibility creates a disincentive for interlocal cooperation, states that seek to promote coordinated planning might consider locking in special district boundaries.

APPENDIX. SUMMARY STATISTICS

TABLE 7.A1. *Summary Statistics*

Variable	Mean	Std. Dev.	Min.	Max.
Dependent Variable				
Revenue agreements	.06	.24	0	1
Water District Boundary Rules				
Boundary change rule index	2.78	.84	1	4
Contiguity requirement	.47	.50	0	1
Fiscal Variables				
Current expenditures (log)	5.39	2.10	0	13.42
Debt finance	.26	.44	0	1
Property taxes per capita ($1,000)	.79	.44	0	5.09
Intergovernmental Variables				
County local governments	57.78	73.75	2	462
Multicounty	.23	.42	0	1
Common boundaries	.12	.33	0	1
Proportion spending on water	.91	.21	0	1
City annexation rules	1.64	1.01	0	3
District formations (per 10,000 people)	.34	1.36	−6.86	14.49
Institutional Variable				
Proportion elected	.74	.44	0	1
Problem Severity Variables				
Precipitation	4.98	1.77	1	9
Temperature	5.08	1.46	2	9
Population growth	.16	.18	−.23	1.85

8

The Political Market for Intergovernmental Cooperation

Kenneth N. Bickers, Stephanie Post, and
Robert M. Stein

The incidence of regional and metropolitan area intergovernmental relations is often explained in terms of efficiency gains for the participating jurisdictions (Stein 1990; Rusk 1993; Waste 1998; Katz 2000; Drier, Mollenkopf, and Swanstrom 2001). It is generally believed that local governments seeking to cut costs or provide a higher quality of services will look to other neighboring jurisdictions and private sector entities to partner with in the provision of goods and services. The economic rationale behind regional and intergovernmental cooperation is well understood. Not obvious are the political and professional motivations that influence decisions to cooperate and collaborate with neighboring jurisdictions.

We theorize that local officeholders view decisions to engage or not engage in intergovernmental cooperation as avenues for promoting their political careers. Two different theories that exist in the literature on intergovernmental cooperation lead to two distinctly different expectations about how intergovernmental cooperation affects electoral trajectories. In one view, local elected officials with ambition for higher office (especially higher political offices that represent a larger geography) may pursue intergovernmental relations as a way to promote themselves to a larger constituency. This view draws on the seminal work of Joseph Schlesinger on ambition theory. In a second view, intergovernmental cooperation reflects the goal of incumbents to protect themselves from electoral threats. In this view, a high incidence of intergovernmental cooperation leads to fewer, rather than more, challenges by quality challengers and is thus associated with fewer opportunities for incumbents at lower levels of government to realize their ambitions for higher office. We test these competing models with data from a sample of U.S. metropolitan area governments and the career trajectories of their elected mayors and council members for the period 2002–2006.

INTERGOVERNMENTAL COOPERATION AND ELECTORAL TRAJECTORIES

Schlesinger (1966) informs us that political ambition can take several forms: discrete, for those who seek office for one term; static, for those who seek office for long tenure; and progressive, for those who seek office as a means of obtaining higher and more attractive elective positions. Each type of ambition predicts a distinct type of political behavior for the incumbent officeholder; "a politician's behavior is a response to his office goals" (Schlesinger 1966, 6). Our focus of interest is on the progressively ambitious elected official. Schlesinger advances the hypothesis that progressively ambitious politicians will seek to advance the interests, prerogatives, and powers of the office(s) they seek to hold in the future (1966, 200).

Prewitt and Nowlin (1969) argue that a politician with progressive ambition "will anticipate holding that office by informing himself of its demands and adopting policy views consistent with the incumbency in it" (1969, 300). Moreover, the progressively ambitious politician will "respond to the constituency which controls access to that office" (1969, 300). The focus of progressive ambition is hierarchical; local politicians seek office at the county, state, and federal level. A hierarchical focus of political ambition produces a specific set of policy orientations for incumbent officeholders. Prewitt and Nowlin suggest that "those aspiring to higher office will have policy perspectives commonly associated with regional, state, or federal levels of government" (1969, 301). Prewitt and Nowlin test their hypothesis with survey data collected from San Francisco Bay area officeholders. They find support for their hypothesis: "the ambitious officeholder more than his unambitious colleague sees problems from a viewpoint we might associate with persons having regional, state, or federal responsibilities" (1969, 301).

What these findings mean for the policy performance of incumbent officeholders and their municipal governments to date has not been explicated. Prewitt and Nowlin and subsequent research continue to focus on the policy preferences and attitudes of ambitious incumbents, not their behavior in office. Yet a reasonable extension of this argument is that some policy actions of municipal governments can propel progressively ambitious local officeholders to seek higher office. Indeed, Schlesinger and Prewitt and Nowlin suggest that progressively ambitious politicians have a strong, positive effect on regional and intergovernmental relations. This attitudinal disposition is thought to be the product of an individual's ambitions for higher office. We extend this argument further and suggest that if this line of argument is correct, there may be strong incentives for progressively ambitious politicians to engage in and support regional and intergovernmental relations. If true, incumbents in cities and jurisdictions that engage in extensive regional and intergovernmental relations should be more likely, ceterius paribus, to seek higher elective office. On this view, intergovernmental agreements allow incumbents to claim credit for services provided to individuals beyond their current constituencies. While it is unlikely that an elected official can single-handedly shape the nature and content of his or her jurisdiction's intergovernmental relations with neighboring jurisdictions, it is nevertheless possible that the presence of a network of extensive intergovernmental relations provides progressively ambitious incumbents a significant opportunity to advance their electoral careers.

An alternative view can be extrapolated from a recent paper by Bickers and Stein (2004). Bickers and Stein report that proximity among local metropolitan area jurisdictions leads to greater intergovernmental cooperation "that stimulates new grant awards that otherwise might not be sought or received by metropolitan area governments" (2004, 818–819). They find that a significantly lower incidence of incumbent members of Congress face quality challengers where intergovernmental aid transfers are most numerous, in particular in geographic areas where local governments are dense and closely proximate. Intergovernmental networks increase the opportunities for credit claiming, but these opportunities are also accompanied by sets of interpersonal relationships among officeholders and attentive publics within the metropolitan area. The thesis is that these relationships tend to dampen the enthusiasm among attentive publics to support or underwrite challenges against incumbents for fear that such challenges might upset a functioning intergovernmental aid system. Ties forged from extensive interactions around issues of governance create strong incentives for cooperation among elected officials rather than electoral challenges.

In sum, this view leads to the expectation that proximity among jurisdictions and the sharing of common borders increases the likelihood of greater interaction and intergovernmental cooperation, which in turn should produce fewer, rather than more, challenges of incumbents by other local officeholders. Challenges against incumbents jeopardize relationships with important political groups including political parties, interest groups, and stakeholders who have an interest in the challenged incumbent. Hence, the likelihood of electoral success is greater when running for an open seat rather than against an incumbent, so the progressively ambitious local officeholder would wait for an open seat rather than challenge a sitting incumbent in areas with highly developed cooperative relationships.

THE NATURE AND CONTENT OF LOCAL INTERGOVERNMENTAL COOPERATION

Local intergovernmental cooperation, broadly defined, includes all policy activities that require some level of policy coordination between local governments. These efforts may include formal or informal agreements among local jurisdictions and may (or may not) require the exchange of revenue. Formal intergovernmental cooperation often includes written agreements among local governments. In some cases, these agreements are codified by one or all of the participating local governments. Formal intergovernmental agreements may dictate a division of labor among local governments which may (or may not) require the transfer of funds between those governments. For example, a city and county may formally agree that the city will provide bus service to both city and county residents, and in return the county will maintain the roads in both areas. Alternatively, the county may simply contract with the city to provide bus service to its residents. This service arrangement would likely require a fee-for-service contract between the two governments, because the county is not providing a service benefit to the city in exchange for the bus service.

Not all local intergovernmental cooperation is formal. Informal intergovernmental cooperation is defined as unwritten agreements among city officials. These intergovernmental agreements are often the result of "handshake" deals among local officials, where the division of service responsibility is understood but never formalized. For example, a city may maintain the county parks within its jurisdiction, based on a mutual understanding between the directors of the city and county parks and recreation departments. Informal agreements often have the effect of functionally coordinating service activities without a written agreement or the exchange of revenue.

The existence of personal as well as professional relationships among local officials increases the likelihood that local governments will enter into informal intergovernmental agreements (Thurmaier and Wood 2002). These types of agreements are most likely to occur when local government officials have worked repeatedly with each other for a number of years or when local government officials know each other through professional and educational networks such as professional associations or graduate/professional school (Bingham, LeBlanc, and Frendries 1981).

Repeat interactions and previous relationships among local officials can generate significant reservoirs of trust and performance expectations that can facilitate local government cooperation (Feiock 2007).

There are several ways in which intergovernmental relations promote the electoral careers of progressively ambition politicians. The product of intergovernmental cooperation includes a set of policy outputs for which elected officials can claim credit, thus advantaging themselves for reelection (Mayhew 1970). Moreover, the subjects of these credit-claiming opportunities are not limited to the constituents of elected officials; they also include the ambitious politician's future constituents, that is, individuals residing in the constituency she might seek to represent. Effective intergovernmental relations provide locally elected officials with a wealth of goodwill with current and potential constituents.

Another important political benefit from intergovernmental relations for the ambitious incumbent is the relationships forged with "gatekeepers who partially control access to the higher office" (Prewitt and Nowlin 1969, 304). The formal and informal nature of intergovernmental relations produces many interpersonal contacts among elected officials at different levels of government. These relationships enable incumbents to advance their electoral ambitions through the current occupants of the office they seek. Intergovernmental relations may also provide the ambitious politician access to the friends and supporters of incumbents whose office is coveted.

Our agnosticism about the direction of the relationship between intergovernmental relations and the decision of incumbents to run for higher office reflects the difference between the opportunity for progressive ambition and the status quo orientation of stakeholders in the intergovernmental aid system. We hypothesize that

H_1 To the extent that progressive ambition is the causal driver, greater intergovernmental cooperation among metropolitan areas will be positively related to the likelihood that incumbents will seek higher offices in a metropolitan area.

H_2 To the extent that the benefits of intergovernmental exchanges lead to extensive interrelationships and hence a status quo orientation among the stakeholders in the intergovernmental aid system, high levels of such exchanges within metropolitan areas will be negatively related to the likelihood that incumbents will seek higher offices in a metropolitan area.

CONTROL VARIABLES AND RIVAL EXPLANATIONS

Cooperation among locally elected officials arises, in part, from the proximity and shared boundaries among metropolitan area governments.

Bickers and Stein (2004) and Post (2002) report a positive and statistically significant relationship between incidence of intergovernmental service agreements and the proximity and shared boundaries of governments within metropolitan areas. It is possible that proximity has an independent effect on the likelihood an incumbent will challenge another incumbent officeholder in the same metropolitan area, independent of the incidence of intergovernmental services agreements.

H_3 The geographic relationship among metropolitan area governments is positively/ negatively related to the likelihood an incumbent will challenge another incumbent in the same metropolitan area.

Term limits removes one path of political ambition. With term limits, a politician cannot hold the same elective office indefinitely. Term limits for local elective office create an inflated supply of potential challengers for all elective offices. If a person is politically ambitious, term limits force that politician to run for a new office every few years. Aggregated across the population of elective offices, term limits increase the supply of quality challengers. Each of these persons has the experience of elective office, which is an important attribute of a quality challenger. The inflated supply of quality challengers is likely to produce a rippling effect across other elective offices. Term limited incumbents might look horizontally at other local offices or look vertically at statewide or federal offices. Consequently, term limits significantly increase the supply of and demand for candidates. We expect that the presence of term limits with a large population of locally elected officeholders is a strong incentive for progressively ambitious officeholders to seek higher elective office.

H_4 The presence of term limits increases the likelihood an incumbent will challenge another incumbent in the same metropolitan area.

Other controls for population size, form of government (council/manager and mayor/council) and office (mayor versus council) are included in our analysis.

RESEARCH DESIGN AND OPERATIONAL MEASURES

To test our explanation of progressive ambition and intergovernmental relations we have constructed a metropolitan level database for a sample of 108 cities in eight Metropolitan Statistical Areas (MSA). Data on the incidence of intergovernmental agreements were collected from a mail survey conducted in 2000. All cities over 25,000 in population and a one in eight sample of cities less than 25,000 in population in eight metropolitan areas were surveyed. The metropolitan areas include San Francisco, Buffalo, Nashville, Phoenix, Dallas, San Antonio, Baltimore, and Houston. The survey replicates the International City Management Association's survey of municipal service responsibility (1999). City Managers in each city were asked to identify from a list of 71 local government services those their city provided. The general service categories of the survey included works and transportation, public utilities, public safety, health and human services, parks and recreation, and administration and services. The appendix to this chapter provides a list of all service categories included in the survey. For each service provided, the city respondent was asked "are any of these services produced by or in conjunction with another local government?" Respondents were asked the governmental unit with which they shared functional responsibility (i.e., city, county, township, or special district) and the geographic relationship between the two jurisdictions (i.e., share a border or overlapping jurisdiction).

Several measures were constructed from the survey:

- The number and proportion of the 71 possible services provided by a city.
- The number and proportion of services provided with another jurisdiction.
- The number and proportion of service partners that share a common jurisdictional border.
- The number and proportion of service partners whose jurisdictions geographically overlap (e.g., county/city, special district/city).

The election data contain electoral information for city council members and mayors from 2002 through the first half of 2006. For each selected city we have constructed the political career path of the city's mayor and council members. The dependent measure is the percentage of mayors and council members who have run for higher office between the years 2002 and 2006. We have full information for 102 of the 108 cities, leading to a loss of six communities in the analysis below.

Our main independent variables are the number and proportion of functions provided with another local jurisdiction, the number and proportion of service partners that share a common border, and the number and proportion of service partners with overlapping jurisdictions. Our measure of intergovernmental service agreements focuses on formal as well as informal relationships between governments. We assume that the foundation of these formal agreements includes a myriad of informal and personal relationships between elected officials at different units and levels of government.

TABLE 8.1. *Proportion of Elected Officials Running for Higher Office*

	Coefficient	t-ratio	Coefficient	t-ratio
Constant	0.645	2.26	0.594	1.94
Number of IGAs across shared borders	−0.010	−0.93		
Number of IGAs with overlapping governments	0.003	0.31		
Percent of IGAs across shared borders			−0.142	−1.02
Percent of IGAs with overlapping governments			−0.055	0.43
City Population (logged)	−0.020	−0.52	−0.021	−0.49
Term Limits (1 = yes, 0 = no)	0.056	0.49	0.060	0.49
Percent by Office (0 = council, 1 = mayor)	−0.409	−4.69	−0.351	−3.83
Percent of Functional Activities	0.070	0.20	0.097	0.25
Observations	102		93	
F-ratio	3.98		2.79	
Prob > F	0.0013		0.0160	
R-squared	0.20		0.16	
Adj R-squared	0.15		0.10	
Root MSE	0.43		0.43	

FINDINGS

The first set of regressions focuses on the impact of intergovernmental cooperation on decisions of local office holders to seek higher offices. The dependent variable is the proportion of a municipality's local office holders that sought higher office at some point during the period from 2002 through mid-2006. Two separate regressions are reported in Table 8.1. The two regressions differ in how intergovernmental cooperation is measured. The first regression measures the number of intergovernmental agreements (both formal and informal) between jurisdictions with shared borders and the number of such agreements between jurisdictions that are overlapping. The second regression measures agreements between jurisdictions with shared borders and jurisdictions that are overlapping as a percentage of the total number of functional activities in which each community is engaged. For both sets of regressions, the other independent variables are the same. Specifically, both sets of regressions include measures for city population (logged), the presence or absence of term limits at the local level, the proportion of local offices held by council members versus mayors, and the scope of the jurisdiction's functional activities.

As Table 8.1 shows, the volume of intergovernmental agreements between jurisdictions that share borders, measured in terms of both the number and the percentage of such agreements, is *negatively* related (albeit with *t*-ratios too small to suggest statistical significance) to the incidence of running for higher offices. The signs on the number and percentage of agreements with overlapping jurisdictions point in opposite directions; and, again, the *t*-ratios indicate a lack of statistical significance. Substantively, the negative sign on this relationship suggests a modicum of support for the hypothesis that intergovernmental aid networks – at least the horizontal networks that emerge among jurisdictions sharing borders – lead to a status quo orientation among incumbents. That is, this finding suggests that the greater the density of agreements with neighboring jurisdictions, the less likely it is that incumbents from that jurisdiction will make bids for offices with larger geographic coverage. Were the progressive ambition hypothesis to be supported, we would have seen evidence exactly to the contrary. We would have seen evidence that as the density of intergovernmental agreements increases, the incidence of running for higher office would also increase.

Interestingly, the variable measuring the scope of functional activities (the proportion of all 71 measured services that are delivered by a given city) is also not significant at conventional levels of significance. But its sign is positive, suggesting that were this relationship to emerge as statistically significant in a larger sample, the incidence of running for higher office would tend to be greater in communities that provide more goods and services, even when controlling for community size. In other words, it suggests that communities that do more things may attract people to elective office who are more progressively ambitious. This is speculative, and, we should add, appears to be offset by the possible appearance of suppressive effects of intergovernmental agreements on progressive ambitions.

Of the other variables in these regressions, two merit special note. One is that there is a highly significant difference in the incidence of council members and mayors making bids for higher office. Given the coding of this variable, the negative sign indicates that council members are far more likely than mayors to run for higher offices. Mayors are significantly less likely to give up their offices to make such bids. Perhaps this is because mayors already hold a position that, at least in local politics, is often viewed as the ultimate political office, whereas a council seat may be viewed as a stepping stone to some other office. It could also reflect the relative paucity of executive-type offices at higher levels to which mayors might plausibly aspire. For people who enjoy the challenges and demands of legislative offices, such as a city council seat, there are many opportunities to seek other offices that are also legislative in orientation, from school boards and county councils, to the state assembly and senate, to ultimately the U.S. Congress. Another possibility is that mayors are more likely to be experienced politicians than are council members and thus more likely to bide their time until an open seat or some other opportunity for elective office comes along that offers a high probability of success. We'll comment more on this possibility below.

What is clear in these data is that the pattern of running for higher office, for mayors and council members alike, is not a function of term limits. The term limits variable is not significantly different from zero. Term limits, at least among local elected officials, neither encourage nor inhibit the likelihood of running for higher office. This is interesting, given how frequently term limits have been touted as a way of encouraging more people to run for office.

The second set of regressions shifts the focus from running for higher offices to successfully winning in bids for higher offices. Table 8.2 contains the same sets of independent variables as in Table 8.1. Here, however, the dependent variable is the proportion of elected officials running for higher office in each community over the 2002–2006 period who actually won. Focusing only on communities in which at least one local incumbent made a bid for higher office narrows the effective sample size for the analysis by quite a lot. The number of observations drops to 32 for the analysis where the measure of intergovernmental agreements is the number of such agreements and to 27 where the measure is the percentage of such agreements (this is because the calculation of percentages involves four communities where the denominator is zero). While the statistical power and possibly the generalizability of these findings are diminished, the results are nonetheless suggestive.

The impact of intergovernmental agreements on electoral trajectories is both clearer and in the opposite direction from what we saw in Table 8.1. The number and percentage of intergovernmental agreements with jurisdictions that share borders continue to carry negative signs, but are not significant. But the number and percentage of intergovernmental agreements with overlapping jurisdictions is significant (t-ratios in excess of 2.0) and positive. This indicates that as the density of intergovernmental agreements with overlapping jurisdictions increases, the incidence of *successful* bids for higher office increases significantly. What does this mean? How is it possible for intergovernmental agreements to help incumbents

TABLE 8.2. *Proportion of Elected Officials Successfully Seeking Higher Office*

	Coefficient	*t*-ratio	Coefficient	*t*-ratio
Constant	1.86	2.36	1.81	2.00
Number of IGAs across shared borders	−0.14	−0.48		
Number of IGAs with overlapping governments	0.47	2.10		
Percentage of IGAs across shared borders			−0.20	−0.50
Percentage of IGAs with overlapping governments			0.72	2.02
City Population (logged)	−0.13	−1.23	−0.07	−0.56
Term Limits (1 = yes, 0 = no)	−0.23	−0.67	−0.29	−0.74
Percentage by Office (0 = council, 1 = mayor)	0.24	0.59	0.30	0.70
Percentage of Functional Activities	0.38	0.41	−0.81	−0.66
Observations	32		27	
F-ratio	1.48		1.52	
Prob > F	0.22		0.22	
R-squared	0.26		0.31	
Adj R-squared	0.08		0.11	
Root MSE	0.66		0.69	

Note: Intergovernmental Agreements are abbreviated as IGAs.

win higher offices but simultaneously suppress the likelihood of running for those offices? Our hunch is that intergovernmental agreements tend to keep incumbents in place (that is, preserve the status quo), but when incumbents jump into higher probability races, such as races for open seats, these agreements help the incumbents make the case for their election.

A piece of evidence in support of this hypothesis is that the difference between council members and mayors largely disappears in this set of regressions. Whereas council members were much more likely than mayors to jump into races for higher office, there is statistically no difference in the likelihood that council members or mayors will actually win. That is, council members and mayors equally benefit from higher densities of intergovernmental agreements with overlapping jurisdictions. Also supportive of this hypothesis is that, as before, term limits are irrelevant in these outcomes. Successful bids for higher office appear to occur without regard to whether the incumbents who enter the race are theoretically term limited, presumably because they are acting strategically rather than simply waiting to run for higher office when they are no longer eligible to run for reelection.

The size of communities does not seem to have an impact on the likelihood of successful bids for higher office, although the coefficient is negative. This suggests that there may be some slightly greater incidence of successful bids in small cities. This raises an interesting conjecture. One might hypothesize that incumbents who serve larger cities would have greater experience and perhaps greater name recognition. But the data suggest this is not the case. Perhaps incumbents in smaller communities enjoy different kinds of advantages, relative to those enjoyed by incumbents in larger communities – for instance, by not having to compete for recognition and attention with as many other politicians.

Once again, the finding from Table 8.1 that cities with greater functional scope do not produce politicians that are more ambitious continues to find support in these regressions. It appears that politicians who are strategic are able to find ways of launching their electoral careers in communities that deliver relatively modest numbers of goods and services as well as in communities that deliver a wide range of goods and services.

SUMMARY

In this chapter, we contrast two different theories about how intergovernmental cooperation alters the electoral trajectories of upwardly ambitious policy makers. In one view, local elected officials with ambition for higher office may utilize intergovernmental relations to promote themselves to a larger constituency. In this view, intergovernmental agreements allow incumbents to claim credit for services that are aimed at potential voters beyond their current constituencies. The expectation is that incumbents in cities and jurisdictions that engage in extensive regional and intergovernmental relations should be more likely, ceterius paribus, to seek higher elective office. In a second view, intergovernmental cooperation reflects the goals of incumbents to protect themselves from electoral threats. The thesis is that intergovernmental cooperation dampens the enthusiasm of attentive publics to support challenges against incumbents for fear that such challenges might upset functioning intergovernmental aid systems. We test these competing expectations with data from a sample of U.S. metropolitan area governments and the career trajectories of their elected mayors and council members for the period 2002–2006.

Our findings support elements of both hypotheses linking intergovernmental aid agreements to electoral trajectories. Intergovernmental agreements, specifically those between communities that share borders, appear to inhibit the likelihood of progressively ambitious locally elected officials from jumping into races for higher offices, although we did not find a significant effect in our relatively small sample. At the same time, intergovernmental agreements, specifically those between communities with overlapping jurisdictions, are significantly associated with a substantially higher incidence of success among local politicians who do enter races for higher office. It appears that intergovernmental agreements make it easier for ambitious politicians to win higher offices, while reducing the likelihood that they will act on those ambitions.

Our argument for these apparently contradictory findings is that in communities where such agreements are numerous, progressively ambitious politicians often are thwarted in their efforts to build support for campaigns for higher office among other incumbents and among attentive publics. But when the time is ripe, as in cases when seats become open or an incumbent in a higher office is perceived to be weak, ambitious politicians are able to utilize the patterns of intergovernmental agreements that have evolved over time in their communities to successfully persuade other incumbents, attentive publics, and electorates more generally to provide support for campaigns for those higher offices. That is, at strategic moments for politicians who are progressively ambitious, intergovernmental agreements are useful in helping build coalitions for higher office.

These findings are based on a relatively small sample. How well these findings will fare when tested in other communities and for other periods of time remains an open question. More interesting, however, is the question of causal direction. In this chapter, we have focused on how intergovernmental agreements might suppress or stimulate bids for higher office. In a sense, we have taken the pattern of intergovernmental agreements as given, at least in the short run. We have not addressed directly the question of how incumbents might seek to create, modify, or eliminate such agreements to enhance the odds of successfully running for future seats. One possibility that emerges from this chapter is that incumbents, while holding one office, might strategically work to devise intergovernmental agreements that are really designed to appeal to a potential future set of attentive publics and voters. How this might play out is an interesting question. Intergovernmental agreements, by definition, are the products of collective action among incumbents in more than one jurisdiction. Why and when one incumbent might be willing to work together with other incumbents on intergovernmental agreements that might advantage the other incumbents in bids for higher office is, for now, an open question.

APPENDIX. SERVICE DELIVERY AREAS

Public Works and Transportation

Residential solid waste collection
Commercial solid waste collection
Solid waste disposal
Street repair
Street/parking lot cleaning
Snow plowing/sanding
Traffic sign/signal installation
Traffic sign/signal maintenance
Parking meter maintenance
Parking meter collection
Tree trimming/planting on public rights-of-way
Administration of cemeteries
Maintenance of cemeteries
Inspection/code enforcement
Operation of parking lots/garages
Operation of bus transit system
Maintenance of bus transit system
Operation of paratransit system
Maintenance of paratransit system
Operation of airports
Water distribution
Water treatment
Sewage collection
Sewage treatment
Disposal of sludge
Disposal of hazardous materials

Public Utilities

Utility operation: electricity
Utility management: electricity
Utility operation: gas
Utility management: gas
Utility meter reading
Utility billing

Public Safety

Crime prevention/ patrol
Police communications
Fire communications
Fire prevention/ suppression
Emergency medical services
Ambulance service
Traffic control/ parking enforcement
Vehicle towing and storage
Vehicle maintenance: emergency vehicles

Health and Human Services

Sanitary inspection
Insect/rodent control
Animal control
Operation of animal
  shelters
Operation of day care
  facilities
Child welfare programs
Programs for the elderly
Operation of hospitals
Management of
  hospitals
Public health programs
Drug and alcohol
  treatment programs
Operation of mental
  health/mental
  retardation programs
  and facilities
Prisons/jails

Parks and Recreation

Operation of
  recreational facilities
Park maintenance
Building and ground
  maintenance
Vehicle maintenance:
  heavy
  equipment
Vehicle maintenance:
  other
Operation of
  convention
  centers/auditoriums
Operation of cultural
  arts programs
Operation of libraries
Operation of museums

Administrative Services

Payroll
Tax bill processing
Tax assessing
Data processing
Collection of
  delinquent taxes
Title reproduction/
  map maintenance
Legal services
Personnel services

PART THREE

INTEGRATING REGIONAL POLICIES THROUGH NETWORKS, JOINT VENTURES, AND PARTNERSHIPS

9

Collaborative Institutions, Functional Areas, and Beliefs

What Are Their Roles in Policy Networks?

Christopher M. Weible

Policy arenas with multiple and interdependent functional purposes are common. Such fragmented policy arenas create institutional collective action (ICA) problems where activities in one functional area interfere with activities in another. This chapter explores the structure of fragmentation and the roles of two mechanisms for mitigating institutional collective action dilemmas: informal policy networks and collaborative institutions.

One of the best case studies for examining fragmentation is San Francisco Bay-Delta water policy, which combines several functional purposes including mitigating flood risks, obtaining water quality standards, protecting endangered species, and supplying water to farmers and urban areas. The San Francisco Bay-Delta water policy arena also involves a large number of actors from local, state, and federal governments and from private and nonprofit organizations. These actors vary in their level of agreement about the seriousness of water-related problems and support for policy alternatives (Munro 1993; Zafonte and Sabatier 1998; Hundley 2001; Heikkila and Gerlak 2005). This chapter examines the structure of the informal networks of allies and opponents in this fragmented and contentious arena, as well as the role of CALFED, a large collaborative institution.

INSTITUTIONAL COLLECTIVE ACTION HYPOTHESES

Analytical frameworks emphasize the important elements to study in a system, enabling the creation of theories and the derivation of hypotheses. A case in point is the ICA framework in *Feiock and Scholz* Chapter 1, which lays out broad guidelines for studying self-organizing governance.

It also offers a theory of political fragmentation, in which the delegation of authority and the need for specialization leads to the partitioning of functional policy areas.

In any functional policy area, decisions are usually suboptimal because externalities arise from other functional policy areas. Cooperative solutions across functional areas is impeded by steep transaction costs that originate from the existing policy fragmentation and from belief heterogeneity among policy participants, and that increase the time and effort required to negotiate, reach, and enforce agreements (Coase 1960; Dahlman 1979). Transaction costs can be mitigated in a number of ways, including informal policy networks and collaborative institutions.

Informal policy networks represent different types of associations or relations. This chapter examines two forms of policy networks: allies and opponents. Ally networks can be defined as actors connected by similar policy orientations, such as beliefs and values (Salisbury et al. 1987; Sabatier and Jenkins-Smith 1993; Zafonte and Sabatier 1998). Ally networks represent the informal associations among actors that enable the exchanging, pooling, and sharing of resources. Ally networks also operate as a hub for reducing transaction costs and coordinating activities to achieve shared goals that simply cannot be done alone (Weible and Sabatier 2005).

The second type of policy network involves shared opponents. Opponents have been studied as a source of political mobilization (Truman 1951). This chapter takes a slightly different angle by focusing on the shared perceptions of opponents as a type of association. As the antithesis of ally networks, opponent networks can be defined as actors who are connected by a common threat, giving them a rationale for overcoming the transaction costs of coordinating their behavior.

This chapter explains the structure of ally and opponent networks in terms of functional area involvement and beliefs. Functional areas can be defined as the purposes or objectives of a policy arena (Chisholm 1989; Zafonte and Sabatier 1998; Fenger and Klok 2001). Most substantive policies and programs splinter into multiple functional areas. Just as most statutes and government agencies have multiple objectives that are often ambiguous and contradictory, policy arenas operate with multiple functional areas that often conflict in means and ends (Moe 1991; Scholz and Stiftel 2005). The transaction costs of interacting across functional areas depend on the types of relations between the functional areas. Following Fenger and Klok (2001), the relations between functional areas can be classified as independent, symbiotic, or competitive.

Independent functional areas are ones that neither overlap nor interfere with each other. Independent functional areas provide no benefits for coordination, making collective action unnecessary. Examples of independent functional areas in water policy might include supplying water to irrigate crops and dredging a water course to maintain navigation.

Symbiotic functional areas are often defined as positive-sum games in which coordination among actors leads to mutually beneficial outcomes. Symbiotic functional areas involve relatively low transaction costs of negotiation because of the mutual gains from coordination and sharing resources. An example of symbiotic functional areas would be maintenance of water quality standards and protection of fish populations, since both are strongly interrelated.

Competitive functional areas can encompass the kinds of conflict described by *Jones,* and are often defined as zero-sum games in which action in one functional area interferes with, or imposes costs on, action in another functional area. Thus, competitive functional areas usually include political struggles over the governance of the same resource or over interrelated resources. Competitive functional areas create steep transaction costs among competing actors, especially in negotiating and reaching agreements. An example of competitive functional areas would be farmers wanting to use water to irrigate crops and environmental advocates wanting to use the same water to maintain adequate stream flow for fish species (Zafonte and Sabatier 1998). This chapter tests the following hypothesis about functional area involvement (either symbiotic or competitive) and networks of allies and opponents.

Functional Area Hypothesis: Policy participants involved in symbiotic functional areas will have similar networks of allies and opponents.

One factor that increases the transaction costs faced by actors in an ICA dilemma is belief heterogeneity among participants. Those with divergent beliefs usually require more time and effort to negotiate, coordinate, and enforce agreements (Lubell 2000). Informal policy networks are expected to involve low-cost exchanges and, thus, connect actors with similar beliefs rather than divergent beliefs. A number of scholars have posited that actors use beliefs to guide behavior and form networks and coalitions (Putnam 1976; Hurwitz and Peffley 1987; Sabatier and Jenkins-Smith 1993). The hypothesis tested in this chapter is that ally and opponent networks will be structured around the shared beliefs of policy participants.

Belief Congruence Hypothesis: Policy participants with similar beliefs will have similar networks of allies and opponents.

Institutional collective action problems are overcome by the formation of collaborative institutions based on principles of open and inclusive participation, consensus-based decision rules, fair rules of negotiation, and joint fact finding (Sabatier et al. 2005; Scholz and Stiftel 2005). Collaborative institutions are designed to bridge interdependent functional areas and to reduce transaction costs of collective action by facilitating coordination and mitigating conflict (Lubell, 2000). They can be thought of as *institutional brokers* among disagreeing organizational affiliations operating in a policy arena. The extent that a collaborative institution shows the following four characteristics (or proxy measures) of a broker is investigated here. First, collaborative institutions will be involved in multiple functional areas to help bridge organizational affiliations that only engage in one or two functional areas. Second, representatives from collaborative institutions will hold inclusive and moderate beliefs to help connect organizational affiliations holding more alienating and extreme beliefs. Third, collaborative institutions will have diverse allies to help bridge otherwise disconnected actors in the arena. Fourth, collaborative institutions will have a relatively low number of opponents. By collapsing these four broker characteristics into a set of dimensions of an institutional broker, the following hypothesis can be tested.

Institutional Broker Hypothesis: Collaborative institutions are more likely to show characteristics of an institutional broker than other organizational affiliations in the policy arena.

AREA OF STUDY

The San Francisco Bay-Delta connects California's Sacramento and San Joaquin rivers to the Pacific Ocean, creating the largest estuary on the Pacific Coast and one of the most important estuaries in the world (BCDC 2007). The Bay-Delta forms the heart of California's water supply system, pumping water to 20 million people and supporting California's agricultural industry (Jacobs et al. 2003).

Water policy in the San Francisco Bay-Delta has a contentious history (Munro 1993; Zafonte and Sabatier 1998; Hundley 2001). In the 1960s, development in San Francisco Bay wetlands was a major issue. It was resolved by the end of the decade with the creation of the Bay

Conservation and Development Commission. This entity was charged with planning and regulating shoreline development and wetlands.

From the late 1960s to the 1970s, policy participants were concerned about pollution from surface runoff and from municipal and industrial dischargers (Sabatier and Zafonte 2007). As a result, the State Water Resources Control Board tried to establish water quality standards from the late 1970s to the 1990s, but it was challenged by a federal appellate decision in 1985, by outraged stakeholders, and by the U.S. Environmental Protection Agency (Zafonte and Sabatier 1998; Hundley 2001).

From the 1980s to the 1990s, stakeholder conflict intensified and shifted to declining fish populations. In the early 1990s, winter-run salmon and the Delta smelt were listed as threatened species under the federal Endangered Species Act. To help remedy fish declines in the context of a severe drought, the U.S. Congress passed the 1992 Central Valley Project Improvement Act. The legislation reserved large quantities of water for the environment and encouraged water marketing with southern California water suppliers (Sabatier and Zafonte 2007). The State Water Resources Control Board responded to the Central Valley Project Improvement Act with limits on water exports, which panicked water users (Jacobs et al. 2003). In 1993, a federal district court ordered the U.S. Environmental Protection Agency to issue water quality standards or be found in violation of the Clean Water Act (Sabatier and Zafonte 2007).

A political stalemate ensued among Bay-Delta water policy players. In 1994, the major policy participants negotiated and reached consensus with the Bay-Delta Accord. It set new water quality standards to protect fisheries while minimizing costs to water users. Part of the solution was CALFED, a collaborative institution designed to coordinate activities among a large number of federal and state government agencies and interest groups.

Conflict did not end with the Bay-Delta Accord, however. Political struggles, especially between northern and southern California interests, continued over CALFED's proposed restoration plans in 1996 (Hundley 2001). The plans offered various options, including creating a peripheral canal, modifying current canals, protecting ecosystems, and strengthening levees. In 1998, CALFED chose a mix of options, excluding the proposed canal. The questionnaire used in this analysis was administered in 1997 after CALFED proposed their restoration plan but before they made their final planning decision.

Zafonte and Sabatier (1998) identified four functional areas in San Francisco Bay-Delta water policy.

1. The *fish functional area* centered on the federal and state fish and wildlife agencies (e.g., the U.S. Fish and Wildlife Service and the California Department of Fish and Game). These agencies were involved in implementing the Endangered Species Act in relation to salmon and Delta smelt. Environmental groups were particularly active in the late 1980s and 1990s in supporting the protection of fish populations and habitats.

2. The *water supply functional area* included two major government agencies: the U.S. Bureau of Reclamation, which operated the central valley water supply project, and the California Department of Water Resources, which operated the state water supply project. Major water suppliers and users included Bay area water suppliers, southern California water suppliers, and local agricultural interests.

3. The *water pollution functional area* involved the U.S. Environmental Protection Agency and state and regional water quality control boards, which were active in setting and regulating water quality standards. Municipal and industrial dischargers were also active in the water pollution functional area.

4. The *shoreline development functional area* included the Bay Conservation and Development Commission, which regulated the development of the shoreline and the protection of wetlands. Private organizations included seaports, the San Francisco airport, and businesses.

METHODS OF DATA COLLECTION AND OPERATIONAL MEASURES

This chapter uses data from a 1997 questionnaire of Bay-Delta policy participants who either directly or indirectly attempted to influence Bay-Delta water policy. The list of policy participants came from actors who testified at Bay-Delta public hearings as well as from staff and leaders of various organizations involved in Bay-Delta water issues. The questionnaire was administered in 1997 by Paul Sabatier and his research group at the University of California, Davis. The 1997 questionnaire was mailed to 1,527 policy participants of whom 671 responded (44% response rate). The appendix provides full operational definitions of all variables used in the analyses.

Ally and opponent networks were measured by asking respondents to name their top three allies and top three opponents out of a list of 23 organizational affiliations. Since the ICA framework focused on the struggles among actors in coordinating across functional areas, it was important to establish the extent that allies coordinate their activities. For each of their three cited allies, respondents were asked if they never, occasionally, or frequently (1) shared information, (2) modified behavior because of expected future reciprocity, (3) modified behavior because of shared goals, and (4) developed joint strategies. The percentage of respondents who occasionally or frequently engaged in each of the four types of activities were, respectively, 94 percent, 50 percent, 75 percent, and 67 percent. These responses provided evidence that the allies, later identified in this analysis, can be linked to different types of coordination. Unfortunately, there was no similar measure of coordination among actors who shared opponents.

Functional area involvement was measured by asking respondents to indicate their involvement in six functional areas, including water pollution, water supply, fish, wetlands, flooding, and dredging (0 = no involvement, 10 = major involvement).

Two types of beliefs were analyzed. The first included four measures of problem severity: fish/wildlife degradation, water quality degradation, flood problems, and water supply problems. The second involved two perceptions about policy proposals: greater protection of wetlands/fish populations and opposition to building a peripheral canal.

The data are analyzed and the results presented with actors aggregated into organizational affiliations. The assignment of the respondents to one of 18 organizational affiliations is discussed in the appendix.

RESULTS

The analysis proceeds in three steps. The first is a background step and presents a descriptive analysis of the means of functional area involvement and beliefs by 18 organizational affiliations. The second step examines patterns of the functional area involvement, beliefs, and ally and opponent networks using multidimensional scaling and cluster analysis. The first two steps show CALFED's relative functional area involvement and beliefs necessary to examine the third hypothesis regarding the extent to which this collaborative institution shows broker characteristics. The third step examines the evidence for or against the first two hypotheses by explaining the variance in ally and opponent networks by functional area involvement and beliefs using a quadratic assignment procedure regression.

Descriptive Analysis of Functional Area Involvement and Beliefs

Table 9.1 presents the mean involvement in each functional area for 18 organizational affiliations, and Table 9.2 reports their beliefs about problem severity and policy positions. In Table 9.2, the organizational affiliations listed in the left column are ordered by their mean beliefs for the severity of fish/wildlife declines. A statistically significant difference among organizational affiliations was found for all functional areas and

TABLE 9.1. *Mean Functional Area Involvement by Organizational Affiliations*

| | o = Not Involved at All, 10 = Extremely Involved | | | | | |
	Water Supply	Pollution	Wetlands	Fish	Flood	Dredging
Env	4.9	4.5	6.1	4.8	2.9	3.9
S/F Fish	4.9	3.2	4.6	7.3	2.3	2.4
EPA	4.3	4.8	5.6	3.3	3.4	2.2
CALFED	8.1	3.7	6.5	6.7	3.8	2.8
BCDC	3.7	4.1	7.6	4.1	3.1	5.7
COE	2.0	1.0	7.3	4.4	6.4	7.6
Sci	3.6	4.7	4.2	3.6	1.8	1.4
SRWQB	3.6	6.7	4.9	2.8	1.3	3.6
Loc Gov	3.8	3.5	4.4	2.4	2.1	0.9
USBR	5.9	5.4	2.0	3.3	2.1	0.1
Mun Dis	3.0	6.8	3.7	2.9	2.5	1.0
SC Water	6.9	2.4	2.5	2.4	1.0	0.7
DWR	6.0	3.0	3.1	5.5	4.0	1.5
Cons	6.2	3.8	2.8	4.0	3.2	1.5
Bay Water	6.6	4.1	3.1	3.4	2.1	1.2
Loc Ag	6.2	4.3	2.8	3.3	3.9	1.1
Bus	2.6	3.7	3.6	3.5	2.7	3.3
Ind Dis	2.5	6.6	2.2	0.4	0.2	2.2
Total	5.0	4.3	4.1	3.9	2.8	2.2

There is a statistically significant difference among organizational affiliations for all beliefs ($p < 0.000$) calculated by a Welch statistic. Env = environmental groups, S/F Fish = state/federal fish agencies, BCDC = Bay Conservation and Development Commission, COE = U.S. Army Corps of Engineers, Sci = scientists, SRWQB = state/regional water quality control boards, Loc Gov = local government, USBR = United States Bureau of Reclamation, Mun Dis = Municipal Dischargers, SC Water = southern California water suppliers, DWR = Department of Water Resources, Cons = Consultants, Loc Ag = local agriculture interests, Bus = businesses/ports, Ind Dis = Industrial Dischargers.

TABLE 9.2. *Mean Perceptions of Problem Severity and Policy Positions by Organizational Affiliations*

| | Problem Severity | | | | Policy Positions | |
| | 0 = Not a Problem at All, 100 = Severe Problem | | | | 1 = Strongly Disagree, 7 = Strongly Agree | |
	Fish Declines	Water Quality	Water Supply	Flooding	Pro-Canal Construction	Pro-Fish/Wetland Protection
Env	93	71	38	60	2.4	6.2
S/F Fish	88	56	34	52	5.1	5.9
EPA	85	55	43	58	4.1	6.5
CALFED	85	43	57	56	5.7	5.3
BCDC	83	68	49	67	2.7	5.8
COE	82	56	55	78	3.6	4.6
Sci	81	60	47	63	3.5	5.4
SRWQB	81	60	44	56	3.8	5.2
Loc Gov	78	63	45	66	2.4	5.4
USBR	76	50	55	67	4.6	4.2
Mun Dis	74	61	54	61	3.4	4.5
SC Water	71	52	72	60	5.7	3.7
DWR	71	53	63	62	5.8	4.1
Cons	68	45	59	62	5.4	4.3
Bay Water	67	53	72	70	4.1	4.2
Loc Ag	58	45	69	68	4.7	3.2
Bus	54	44	49	52	3.6	4.1
Ind Dis	52	48	56	53	2.0	3.8
Total	74	55	54	62	3.9	4.7

There is a statistically significant difference among organizational affiliations for all beliefs ($p < 0.000$) calculated by a Welch statistic. Env = environmental groups, S/F Fish = state/federal fish agencies, BCDC = Bay Conservation and Development Commission, COE = U.S. Army Corps of Engineers, Sci = scientists, SRWQB = state/regional water quality control boards, Loc Gov = local government, USBR = United States Bureau of Reclamation, Mun Dis = Municipal Dischargers, SC Water = southern California water suppliers, DWR = Department of Water Resources, Cons = Consultants, Loc Ag = local agriculture interests, Bus = businesses/ports, Ind Dis = Industrial Dischargers.

beliefs using a Welch test ($p<0.000$). Organizational means higher than the total means in a given column are highlighted in bold to help readers interpret patterns in the tables. Five conclusions are drawn from the two tables.

First, the starkest division is between actors involved in, and with beliefs supporting, water quality and fish/wetlands versus actors involved in, and with beliefs supporting, water supply. In Table 9.1, organizational affiliations most heavily involved in water supply include southern California water suppliers, the Department of Water Resources, consultants, San Francisco Bay water suppliers, local agricultural interests, the United States Bureau of Reclamation, and CALFED (means > 5.9). For the most part, these water supply organizational affiliations show less concern about fish and water quality problems and about fish/wetland protection as reported in Table 9.2.

In contrast, Table 9.1 indicates that nine organizational affiliations (environmental groups, state/federal fish agencies, the Environmental Protection Agency, Bay Conservation and Development Commission, the Army Corps of Engineers, Scientists, state/regional water quality control boards, local governments, and CALFED) report high involvement in wetlands. Generally these nine organizations are concerned about fish/wildlife declines and about water quality problems, but less so about the water supply problems in Table 9.2. Five of these pro-fish/wetland organizations are highly involved in the fish functional area, including environmental groups, state/federal fish agencies, Bay Conservation and Development Commission, the Army Corps of Engineers, and CALFED. This first point supports previous research on Bay-Delta water policy (Munro 1993; Zafonte and Sabatier 1998; Hundley 2001).

Second, the lowest level of involvement is in dredging and flooding and the least amount of disagreement is about floods. In Table 9.1, only the Army Corps of Engineers scores higher than 5 in flooding and dredging. The Bay Conservation and Development Commission, which was originally charged with regulating shoreline development, is also involved in dredging. Additionally, Table 9.2 shows that the least amount of disagreement occurs with flood problems. The means for flood problems ranged from 52 to 78 on 100-point scale with 100 equal to a perceived severe problem. Dredging and flooding are neither the most salient issues nor the major sources of conflict.

Third, beliefs about the peripheral canal produce a different lineup of supporters and opponents. Support and opposition to the peripheral canal have always created odd alliances in the Bay-Delta (Munro

1993). The results from the 1997 questionnaire are no different. Strongly opposing the canal are environmental groups, local governments, and industrial dischargers (means >= 5.6). Strongly supporting the canal are CALFED, southern California water suppliers, the Department of Water Resources, consultants, and state/federal fish agencies (means < 3). This lineup of canal opponents and supporters has some validity. Many environmental groups oppose the canal because they perceive it might have adverse impacts on diverting fresh water from the Bay-Delta. At the time, CALFED had been advocating a plan to build the canal. Southern California water suppliers have always been the principal recipients of peripheral canal water and have traditionally been supporters. The state/federal fish agencies support the canal because they believe that diverting water into a canal would protect fish species from dying in water pumps (Sabatier and Zafonte 2007).

Fourth, CALFED appears to play their intended role as a broker, based on its high involvement in most functional areas and on its diverse beliefs. CALFED is the only organizational affiliation with high involvement in the three major functional areas: wetlands (mean = 6.5), fish (mean = 6.7), and water supply (mean = 8.1). CALFED shows concern about fish/wildlife declines (mean = 85) and about water supply problems (mean = 57). At the time of the questionnaire, CALFED supported fish/wetland protections and the peripheral canal. Based on the organization's beliefs and functional area involvement, it would be difficult to place CALFED on one side or the other in this debate, which suggests that CALFED is in a position to broker disputes among rivals.

Fifth, the results corroborate Zafonte and Sabatier (1998), who studied the same population four years earlier using different operational approaches. Zafonte and Sabatier (1998) used a 1992 questionnaire and approximated functional area involvement by belief severity. They found many of the same pro–water supply and pro–fish/wetland organizational affiliations. Zafonte and Sabatier (1998) found a water pollution functional area with the major players being state/regional water quality control boards, municipal dischargers, and industrial dischargers. They also found that the Army Corps of Engineers, the Bay Conservation and Development Commission, and businesses were active in dredging and flooding issues. However, Zafonte and Sabatier (1998) were not as precise in estimating participation in functional areas because their measure for functional area involvement was based only on perceived severity of beliefs. Note that Tables 9.1 and 9.2 show that beliefs about problem severity do not reflect environmental groups' high involvement in water supply and scientists' low involvement across all functional areas.

Multidimensional Scaling Maps and Cluster Analysis

To provide a simpler image of this pattern of relationships, Figures 9.1 to 9.4 present multidimensional scaling and cluster analyses to investigate the similarity in functional area involvement, beliefs, ally networks, and opposition networks among the 18 organizational affiliations. Combining the scaling and cluster analyses is common for identifying actors with similar network ties (Knoke et al. 1996).[1] Multidimensional scaling simplifies a high-dimensional matrix of *n* by *n* objects into a lower dimensional space, usually two or three underlying dimensions that minimize the distance among all pairs of objects. The dimensional coordinates can then be graphed to form a spatial representation or map of the matrix with objects close to each other being more similar in their ties than objects that are far away. In Figures 9.1 through 9.4, the objects are the same 18 organizational affiliations found in Tables 9.1 and 9.2. The goodness of fit of a multidimensional scaling map is a stress value. The stress values for Figures 9.1 through 9.4 range from 0.12 to 0.19.

Groupings of organizational affiliations on the multidimensional scaling maps are encircled by a Tabu search cluster analysis (Hanneman and Riddle 2001; Borgatti et al. 2002). The Tabu search cluster analysis is an iterative clustering method that reorganizes the objects (i.e., affiliations)

---

[1] I begin with four matrices with 18 organizational affiliations and either six functional areas (18 by 6 matrix), six beliefs (18 by 6 matrix), or 18 allies and 18 opponents (18 by 18 matrices). For the ally and opponent networks, I first normalize the citations to percentages so that a given cell represents the percentage of the total citations from a given affiliation to another affiliation. Each row in the normalized matrix then adds to one. For all four networks, I then create a symmetric matrix by calculating the Pearson's correlations between rows, diagonals included. The numbers in the resulting symmetric matrix are thus Pearson's correlation coefficients indicating the similarity between pairs of citing organizational affiliations, and the diagonals equal one. This 18 by 18 symmetric matrix is used in a multidimensional scaling procedure using Gower's classical metric ordination. The number of dimensions is set at two even though the stress value decreases to 0.10 or less when the number of dimensions increases to three. This certainly indicates a better fit but I keep the number of dimensions at two to simplify the presentation of the data, since stress values less than 0.20 are acceptable. I also use the 18 by 18 symmetric matrix to create the encircled clusters of the organizational affiliations using a Tabu search cluster analysis. Both the multidimensional scaling procedure and the Tabu search cluster analysis are conducted with UCINET.

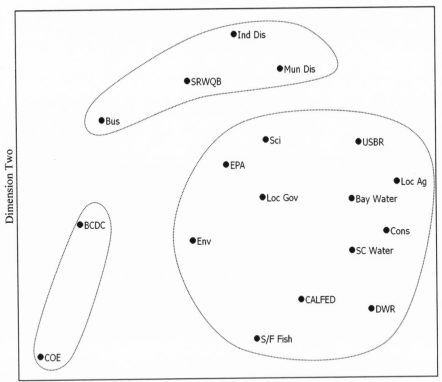

FIGURE 9.1. Multidimensional Scaling Map of Functional Area Involvement. *Notes:* Stress = 0.12. Clusters optimized at three (R^2 = 0.64). Env = environmental groups, S/F Fish = state/federal fishagencies, BCDC = Bay Conservation and Development Commission, COE = U.S. Army Corps of Engineers, Sci = scientists, SRWQB = state/regional water quality control boards, Loc Gov = local government, USBR = United States Bureau of Reclamation, Mun Dis = Municipal Dischargers, SC Water = southern California water suppliers, DWR = Department of Water Resources, Cons = Consultants, Loc Ag = local agriculture interests, Bus = businesses/ports, Ind Dis = Industrial Dischargers.

into clusters, the number of which is set by the researcher. Given a matrix of organizational affiliations, the Tabu search cluster analysis rearranges the matrix such that affiliations with highly correlated ties are in the same cluster and those that have uncorrelated ties are in a different cluster. Tabu search cluster analysis provides a goodness-of-fit measure (R^2), which can be used to find the optimal number of clusters. The goodness of fit peaks at three clusters for all four figures. The major difference between the Tabu clusters and the multidimensional scaling maps is that

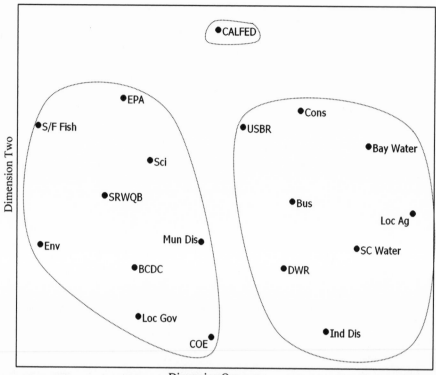

FIGURE 9.2. Multidimensional Scaling Map of Beliefs. *Notes*: Stress = 0.19. Clusters optimized at three (R^2 = 0.38). Env = environmental groups, S/F Fish = state/federal fishagencies, BCDC = Bay Conservation and Development Commission, COE = U.S. Army Corps of Engineers, Sci = scientists, SRWQB = state/regional water quality control boards, Loc Gov = local government, USBR = United States Bureau of Reclamation, Mun Dis = Municipal Dischargers, SC Water = southern California water suppliers, DWR = Department of Water Resources, Cons = Consultants, Loc Ag = local agriculture interests, Bus = businesses/ports, Ind Dis = Industrial Dischargers.

multidimensional scaling identifies a low number of dimensions that minimize distances among objects, whereas the Tabu search partitions and rearranges the objects in a given matrix to maximize within-cluster similarities (or to minimize within-cluster variance).[2]

Figure 9.1 provides a map for functional area involvement and Figure 9.2 provides a map for beliefs. Figures 9.3 and 9.4 provide maps for ally and

---

[2] I also cluster using hierarchical clusters and find that the branches splinter in a similar manner as provided by the Tabu Search cluster.

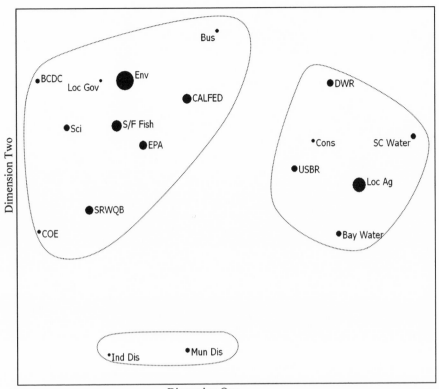

Dimension One

FIGURE 9.3. Multidimensional Scaling Map of Ally Networks. *Notes*: Stress = 0.19. Clusters optimized at three (R^2 = 0.64). The size of the node indicates the sum of all ally citations received by an organizational affiliation. Env = environmental groups, S/F Fish = state/federal fishagencies, BCDC = Bay Conservation and Development Commission, COE = U.S. Army Corps of Engineers, Sci = scientists, SRWQB = state/regional water quality control boards, Loc Gov = local government, USBR = United States Bureau of Reclamation, Mun Dis = Municipal Dischargers, SC Water = southern California water suppliers, DWR = Department of Water Resources, Cons = Consultants, Loc Ag = local agriculture interests, Bus = businesses/ports, Ind Dis = Industrial Dischargers.

opponent networks, respectively. The nodes in Figures 9.3 and 9.4 vary in size to represent the number of ally and opponent citations received by each organizational affiliation. For example, in Figure 9.3, the biggest node represents environmental groups, indicating that this organizational affiliation received the most ally citations compared to any other organizational affiliation (18% or 261 out of 1,417). Industrial dischargers are represented by the smallest node, indicating that this organizational affiliation received the

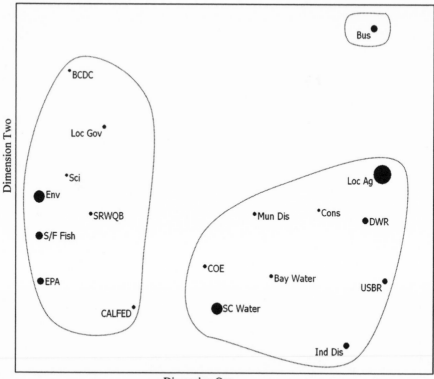

FIGURE 9.4. Multidimensional Scaling Map of Opponent Networks. *Notes:* Stress = 0.13. Clusters optimized at three (R^2 = 0.62). The size of the node indicates the sum of all opponent citations received by an organizational affiliation. Env = environmental groups, S/F Fish = state/federal fish agencies, BCDC = Bay Conservation and Development Commission, COE = U.S. Army Corps of Engineers, Sci = scientists, SRWQB = state/regional water quality control boards, Loc Gov = local government, USBR = United States Bureau of Reclamation, Mun Dis = Municipal Dischargers, SC Water = southern California water suppliers, DWR = Department of Water Resources, Cons = Consultants, Loc Ag = local agriculture interests, Bus = businesses/ports, Ind Dis = Industrial Dischargers.

fewest ally citations (1% or 14 out of 1,417). Similarly, for opponent networks in Figure 9.4, agricultural interests are represented by the biggest node because they received the most mentions as an opponent (25% or 310 out of 1,254). In contrast, scientists are represented by the smallest node for receiving the fewest opponent citations (1% or 8 out of 1,254).

Looking across the four figures, two groups of organizational affiliations always cluster together. One cluster includes some of the same organizational affiliations active in the water supply functional area who also hold pro–water supply beliefs. These pro–water supply organizational affiliations include consultants, San Francisco Bay water suppliers, local agricultural interests, southern California waters suppliers, the United States Bureau of Reclamation, and the Department of Water Resources.

Figures 9.1 through 9.4 locate these water supply organizational affiliations in clusters on the right end of the horizontal dimension. The most common ally among water supply advocates is agricultural interests. The pro–water supply organizational affiliations name agricultural interests with at least 15 percent of each of their ally citations. Among all organizational affiliations, agricultural interests receive 192 out of 1,417 ally citations (or 14%), ranking them second behind environmental groups. The pro–water supply organizations most frequently mention environmental groups as opponents with at least 22 percent of each of their citations.

The second cluster includes some of the same organizations who supported the fish/wetland problems and policies. These pro–fish/wetland organizations include environmental groups, scientists, the Environmental Protection Agency, state and federal fish agencies, and San Francisco Bay-Delta local governments. These organizations always cluster together in all four figures. They most frequently mention environmental groups as allies with at least 15 percent of each of their ally citations, and they most frequently mention agricultural interests as opponents with at least 32 percent of each of their opponent citations.

One interesting finding from Figure 9.1 is that organizations involved in the water supply and fish/wetland functional areas cluster together. This giant cluster encircles actors from two opposite sides of the debate, which is expected when functional areas are either symbiotically or competitively interdependent. A close look at Table 9.1 shows that some of the fish/wetland organizations are also involved in water supply. For example, environmental groups, the Environmental Protection Agency, and state/federal fish agencies report high involvement in the water supply functional area. Showing involvement in both the water supply and the fish functional areas are the Department of Water Resources and consultants.

The vertical dimension in Figure 9.1 separates a cluster of organizational affiliations involved in the water pollution functional area. The water pollution organizational affiliations include municipal dischargers, industrial dischargers, state/regional water quality control boards, and business/ports.

For the ally networks in Figure 9.3, the vertical dimension of the multidimensional scaling map and the cluster analysis also separate a part of the water pollution cluster by encircling industrial dischargers and municipal dischargers. Likewise, in the opponent networks in Figure 9.4, the vertical dimension isolates business/ports from the remaining organizational affiliations.

Some of the members of the water pollution cluster (in Figure 9.1) appear as members of the pro–fish/wetland cluster and the pro–water supply cluster. Industrial dischargers are located in the pro–water supply cluster in Figures 9.2 and Figure 9.4. Municipal dischargers are located in the water supply cluster in Figure 9.4 but in the pro–fish/wetland cluster in Figure 9.2. The state/regional water quality boards (SRWQB) are located in pro–fish/wetland cluster in Figures 9.2, 9.3, and 9.4.

A third cluster in Figure 9.1 is on the left of the multidimensional scaling map and includes the Army Corps of Engineers and the Bay Conservation and Development Commission. As shown in Tables 9.1 and 9.2, these two organizational affiliations are primarily involved in, and concerned about, dredging and flooding. This flooding and dredging cluster is not isolated as a separate cluster in the remaining figures. However, the Bay Conservation and Development Commission and the Army Corps of Engineers are both located on the far left of the ally map in Figure 9.3.

Evidence that CALFED is playing a brokerage role is mixed. They are centrally located in the large central cluster in Figure 9.1 and as an isolate between the two clusters in Figure 9.2. However, CALFED is also located in the pro–fish/wetland cluster in Figures 9.3 and 9.4.

The Impact of Functional Overlap and Beliefs on Ally and Opponent Networks: Quadratic Assignment Procedure (QAP) Regression Analysis

The quadratic assignment procedure regression provides a systematic means for analyzing the relative impact of functional area involvement and beliefs on ally and opponent networks.[3] The QAP approach is useful for analyzing networks because the procedure corrects for multicollinearity and does not require an assumption of random sampling or independence between observations (Krackhardt 1988; Borgatti et al. 2002). All matrices used in the QAP regression were normalized and symmetrized by calculating Pearson's correlations as a measure of similarity.

The QAP regression analysis proceeds in two steps. In the first step, it conducts the usual multiple regression analysis by explaining the

---

[3] The multiple regression QAP is conducted in UCINET Version 6.153 using the Double-Dekker Semi Partialing technique (Dekker et al. 2003).

TABLE 9.3. *QAP Regression*

	Ally Networks	Opponent Networks
Beliefs	0.33**	0.50***
Functional Areas	0.37***	0.14
Adjusted R^2	0.25	0.27

Note: All numbers are standardized coefficients. * <0.10, ** <0.01, ** <0.001.

dependent matrix (ally or opponent networks) with the explanatory matrices (functional areas or beliefs). This first step calculates the regression coefficients and R^2. The second step randomly permutes (2,000 per explanatory matrix) the rows and columns of the dependent matrix in order to test the assumption that the observed estimates are significantly different than would be produced by random variations of the dependent matrix. The regression model is then rerun using the static explanatory matrices on each permutated dependent matrix. After each permutation and regression, all coefficients and R^2s are recomputed and saved into a distribution from which inference and standard errors are computed. Significant p values are calculated as the number of times that a coefficient or R^2 is greater than the values calculated in the random permutations. Standardized coefficients, which are shown in Table 9.3, can be interpreted the same as in ordinary least square regression as the unique effect of the explanatory matrix on the dependent matrix.

Table 9.3 shows the QAP regression analysis for ally and opponent networks. Supportive results would be evidenced by coefficients with positive signs and statistical significance. Contradictory results would be significant coefficients with negative signs, which would indicate that similar functional area involvement or similar beliefs is associated with different networks of allies and opponents.

For ally networks, both functional areas and beliefs are significant. Similar functional areas explain about the same variance in the ally networks (std. coef. = .37) as does similar beliefs (std. coef. = 0.33). The significance of both functional area involvement and beliefs on ally networks supports the findings from the maps in Figures 9.1, 9.2, and 9.3, which all show similar clusters along the horizontal dimension between the pro–water supply organizations and the pro–fish/wetland organizations. Only the functional area map in Figure 9.1 and the ally map in Figure 9.3, however, show the separation of a water pollution cluster by isolating municipal and industrial dischargers, which might explain the slightly stronger explanatory power of functional area involvement.

For opponent networks, only beliefs are significant. (std. coef. = 0.50). The insignificance of functional area involvement to explain opponent networks makes sense when comparing Figures 9.1 and 9.4, since the opponent networks in Figure 9.4 provide no semblance to any of the functional area clusters highlighted in Figure 9.1. However, both the belief map and the ally map show the division between the pro–water supply organizational affiliations and the pro–fish/wetland organizational affiliations.

SUMMARY

This chapter considers two of the mitigating mechanisms capable of resolving the ICA problems that arise from functional fragmentation and transaction costs (*Feiock and Scholz*). The first is informal policy networks, such as ally and opponent networks. The second is collaborative institutions, specifically CALFED. The results provide strong confirmation that ally networks are best understood as bridging symbiotic functional areas that involve actors with similar beliefs and low transaction costs. Opponent networks, on the other hand, are unrelated to functional areas and are better understood as binding actors together who share similar threats, but only when similar beliefs ensure that transaction costs are low.

Collaborative institutions, in contrast, probably work best in mitigating situations with high transaction costs among competitive functional areas, as found between water quality and water supply. One implication of the findings reported in this chapter is that informal policy networks and collaborative institutions play different roles in mitigating transaction costs and enabling collective action to address ICA dilemmas.

More specifically, the findings reported here provide strong support for the belief congruence hypothesis by demonstrating that shared beliefs shape both ally and opponent networks. This is also consistent with the extant literature linking ally and opponent choice and beliefs (Salisbury et al. 1987; Sabatier and Jenkins-Smith 1993; Knoke et al. 1996). To the extent that differences in beliefs provide a source of friction in negotiating agreements, as noted in the ICA framework, belief heterogeneity will increase transaction costs across different clusters of actors while reducing them within each cluster.

Support for the functional area hypothesis is mixed, since functional area involvement appears to shape ally but not opponent networks. One lesson from this finding is that opponent networks are simply not an antithesis of ally networks. The major conceptual difference between the two networks is that ally networks derive from common policy objectives while opponent networks derive from common threats. The findings suggest that both shared policy objectives and threats relate to similar beliefs, but that only shared policy objectives relate to similar functional area involvement. If Fenger and Klok (2001) are correct that interdependent functional areas provide a rationale for interorganizational coordination, then ally networks represent a better approximation for coordination among actors in response to ICA problems than do opponent networks. Such an explanation supports the findings in another study that found a significant correlation between ally and coordination networks in a California marine policy subsystem (Weible and Sabatier 2005).

A third hypothesis investigates the extent that CALFED serves as an institutional broker. The expectation is that CALFED would link different functional areas, show inclusive beliefs, avoid extreme policy positions, serve as an ally among warring affiliations, and avoid opposition. This chapter provides some empirical support for the expectation that CALFED plays a broker role. CALFED is highly involved in three functional areas, more than any other organizational affiliation. CALFED representatives may not always hold moderate beliefs, but they are diverse in the range of their beliefs. For example, they agree about the severity of fish declines and about water supply problems. CALFED aligns with environmentalists in their support for greater fish protection policies, but also with southern California water users in support of building a peripheral canal. CALFED is associated more with the pro–fish/wetland cluster than with the pro–water supply cluster, but no organization named CALFED in more than 15 percent of their opponent citations.

The techniques of network analysis demonstrated in this chapter provide a means to observe and simplify the description of the complex relationships that develop among actors in fragmented policy arenas as well as to analyze systematically the interactions across different dimensions of these relationships. These relationships in turn provide a critical foundation for understanding the dynamics of self-organizing institutions and their role in the American federalist system.

APPENDIX

Organizational Affiliations

Organizational affiliations were coded using three techniques. First, respondents were placed into categories based on the mailing address of

TABLE 9.A1. *Frequency and Percentages of Organizational Affiliations*

	Frequency (n)	Percent
Local Agricultural Interests (Ag)	101	15%
Department of Water Resources (DWR)	30	5%
U.S. Bureau of Reclamation (USBR)	11	2%
Southern California water suppliers (SC Water)	23	3%
Bay water suppliers (Bay Water)	17	3%
Consultants (Con)	53	8%
Chamber of Commerce/Businesses (Bus)	9	1%
Municipal Dischargers (Mun Dis)	32	5%
Industrial Dischargers (Ind Dis)	17	3%
Environmental groups (Env)	49	7%
State/Federal Fish Agencies (S/F Fish)	48	7%
CALFED	10	2%
State/Regional Water Quality Control Boards (SRWQB)	41	6%
U.S. Environmental Protection Agency (EPA)	9	1%
Sporting and fishing groups (combined w/ Env)	12	2%
University Scientists (Sci)	39	6%
Bay Conservation Development Commission (BCDC)	28	4%
U.S. Army Corps of Engineers (COE)	9	1%
Bay Delta local governments (Loc Gov)	32	5%
Shoreline developers and ports (combined w/ Bus)	7	1%
Miscellaneous/Other	91	13%
Totals	668	100%

their organization. The mailing addresses were collected at public hearings or by suggestions of an advisory committee. Second, the coded organizational affiliations were checked for validity by examining reported employer and level of government for government officials on the questionnaire. For employer, respondents were asked the following question: "Which of the following best describes your principal employer? 1. Private/industrial waste discharger or discharger-related interest group [Bus / Private Water users]; 2. Publicly owned waste treatment facility; 3. Port or airport; 4. Water-related business (e.g., developer or marina, but not a major discharger); 5. Chamber of commerce / business group; 6. Urban water supply district or user interest group; 7. Irrigation/reclamation district or user interest group; 8. Agricultural firm or interest group; 9. Government (state, federal, or general purpose local); 10. Media (newspaper, television, radio); 11. Consulting firm (principal client, if any);

12. University; 13 Environmental interest group; 14. Fishing or sporting group; 15. Upstream local government or watershed group; 16. Not employed for monetary compensation; 17. Other (please specify)." Third, to verify the validity for government officials, the results were checked with the respondents who worked in the government and their cited level of government. The question wording was "Do you hold a public office or governmental position? [1 = Yes, 2 = No] If yes, is the level: 1 = Local; 2 = Regional; 3 = State; 4 = Federal."

Functional Area Involvement

For functional area involvement, respondents were given the question: "Water policy surrounding the Bay-Delta has many dimensions. On the scale below, please indicate your involvement over the last 5 years in each of the following aspects of Bay-Delta water policy. A score of 10 indicates extremely involved, while a score of 0 indicates not involved at all." The functional areas included "a. Water pollution, including agricultural drainage; b. Water supply and flows; c. Wetlands habitat and fill; d. Fisheries; e. Flood control; and f. Dredging."

Ally and Opponent Networks

The ally and opponent networks were identified using the following statement: "Below is a list of twenty-three groups of people concerned with Bay-Delta water policy: 01. CALFED, 02. U.S. Environmental Protection Agency, 03. State / regional water quality boards, 04. Army Corps of Engineers, 05. Bureau of Reclamation; CVP operators, 06. DWR; SWP operators, 07. State / federal fish and game agencies, 08. BCDC, 09. Bay-Delta city and county land use officials, 10. Southern California urban water suppliers, 11. Bay-Delta urban water suppliers, 12. Agricultural interests: Delta, 13. Agricultural interests: Sacramento Valley, 14. Agricultural interests: San Joaquin Valley, 15. Municipal dischargers (POTWs), 16. Industrial dischargers, 17. Shoreline developers and ports, 18. Chambers of commerce/business groups 19. Environmental groups 20. Fishing and sporting groups, 21. Upstream local govt. or watershed groups, 22. University researchers, 23. Consultants." To create the agricultural interests, organizational affiliation choices 12, 13, 14, and 21 were combined.

Respondents were then asked to answer two questions: "1. Using the above list, please identify up to three groups that you regard as allies by putting the appropriate numbers in the boxes below. 2. Please indicate up to three groups that you regard as your principal opposition."

Beliefs of Severe Problems

The four severe problems scales were created from a battery of potential problems. The complete wording and presentation follows. "The following items have been suggested as problems related to Bay-Delta water policy. Please indicate your assessment of the seriousness of each problem on the thermometer scale below. A score of 100 indicates an extremely serious problem, while a score of 0 indicates not a problem at all. a) Shrinkage of the Bay's surface area (e.g., through fill). b) Water pollution in the Bay-Delta. c) Poor quality of Delta water for urban and/or agricultural users. d) Inadequate water storage. e) Impediments to water transfer users. f) Uncertainty of long-term water supply for urban and agricultural users. g) Delta levee susceptibility to sudden catastrophic collapse. h) Loss of wildlife/fisheries habitat in the Bay-Delta. i) Disposal of dredge material. j) Salmon decline in the Bay-Delta and Central Valley. k) Introduced species. l) Flood control on Central Valley rivers and in the Delta. m) Loss of property rights because of environmental restrictions. n) Uncertainty and financial costs due to government regulations."

From the items, four problem severity scales were created:

1. Water supply problems (Cronbach's alpha = 0.81): (1) Inadequate water storage (factor loading = 0.87); (2) Impediments to water transfers (factor loading = 0.80); and (3) Uncertainty of long-term water supply for urban and agricultural users (factor loading = 0.88).
2. Water quality problems (Cronbach's alpha = 0.70): (1) Shrinkage of the Bay's surface area (e.g., through fill) (factor loading = 0.83); (2) Water pollution in the Bay-Delta (factor loading = 0.79); and (3) Disposal of dredge material (factor loading = 0.75).
3. Fish Problems (Cronbach's alpha = 0.86): (1) Loss of wildlife/ fisheries habitat in the Bay-Delta (factor loading = 0.94); and (2) Salmon decline in the Bay-Delta and Central Valley (factor loading = 0.94).
4. Flooding Problems (Cronbach's alpha = 0.65): (1) Delta levee susceptibility to sudden catastrophic collapse (factor loading = 0.86); and (2) Flood control on Central Valley rivers in the Delta (factor loading = 0.86).

Policy Proposal Beliefs

The policy proposal beliefs were created by variables introduced with the following statement: "Please indicate your opinion concerning the following policy proposals regarding the San Francisco Bay-Delta. Circle the response which best reflects your opinion from 1 = strongly disagree to 7 = strongly agree. Circle 9 if you have no opinion." The two policy proposals include

1. Pro-Fish (Cronbach's alpha = 0.91): (1) In-stream flow requirements from the Sacramento River to the Bay-Delta should be set at levels sufficient to restore fish populations to pre-1976 levels (factor loading = 0.82); (2) The EPA water quality criteria to protect the most sensitive species in ambient Bay waters are too costly for the benefits produced (factor loading = 0.88); (3) The Endangered Species Act should be amended to include economic feasibility in the list of species (factor loading = 0.88); (4) The Delta smelt should be delisted as a threatened species (factor loading = 0.87); (5) BCDC's de facto policy of no net fill – i.e., requiring fill projects having significant environmental impacts to return to tidal action an area of comparable habitat value irrespective of the nature of the applicant – should be continued (factor loading = 0.74); and (6) Restrictions on development in salt ponds and managed wetlands now within BCDC jurisdiction should be eased (reversed) (factor loading = 0.75).

2. Anti-Canal (Cronbach's alpha = (0.91): (1) A facility should be constructed to divert Sacramento River freshwater around the Delta to meet the needs of central and southern California water users and Delta fisheries (reversed) (factor loading = 0.96); and (2) If environmental guarantees with high degrees of permanence could be developed (e.g., via a combination of multiparty private contracts and federal legislation), a peripheral canal should be a major component of solving Delta water problems (reversed) (factor loading = 0.96).

Sustaining Joint Ventures

The Role of Resource Exchange and the Strength of Interorganizational Relationships

Ramiro Berardo

Understanding how political actors engage in collaborative behavior in fragmented policy arenas is extremely important, particularly when the use of finite public goods is at stake (*Feiock and Scholz*). Collaboration may reduce the potential occurrence of conflict among users by informing parties about better ways to avoid negative externalities and to take advantage of positive ones, creating the conditions under which more extensive cooperative behavior can develop. Given the important effects that collaborative initiatives may produce, it is only logical that the bulk of research in political science and public administration concentrates on studying how to overcome the initial obstacles to collaboration in the presence of excessive fragmentation.

However, less attention is paid to answering the question of *how collaboration can be sustained over time.* This is unfortunate, since the continuation of these practices, rather than their mere emergence, is what makes the solutions to institutional collective action (ICA) problems more valuable to stakeholders. Fortunately, important progress has recently been made by scholars in both political science and public administration on how collaboration can be achieved and extended (cf. Feiock 2004, 2007; Koontz et al. 2004; Sabatier et al. 2005; Scholz and Stiftel 2005). This research continues this trend by explaining how collaboration can be sustained when actors exchange resources that are needed for the successful implementation of joint ventures, one of the self-organizing mechanisms to solve ICA problems that are explored in this book.

In particular, I will analyze the behavior of organizational actors engaged in collaborative projects sponsored by the Southwest Florida

Water Management District (SWFWMD).[1] These projects are joint ventures designed to protect water quality, ensure water supply, protect natural habitats, and prevent flooding in the southwest region of Florida – an area that demands highly coordinated efforts to protect natural resources efficiently in the presence of rapid urban development.

Collaborative projects are particularly important to overcome the negative effects of individually rational and noncoordinated behavior by local governmental and nongovernmental actors on the maintenance of ecological balance in water-rich Florida. Collaborative projects function as forums where actors build and maintain joint visions on how to protect natural resources, hence making ICA problems less likely to develop. Knowing how actors in these joint ventures create the basis for sustained collaboration is important because it is this sustainability that eases the path to the solution of other problems that may appear in a more or less distant future.

Studying the sustainability of collaboration is crucial in relatively small policy arenas where the possibilities for "shopping around" for collaborative partners are limited and where the breakdown of collaborative relationships can spiral rapidly toward conflict. Once relationships deteriorate, it is extremely costly and time-consuming to rebuild them – if they can be reconstructed at all. By explaining what factors increase the likelihood of future collaboration, this research will identify some initial conditions under which the costly results of institutional defection are avoided.

Specifically, I ask how the exchange of needed resources among partners in these projects affects participants' opinions about the likelihood of sustaining collaborative efforts in the future. I then determine whether some resources are more important than others for influencing actors' adoption of collaborative attitudes.[2] In so doing, I apply resource exchange theory, an underutilized approach in policy studies (O'Toole 1997), to examine how cooperation takes place when actors lack natural incentives to avoid free-riding behavior. In addition, I explore how the strength of the ties that are developed among partners in the joint ventures explains the sustainability of collaborative behavior. Observing both the

---

[1] Henceforth "the district" or "SWFWMD."

[2] It should be noted that the indicator for the dependent variable is not an objective measure of sustained collaboration but rather a proxy for it based on the perceived likelihood of sustained collaboration stated by organization members participating in the projects. In this respect, I claim that the study uncovers some of the conditions that might *facilitate* sustained collaboration.

exchange of resources *and* the strength of interactions among partners in joint ventures can enhance our understanding of how collaboration can be more effectively sustained.

I start by describing the uses of water in Florida in general and southwest Florida in particular. The state is known for the large availability of the resource, but high rates of development and rapid increase of the population create the typical problems of overuse of common-pool resources (see Ostrom 1990; Ostrom et al. 1994). I next present the main hypotheses to be tested and describe the data collection process, measurement of variables, and estimation technique. Finally, I present the results of the empirical analysis and discuss their relevance for understanding how collaboration is sustained in the presence of natural incentives to engage in disjointed decision making.

THE EMERGENCE OF COLLABORATIVE PROGRAMS FOR WATER IN SOUTHWEST FLORIDA

Florida is one of the water-rich states in the United States par excellence. The level of precipitation amounts to an average of 53 inches per year, and the state's territory contains approximately 3 million acres of wetlands, 7,700 lakes greater than 10 acres, and more than 1,700 streams (Fernald and Purdum 1998).

While rich in the gross availability of the resource, the state is increasingly faced with the need of carefully managing its water, mainly because population continues to grow at rapid rates. Almost 16 million inhabitants lived in Florida at the beginning of the new millennium according to the U.S. 2000 Census, and this number is expected to climb to almost 26 million by 2030.[3] A growing population demands more water and forces policy makers to adopt innovative measures to cope with the dangers of overuse. According to the U.S. Geological Survey (USGS), in 2000 Floridians withdrew more than 20 million gallons of water per day from both saline and fresh sources (Marella 2004). Freshwater came from both groundwater and surface sources; the biggest withdraws from groundwater sources were destined to public supply (43% of the total groundwater withdraws), while the main utilization

---

[3] Source: Demographic Estimating Conference Database, updated July 2005. For more information on demographic composition in the State of Florida, visit the Web site of the "Office of Economic & Demographic Research" of the Florida Legislature at http:// edr.state.fl.us/conferences/population/demographic.htm (last accessed April 10, 2009).

of surface sources was made for agricultural purposes (62% of the total surface water use).

Southwest Florida – the site for this study – contains approximately one-quarter of the state's population: 3.99 million people live in the region, with the majority populating the Tampa Bay metropolitan area. By the year 2000, water users in the region were the largest withdrawers of freshwater for commercial-industrial use in the state, as well as the largest consumers of saline water utilized to cool power-generating plants (Marella 2004).

The magnitude of these uses poses increasing threats to the stability of ecosystems. For instance, excessive withdrawal of water from underground sources can lead to reduction of spring flows (affecting the ecosystems around them) and to the invasion of saltwater into underground aquifers. Excessive utilization of surface water can also have negative consequences. Over-irrigation of fields, for instance, is very likely to result in the impoverishment of the quality of both surface and groundwater sources, since the excess water from the irrigation can carry pollutants like residuals of pesticides and soluble nutrients back to those sources.

In the past, water issues have been highly conflictual, even producing widespread conflict among groundwater users that resulted in the highly publicized "water wars" of the 1970s and 1980s, when users spent considerable amounts of money settling their disputes in court (Dedekorkut 2005). In part to reduce potential sources of conflict, the Southwest Florida Water Management District – the main authority responsible for water-related issues in the area – has created a set of collaborative programs that encourages water users to engage in cooperative practices.[4] The Cooperative Funding Initiative (CFI) is one of the most important of these programs

---

[4] There are five water management districts (WMDs) in Florida, which have regulatory capabilities to deal with the protection of water resources in the state. They can create and collect ad valorem taxes and operate with a relatively extended autonomy from other agencies and actors at the state and local levels. The SWFWMD was created in 1961 to deal with the flooding problems occasioned by hurricane Donna, but with the passing of the Water Resources Act in 1972 its powers were extended beyond that specific area. Nowadays, in addition to the goal of flood protection, the district extends its regulatory capabilities to three other main areas: (1) water supply, (2) water quality management, and (3) protection and restoration of natural systems. The organization is governed by a governing board composed of 11 members, which appoints the executive director. Territorially, the district is divided in nine basins according to hydrologic criteria, each of which is governed by a board composed by members appointed by the governor to serve three-year terms.

in terms of budgetary allocations for projects and comprehensiveness of water-related problems addressed by the projects.

Under the CFI umbrella, organizations submit project proposals linked to the main areas of the district's responsibility, which include the protection of natural systems, the prevention of flooding, the enhancement of water quality, and the provision of water for human uses. The applicants can apply for up to half of the project budget from the district, reducing the high costs of solo responses to water management problems. The district also obtains clear benefits by taking advantage of local water management expertise, by reducing the potential sources of conflict with the partners, and by sharing the financial cost associated with the projects.

The program is carried on at the basin level (see note 4), which means that applicant organizations present their projects for consideration to the district's basin boards, which make individual decisions on whether funds will be allocated to each project. The process of obtaining funding is relatively straightforward and takes place over a one-year cycle that starts every October, when the district holds informational workshops for potential partners interested in obtaining funds. The deadline for the presentation of applications is the first Friday of December. The district's staff reviews the applications and determines a final ranking by April. The Basin Board meets in June to review projects and in August to approve the final budget for selected projects for the following fiscal year. Based on these decisions, contracts are awarded for the following fiscal year in the month of October, when the annual process comes to an end.

Cooperative Funding Initiative projects are ideal scenarios for studying collaboration because the actors involved benefit greatly from their participation in the program and the issues addressed by the projects are of the greatest interest for stakeholders in the area. Also, often the CFI program promotes collaborative relationships between stakeholders from different local jurisdictions. For instance, cities, towns, or county governments usually present joint projects. Therefore, the study of the CFI projects provides a great venue to study how collaboration may unfold when stakeholders in highly fragmented systems craft joint ventures to address ICA problems.

RESOURCE EXCHANGE, TIE STRENGTH, AND SUSTAINABILITY OF COLLABORATION

When actors build relationships they become increasingly dependent on each other as they exchange resources necessary to reach whatever goals they may have in the beginning of their association. Scholars have proposed and tested different versions of the resource dependence approach (Blau 1964; Benson 1975; Cook 1977; Galaskiewicz 1979; Cook et al. 1983; Markovsky et al. 1988; Cook and Yamagishi 1992), and students of public policy have timidly explored the applications of this theoretical tool (Rhodes 1981, 1986; Hanf and O'Toole 1992; Marsh and Rhodes 1992; Agranoff and McGuire 1998; Wondolleck and Yaffee 2000; Scholz, Berardo, and Kile 2008), but it remains underutilized.[5]

The working assumption of scholars in this tradition is that organizations are not self-sustained or independent from their environment, in the sense that they rarely have all the resources they need to guarantee their own survival or reach their goals.[6] As a result of this scarcity, organizations need to secure access to resources from "suppliers" in their environment that can provide the resources in question. In interorganizational studies, those suppliers are just other organizations that are members of the larger system (the *environment*) on which the organization in need depends.

Of course, the crucial implication for those interested in the study of ICA problems is that the development of resource exchange can affect behavior. An actor receiving resources from another one obviously benefits from this exchange and should respond accordingly by becoming more trustworthy and by potentially engaging in further cooperative actions. Is this reasoning applicable to partners in CFI projects? Does the exchange of resources between partners affect the willingness of the receiving organization to sustain collaboration with the supplier of such resources? If this is the case, which are the resources that are more important in producing sustained collaboration? Answering these questions will provide valuable insight to more

---

[5] These theoretical efforts have been grouped under different names, but "resource dependency theory" and "resource exchange theory" are the most common. Other denominations include "political economy model" and "dependence exchange" (see Aldrich and Pfeffer 1976 for more details). For the purposes of clarity, I will refer to the theory simply as resource exchange theory in the rest of this chapter.

[6] Resources are varied and can be of both a material and a nonmaterial nature, although in studies of resource exchange the utilization of material resources is much more common. Material resources may include financial resources, information or knowledge of different kinds (depending on the types of actions performed by the organization), personnel to carry on the organization's tasks, and so on. Nonmaterial resources may include legitimacy of the organization's goals, symbolic power or prestige enjoyed in the presence of competitors, and similar assets.

fully understand the circumstances in which partners in joint ventures can overcome ICA dilemmas that tend to develop in excessively fragmented systems.

Identifying "Needed" Resources: A Contextual Issue

To answer the questions presented in the previous paragraph, it is first necessary to identify the resources to be exchanged. Emerson claimed that the definition of a resource depends on the context, and that "any ability possessed . . . [by an actor] is a resource only in relation [to] . . . specific other [actors] who value it" (Emerson 1976, 348). Researchers testing hypotheses derived from the resource exchange theory deal with this issue regularly and must carefully define what a resource is, depending on the topic of study or the nature of the relationships they observe.

In this work, I study the exchanges that take place in projects seeking funding under the CFI. Hence, critical resources are those that are *more likely to ensure the successful design and implementation of the projects*. These resources were identified initially with the assistance of an advisory board of active policy makers in southwest Florida.[7] The board did not rank resources in order of importance but rather identified the main areas in which project participants need to accumulate adequate resources if they are to succeed in the design and implementation phases of the project. The kinds of resources identified in this context include funding availability, technical information, public buy-in and/or political support for the project, and finally,

---

[7] The members of this board are Dick Eckenrod, executive director of the Tampa Bay Estuary Program; George Henderson, senior scientist at the Florida Fish and Wildlife Commission; Andy Squires, director of the Pinellas County Department of Environmental Management; Janet Kovach, former member of the SWFWMD Governing Board, and Mark Hammond, director of the Resource Management Department, SWFWMD. In addition to identifying critical resources for projects, the members of the board unanimously suggested studying exchange of resources in the projects at the very initial stage of the application for CFI funding – in the period of time preceding the final decision of the basin boards on whether to provide funds. According to the opinion of the advisory board members, the application process is actually the most critical stage for the development of collaboration. It is during this stage that political negotiations take place, roles in the project for the different participants are defined, and the exchange of resources is just being established with the goal of making the project's application successful.

assistance to meet regulatory requirements that make the project legally viable.

I interviewed district staff to further validate the choice of resources and verify their importance during the application process for CFI funding.[8] All four areas of resource exchange were acknowledged as important, although political support and technical information were seen as the most important. Gathering political support from stakeholders in the areas is critical to gain the required sponsorship of local government, since local governments face multiple demands for allocating their limited funds.[9] Obtaining sufficient technical information and expertise is necessary develop the kind of "polished" application that tends to be ranked higher during the review process.

To the extent that public buy-in and/or political support for the project and the availability of technical information become crucial, a receiver of these resources would presumably be more willing to sustain collaboration with the provider than with nonproviding partners. The other resources are obviously still important, but they should be less critical in explaining why partners in these joint ventures perceive that collaboration will be sustained over time. Thus, it is hypothesized that there should be a positive relationship between the reception of resources in each of the four areas identified above and the willingness to sustain collaboration with the provider, but that this positive relationship should be of a *greater magnitude* when the resources being exchanged are technical information and public buy-in and/or political support for the project. In other words, respondents should express a greater willingness to sustain collaboration with those partners who provide the resources that are more likely to make a project successful.[10]

The Strength of the Interorganizational Ties

Studies of tie strength and its effect on dyadic relationships have developed steadily ever since Mark Granovetter's (1973) seminal study of job search showed that contacts maintained with distant acquaintances

---

[8] I am particularly indebted to Mr. Rand Baldwin, Community Affairs Coordinator with the district for his invaluable help during this stage of my research. Michael Holtkamp and Janie Hagberg, project managers with the district, also provided valuable insight about these issues.

[9] In 40 out of the 41 projects studied in this paper, the applicant was a local government in southwest Florida.

[10] The measurement of the variables will be described in a later section.

("weak ties") provided more productive information for finding jobs than contacts maintained with friends ("strong ties"). Granovetter attributed these findings to the fact that weak ties allow the actors to gather nonoverlapping information by reaching distant parts of a network and concluded that weak ties "are the channels through which ideas, influences, or information socially distant from ego may reach him" (Granovetter 1973, 1370).

While subsequent work has demonstrated the advantages of weak ties for information transfer in both interpersonal and interorganizational relationships (Lin, Ensel, and Vaughn 1981; Roch, Scholz, and McGraw 2000), evidence of the importance of strong ties for enhancing credibility and ensuring the exchange of critical information in groups has also accumulated rapidly (Friedkin 1982; Hansen 1999; Carpenter, Esterling, and Lazer 2003). In politically fragmented systems the credibility of a partner's commitment to collaborative action is highly uncertain. In the specific case of the joint ventures that I study here, one way of reducing this uncertainty could consist in the establishment of solid or "strong" relationships through which the actor can learn more about the partner's behavior, interests, and goals. In this sense, strong ties allow for an easier determination of how credible and trustworthy partners are (Scholz et al. 2008) and should help partners build relationships characterized by sustained collaboration. Hence, it is hypothesized that partners will show a higher propensity to maintain collaboration with those partners with whom they share strong ties.

OTHER FACTORS AFFECTING THE SUSTAINABILITY OF COLLABORATION

To test the influence of resource exchange and tie strength on the willingness of project partners to sustain collaboration in the future, we need to control for other factors likely to influence future collaboration.

The District as a Partner

While the involvement of the district in the projects is always secured through its provision of funds to implement projects whenever they are approved, in some cases the district gets involved to a greater extent by providing other types of resources, mainly input in technical issues to make the projects more viable. The district assigns project managers to all the projects that apply for funding and in some cases the participation of these managers is so central that applicants identify the district as a "formal partner" in the project.

I introduce this variable in the analysis to control for the possibility that the presence of the district as a partner in a project conditions the responses about likelihood of sustained collaboration. Pfeffer and Salancik (2003 [1978], 49) contend that "the final source of control (of an organization over its environment) derives from the ability to make rules or otherwise regulate the possession, allocation, and use of resources and to enforce the regulations." The district is the organization with the highest regional authority to regulate the use of the water resources in southwest Florida and the sponsor for the CFI. In fact, the district's provision of funds makes it an indispensable actor for the viability of projects. Hence, it is plausible that respondents from other organizations exhibit a higher willingness to sustain collaboration when the district is the provider of the resources that are important to make the project viable.

Meeting the Organizational Expectations when Participating in the Project

Another variable associated with the reduction of transactional costs through the establishment of solid relationships with partners in these joint ventures is the expectation of respondents that their organizations will meet their goals when participating in the projects. When an organization meets its expectations, a positive precedent is created in its relationship with the partners. This could help reduce the costs of searching for potential counterparts for new partnerships by allowing the searcher to narrow its choices rapidly to those actors with whom there is a history of past successful collaboration. If this is the case, we should observe a positive relationship between the belief that the organization is meeting its goals in the project and the stated willingness to extend collaboration with any partner in the project.

Project Size

I also control for the size of the project in which the partners interact, since projects funded under the CFI program are not uniform in terms of their financial requirements. Some of these projects are very small and require less effort by the partners to design and implement the project. On the other hand, other projects are very large in size and require greater investments to be implemented, as in the case of city- or countywide water management plans that use extensive financial support and human resources.

To some extent, participating with a partner in a project of a large magnitude signals the willingness to take larger risks with that partner, and this is another way of indicating how solid their relationship is. Thus, including the size of the project in my analysis to explain the willingness of respondents to sustain collaboration with the partners allows me to control for the possibility that the responses are affected by the fact that the relationship has progressed toward the elaboration and execution of projects that demand a stronger link between the parties. Therefore, I expect a positive relationship between the size of the project and the willingness to sustain collaboration.

Individual Perception of the Importance of Water Issues

Up to this point, the independent variables capture features of the respondents' organizations or characteristics of their relationships with their partners in the joint venture. Putting the burden of the analysis on these variables is a natural choice, since this is basically a study of inter-organizational relationships. Nevertheless, we also need to account for the attitudes of respondents that may affect their responses. I specifically control for one of these attitudes: the perception of importance of water issues in the area under study. It is possible that individuals who are more concerned about water issues feel the need to extend collaboration, which is just a reflection of their interest in solving these problems and not of the attributes of the partners they evaluate.

In the case of water management in the area under study, the projects designed under the Cooperative Funding Initiative prioritize four main areas of management: water supply, water quality management, flood control, and protection and restoration of natural systems. Hence, if the argument described above holds, individuals who perceive these issues to be highly important should also show a greater tendency to extend collaborative practices.

DATA, MEASUREMENT, AND ESTIMATION TECHNIQUES

I test the hypotheses with data collected from respondents participating in 41 projects that applied for CFI funding in December 2004 and December 2005. The decision to restrict the study to these projects was determined by data reliability concerns. After a multistage selection process designed to obtain reliable data,[11] 156 project participants were asked to answer a 16-question survey detailing their participation in the projects and their relationships with the other project partners. We received a total of 99 replies, which represents a response rate of 63.5 percent. Since the respondent is asked to provide information about each one of the partners in the project, each survey provides as many cases for the analysis as there are partners in the project. The 99 surveys that I collected provide a total of 182 cases for the analysis, which I use to test the hypotheses presented above.

Variables

The Dependent Variable: Sustained Collaboration. Respondents answer the following question: "Based on your participation in this project and

---

[11] The list of projects that applied for funding in these two years initially included 230 cases. Since several projects can share the same personnel, only a total of 112 individuals were identified as "contact person" in the application forms presented to the different basins of the district. The application form contains information including the name of the organization acting as "cooperator" and the "contact person" in the organization (usually the individual who is more involved in the design of the project). The information about the applications is contained in the so-called Budget Notebook of each of the basins. These documents are released after each of the six bi-monthly meetings that basin boards hold in the months of February, April, June, August, October, and December. The notebooks contain information on CFI projects being funded, but also information on projects that are applying for funding for the next fiscal year. This information is gathered from the application forms filled in December.

Since applications do not include a detailed list of individuals or organizations participating in the projects as partners, the "contact persons" are the best available source that could provide this information. Of course, the fact that 112 individuals function as "contact person" for 230 projects means that some of them take on liaison roles between the applicant and the district in more than one project. This led to a two-stage data collection process. In the first stage developed between March and May of 2006, we contacted the 112 individuals by e-mail and telephone and asked them to answer a short survey providing the names of all the organizations participating in the projects (partners) as well as the names and contact information for individuals representing each of those organizations. By mid-May, we had obtained responses from 67 of the 112 individuals (59.82%) who provided information about the organizations and individuals involved in 99 of the original 230 projects applying for CFI funding in the last two years.

A number of individuals participate in different projects at the same time, so it was necessary to choose the projects in a way that would minimize the number of survey requests to these individuals while at the same time maximizing the number of projects available for analysis. We adopted the rule of selecting projects in a way that would ensure that respondents were not asked to answer more than two surveys, which brought the number of projects to 41. The list of respondents for these projects included 156 individuals: 129 one-time respondents, and 27 two-time respondents (individuals who participated in two projects). Individuals in this last group who returned their first survey were then contacted by e-mail and asked if they were willing to answer a second survey. If they did not reply to the e-mail request in three days, a phone call followed.

your relationship with the partner, would you say that you are more likely to engage in future collaborative efforts, or less likely to do so?" The answer ranges from 1 to 7, where 1 represents "less likely to collaborate" and 7 represents "more likely to collaborate."

To simplify the estimation of the model and the interpretation of the results, I recoded the dependent variables into four categories.[12] The initial distribution of the values of the variable is skewed toward the higher values of the scale, with fewer cases in the lower values of the scale. It is fair to speculate that this is a result of the context in which the respondents answered the question. The fact that they were engaged in a common project is a sign that the main obstacles for collaboration have already been removed. Hence, there should be a tendency for respondents to favor sustained collaboration because, everything else being equal, current collaboration should be a good predictor of future collaboration. Descriptive statistics for this and other variables are available in the appendix.

The Main Independent Variables: Exchange of Resources with the Partner. To capture the exchange of resources with the partner for each of the four areas of interest – technical information, funding, public buy-in and/or political support, and solution of permitting and regulatory hurdles – I combine two observations:

1. Whether the respondent gathered the resources from the partner, but also
2. The number of outside suppliers not formally participating in the project that provided the resources to the respondent's organization.

For the first observation, the respondents were asked whether the partner organization provided each of the four resources. Respondents answered "yes" (coded 1) or "no" (coded 0) for each case.[13] For the second observation, respondents were presented with a list of 51 organizations that consistently participate in water-related policies and projects in southwest Florida and they were asked again to answer whether each

---

[12] Values 1 through 4 of the original variable were grouped and assigned a new code of 1 (15.4% of responses). The remaining values in the original scale 5, 6, and 7 adopted a new code of 2 (9.3%), 3 (25.8%), and 4 (49.5%), respectively.

[13] The survey used this simplified measure rather than asking respondents about the amount of assistance in each of these areas as a compromise between the length of the survey and the relative gain from asking more detailed questions; respondents were asked to provide information about every partner in the project, so the answer to this and other questions could have been extremely cumbersome for respondents had we asked them to provide more details.

of these organizations provided assistance.[14] As before, respondents answered "yes" or "no" (coded 1s and 0s) for each one of the organizations in each of the four areas. I then proceeded to add the positive mentions (the 1s) for each area, so for every respondent I could count the number of outside suppliers that provided any given resource.

With these two pieces of information, the next step consists in performing the following calculation:

$$\frac{\text{Resource from Partner}}{\sum \text{Outside Source}} \tag{1}$$

The calculation is repeated in each of the four areas. For instance, a respondent that received technical information from the partner and 10 other organizations outside the project obtains a score for exchange of technical information for the partner that equals 0.1, while a respondent that receives the resource from the partner but only from two outsiders has an exchange score that equals 0.5. Of course, when the numerator equals 1 and the denominator is 0 (the respondent receives the resource from the partner but not from outside sources), the result of the calculation is undefined. However, this is the representation of the maximum possible level of exchange with a partner, since there are no alternative suppliers. Thus I recode those cases, giving them a value of 2. This value is chosen because it represents double the amount of dependency on the partner in comparison to the case in which the partner provides the resource and there is exactly one outside source, in which case the score for exchange equals 1. Hence, the ideal values of this variable range from 0 (no exchange with the partner) to 2 (highest exchange).

This calculation reflects the fact that the value of a partner as a supplier of resources is relative to how much the respondent's organization obtains the resources from other suppliers. Complete reliance on one partner to gather the resource (no outside suppliers) represents a situation in which there is the maximum possible interdependency between the two organizations, and hence the score for the exchange is maximized.

Strength of Interorganizational Tie. There is lack of consensus on how best to measure the strength of interorganizational ties, given the

---

[14] The list contained organizations grouped under the following categories: (a) Federal Government, (b) State Government, (c) Regional Government, (d) Local Government, (e) Private and Non Governmental Stakeholders.

multitude of dimensions that the definition of tie strength contains. In his seminal article, Granovetter stated that the strength of a tie is "a [probably linear] combination of the amount of time, the emotional intensity, the intimacy [mutual confiding], and the reciprocal services which characterize the tie" (Granovetter 1973, 1361). Granovetter himself performed his analysis on the effects of weak ties in the search of jobs by capturing only one of these dimensions and measuring strength based on frequency of contacts.[15]

I measure the *frequency* of the relationship between the respondent's organization and the partner in the project under study by asking the respondent to "please indicate how frequently you have contacted the partner in the year prior to the basin boards' decision on whether to fund the project or not." Respondents chose their answers from the following five options: (a) weekly, (b) monthly, (c) quarterly, (d) annually, or (e) never. Responses were coded with a "5" when the option chosen was "weekly" and with a "1" when the respondent picked the answer "never." Hence, a higher value in this variable represents more frequent contacts between the organizations in the project.

Although I do not have data for each of Granovetter's indicators of tie strength, I can also measure the *closeness* or intensity in the relationship by observing how many common projects are shared between the respondent's organization and the partner. The common participation in a larger number of projects is a good indicator of how much interaction occurs between the organizations, hence informing us about the intensity of the relationship – one of the dimensions of the strength of a tie identified by Granovetter. Specifically, I asked "in how many other water-related projects your organization is participating with the partner." The menu of choices was (a) none, (b) 1 project, (c) 2 to 5 projects, (d) 6 to 10 projects, and (e) more than 10 projects. In this case, a coding of 5 was assigned to respondents choosing option "e"

---

[15] The difficulties researchers may face in collecting information in all of these dimensions to measure tie strength has been reflected in studies that assume that a tie is strong or weak based on labels assigned to counterparts in interpersonal relationships (like *friend, neighbor, acquaintance*, etc.). However, the problem is that there is also a lack of agreement on how these labels should be interpreted. For example, Lin et al. (1981) in their study of the search of higher status jobs consider relatives, friends, and neighbors as strong ties, while acquaintances and indirect ties (friends' relatives, etc.) are considered weak ties. However, Marsden and Hurlbert (1988) classify neighbors as weak ties. Others do not even consider friends as strong ties (Roch et al. 2000).

and a coding of 1 was assigned for option "a," so the higher the score, the stronger the tie.

District as a Partner. This dichotomous variable was coded 1 if the partner was the district and 0 if the partner was any other organization.

Meeting the Organizational Expectations when Participating in the Project. The following statement was presented to the respondents: "*At this point*, it is certain that the project will meet my organization's expectations." They then located themselves on a 7-point scale, where 1 corresponded to the option "I strongly disagree with the statement" and 7 "I strongly agree with the statement."

Project Size. The size of the project was measured by the total estimated budget (in thousands of dollars) to implement it. These data are obtained from the applications contained in the "budget notebooks" of each of the district's basin boards.

Individual Perception of the Importance of Water Issues. The district prioritizes four areas of action: water supply, flood control, water quality management, and protection and restoration of natural systems. We asked respondents, "Please indicate how important are each of (these) issues in your region." For each of these four areas, respondents placed themselves along a 7-point scale where 1 means "not important" and 7 "very important." I then averaged these responses and assigned this value to the respondent.

Estimation Technique

I estimate an ordered logit model, which is specially suited for the ordinal dependent variable that I described above. In ordered logit models (and other models utilized for ordinal dependent variables), it is assumed that the categorical dependent variable (y) is a particular realization of an underlying continuous latent variable (y^*) that generates the observed values. In other words, the observed values of sustained collaboration (y) are assumed to be some categorical representation of the underlying continuous variable "sustainability of collaboration" (y^*).

A Note on Missing Data

The rate of missing data for the 182 observations was never higher than 8 percent for any individual question. However, the missing information was scattered across the observations, which means that proceeding with the analysis utilizing only those cases with complete information would have produced a significant reduction in the explanatory power in the model, in addition to the known problems of inefficiency and bias that come with a listwise deletion approach.[16]

To avoid these limitations, I utilize Amelia II, which implements a bootstrapping-based algorithm designed for "multiple imputation" of missing data (see Honaker, King, and Blackwell 2006 for more details). The program imputes h values for each case or cell in which missing data exist, finally creating h databases that can be used together to estimate the model of interest.[17] With the utilization of this software, I obtained data for a total of 182 observations.

RESULTS

Table 10.1 reports the ordered logit results performing the analysis across the five multiply imputed databases produced by Amelia II. The analysis was performed with Stata (version 10), a statistical software program widely used in the social sciences. Stata returns the average of the five different results obtained from each individual estimation. Available tests indicate that the model performs adequately.[18]

The clustering of the standard errors by project seeks to correct for potential problems that would be caused if the dependent variable were affected by some unobserved explanatory variable operating at the project level that is relegated to the error term in the equation. Estimation of the model without clustering produces similar results,

---

[16] 117 observations contain no missing information in any of the variables utilized in the analysis.

[17] The default number for this quantity h estimated by Amelia II is five. Amelia II can be downloaded for free at http://gking.harvard.edu/amelia/.

[18] Since the results presented here are an average for the five separate estimations, Stata does not produce measures of fitness for the final output. All five individual estimations converged properly, and Wald tests for each of them reject the null hypothesis of all the coefficients being simultaneously equal to zero. I also conducted Brant tests to check whether the "parallel regression assumption" holds. The assumption is central to the use of ordered-logit models and states that the effects of the different independent variables are equal across the different categories of the dependent variable. The Brant procedure (Brant 1990) compares the slope coefficients for all the independent variables in the j-1 binary logits that are implied by the ordered regression, where j equals the number of categories in the dependent variable. Significant values for the test signal a violation of the assumption. In every one of these tests, there was no evidence of a violation of the assumption.

TABLE 10.1. *An Ordered Logit Estimation of Sustained Collaboration with Exchange of Resources Disaggregated*

Dependent Variable: Likelihood of Extending Collaboration with Partner	
Exchange of Resources	**Coefficients**
Resources respondent's organization received from partner:	
Assistance in Technical Information	0.15 (0.34)
Assistance in Funding Issues	−0.06 (0.33)
Assistance in Enhancing Public Buy-in and/or Political Support	0.83*** (0.26)
Assistance in Permitting/Regulatory Requirements	0.29 (0.25)
Tie Strength	
Intensity of Interorganizational Relationship	0.41** (0.22)
Frequency of Interaction in the Project	0.27** (0.15)
District as a Partner	0.43 (0.39)
Achievement of Organization's Expectations when Participating in Project	0.41*** (0.14)
Size of the Project (in thousands of dollars)	−.00004 (0.0001)
Individual Perception of the Importance of Water Issues	0.48** (0.24)
Threshold1	5.63*** (1.77)
Threshold2	6.38*** (1.81)
Threshold3	7.80*** (1.87)
N 182 Number of Projects 41	

** $p<0.05$; *** $p<0.01$ (one-tailed).
Note: The entries are maximum likelihood estimates. Robust standard errors are given in parentheses (clustered by project).

but the robust standard errors are reported since this is technically more appropriate.[19]

Dependency for Public Buy-in Increases Collaboration

When I introduced the arguments linking exchange of resources to the sustainability of collaboration, I predicted that more exchange dependency with a partner should positively affect the willingness to sustain collaboration with that partner, particularly for technical information and public buy-in and/or political support for the project. The evidence supports the prediction for public buy-in and/or political support for the project, but not for technical support.

---

[19] Alternatively, and as a test of the robustness of the results shown in Table 10.1, I have estimated the model clustering the standard errors by (a) individual id of the respondents, and (b) organization name. I have observed no substantial differences in the magnitude or significance levels of the coefficients obtained in those estimations in comparison to those that I report here.

But how large is this effect? I will illustrate the effect by analyzing how a change in the independent variable from its minimum to its maximum value affects the *predicted probability* of a respondent scoring the highest value of 4 in the scale measuring "likelihood of future collaboration with the partner." Almost 50 percent of the cases scored this value, so I choose to show the predicted probability of respondents falling into this category to preserve the simplicity in the analysis.[20]

I will calculate both the probability of obtaining a value of 4 in the dependent variable when the value of the exchange with the partner for public buy-in and/or political support is at its maximum (value of 2), and the probability of obtaining a value of 4 in the dependent variable when the value of the exchange with the partner is at its minimum (value of 0). The effect of the independent variable on the dependent can be assessed by comparing these two quantities. I utilize the Clarify software (Tomz et al. 2001) to produce these calculations.[21] In order to "isolate" the effect of the independent variable, the remaining independent variables in the model are fixed at their mean value, with the exception of the dummy variable "District as a Partner" which is set at its modal value of zero (the partner is not the district) – I repeat this procedure for each statistically significant independent variable to assess their importance and report the results of the calculations in Table 10.2.

When the level of dependency on the partner is at its minimum, the likelihood that the partner was rated at the highest level equals .36, compared with a sizable .74 when the respondent is highly dependent on the partner for obtaining assistance in public buy-in and/or political

---

[20] The formula for the calculation of predicted probabilities in an ordered-logit model depends on the number of categories of the dependent variable. In this specific case, the formula to obtain the predicted probability that the outcome of the dependent variable will be 4 is

$$\Pr(y = 4) = 1 - \frac{1}{1 + e^{(X_i\beta - \tau 3)}} \tag{2}$$

where e is the base of the natural logarithm, β is the vector of coefficients capturing the effects of the different independent variables in the model, and $\tau 3$ is the cut-point or threshold separating the third from the fourth category in the dependent variable.

[21] The software can produce a variety of "quantities of interest," including expected and predicted values, under different conditions set by the user. To calculate the predicted probabilities presented here, Clarify draws a number of simulations (1,000 by default) of the main and ancillary parameters in the model (the thresholds separating the categories of the dependent variable) and calculates the predicted probabilities for the values of the dependent variable, reporting the mean of those simulations with a 90 percent confidence interval.

TABLE 10.2. *Predicted Probabilities of Stating that Future Collaboration is "More Likely" for Extreme Values of Significant Independent Variables*

Independent Variables	Future Collaboration "More Likely"*
Dependence on Partner for Obtaining Public Buy-in and/or Political Support	
Lowest Dependence	.36 [.29 – .46]
Highest Dependence	.74 [.63 – .82]
Net Difference	.38
Tie Strength	
Lowest Tie Strength	.16 [.08 – .26]
Highest Tie Strength	.72 [.50 – .84]
Net Difference	.56
Achievement of Organization's Expectations when Participating in Project	
Lowest Achievement	.18 [.10 – .33]
Highest Achievement	.61 [.47 – .73]
Net Difference	.43
Individual Perception of the Importance of Water Issues	
Lowest Perceived Importance	.24 [.12 – .39]
Highest Perceived Importance	.59 [.45 – .71]
Net Difference	.35

* 90% confidence intervals in-between brackets.

support for the project. The difference in the probabilities is equal to .38, an important amount that is also significant as proven by the non-overlapping confidence intervals for the two separate quantities.

This outcome helps us obtain a clearer picture of the types of problems that are critical for stakeholders in the management of water in southwest Florida, an area where the lack of agreement on how to protect the resource has resulted in extended conflict in the past. Different actors have different interests in the highly controversial area of water management, and local governments – the applicants in all but one of the projects studied in this chapter – face great pressure to attend to multiple and usually conflicting demands. Money spent in building another retention pond to treat stormwater runoff or in restoring wetlands to enhance wildlife will almost certainly generate endorsements by environmental groups and individuals concerned with the protection of the ecological balance of the area. Nevertheless, this same type of project could easily antagonize others interested in directing public funds to other areas that might need attention from the local government. Thus, gathering political support or enhancing the public buy-in for a project is almost always a top priority for decision makers, and finding a key partner that can assist in such a critical area affects their willingness to engage in cooperative behavior.

Stronger Ties Enhance Collaboration

I hypothesized that the sustainability of cooperation is related to the strength of interorganizational relationship both inside and outside of the specific project being studied. The evidence supports these expectations. Both coefficients capturing the relationship between the strength of tie and the dependent variable are positive as predicted and statistically significant at the .05 level. As indicated in Table 10.2, positive changes in the scales measuring strength of the tie also produce a sizable change in the probability of respondents falling in the fourth category of the dependent variable (more likely to sustain collaboration with the partner in the future). The calculated probability of scoring the highest value in the dependent variable grew from .16 with both variables at their lowest values to .72 with both variables at their highest values for a net positive effect of .56.

Together, these results confirm that strong interorganizational ties should be recognized as an important component of collaborative behavior needed to resolve ICA dilemmas. The reduction of uncertainty about a counterpart that comes with having shared other cooperative efforts and having established frequent interactions in the project provide distinctive opportunities to address common problems and speculate about potential solutions to them. It is easier for actors to recognize the advantages of synergetic action when these conditions are created, which probably affects the willingness to sustain collaboration in the future through common participation in other joint ventures.

Other Impacts on Collaboration

The achievement of the expectations of the organization when participating in the project also significantly influenced the sustainability of cooperation. Moving from "strongly disagree" to "strongly agree" produces a .43 increase in the probability that that sustained collaboration with the partner is more likely. Stated differently, a failure to meet expectations in a project considerably decreases the likelihood of sustained collaboration with any of the project's partners. The main lesson here is that collaborative relationships need to be built and nurtured one step at a time, and that the continued collaboration that is so central to effectively solving ICA dilemmas can be hampered if individual projects become problematic for a partner. This could have an overall negative effect on the search for solutions to the problems of fragmentation and disjointed decision making. Even if the disappointed organization decides to develop new collaborative projects, the task of finding trustworthy partners is more onerous if no history of previous cooperation exists. This frailty of the collaborative relationships needs to be taken into account by decision makers with a role in the promotion of initiatives such as the CFI program that strongly rely on the collaborative intentions of the participants. Every collaborative project should be approached as an opportunity for finding consensual responses to common problems, but under the explicit acknowledgment that the costs of not meeting expectations can be high, resulting in the deterioration of relationships among stakeholders.

The last significant coefficient in the model links the respondents' concern with water-related problems to the dependent variable. Individuals more concerned with problems in water management have more chances of stating that future collaboration with the partners in the projects is more likely. Taking the independent variable from its minimum (3.75) to its maximum (7) produces a positive change in the probability of sustained collaboration being more likely of .35 (.24 for the minimum and .59 for the maximum). This relationship could be the result of the personal interest that respondents have in solving water-related problems, but also of a more or less objective assessment of these problems in southwest Florida that can actually fuel real collaborative efforts in the future. In any case, the positive relationship between the two variables feeds the optimistic view that the community of stakeholders in the area is highly motivated to deal with the problems that human activities impose on the natural systems.

The District as a Partner does not produce a higher likelihood of sustained collaboration. This result is surprising, given that the district is such an important source of financial resources for each of these projects. On the other hand, this finding couples nicely with the idea that a greater willingness to engage in future collaboration depends primarily on the overall benefits that the respondent's organization obtains from the project and the contributions that the partners make to increase the likelihood of successful implementation. The formal power held by those partners is not important in explaining the dependent variable.

Finally, the size of the project measured in thousands of dollars was negative but insignificant, suggesting that individuals working in larger projects are not more prone to sustain collaboration with their partners. Putting together projects of a larger magnitude does not seem to be enough to engage actors in extended collaboration.

SUMMARY

This chapter identifies the conditions under which sustained collaboration becomes more likely in multiparty joint projects, one of the mitigating mechanisms to ICA problems identified in this volume. Joint projects allow governmental and nongovernmental organizational actors alike to appropriate the benefits of coordinated behavior. But rather than studying how joint projects come to life, this chapter aims at discovering what aspects of informal relationships within *ongoing* projects enhance the likelihood of *sustaining* collaboration among the organizations in the future.

The chapter brings together two theoretical perspectives to study this issue; the first one emphasizes resource exchange and dependency, while the second emphasizes the strength of relationships. This empirical study of 41 water-related projects in southwest Florida sheds new light on how stakeholders create the conditions under which the likelihood of collaboration in future interactions can grow. Future collaboration can minimize the ever-costly outcome of uncoordinated behavior in fragmented decision-making arenas and can ease the path to the solution of ICA dilemmas. Both a partner's ability to provide political support for the project and a strong tie between participating organizations increase the perceived likelihood of future collaboration.

The results have shown that the perceived likelihood of sustained collaboration with a partner grows when that partner can provide public buy-in and/or political support for the joint venture. Surprisingly the exchange of technical expertise, financial resources, and regulatory and permitting assistance did not significantly influence the sustainability of collaborative practices, suggesting that they are more widely available and less likely to be the critical resource required for project success.

Overall, the results suggest that the quality of the informal relationship is at least as important as the dependency on exchanged resources in enhancing the likelihood of future collaboration. This outcome supports the speculation that strong informal linkages are crucial to overcome the natural tendency to disengage from cooperative practices in the presence of excessive fragmentation in the policy system.

The results presented here can help political science and public administration scholars better understand the types of resources that are critical to creating conditions for institutional actors to overcome collective action problems resulting from fragmentation of policy and authority. Particularly in local venues where constituencies demand the attention to multiple policy issues at the same time, policy makers face the challenge of finding political support and public buy-in for their ideas and initiatives. When this is the case, it seems likely that other resources that might be important to secure the successful implementation of those initiatives take a back seat in favor of the search for legitimacy for the new efforts. In other words, sustained collaboration is not the product of exchanging resources – even important ones – to make a project success-ful, but exchanging those that facilitate "selling" the project to the local constituencies. This result adds an extra layer to the already complex issue of how to deal with authority fragmentation and reminds us that ICA problems may in fact be exacerbated by the failure to recognize and neutralize the opposition that the principal may have to the actions that the governmental agents perform.

This study has also found that the strength of the tie linking project partners helps explain the likelihood of sustaining collaboration. This sug-gests that the extension of collaborative practices is more likely when organizations participate in multiple projects together, and when they are represented by concerned individuals who frequently meet their partners to discuss project-related issues. Furthermore, the achievement of the orga-nization's expectations when participating in the project and the individual perception of the importance of water issues in the area of study also contribute to an improved understanding of when stakeholders manifest their intentions to continue with collaborative efforts. In general, the over-all results support the claim that common visions are more easily built and cooperation becomes more likely when actors face each other directly and fulfill mutual needs (Ostrom 1990). It is under these circumstances that partners get to know each other better, which in most cases may reduce at least the costs of their negotiated transactions. This is what leaves room for an increase in the net gain that the relationship may produce.

In closing, I would like to emphasize that more research is needed to overcome limitations in our knowledge of how resources interdependen-cies limit the dangers of selfish behavior. For instance, obtaining complete information on how every partner in a project relates to *every* other one would allow us to answer important questions. Do projects perform bet-ter when each partner interacts frequently with every other partner? Alternatively, is the existence of a central actor functioning as a coordi-nator in a star-like structure a better way of securing successful imple-mentation of the project? Are projects that attract more resources from outside sources more likely to produce the conditions under which the partners are more likely to extend collaboration, or do projects create these conditions when they function as self-sustained entities? These questions cannot be answered without full knowledge of how *all the partners interact with each other* in each of the 41 projects under study.

In addition, a systematic study of how projects evolve would improve our chances of assessing in more detail how collaboration actually unfolds. This study is limited to the linkage between resource exchange during the application process and opinions about likelihood of collaboration. Documenting carefully how exchanges take place in a project during the whole implementation process and whether organizational actors extend their participation in similar types of collaborative efforts after their participation in that project would provide more definitive information on the link between exchange of resource and sustainability of collaboration.

APPENDIX. DESCRIPTIVE STATISTICS

Variable	Mean	Standard Deviation	Minimum	Maximum
Likelihood of Future Collaboration	3.085	1.098	1	4
Resource Dependence				
Assistance in Technical Information	0.45	0.64	0	2
Assistance in Funding Issues	0.69	0.81	0	2
Assistance in Enhancing Public Buy-in and/or Political Support	0.45	0.70	0	2
Assistance in Permitting/ Regulatory Requirements	0.28	0.57	0	2
District as a Partner	0.23	0.42	0	1
Tie Strength				
Intensity of Relationship	2.950	1.120	1	5
Frequency of Interaction in the Relationship	3.612	1.045	1	5
Achievement of Organization's Expectations when Participating in Project	5.301	1.301	2	7
Size of the Project (in thousands of dollars)	1006.423	1327.022	16	9117
Individual Perception of the Importance of Water Issues	5.807	.751	3.75	7
N = 182				

Note: The means and standard deviations presented in this table are the averages of those values for the five databases utilized in the analysis.

Institutional Collective Action in an Ecology of Games

Mark Lubell, Adam Douglas Henry, and Mike McCoy

The main goal of this volume is to explain how governance authorities in a particular policy arena overcome fragmentation and solve vertical and horizontal collective action problems. Our chapter addresses this goal in two ways: first, we apply Norton Long's (1958) analysis of the ecology of games played in territorially defined metropolitan areas to regional governance, and second, we analyze the relationships between collaboration networks, trust, and political influence in the context of regional land-use and transportation policy. The central argument of the ecology of games framework is that local political outcomes emerge from actors pursuing their self-interest in multiple, interdependent, and rule-structured games. The resulting decisions lead to the type of fragmentation and decision externalities discussed throughout this volume. Collaborative partnerships and networks are considered potential self-organizing mechanisms for overcoming these dilemmas, and our empirical study explicitly examines the resulting patterns of cooperation, trust, and political influence.

Our use of the ecology of games metaphor is partly a reaction to the burgeoning social science literature that examines the dynamics and effectiveness of collaborative processes as new institutions for political decision making. This literature itself has emerged in response to (and perhaps also partly caused) the widespread appearance of collaborative policy and its aliases in nearly every policy subsystem, especially environmental policy (O'Leary, Gerard, and Bingham 2006). These collaborative institutions are designed to alleviate many symptoms of institutional collective action (ICA) problems discussed in this book.

However, there is currently no scientific agreement on the effectiveness of collaborative institutions relative to other types of institutional structures, such as traditional command-and-control policies. One very important reason for this lack of agreement is the great difficulty in measuring actual policy outcomes such as changes in environmental quality (Koontz and Thomas 2006) that can be attributed to the institution being studied. Instead, most research on collaborative policy has focused on more measurable evaluative criteria such as attitudes (e.g., policy satisfaction), behaviors (e.g., levels of collaboration), or project implementation (e.g., scope of project).

Another reason for the continued disagreement is that even the very best studies on collaborative policy make a simplifying assumption that completely ignores the true complexity of decentralized, regional governance. This is the central concern of this chapter, and also the primary advantage of the ecology of games perspective. The vast majority of research on collaborative policy is limited to qualitative (and sometimes quantitative) case studies of a single or small number of collaborative processes (see Sabatier et al. 2005 for discussion). Only a few studies use large-N, comparative research designs (Leach, Pelkey, and Sabatier 2002; Lubell 2003; Heikkila and Gerlak 2005), and among these studies, few directly compare collaborative institutions to some other type of alternative institutional structure. For example, Leach and Sabatier's watershed partnerships project looks only at watersheds with partnerships and not those without partnerships. Lubell's (2003, 2004; Schneider et al. 2003) National Estuary Program study is perhaps the only truly comparative, quasi-experimental study on collaborative policy – it directly compares estuaries with and without a collaborative planning process. However, it does not directly measure or take into account any of the other policy processes or institutions that are in operation in a particular estuary, and estuaries without the National Estuary Program certainly do not exist in an institutional vacuum.

The implicit assumption of this previous research is that the collaborative policy institution under study somehow stands alone as a comparative concept, similar to an experimental treatment. What is ignored is the often vast diversity of institutions that actually exist in any given region, ranging from local government planning, to informal citizen forums, to on-the-ground implementation of state/federal policies. Policy outcomes are really the aggregate consequence of decisions and behaviors that occur within this ecology of policy games. In this chapter we will demonstrate why any single collaborative policy institution should be understood within this ecology.

Furthermore, the literature on partnerships assumes that the idea of cooperation is somehow the exclusive purview of collaborative policy and that other institutions are "noncooperative." We explicitly reject this assumption and posit that building cooperation is the goal of all governance institutions – every institution is trying to solve some type of underlying collective action problem such as a public goods or common pool resource dilemma. Thus, good governance requires the evolution of cooperation in not just collaborative policy venues but across the whole range of other governance games in a particular area, such as city-county planning, natural resources planning, and so on. This is exactly the situation that the ecology of games perspective is best suited to analyze.

Land-use and transportation planning in California, which is the empirical setting for this research, is an excellent example of the ecology of games. We study the emergence of collaborative planning in two regions of California: Merced County in the Central Valley and Amador, Alpine, and Calaveras counties in the Sierra foothills (the Tri-County region). These regions define the territorial policy subsystems in which the ecology of games occurs, and each region has several games related to land-use and transportation planning including a specific collaborative policy process. In our survey, we operationalize these games as city and county planning, environmental review processes, natural resources planning, and the collaborative process at hand. Each of these games derives political authority from some type of legislative or administrative act, with specific policy decisions and resource allocations made in each game. These are also the primary set of games that influence transportation and land-use outcomes in a given region. The ecology of games constitutes the set of governance institutions at hand in each region, which may succeed or fail in facilitating cooperation and solutions to regional collective action problems.

The next section describes some of the main theoretical assumptions of the ecology of games model. The purpose of the theoretical discussion is to motivate a small set of empirically testable hypotheses about the structure of interactions within games and interconnections between games. We then describe in more detail the ecology of games being played in land-use and transportation planning in California, including the role of collaborative planning. The empirical analysis uses survey data from policy elites in two regions of California to estimate the marginal influence of collaborative planning on cooperation throughout the ecology of games as well as the interconnections among policy networks across the ecology of games. The results of this analysis have important implications for the understanding of ICA.

THE ECOLOGY OF GAMES AND COLLABORATIVE PLANNING
IN CALIFORNIA

This section begins by laying out the three main theoretical concepts of
the ecology of games perspective: the structure of games, how community
or regional policy outcomes emerge from the play of multiple games
within a subsystem, and how games are potentially interconnected. We
then develop theoretical hypotheses about collaborative policy and
describe the ecology of games involved in our research setting of collaborative regional land-use and transportation planning in California.

Theoretical Assumptions of the Ecology of Games Framework

Norton Long's fundamental notion of a game, especially as expressed by
Dutton (1995), has many similarities to game-theoretic models. Games
are "arenas of competition and cooperation structured by a set of rules
and assumptions about how to act in order to achieve a particular set of
objectives" (Dutton 1995, 381). Each individual game derives its authority from some type of legislative, administrative, or judicial decision made
at higher levels of the political system.

Political players in games are self-interested, with utility functions
defined by their individual goals. Thus, different players might have different objectives – bureaucrats may seek to maximize budgets, elected
officials may seek votes, and interest groups may seek members. The idea
of a game does not require pitting the efficiency gains from solving collective action problems versus payoffs available from gaining political
influence – both are potentially available and linked in a policy game.
The rules of the game define the available behaviors and payoffs contingent on the choices of other actors.

Although not stated explicitly, Long's idea of game play does not
adhere to the narrow rationality model used by simple game theory models. Players are not necessarily aware of all possible moves and payoffs
associated with all outcomes that allow for rational strategic choice.
Rather, players operate according to a boundedly rational model
with limited cognitive capacities, information, and issue attention
(Baumgartner and Jones 1991). They adapt their strategies and learn over
time as the history of any particular game unfolds, where "random adjust-
ment and piecemeal innovation are the normal methods of response"
(Long 1958, 254) to uncertainty and changes in the political environment.
At any given time, the actors can pay attention to only a small subset of

the entire ecology (Liu and Jones 2005). The uncertainties faced by actors within a particular game are multiplied by the complexity of an ecology of games.

The second theoretical assumption moves from the idea of an individual game to an ecology of games, where the outcomes within any territorially defined political system are a product of interactions within two or more local games. The territorially defined subsystem is not the same as a functional policy arena like "water policy." Rather, multiple issues may be encompassed within a region and the issues may be interconnected through physical, economic, or social processes such that changes in one issue affect parameters in other issues. Individual games may also address single or multiple issues. Decisions and actions within each game produce policy outputs and outcomes, which in turn have consequences for the utility of the actors involved. Sometimes the actors are aware of the consequences of their decisions, but often it is difficult to know all of the relevant outcomes. For example, it is very difficult to evaluate the environmental outcomes of collaborative or other environmental policies. In addition, the outcomes from one game may affect choices and outcomes in other games; hence, the overall outcome for any given policy subsystem is an emergent property of the multiple games at play in the ecology.

An important characteristic of the ecology of games is that there is no institutional mechanism for coordinating action across games within a particular subsystem. In Long's words (255, italics added): "Games go on within the territory, occasionally extending beyond it, though centered in it. But, while the particular games show clarity of goals and intensity, few, if any, treat the territory as their proper object. The protagonists of *things in particular* are well organized and know what they are about; the protagonists of *things in general* are few, vague, and weak." Hence, overall outcomes within a policy subsystem are largely unplanned and unconscious results of behavior within individual games, even though actors may consciously try to pursue combined strategies and coordinate outcomes across multiple games in their own interest. At the same time, actors within individual games will typically ignore the social consequences of their decisions: "The common interest, if such there be, is to be realized through institutional interactions rather than through the self-conscious rationality of a determinate group charged with its formulation and attainment."

The uncoordinated nature of the individual games and actors is, of course, a recipe for the types of institutional collective action problems that are the focus of this book. Fragmentation and decision externalities occur because there are multiple public agencies, elected officials, local governments, and interest groups, each seeking to achieve their own particular objectives. These actors operate within games established by various constitutional, legislative, and administrative laws, such as city planning, regional transportation planning, and environmental impact reporting. The decisions made in each game potentially generate positive or negative externalities that are experienced either vertically or horizontally within the federal system. The ecology of games perspective suggests that actors are often unaware of or ignore these externalities, thus resulting in cumulative policy decisions that have negative effects for an entire region (e.g., increased air/water pollution, traffic, urban sprawl), or fail to engage in mutually beneficial policies (e.g., building a highway project that serves multiple jurisdictions).

The third and last theoretical assumption is that games are possibly interconnected in important ways. We already mentioned that outcomes in one game could affect payoffs or strategies in other games. For example, if a new highway built in the transportation game destroys vernal pool habitat for endangered invertebrate species, then the payoffs and actions in the Endangered Species Act recovery planning game are much different. Games can also be interconnected by actors who play in multiple games, where each game offers different possibilities for achieving particular goals. Actors who play in multiple games may also make use of other actors within one game to achieve goals in another, for example, by gaining political influence or economic resources that could be brought to bear in another arena. As will be seen in the next section, our empirical research is largely driven by trying to understand how the structure of policy interactions varies across games and how collaborative policy can serve as a bridge to connect several games.

But before turning to the hypotheses for collaborative policy, it is important to note some major advantages of the ecology of games perspective for understanding policy and governance in general. The ecology of games perspective encompasses several existing ideas in policy theory, such as Ostrom's (2005) idea about institutional diversity, Baumgartner and Jones's (1991) idea of venue shopping, Blomquist and Schlager's (2005) discussion of polycentric governance, and Feiock's (2007) conceptualization of ICA. The ecology of games perspective also brings the idea of political power and influence back into institutional studies of collective action – actors in the ecology of games are not only interested in solving cooperation dilemmas but may also seek political power to serve their own selfish ends, even at the expense of economic efficiency. Future studies using the ecology of games perspective will need to think hard about how to trace the trade-offs between solving collective action problems and attaining political power – *Bickers et al.*'s chapter in this volume, for example, discusses the potential role of electoral incentives in shaping the interest of local officials in cooperating with those in neighboring municipalities. Finally, the ecology of games framework provides the raw material to begin thinking about a more formal game theoretic or agent-based model analysis. Given the complexity of the ecology of games, we suspect that agent-based evolutionary models will provide the greatest initial insights into ecological dynamics.

COLLABORATIVE POLICY AS SELF-ORGANIZING GOVERNANCE

This section uses the ecology of games perspective to derive hypotheses for two main empirical research questions regarding the ability of collaborative institutions to solve institutional collective-action problems: (1) What is the marginal effect of collaborative policy for improving cooperative attitudes (consensus, fairness, policy satisfaction) and behaviors (cooperative policy implementation)? (2) How are networks of collaboration, trust, and political influence linked across the ecology of games?

The first question directly targets whether collaborative institutions can effectively alleviate the ICA dilemmas that emerge from the fragmented set of policy games in a particular region. The ecology of games perspective suggests two reasons that collaborative institutions may not be very effective. First, Long's argument is at best silent on the ability of governance institutions to integrate across policy games. Long does argue that political leadership and public opinion may provide ways to integrate across games, but governing structures largely emerge as epiphenomena of uncoordinated behavior within the game ecology. The ecology of games argument implicitly rejects institutional theories of politics that assume that higher level institutional structures, such as federalism, can shape cooperation and conflict in lower level games. Even more worrisome is the possibility that collaborative institutions are merely another game added to the ecology and thus may actually reduce the effectiveness of other existing games by straining the resources available to any particular actor for participating in policy decisions. In this sense, collaborative institutions compete with rather than complement existing institutions. If these arguments are true, participation in a collaborative institution at best will not affect overall levels of cooperative attitudes and behaviors, and at worse may decrease cooperation throughout the ecology.

Second, collaborative institutions may serve a function that is similar to Edelman's (1971; see also Lubell 2004) theory of symbolic politics, which provides a pessimistic view that collaborative policy is merely a symbol of political agreement that quells political discontent but does not alleviate the underlying ICA problems. Similarly, in reference to political leadership, Long argues that "to some extent it is clear that the ancient and modern practice of civic magic ritual is functional – functional in the same sense of a medicinal placebo." Civic rituals can function to "tranquilize anxieties" and keep "people from tearing each other apart in the stress of their anxieties" (Long 1958, 257).

There is some empirical evidence that collaborative policy may provide the symbolic function of a civic magic ritual. Lubell (2004) finds that policy actors in estuaries that are within the collaborative National Estuary Program (NEP) have higher levels of consensus but the same levels of cooperation as estuaries outside the NEP. In this case, the collaborative policies of the NEP appear to lead to more positive attitudes but lack any behavioral follow-through. If collaborative policy is only symbolic, then any resources spent engaged in such process are wasted because they only deflect attention away from underlying problems.[1] In the context of this study, symbolic policy would predict that participants in collaborative planning should have more positive attitudes toward policies but should not engage in higher levels of collaboration.

The ecology of games arguments stand in contrast to institutional rational choice (IRC) (North 1990; Ostrom 1990; Libecap 1994; Lubell et al. 2002) approaches, which argue that collaborative policy reduces the transaction costs of cooperation by providing a venue for building agreement on issues, developing social capital among stakeholders, and improving the scientific/information basis of decision making. Extending this argument to the multigame setting, collaborative partnerships provide cross-cutting governance institutions that help actors operating in different games address decision externalities. This hypothesis reflects

---

[1] Long basically assumes that the underlying problems generating the anxiety typically disappear with time, so that symbolic policies reduce conflict until the problem passes. Symbolic policy argues that the problems will continue, which is the more likely case with most environmental problems; for example, an endangered species that goes extinct usually does not reappear some years later.

Coase's idea that externalities cause inefficiencies only when transaction costs prevent voluntary exchange, and also Ostrom's theory that higher level institutions constrain lower level institutions. If the optimistic IRC hypothesis is true, then participants in collaborative planning should have higher levels of cooperative attitudes and behavior.

In addition, the ecology of games perspective allows consideration of potential interactions among games. The optimistic IRC hypothesis suggests the possibility of positive spillovers and synergies between the collaborative process and other traditional policy venues. If collaborative partnerships provide a crucible for crafting social capital and reducing transaction costs, then participation in the collaborative process should also lead to more cooperation in other games. However, many critics of collaborative processes believe they are just a waste of time; they would rather spend their time in the traditional process instead of burdening themselves with collaboration. Furthermore, some actors simply question the effectiveness of the voluntary and inclusive policies emphasized by collaborative groups. If there are negative feedbacks between collaborative policy and more traditional policy games, then participation in collaborative processes will *reduce* the effectiveness of traditional processes. The potential for spillover effects will be analyzed with interaction terms in the empirical models below.

The ecology of games perspective also implies that networks of collaboration, trust, and political influence are potentially linked throughout the ecology of games. As noted in the introduction, successful governance probably requires cooperation across all the games in the ecology, and specific collaborative processes may help build the necessary social capital. If this is true, there should be a positive correlation between networks of collaboration and trust. However, the ecology of games also supposes that actors collaborate in order to gain political influence and achieve their policy preferences. At the very least, actors seek to secure the most favorable distributional outcome from the range of different Pareto-improving possibilities. But the availability of political power also raises the possibility of rent-seeking, so that collaboration can create winning coalitions that implement policies where the costs to losers outweigh the benefits to the winners (Pareto-inefficient). However, this is not a necessary consequence of political power because it can also be used to help secure more widescale and socially efficient cooperation. Although this study cannot empirically distinguish between the socially beneficial versus harmful uses of political power, the prediction asserts a positive correlation between collaboration networks and political influence networks.

The Ecology of Transportation and Land-Use Planning in California

In California, several counties or multicounty regions have put together collaborative processes at regional levels in an attempt to integrate land-use and transportation planning. These collaborative institutions are designed to respond to state and federal transportation law and to alleviate the ICA problems that occur when local jurisdictions make independent land-use and transportation decisions, ignoring regional costs/benefits and cross-domain effects. These are exactly the types of ICA problems predicted by the ecology of games perspective when actors attend only to the outcomes of a narrow, particular game.

Many of the collaborative processes are centered on councils of government (COGs), metropolitan planning organizations (MPOs), or regional transportation planning agencies (RTPAs). Each of these is a regional institution that has attempted to coordinate across multiple local governments on a variety of issues. COGs are voluntary associations of city and county governments, with boards of directors consisting of elected officials from member jurisdictions. The main function of COGs is to assist member local governments with regional planning for issues of multijurisdictional interest, such as housing. Along with a variety of information and data analysis services, COGs often formulate specific policy recommendations to be considered by member governments. However, COGs play a strictly advisory role in planning and the member governments retain all authority for land-use planning.

MPOs and RTPAs both exist to distribute transportation funding to regional and local needs, with MPOs largely handling federal funding and RTPAs state funds. Transportation plans are the key policy instrument of these regional organizations; funding will flow only to approved plans. MPOs exist only in larger metropolitan regions; there are 12 single county MPOs and 4 multicounty MPOs in California. California RTPAs are statutorily required to create regional transportation plans (RTPs) for the area of their jurisdiction every three years in urban areas and every four years in nonurban areas. These regional transportation plans serve as guidelines for the distribution of federal transportation funds to local and regional projects. In regions with MPOs such as Merced, RTPAs and MPOs are combined into the same planning institution. In regions without MPOs, such as the Sierra Tri-County area, RTPAs are the only regional transportation planning agencies. Also, in some cases the COG, RTPA, and MPO are all combined into a single planning entity.

While councils of government, metropolitan planning organizations, and regional transportation planning agencies are the closest thing California has to regional planning institutions, local land-use planning remains the exclusive domain of California's 528 incorporated and chartered cities and, for unincorporated land, planning is the domain of its 58 counties. The only real authority of MPOs and RTPAs comes from the development and approval of regional transportation plans and the distribution of state and federal transportation funds. Along with regional planning entities and local government planning, land-use decisions are also affected by environmental impact statement/review requirements, natural resources planning under laws like the Endangered Species Act, and a variety of other environmental and resource laws and rules. Each law or rule generally determines who can participate in the games and what types of resources are subject to collective decision making.

The actual outcomes of land-use and transportation emerge from a very large ecology of games in a particular region. For example, the outcome of a regional road building project is affected by existing federal and state transportation plans, the land-use plans of local governments in whose jurisdiction the road will go, and a variety of environmental requirements. These same sets of games will affect many other infrastructure or environmental projects in the same region. These games are at best loosely connected across the physical and legal landscape of a particular region, leading to the types of collective action problems and unintended consequences described by the ecology of games.

The collaborative processes in the Merced and Tri-County regions have emerged within this complex ecology of games, and are following a larger statewide trend to build on the existing authorities of councils of government, regional transportation planning agencies, and metropolitan planning organizations as forums for broader collaboration. The collaborative process in Merced County is called the Partnership for Integrated Planning. It started in 2001 as an interagency initiative headed by the Merced County Association of Governments (MCAG – the COG/MPO for this region) and funded by the California Department of Transportation. The goal of the partnership was to collaboratively develop a long-term regional transportation plan for Merced County. Such a plan is the ordinary province of a COG/MPO but this process was expanded to include a much broader range of stakeholders and policies associated with transportation. Even though care was taken to position the institution and process as voluntary and not primarily based on land-use planning, the project did indeed explicitly address the regional links among land-use and transportation policies (McCoy and Steelman 2005).

The Tri-County collaborative planning effort started much later (2005) and is less well known among the actors. Alpine, Amador, and Calveras counties are located in the foothills and mountains of the Central Sierra Nevada. The three counties, along with neighboring Tuolumne County, belong to a common council of government, the Central Sierra Planning Council and Economic Development District, but each county has its own RTPA and conducts its own transportation planning through its individual RTPA arrangements with the cities and the county government in its RTPA jurisdiction. The three regional transportation planning agencies have had some experience in sharing transportation planning as they found that historically scarce transportation funds could be better managed by cooperation than competition. This informal cooperation led to a series of revenue sharing memorandums of understanding (MOU) over the years, but no formal joint planning structure ever evolved from these ad hoc arrangements. In 2005 the California State Department of Transportation proposed that a collaborative transportation planning effort including land use considerations adjunct to transportation planning be undertaken by these RTPAs. The RTPAs agreed to the proposal and received funding from the California Department of Transportation (CALTRANS) to begin a process of joint transportation planning through land use/land cover mapping, growth modelling, and public outreach. At the time of our survey in late 2006 the boards of all three RTPAs and the boards of the relevant counties and most of the cities had considered and approved of the process through an MOU. The mapping and modeling efforts had also begun but organized public outreach had not.

The key insight of the ecology of games perspective is that these collaborative processes in Merced and Tri-County cannot be understood in isolation from all of the other traditional planning processes in those regions, and the outcomes of any collaborative plan do not determine the full range of policy outcomes. Many different actors participate in these games, ranging from state agencies like the California Department of Transportation to local government officials, and environmental and economic development interest groups. Most of these actors participate in more than one policy game, and each game has opportunities for stakeholder participation, requires information gathering from other actors, and sometimes mandates coordination from other agencies. In other words, all of the traditional planning processes have multiple opportunities for cooperation and political discussion. The ecology of games essentially constitutes the governance institutions in these regions, and these governance institutions may succeed or fail in solving regional collective action problems.

SURVEY RESEARCH DESIGN AND EMPIRICAL ANALYSIS

We conducted an Internet/telephone survey of land-use and transportation stakeholders in the Merced and Tri-County regions in the fall of 2006. The survey population was constructed from five separate lists: a state directory of city/county planning officials in each region, lists of participants in the respective collaborative process, all stakeholders in the region identified as participants in environmental impact statements from 2001 to 2006 in the California Environmental Quality Act database, all stakeholders and all planning staff/elected officials from city and county governments within the region, and all project managers listed in the Natural Resources Project Inventory from 2001 to 2006. The population was constructed to reflect our best guess at the entire universe of policy actors associated with land-use and transportation planning in these areas. This is the only way to attempt measuring participation in the ecology of games, as opposed to a specific game. Because we were attempting to measure policy networks as completely as possible, the survey was delivered to all identified stakeholders. The response rate to the survey was 44 percent for Merced and 43 percent for Tri-County.

We conduct two basic types of analyses. First, we estimate the marginal influence of collaborative policy using individual-level cooperative attitudes and behaviors as the dependent variables, with various measures of participation in collaborative policy and traditional planning venues as the main independent variables. The specific collaborative process for Merced is the Partnership in Integrated Planning, and for Tri-County it is mainly the series of MOUs. The traditional planning processes include environmental review processes, city/county planning, transportation planning, and natural resources planning. Each of the traditional processes has a different political authorization, but the decisions made in all of them have historically combined to influence land-use and transportation outcomes. Interaction terms are included to test for negative or positive feedback between collaborative policy and traditional venues. Second, we conduct a series of policy network analyses based on the correlation between networks of collaboration, trust, and perceived influence that have emerged from the total ecology.

Measurement of Cooperative Attitudes and Behaviors

Our dependent variables are four different types of cooperative attitudes and behaviors that are conceptualized as measures of the effectiveness of collaborative policy: cooperative policy implementation, perceived consensus, perceived policy fairness, and policy satisfaction. Following the ecology of games framework, these questions are asked about land-use and transportation policies in general within a particular region, which can be affected by all of the games. This allows us to estimate the marginal influence of participation in different games on the overall indicators of cooperation within a region, as opposed to one specific policy venue.

Cooperative implementation is a scale ranging from 0 to 7 that sums the number of "yes" answers from a list of seven joint policy implementation activities: sharing information/data, sharing personnel, participating in joint research projects, participating in joint grant/funding proposals, participating in interagency taskforces, signing a MOU, or sharing permitting activities. These implementation activities are conceptually distinct from participation in the collaborative process, where the actors are engaged in planning activities. The distinction is similar to Ostrom's (1990) distinction between collective choice (the collaborative process) and operational rules (implementation activities).

The attitudinal scales are all multi-item Likert scales ranging from 1 to 7; responses to individual items are averaged to form the overall scale. *Perceived consensus* (alpha = .85) asks about the level of consensus on seven problem dimensions: severity and causes of problems, research needed, appropriate public policies, economic consequences, environmental consequences, and social consequences of policies. *Perceived fairness* is a three-item scale (alpha = .69) that asks the respondent to rate the overall fairness of regional policies, how well their interests are represented, and whether their participation influences outcomes. This measure of fairness thus includes notions of efficacy. *Policy satisfaction* is a three-item scale (alpha = .78) that asks whether regional policies will resolve problems, have effective leadership, and generate innovative solutions.

Measurement of Policy Game Participation and Control Variables

The most important independent variables are questions that ask the respondent to rate their frequency of participation (0 = Never, 1 = Annually, 2 = Monthly, 3 = Weekly, 4 = Daily) in six policy games: environmental review processes, city/county planning, transportation planning, natural resources planning, any "other" process not listed, and the collaborative process in that region. For Merced, the frequency battery asks specifically about the Partnership for Integrated Planning, while for Tri-County the respondent could name any collaborative process. Our measure of *traditional planning participation* is constructed by a weighted average of the first five games from the above list plus any mention of an "other" process: $\sum_{i=1}^{5} freq_i/4$ where the value of frequency is coded as indicated above. The scale ranges between 0 and 5 with a mean of 1.8, where a 5 indicates daily participation in all five activities.[2]

We measure *collaborative policy participation* by combining the frequency question with a second question that asks about 12 different types of process participation such as speaking with representatives, reading materials, going to meetings, writing plan alternatives, and so on. These two scales are normalized to range between zero and one, and then averaged (alpha = .74; correlation = .61) to provide an overall summary measure. The process participation question asks specifically about the collaborative processes in Merced and Tri-County, as distinct from the traditional processes.

Following Sabatier and Jenkin-Smith's (1993) Advocacy Coalition Framework and previous studies (Lubell 2003; Weible 2006) that have examined the relationship between belief systems and policy perceptions, we include four measures of political values as control variables: environmentalism, economic conservatism, inclusiveness, and smart growth values. *Environmentalism* (alpha = .78) is a three-item scale derived from Dunlap et al.'s (2000) New Ecological Paradigm battery. *Economic conservatism* is a four-item scale (alpha = .65) measuring whether the respondent believes government should not interfere with private property rights. *Inclusiveness* (alpha = .61) is a three-item scale measuring preferences about the appropriate breadth of public participation in policy, with higher values indicating a broader range of interests. *Smart growth* (alpha = .73) is a five-item battery measuring agreement with five smart growth principles: affordable housing, livable communities, cultural diversity, in-fill development, and alternative

---

[2] Note that lower numbers on the traditional planning participation scale could indicate a high level of participation in just one game, or low levels of participation across multiple traditional games. Given the high correlations among participation in the traditional processes, we do not try to quantitatively distinguish among them in this analysis.

transportation. The overall model also includes a dummy variable to differentiate between regions.

Measurement of Policy Networks

The survey includes a battery of social network questions that present each respondent with a list of 53 agencies (e.g., U.S. Department of Transportation) or classes of actors (e.g., developer/real estate), and then asks the respondent to check off the actors with whom they collaborate, whom they trust, and who they believe has the most influence on policy outcomes. It is important to remember that a separate survey question is used to elicit each type of network relationship. The social network battery allows the respondent to name multiple local governments as well as actors not on the original list. This has produced a total of 116 organizational names or classes of actors for Merced and 115 for Tri-County, where each organization represents either the respondent's primary affiliation or the organization/class of actors they checked in a network checklist.

We use the respondent-level survey data to construct organization-to-organization networks, where, consistent with the ICA framework, respondents are assumed to represent the organizations with which they are affiliated. For a given type of network relationship (e.g., trust, collaboration, policy influence), a link exists between organization A and organization B when a respondent affiliated with A reports a relationship with organization B. If more than one respondent from organization A indicates a relationship with organization B, then the value of the link is increased by one; this produces valued networks. For the collaboration networks, these ties are undirected because we assume that collaboration links are reciprocated; the values of any reciprocated ties are averaged across both organizations. For the political influence and trust networks, the ties are directed; if organization A thinks organization B is influential (or trustworthy), we do not assume organization B thinks A is influential (or trustworthy).

We use the network data to construct several metrics for use in the analysis. For the collaboration network, *collaboration degree centrality* is the total number of undirected, valued links for a particular organization. For the trust and policy influence networks, we calculate *in-degree centrality* as the total number of times a particular organization is mentioned as being trusted or influential. The trust and policy influence networks are *directed* networks, where one organization can mention another as trustworthy or influential without a reciprocal mention. These degree centrality measures will be used at the level of the organization. These network measures do not consider participation in different games but rather reflect participation in the overall ecology. However, the assumption is that these networks are a function of all the games combined; it leaves the exact structure of participation across the ecology as implicit.

Last, for first stage of the analysis, we also calculate *trust betweenness centrality*.[3] Betweenness centrality is a social network measure defined as the number of paths between two organizations that pass through the focal organization; for example, if the U.S. Fish and Wildlife Service is connected to CALTRANS through the Environmental Protection Agency (EPA), then the EPA is "between" those two agencies and the path would add one to EPA's betweenness score.

We include trust betweenness for two reasons. First, most theories of collective action suggest that trust provides a critical source of "social capital" that encourages cooperation, and thus organizations that are central in the trust network should also have higher levels of cooperation. Second, the placement in the trust network also reflects the structural opportunities for collaboration experienced by a particular organization vis-à-vis the entire ecology of institutional games at play in a region. For example, CALTRANS is involved with many different policies and projects and therefore is likely to interact with many other actors, which at least provides the opportunity for forming trust-based relationships. Often, empirical studies attempt to capture these types of embedded structural incentives by differentiating between federal, state, and local agencies or some other natural organizational classification that may reflect differences in structural opportunities for collaboration. Network measures may be better indicators of these structural opportunities because they empirically represent how central a particular organization is without relying on assumptions about a particular organizational category.

REGRESSION ANALYSIS: THE MARGINAL EFFECTS OF COLLABORATIVE POLICY

Table 11.1 grounds the analysis by reporting the frequency of participation in the five different policy games and the correlation between

[3] Trust betweenness-centrality is calculated from an undirected, symmetric network in which we assume trust ties are reciprocated. Preliminary analyses include organizational-type dummy variables as well as number of years involved in planning as additional control variables; these variables do not change the main theoretical findings about the effects of participation in different venues.

participation and the four policy outputs. As can be seen, respondents participate on average somewhere between annually and quarterly (column 1, first five rows) in the four traditional planning processes, with the frequency a bit lower for collaborative processes. "Regular" participants are defined as participating at least monthly in a particular venue. The smallest percentage (32.7%) of regular participants is in the local collaborative process, while the largest percentage (59.2%) is in city/county planning. On average, survey respondents report being regular participants in 2.5 policy games.[4] The respondents also indicate participating in an average of 3.8 collaborative process activities in the past three years (column 1, last row). It is important to note that 47 percent of the respondents did not participate in the collaborative process at all (zero activities); among those respondents who did participate, they engaged in an average of 7.3 planning-related activities.

The correlations presented in the last three columns of Table 11.1 provide the first evidence that while collaborative process participation is associated with more positive policy outputs, so are the traditional planning venues. All the traditional venues except city/county planning are positively correlated with cooperative implementation, and all of them have a positive effect on fairness. Participation in transportation planning produces higher levels of satisfaction, but at least according to this bivariate evidence, only collaborative processes have a positive correlation with consensus. Table 11.1 does show collaborative processes make a difference in levels of cooperative behavior – but so do all of the traditional planning processes. Cooperation is not limited to a particular institutional structure that has the label of collaborative planning.

Table 11.2 provides a more robust analysis with linear regression models for all four of the dependent variables, combining data for both regions. Importantly, Table 11.2 contains an interaction term between traditional and collaborative process participation in order to estimate any positive or negative feedbacks discussed in the theory section. With the interaction term included, the coefficients for traditional and

---

[4] Average number of games played is not reported in Table 11.1. The respondents are approximately evenly distributed across game numbers: 16.8 percent are not regular participants in any game; 16.8 percent in one game; 17.2 percent in two games; 13.4 percent in three games; 19.7 percent in four games; and 16 percent in five games.

TABLE 11.1. *Venue Participation Frequency and Relationship to Policy Outputs*

	Mean Participation Level	Percentage of Regular Participants	Cooperative Implementation Activities	Consensus	Policy Satisfaction	Policy Fairness
Environmental Review Processes	2.85	56.3%	.27*	.07	.11	.28*
City/County Planning	2.86	59.2%	.12	.05	.06	.26*
Transportation Planning	2.55	49.1%	.22*	.09	.25*	.31*
Natural Resources Planning	2.76	52.9%	.33*	-.01	.01	.15*
Collaborative Process Frequency	2.03	32.7%	.34*	.14*	.27*	.35*
Collaborative Process Activities	3.84	N/A	.35*	.08	.18*	.23*

Notes: Cell entries in Column 2 are average scores for frequency of participation in policy venues as measured on 5-point scale (Never, Annually, Monthly, Weekly, Daily) and collaborative process activities selected from a checklist of 13 options. "Regular" participants are defined as participating at least monthly in a particular venue. Columns 3 through 6 show correlations between venue participation scores and policy outputs. * Reject null hypotheses of correlation = 0, $p<.05$.

TABLE 11.2. *Regression Analysis of Policy Outputs*

	Cooperative Implementation	Perceived Policy Fairness	Policy Satisfaction	Perceived Consensus
Policy Game Participation				
Traditional Policy Processes	.82(.16)*	.54(.10)*	.29(.11)*	.19(.11)^
Collaborative Processes	6.11(1.10)*	2.75(.70)*	2.55(.79)*	1.52(.76)*
Interaction: Traditional × Collaborative Process	−1.66(.44)*	−.89(.28)*	−.18(.06)*	−.43(.30)
Policy-Core Beliefs				
Environmental Values	−.003(.09)	−.16(.06)*	−.18(.06)*	.02(.06)
Inclusiveness	−.12(.13)	.11(.08)	.17(.09)^	−.12(.09)
Economic Conservatism	−.14(.10)	.06(.06)	.09(.07)	.28(.07)*
Smart Growth	.13(.16)	−.12(.10)	.20(.11)^	.03(.11)
Control Variables				
Trust Betweenness Centrality	.002(.0007)*	.0002(.0004)	−.0003(.0005)	−.0006(.0005)
Tri-County Region	−.15(.26)	.12(.17)	.27(.19)	.02(.18)
Constant	2.22(.99)*	3.25(.63)*	1.12(.71)	3.29(.68)*
Model Fit	$F = 4.47^*$ Adj. $R^2 = .13$	$F = 9.10^*$ Adj. $R^2 = .25$	$F = 4.47^*$ Adj. $R^2 = .16$	$F = 2.99^*$ Adj. $R^2 = .08$

Note: Table entries are unstandardized slope coefficients from linear regression model; standard errors in parentheses. * Reject null hypothesis that coefficient = 0, $p<.05$, ^ $p<.10$, one-tailed tests.

collaborative process participation should be interpreted as the marginal effect of that particular process when participation in the other process is zero. When participation in the traditional processes is zero, then collaborative processes do indeed have a positive marginal effect on cooperative implementation, perceived fairness, policy satisfaction, and consensus. At the same time, when participation in collaborative processes is zero, then traditional planning processes increase the levels of all the cooperative behaviors and attitudes. Remember that the traditional process scale ranges from 0 to 5 while the collaborative process scale ranges from 0 to 1. Therefore, multiplying the traditional policy coefficient by its range allows comparison of the magnitudes of the effects across the range of the scales. By this calculation, the main effects of the two different types of processes are about equal for each independent variable.

However, the interaction term is negative, statistically significant, and large in magnitude in all but the consensus model (where it is still negative but not significant). As participation in the collaborative process increases, the positive relationship between traditional processes and cooperative attitudes/behaviors decreases. The interaction effect can also be interpreted in reverse: as participation in traditional processes increases, the marginal positive effect of participation in collaborative processes decreases. The *negative* feedback between collaborative and traditional processes is consistent with two hypotheses. The collaborative process may be *raising* transaction costs by increasing the workload and time demand of policy actors with limited resources. Or actors who choose to participate in a collaborative process might find the traditional processes ineffective; one of the traditional justifications for collaborative processes is that they can address problems that traditional processes have failed to solve. At the same time, actors who prefer traditional processes may disagree with the decision style of collaborative processes.

A more detailed picture of the interaction effects is provided by analyzing the data using separate regression equations for each region. Institutional rational choice theories, rightly understood, are centrally concerned with matching the appropriate institutional structure to the particular circumstances of a given collective action problem. In some cases, there may be positive interactions between collaborative and traditional processes, while in other cases there may be negative effects.

Figure 11.1 maps the interaction effects by showing for each region how the marginal influence of the collaborative process varies as a function of traditional process participation.[5] The dependent variables are cooperative implementation, policy satisfaction, and fairness. For lower levels of traditional process participation, collaborative policy appears to have a greater effect on cooperative attitudes and behaviors in the Tri-County region (e.g., coefficient of 4.12 for Merced versus 7.6 when traditional process participation is zero). At the same time, the slopes of the interaction effects are steeper in Tri-County than in Merced, suggesting a more severe negative trade-off between collaboration and traditional processes.

Furthermore, in both cases, the marginal effect of the collaborative process is actually *negative* at very high levels of participation in traditional planning processes. A collaborative process will actually reduce

---

[5] The formulas for these lines are the derivative of the regression results taken with respect to the collaborative process variable, which have the following basic format: dy/d (collaboration) = collaboration coefficient + (interaction coefficient) * (level of participation in traditional planning).

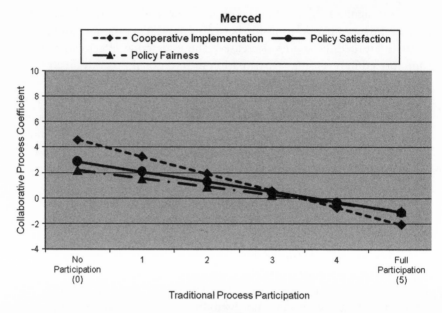

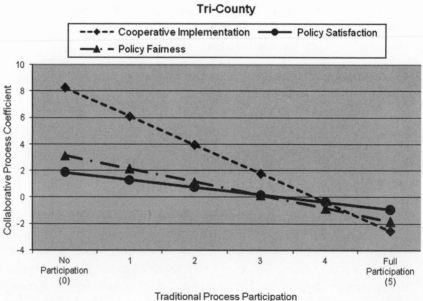

FIGURE 11.1. Marginal Effect of Collaborative Process as Function of Traditional Process Participation.

cooperative attitudes and behaviors among those actors heavily committed to other policy games. The structure of the interaction terms indicates important trade-offs between traditional and collaborative processes in terms of their effects on cooperation. For example, Figure 11.2 shows the predicted number of cooperative implementation activities as a function of collaborative process participation for four different levels of traditional process participation: minimum, low, high, and maximum. The predicted values are derived from the model in Table 11.2 (combining both regions); the other independent variables are held at their mean values. Similar graphs could be drawn for the attitude variables.

Figure 11.2 shows that the highest level of cooperation occurs when traditional policy process participation is at the minimum and collaborative process participation is at the maximum. The lowest level of cooperation occurs when participation is at a minimum in both types of games. But at the same time, cooperation is also relatively high when traditional process participation is at the maximum and collaborative process participation is at the minimum. And because of the negative feedback, low levels of cooperation also occur when participation in both games is at the maximum. This suggests an either/or situation – to increase cooperation, either fully participate in collaborative processes or traditional processes. Do not completely avoid participation, but do not fully commit to both processes at once. Interestingly, the predicted levels of cooperation from the actual sample range from 1.5 to 7.8, with a mean of 4.2 – these actors are not maximizing opportunities for cooperation. These patterns may emerge because of strategic venue selection or because there is a budget constraint on cooperation. However, a positive correlation (Pearson's $r = .40$) between traditional process and collaborative process participation supports the budget constraint interpretation.

In terms of the Advocacy Coalition Framework and policy-core beliefs, environmentalists, in general, are less satisfied with regional policies and believe they are less fair. Inclusiveness increases the level of perceived satisfaction; people who want to include a wide range of interests tend to believe that some common ground can be found among them. Economic conservatism increases the level of perceived consensus; we are not sure exactly why this occurs although it may be a signal of satisfaction with the status quo. For example, growth machine theories suggest that local policy generally favors economically conservative development interests; this would be consistent with unhappy environmental interests.

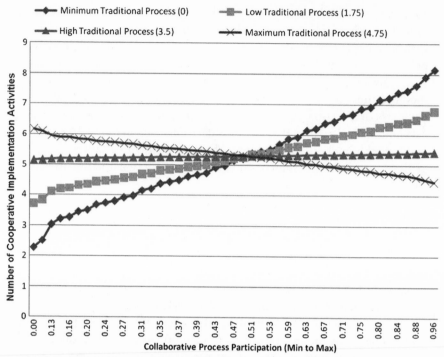

FIGURE 11.2. Predicted Number of Implementation Activities.

It is interesting to note that policy-core beliefs are significant only in the attitudinal models and do not affect collaborative behavior at all. The structural incentives for cooperative behavior provided by the ecology of games may override the influence of policy-core beliefs. There are plenty of environmentalists working in the U.S. Forest Service who are forced to collaborate with ideologically distant actors just because of regulatory requirements such as Section 7 of the Endangered Species Act. More fine-grained analysis of ideological differences among actors is needed to understand how ideological beliefs shape collaborative networks.

Network Analysis: The Structure of Collaboration, Trust, and Political Influence

The central question in this section is whether networks of collaboration are associated with greater levels of political influence, or greater levels of trust, or both. The first step is to analyze differences in the network structure for each type of network relationship. The network diagrams in Figures 11.3a and 11.3b show the top 10^6 most connected actors for the collaboration, trust, and perceived influence networks in both regions. The lines (collaboration) and arrows (perceived influence/trust) show which actors are connected, and the size of the circles is proportional to the numbers of connections; larger circles mean more connected actors.

Four basic categories of actors appear to be central players throughout these different types of networks. A variety of California state agencies are involved, most notably the Department of Transportation (CALTRANS), California Fish and Game, the Regional Water Quality Control Board, and the Air Pollution Control District. These state agencies are central players in policy implementation given their authority to approve transportation plans, grant permits, and provide funding. Federal agencies are more involved in the Tri-County region, which, due to the location in the Sierra foothills, has more of an interface with federal public lands. A second category is the regional governance institutions such as the Merced Council of Governments and the regional transportation planning authorities, which have always been at the center of transportation planning and intergovernmental coordination. Third, the local governments themselves, both counties and cities, are generally the entities that directly experience the costs and benefits of specific transportation projects and also have the most control over land-use decisions. Last, there are some specific interest groups involved in the process, especially real estate development and farming/ranching, which often directly benefit from increased development. Environmental groups do not appear to be central players except that land trusts are influential in Merced, most likely because they are involved with preserving agricultural landscapes through conservation easements. The lack of environmental interest groups suggests that "growth machine" politics are at play in land-use and transportation planning; this may explain the negative coefficients on environmental values seen in Table 11.2.

Examining the network diagrams alone is not sufficient to understand the role of collaborative institutions within the ecology of games; the diagrams rely heavily on visual interpretation. The next step is to examine the relationships between collaboration degree centrality, trust in-degree

---

[6] If there is a tie for tenth, we include all the tied organizations.

Merced Collaboration Network

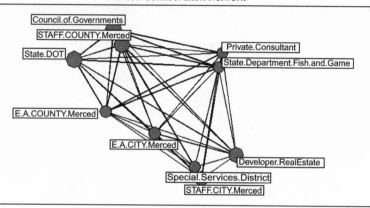

Merced Trust Network

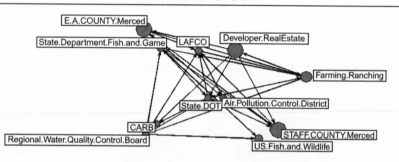

Merced Perceived Influence Network

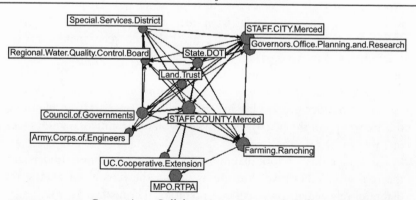

FIGURE 11.3a. Comparing Collaboration, Perceived Influence, and Trust Networks in Merced County. *Note*: E.A. refers to elected/appointed officials.

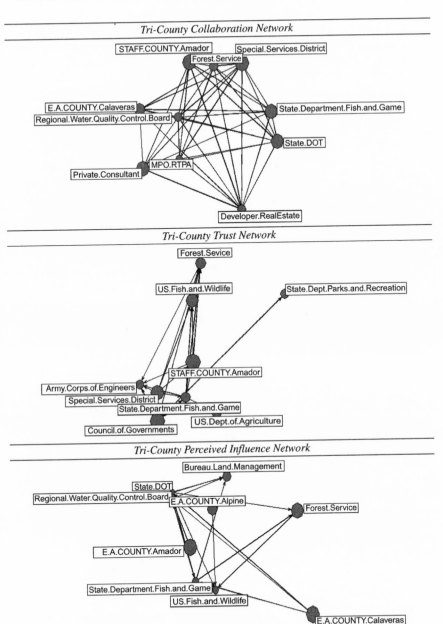

FIGURE 11.3b. Comparing Collaboration, Perceived Influence, and Trust Networks in Tri-County. *Note*: E.A. refers to elected/appointed officials.

centrality, and perceived influence in-degree centrality throughout the ecology of games. Are collaborative relationships more associated with political influence or trust networks? The question is predicated on the assumption that these networks evolve over time from the underlying ecology of games and not just one single game. The earlier analyses support this claim by showing how both participation and collaboration are spread throughout the different games. However, the ecology of games framework also implies that game-specific networks are formed among those actors who participate in particular games. The best way to measure such game-specific networks would be to ask network question for each game in which an actor participates (e.g., Whom do you trust in the collaborative process? Whom do you trust in city/county planning?). The global networks measured here are essentially accumulated from the underlying set of game-specific networks.

Figure 11.4 shows three scatterplots, with collaboration degree centrality on the x-axis and trust in-degree centrality and perceived influence in-degree centrality as points on the y-axis. The figure shows the observations for Merced and Tri-County separately, as well as the combined observations. The fitted bivariate regression lines reveal the interesting pattern that while both relationships are positive, collaboration has a stronger influence on perceived influence. Table 11.3 presents a more precise analysis by reporting the correlation coefficients between trust, perceived influence, and collaboration degree distributions as well as regression results with collaboration degree centrality as the dependent variable and trust and perceived influence as independent variables. The regressions control for the total number of games participated in by each actor and the region.

The correlations confirm the positive relationships between collaboration, trust, and perceived influence, although the correlations are about equal. The regression coefficients are a more direct reflection of the scatterplots in Figure 11.4, with collaboration having the strongest effect on perceived influence. The difference between the correlation and regression results highlights the critical causal assumption in Figure 11.4 and the regression analysis: collaboration networks are producing trust and political influence. If this assumption is accepted, the results suggest that collaboration is even more important for producing political power than for trust. This is consistent with the ecology of games framework but would be surprising to the more prevalent argument that collaboration produces social capital.

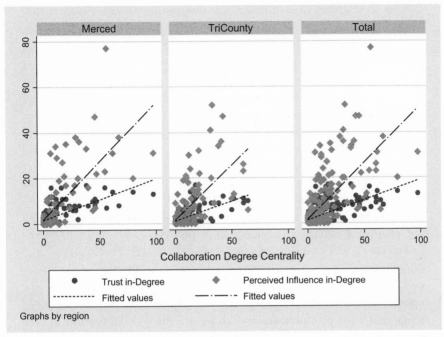

FIGURE 11.4. Scatterplots of Collaboration Degree Centrality and Trust/Perceived Influence In-Degree.

TABLE 11.3. *Relationships among Collaboration, Trust, and Perceived Influence Degree Distributions*

	Trust in-Degree		Perceived Influence in-Degree	
	Correlation	Regression	Correlation	Regression
Collaboration Degree Centrality	.68*	.16(.02)*	.68*	.46(.04)*
Number of Games	n/a	.11(.11)	n/a	−1.25(1.19)
Tri-County Region	n/a	−.66(.43)	n/a	.48(.31)
Constant	n/a	1.52(.32)*	n/a	1.72(.89)*
Model Fit	n/a	F = 66.95* Adj. R² = .46	n/a	F = 69.97* Adj. R² = .47

Note: Table entries are pairwise Pearson correlation coefficients and unstandardized slope coefficients from linear regression model; regression standard errors in parentheses. * Reject null hypothesis that coefficient = 0, $p<.05$, ^ $p<.10$, one-tailed tests.

The correlations do not make any assumption about causality; they allow for the very realistic possibility of reciprocal relationships. A given actor may develop collaborative relationships in order to earn trust or political influence. However, actors might also be invited to collaborate because of existing levels of trust or political influence. We would predict the existence of these types of reciprocal dynamics, and how they play out between types of network relations and among different games is an important avenue of future research. Untangling these relationships will require better instrumental variables (which we do not have) or, more likely, panel analysis that allows observation of change over time. Game-specific networks will help further understanding of how different games are interconnected. Intriguingly, a regression with the collaboration degree as the dependent variable produces the following estimated equation: *Collaboration in-Degree* = $-.64 + 1.36 *$ *Trust in-Degree* $+.49 *$ *Perceived Influence in-Degree* $-1.42 *$ *Tri-County* $+1.49 *$ *Number of Venues*.[7] These results suggest that trust produces more collaboration than perceived influence, which is consistent with the equality of the correlation coefficients. This raises the tantalizing possibility that trust produces collaboration, and then collaboration in turn produces political power. While it is impossible to conclude that such an asymmetry exists, it is clear that both trust and political power are at play within the ecology of games.

SUMMARY

The hypotheses and analyses in this chapter are driven by the fundamental insight that institutional collective action can only be understood within a context of the complex ecology of policy games being played within a particular territorially defined policy subsystem. This ecology is what really constitutes governance within a subsystem – there is no single governance institution. Overall policy outcomes emerge from the collective decisions about the allocation and use of resources being made in each of these games. At the same time, actors participate in different games to earn both social capital and political influence; it is likely that social capital and political influence also lead to more cooperation. The lack of coordination among individual games leads to the types of ICA

---

[7] All the coefficients are statistically different from zero at p<.05 except for the Tri-County dummy variable.

dilemmas often ascribed to fragmented governance, as reflected in unintended consequences and uncontrollable cumulative effects.

To what extent can a collaborative process serve as a self-governance mechanism, and what are the feedbacks between collaborative institutions and other games? Our analysis suggests that collaborative processes do indeed have a positive marginal influence on cooperation – stakeholders who participate in collaborative processes appear to have higher levels of collaborative implementation activities, think the regional policies are fairer, and are generally more satisfied with policy effectiveness. But the positive influence of collaborative processes faces diminishing returns in its contribution over and above the impact of participation with other policy venues. Expending resources in the context of a collaborative process appears to reduce the availability of those resources for building relationships in the context of other policy games. This is because cooperation is not limited to collaborative processes. Every other traditional policy venue has structural requirements and opportunities for cooperation. In some sense, regional governance has always required cooperation among multiple actors; the necessity for cooperation is by no means new. The benefits of collaborative processes must be balanced with the necessity of developing cooperation in other venues.

To what extent are actors instrumentally using participation in collaborative processes to earn social capital or political influence in other games? Our analysis suggests that both political influence and trust are important resources for actors who span multiple games. There is also circumstantial evidence that collaboration networks are more important for producing political influence than for building new social capital. Unfortunately, our data and research design are not yet sophisticated enough to conclusively disentangle the dynamics among cooperation, trust, and political influence, nor to show how these network relationships emerge from different games within the ecology. However, the importance of political influence is not necessarily a negative phenomenon from the perspective of social welfare, because governance may be most effective when the actors with the most political authority are able to form sets of institutions that allow them to capture gains from cooperation. Political influence would only conflict with solutions to collective action problems when it is used to benefit one actor or coalition at the expense of others, especially when the social costs outweigh the individual benefits.

We believe that Long's ecology of games framework deserves a more central place in the study of ICA. Even at this early stage in the empirical research, we think the framework provides a stronger theoretical foundation for understanding the causes of fragmentation and decision externalities. The ecology of games framework requires considering how all of the institutions combine to solve – or cause – collective action problems. Future research needs to include better identification of games and measurement of game-specific behavior, dynamic analyses that show the consequences of leaving and joining games over time for the structure of policy networks and the availability of political resources, and more formal mathematical or computational analyses of game ecologies that can sharpen the theory and hypotheses.

12

Enhancing Vertical and Horizontal Self-Organization

Harnessing Informal Networks to Integrate Policies within and between Governments in the European Union

Paul W. Thurner

The European Union (EU) faces considerable challenges in developing efficient institutions to integrate preferences of many state and substate units for decisions ranging from constitutional to minor policy decisions. Existing approaches tend to focus exclusively on the formal allocation of power, thereby completely neglecting the informal forces at work in decision-making processes. In this chapter I argue that the informal, self-organizing administrative networks already developed within the formal framework of European Union decision making provide a natural model for designing more effective and efficient decision frameworks for negotiations during intergovernmental conferences dealing with constitutional treaty-making. I first analyze the institutional collective action (ICA) problems encountered by the existing formal negotiating structures in terms of the collective action problems they imply. I then demonstrate how existing administrative networks can be identified on both the national and the EU level, and argue that these networks could provide the basis for selecting negotiation teams and creating better decision structures. The analysis focuses on the EU, but the basic argument applies in metropolitan, regional, national, or supernational settings whenever existing units of government facing horizontal ICA problems attempt to negotiate a constitution to resolve them.

ICA AND THE SECOND-ORDER FREE-RIDER PROBLEM IN CONSTITUTIONAL DEVELOPMENT: THE EUROPEAN UNION

The European Union is a hybrid multi-tiered political system with marked problems of fragmentation of authority and extensive ICA

problems. Experts on EU regional integration are divided on the following main questions: what is the optimal amount of centralized joint
decision-making rights and how should policy-specific competencies
(legislative initiative and adoption, implementation) be allocated to
the different levels of government? Authors like Hix (2005) or Dann
(2007) designate the present political system of the EU as a de facto
"executive federalism"[1]: national governments more and more initiate
and adopt legislative acts at the EU level whereas implementation continues to be strictly reserved to the national levels. There is a constant
competition between the European Commission as the supranational
agenda setter and the national governments and their administrations.
An open question is therefore how the member states achieve consensus
on explicit stipulations on the formal allocation of rights to be inserted
in a constitutional treaty.

The history of negotiations illustrates the great difficulty in reaching
an agreement. In 1996/7, 210 years after the adoption of the U.S. constitution, the fifteen EU nations (EU-15) negotiated an intergovernmental treaty that was intended to prepare the institutional architecture for
an enlarged union of 25 to 27 member states. Due to irresolvable conflicts, many of the negotiation issues with regard to the future institutional design had to be postponed to the next EU Intergovernmental
Conference in 2001 in Nice, which again resulted in the adoption of
only provisional decision rules. Note that the Amsterdam and the Nice
treaty stipulation set the stipulations for the current institutional status
quo so far. This is due to the fact that the 2003/2004 intergovernmental
conference finally adopted a constitution for Europe, but referendums in
two of the founding member states failed to ratify it in 2005. Despite
having changed the procedure by involving nongovernmental experts
in the European Convention, the constitution project was aborted. In
2007, after renegotiating parts of the constitutional text, member states
finally agreed that the notion of a constitution will be avoided in the
next intergovernmental treaty. Even the future of this so-called Lisbon
treaty remains uncertain after a rejection by the Irish electorate in June
2008.

Where does this inconsistency between official declarations, intergovernmental agreements, and actual support of a European constitution by

---

[1] For a discussion of the federal character of the political system of the EU, cf. Bednar,
Ferejohn, and Garrett 1996, and Keleman 2003.

the member states come from? How could a decision-making process be designed to reach a renegotiation-proof or optimal contract? To answer these questions, my analysis draws on the literature on informal structures in bureaucratic hierarchies (Breton and Wintrobe 1982; Wintrobe 1997; Breton 1998)[2] and their role in formal constitution-building (Coleman 1990; Knight 1992). In particular, I focus on how to create teams (Holmstrom 1982) responsible for the intragovernmental (national) coordination of multiple task completion (Holmstrom and Milgrom 1991) and vested with the mandate to negotiate intergovernmentally. Note that tasks in the following context consist of preparing domestically negotiation positions for a series of constitutional issues to be negotiated intergovernmentally.

In the view of sociologist James Coleman (1990), constitutions represent a way to allocate the decision and control rights between the participating "elementary individuals" and the resulting corporate actor. Setting up such contracts can be considered a joint project of the group. Therefore, creating and implementing norms and constitutions amounts to producing public goods which can be represented as an n-person prisoner's dilemma game: everyone benefits from the norms, but no single actor can decide and implement them alone. Those who take the initiative have sure costs without certainty that the contract will be successful and profitable, so not investing in the process of institutionalization is a dominant strategy. Thus, the process of negotiating a contract to create a new corporate actor involves the well-known second-order free-rider problem of developing institutions. Therefore, to induce a successful constitution-creation process in self-organizing settings, it is important to minimize this problem by keeping the transaction costs of institutionalization as low as possible and developing adequate incentives to participate for self-organizing subsets of actors.

Most of the time small groups of elites, later considered to be founding fathers, develop and consent to a constitutional contract. In the case of the EU, these elementary individuals intending to invent a constitution are corporate actors with complex internal principal-agent relations

---

[2] "Informal structures are the coalitions or networks of unofficial relationships which play a continuous role, sometimes positive and sometimes negative, in the transmission of commands, in the collection and communication of information and in the coordination of tasks inside and, at times, beyond the confines of organizations" (Breton 1998, 187).

themselves.[3] Under current practice, EU intergovernmental conferences are conducted under the responsibility of the heads of state or government, assisted by their foreign affairs ministries. The foreign affairs ministries have the formal monopoly to represent the nation-states externally and they have a mandate to negotiate an intergovernmental constitutional contract.

A crucial second-order problem of public good provision (see Heckathorn 1989; Coleman 1990, 270–286) and of task-related information provision arises during the phase of preparing the negotiation issues. Functionally specialized ministries maintain a monopoly of expertise with regard to the impact of task-related policy externalities, leading to asymmetric information (Hayes-Renshaw and Wallace 2006). Specialized ministries regularly meet in the Council of Ministers. Currently, the Council of the EU is represented by the sectoral ministers of the member states and is therefore also called the Council of Ministers: "Depending on the issue on the agenda, each country will be represented by the minister responsible for that subject (foreign affairs, finance, social affairs, transport, agriculture, etc.)."[4] These formal meetings resulted in the development of informal transgovernmental networks among ministries and their officials that potentially undermine the foreign affairs ministries' formal monopoly of communication during intergovernmental conferences.

Given these institutional preconditions, how then can an optimal constitutional contract be achieved? According to Coleman, "a constitution is optimal if, in the system that results, rights for each class of actions are allocated in accordance with the interests of those who, post-constitutionally, have power-weighted interests that are stronger than the opposing power-weighted interests" (Coleman 1990, 355). As long as constitutional contracts do not mirror the power relations of the pre-constitutional power relations, they are not sustainable. As "formal

---

[3] "The U.S. Constitution recognized two sets of elementary actors explicitly by establishing two representative assemblies: the House of Representatives, in which each citizen was to be equally represented, and the Senate, in which each state was to be equally represented by two senators, regardless of the number of citizens within it. . . . In fact, the debates of the Constitutional Convention of 1787 concerned not the balance between the rights of persons and those of the federal government, but the balance between the rights of states and those of the federal government. For most purposes, one can say that in the constitutional deliberations leading to the formation of the United States, the constituent states were more nearly the relevant individuals than were natural persons" (Coleman 1990, 367).

[4] Cf. http://www.consilium.europa.eu/showPage.asp?id=242&lang=en&mode=g.

constitutions have their sociological origins in informal norms and rules" (Coleman 1990, 327; Knight 1992), it is necessary to take account of the pre-constitutional informal interaction process (Breton 1998) in order to create positive incentives and governance schemes post-constitutionally.

The preparation of such constitutional agreements and their effective implementation requires that ministerial jurisdictions of the involved states work together both within and between states. Informal administrative cooperation facilitates the provision of second-order public goods (cf. Lazega 2000; Panchanathan and Boyd 2004). To the extent that transaction costs are small, subsets of administrative actors collaborate in constitutional norm creation and implementation. These subsets may become power cores of a constitutional process. The theory of efficient bureaucratic hierarchies postulates that superiors in the process should actively accumulate vertical power and control the horizontal networks (Breton 1998, 188). A crucial prerequisite is the implemention of a design that ensures efficient and effective information extraction (Holmstrom 1982). To avoid moral hazard problems,[5] Holmstrom (1982, 325) proposes an incentive scheme in which "aggregate measures like peer averages provide sufficient information about common uncertainties." In short, the design of a new constitutional negotiation process must adequately reflect the existing informal control of critical information and the incentives of those controlling the information.

I propose an integrated perspective on how to reduce the second-order free-rider problem by creating structural incentives that encourage administrations to engage in costly inter-institutional cooperation. To illustrate this perspective, I apply a historical counterfactual thought experiment (Tetlock and Belkin 1996) to a real case, that is, to the Intergovernmental Conference 1996 leading to the Amsterdam treaty. I show how teams with the mandate to negotiate such contracts could have been composed in a way that would meet the double criteria of within-governmental communicative effectiveness and efficiency as well as of transgovernmental interface legitimacy.

I begin this exercise by determining for each country the preexisting formal assignments of ministerial authority to develop the country's

---

[5] "Moral hazard refers to the problem of inducing agents to supply proper amounts of productive inputs when their actions cannot be observed and contracted for directly" (Holstrom 1982, 324).

negotiation positions on each treaty negotiation issue. To understand the informal networks that evolved under the formal structure, I next survey all involved ministerial jurisdictions to identify the peer-perceived real authority of the administrative agents with regard to the same issues. I then use the survey information to compose our virtual negotiation teams based on perceived authority, which differ significantly from the formally designated authorities in 1996–1997.

My proposed governance form is called a *process management of functional specialists*, which maintains the social capital of established ministerial divisions while enhancing flexibility as well as incentive compatibility. After introducing the case study to be analyzed and discussing the organizational concept in this section, the following two sections illustrate how results of the case study can be used to design national teams as well as federal teams according to the process management concept.

THE CASE STUDY

The Intergovernmental Conference (IGC) of 1996 represents one step of EU institutional reform comparable to the Maastricht Treaty (1992) or the Nice Treaty (2000). The IGC began in March 1996 and concluded with the Amsterdam summit in June 1997. The IGC assembled 15 national delegations mostly comprised of four to five top officials of the respective foreign ministries and of the permanent national diplomatic representations in Brussels, so the negotiation teams were dominated by the foreign affairs departments.[6] The public portrayal of IGC negotiations suggested that issues were resolved by heads of states over the course of a few days (and nights), but this portrayal obscured the lengthy preparations that preceded the summit. Negotiations took place over the course of 16 months and relied on formal and informal coordination between and within the member states.

As part of the negotiations, each nation had to develop nationally acceptable positions as a basis for the highly strategic international meetings. Positions were required for 46 predetermined negotiation issues, which I consolidate into nine policy domains I will refer to as tasks for

---

[6] The list of all delegation members is documented in Thurner, Pappi, and Stoiber (2002).

this analysis.[7] The interministerial preparation of negotiation positions can then be understood as a problem of managing distributed, specialized decision making, where the divisions are ministries and their respective bureaucracies and clients. To develop these positions, each nation delegated the task of developing national positions to relevant ministries. The pattern of delegation was quite important because ministries represent different constituencies. The assumption of simple jurisdictions as well as of exclusive competencies (the "minister as a dictator," see Laver and Shepsle 1996) does not apply to cabinets in the real world. Cabinets, as a rule, consist of complex jurisdictions with multiple, cross-cutting, and shared formal competencies. Determining which ministry would be the agenda setter and which would be an agent with competing or no responsibilities, respectively, was critical in determining the motivations of the ministries and their constituencies.[8]

The complexity of the resultant delegation is illustrated in Figure 12.1, which presents the ministerial interdependencies within the German government for IGC preparations. The agenda setting rights and competing responsibilities for these tasks presented in Figure 12.1 were reconstructed from official documents.[9] Circles represent each ministry, and squares represent the nine tasks. Lines connecting the ministries and tasks indicate the formal assignment of responsibilities and competencies. The two offices in the middle – Ministry of Foreign Affairs (MFA) and Ministry of Economics (MEco) – are assigned formal authority for the most tasks. Additionally, the parliamentary committee

---

[7] The tasks include 46 negotiations issues that have been regrouped into homogenous groups comprising N negotiation issues: Task 1: Fundamental Legal Questions (N = 8), Task 2: Common Foreign and Security Policy (N = 7), Task 3: Justice and Home Affairs (N = 6), Task 4: Collective Decision-Making within the Institutional Bodies of the EU (N = 9), Task 5: Balance of Power between the Institutional Bodies of the EU (N = 5), Task 6: Transferring Further Competences to the EC in Matters of (a) Employment, (b) Environment, (c) Energy, Civil Protection, and Tourism, (d) External Economic Relations (N = 6). The negotiation issues and the legal options have been prepared by the Legal Service of the Council and have been distributed to the Foreign Ministries.

[8] The following acronyms will be used for indicating the subgovernmental units: Premiers Offices = PO; Ministries of Agriculture = MAgr; Ministries of Defence = MDef; Ministries of Foreign Affairs = MFA; Ministries of the Interior = MI; Ministries of Justice = MJ; Ministries of Finance = MF; Ministries of Economy = MEco; Ministries of Labour = MLab; Ministries of Social Affairs = MSoc; Ministries of the Environment = MEnv; EU-Committee of the Parliament = EU-C; Chamber of the Federal Status = FS.

[9] According to §15 and §19 of the Joint Standard Operating Procedures of the German Government.

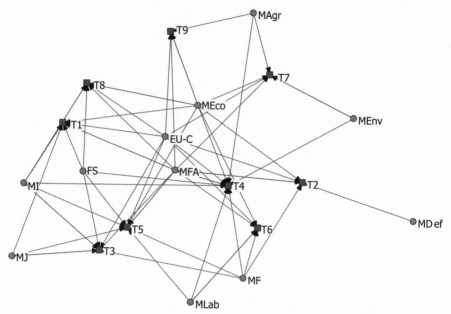

FIGURE 12.1. Formal Competences as a Network: Agenda Setting and Competing Responsibilities. *Notes*: T: Tasks 1-9; Ministries of Agriculture = MAgr; Ministries of Defense = MDef; Ministries of the Interior = MI; Ministries of Justice = MJ; Ministries of Finance = MF; Ministries of Economy = MEco; Ministries of Labor = MLab; Ministries of the Environment = MEnv; EU-Committee of the Parliament = EU-C; Chamber of the Federal States = FS.

responsible for European Affairs (EU-C) had to be involved – and was therefore a central player formally. The Premier's Office (PO) does not appear because it had a general supervisory role but no direct task competencies.

Figure 12.1 shows how the official authority structure of government can be represented as a "two-mode" network. Contrary to the simplifying assumption of governments as unitary actors and cabinets as consisting of simple jurisdictions, network analysis is capable of representing complex interdependencies in nonhierarchical as well as hierarchical structures. The analytical divide I emphasize is therefore not between official hierarchies and networks but between different network structures representing administrative hierarchy and self-organizing information networks. Nor do I support the common juxtaposition of markets and hierarchies as the ends of a spectrum with networks as a governance form that falls between the ends, since network analysis can be applied to markets and hierarchies as well as all intermediate forms. The complex externalities arising from overlapping responsibilities in Figure 12.1 cannot be internalized into a hierarchical form by simply restructuring the departments and requires the more sophisticated forms of coordination that network analysis is capable of representing.

PROCESS MANAGEMENT WITH FUNCTIONAL SPECIALISTS: ANALYZING INFORMAL ADMINISTRATIVE NETWORKS TO SELECT NEGOTIATION TEAMS

Using a thought experiment I next provide a counterfactual answer to the following question: how can national teams vested with the mandate to coordinate domestically and to negotiate internationally be composed to maximize both communicative efficiency and communicative effectiveness within governments as well as communicative interface legitimacy between governments? The organizational design of process management with functional specialists is based on informal administrative networks. The result, as will be shown, stands in clear contrast to the negotiation teams that were mostly composed of Foreign Affairs officials.

The coordination of multiple governmental agents with responsibilities for multiple tasks requires interjurisdictional cooperation within governments as well as between governments. Functional divisions clearly complicate administrative cooperation. Central coordination by the foreign ministries in the traditional project management schemes actually may aggravate moral hazard problems in such circumstances for the reasons we have shown. Recent theories of organization recommend new forms of a so-called business process management (Becker 2003) in which existing functional divisionalizations are broken up and appropriate chains of value production for given tasks are flexibly implemented. That is, specific sequences of the chain of value production are reintegrated into a new process. These new forms guarantee a higher degree of accountability and they reduce moral hazard problems of team production. Integration may be achieved at high executive levels as well as at the operational level. All kinds of vertical and horizontal boundaries of an organization are treated with flexibility.

A prerequisite for an incentive compatible design of processes is the identification of so-called critical value-adding processes that are critical for the completion of tasks. Having identified these critical processes it is possible to redesign the organization vertically as well as horizontally and to build and empower new organizational units. However, it is advised not to completely reconstruct processes from scratch and to appoint a case manager with extensive responsibilities, particularly when the existing functional divisions represent established "knowledge disciplines" producing indivisible know-how and technologies. In such cases it is recommended to rely on so-called process teams of functional specialists (Picot, Dietl, and Franck 2005, 295). With the support of new information and communication technologies it is possible to design completely new organizational forms.

Viewed from a historical perspective, nation-state governments developed more or less equivalent functional departments that institutionalize a political division of labor, which proved to be more or less useful (North 1981, 1990). Every ministerial division incorporated a specific value chain of political production required for the maintenance of the state as an organization. However, the institutionalized divisions of labor within each state were ill-equipped for international and especially for transnational challenges, since internal coordination of specialized ministries imposes considerable transaction costs. Task specific interdependencies may remain unrecognized, resulting in redundancies and delay. And transgovernmental relations challenge traditional hierarchies.

There is a trade-off between maintaining functional specialization and flexibility, and network analysis is an appropriate tool to consider this trade-off, to support reorganization processes (Borgatti and Foster 2003), and to identify "critical production processes." Applied network analysis allows the representation of formal as well as of informal organizational structures. From an institutional economics perspective, informal interactions of organizational members in task processing can be seen as implicit and incomplete contracts (Furubotn and Richter 2005). If they are acknowledged as useful by the executive, they may be actively and gradually stabilized and institutionalized (Stinchcombe 2001).

Network analysis enables us to identify actual task-specific authorities in informal business and administration processes (Thurner 2006; Thurner and Binder 2008; Thurner and Pappi 2009) by evaluating "the relative centrality of different teams or departments within an organization" (Everett and Borgatti 2005, 54). If "communities of practice" prove capable of integrating policies across the existing jurisdictional and national boundaries, then they can be used to create a process design and to be empowered with positional goods. Successful officials can become "process owners." The question is then how to assign rights efficiently and effectively such that the costs of reorganization are minimized? Applied network analysis recommends us to focus on central groups:

A manager may want to assemble a team with a specific set of skills, if the team were charged with some innovative project, it would be an additional benefit, if they could draw on the wider expertise available within the organization. The more central the group, the better positioned they would be to do this. (Everett and Borgattti 2005, 58)

Tracking and monitoring the work flows can help determine the appropriate members for a process team. Network analysis offers specific concepts of communication efficiency, communication effectiveness, and communicative authority. For example, network efficiency reduces communication redundancies and can be measured by the betweenness centrality of actors and groups.[10]

Effective communication positions are taken by those actors and groups who are near to all others: "The effectiveness of the group is a function of the shortest distance that any informer is from the origin of any bit of information" (Everett and Borgattti 2005, 62). Accordingly, it is measured by the concept of closeness centrality (Wasserman and Faust 1994, 184ff). Informal legitimacy – the accepted, real authority – can be operationalized by the concept of popularity or prestige. This concept takes into account not only the number of direct relations between actors but also the indirect ties (Wasserman and Faust 1994, 205 ff).[11] In short, criteria like efficiency, effectiveness, and intercultural legitimacy can be consistently defined and operationalized and used for an evidence-based reorganization of administrative processes.

Applying these criteria to the informal interaction between ministries within governments and between governments, that is, between institutional actors, I will identify an optimal process team representing the governments externally. My question is counterfactual because I ask what the team composition would have been had governments applied these criteria in selecting team members.

---

[10] "If an individual's ties are redundant with those of others, they can be removed from the group without reducing the group's centrality, creating more efficient groups in this respect" (Everett and Borgatti 2005, 58), and "Efficient groups do not have redundancy in terms of supporting actors who do not contribute" (Everett and Borgatti 2005, 60). "Betweenness-centrality measures the degree of information control: . . . an actor is central if it lies between other actors on their geodesics, implying that to have a large 'betweenness' centrality, the actor must be *between* many of the actors via their geodesics" (Wasserman and Faust 1994, 189).

[11] "An actor's rank depends on the ranks of those who do the choosing; but note that the ranks of those who are choosing depend on the ranks of the actors who choose them, and so on" (Wasserman and Faust 1994, 206). In the following I will rely on the page rank algorithm.

ADMINISTRATIVE PROCESS MANAGEMENT IN PRACTICE:
SELECTING NEGOTIATION TEAMS

"The Foreign Office always heads delegations in those cases in which negotiations are of particular foreign policy relevance" (Andreae and Kaiser 2001, 41). This is the explicitly stipulated rule of the joint rules of procedure of the German government. It has quite similar analogies in the other countries. But assume that the government executives of our counterfactual case study decide to restructure the assignment of competencies for external relations and reorganize the respective organizational unit, that is, the delegation team for the Intergovernmental Conference. We know from organizational studies that top-down executive interventions are successful only in cases with a high concentration and explicitness of the relevant distributions of knowledge, with a high centralization of power, with high degrees of flexibility of the organizational members, and with no conflicting interests (cf. Picot et al. 2005). Naturally, most of the time, these requirements are not fulfilled.

It is under these circumstances that self-organizing relationships become increasingly important. Harnessing the process requires incentive compatibility that in turn rests on knowledge about the preferences and the interactions of the officials. One fundamental trade-off arises between integrating as many members as possible in order to get the necessary local information and keeping the number low to minimize the resultant problems of rent seeking, manipulation of information, and shirking (Picot et al. 2005, 398). Therefore, a well-reasoned reduction of participation rights is advisable. In our case this means that we restrict the number of participating ministries. We maintain the originally implemented size of four delegates. However the algorithm to fill the team will be completely different.

Since it was not possible for us to monitor the work flows in the ministerial bureaucracies in real time we reconstruct these work flows from our data. We interviewed 140 top officials of relevant government ministries, premiers' offices, and presidents' offices and asked them what their ministries most preferred position was with respect to the nine tasks being negotiated. Additionally, we surveyed involved domestic parliamentary and federal committees and councils. One of the network questions was the reputation item: "Who was in your opinion especially influential in Task [xyz]?" This question was asked to all involved ministries of a government. I argue that using this item, it is possible to trace validly the effective informal interaction processes. Figure 12.2 presents the informal reputational network revealed by this

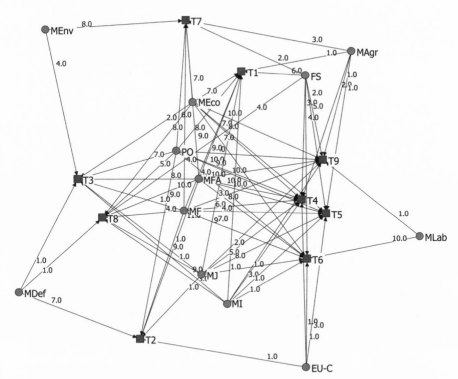

FIGURE 12.2. Tracing Critical Processes (Germany). *Notes*: T: Tasks 1-9; Premiers' Offices = PO; Ministries of Agriculture = MAgr; Ministries of Defense = MDef; Ministries of Foreign Affairs = MFA; Ministries of the Interior = MI; Ministries of Justice = MJ; Ministries of Finance = MF; Ministries of Economy = MEco; Ministries of Labor = MLab; Ministries of the Environment = MEnv; EU-Committee of the Parliament = EU-C; Chamber of the Federal States = FS.

question for the German case whose formal authority network was presented in Figure 12.1.

The links in this two-mode network represent the number of times the ministry has been reported to be influential for each indicated task; for example, the ministry of environment (MEnv) was considered to be influential in Task 7 by eight of the ten within-governmental peers. Note that the subjective attribution of influence is not necessarily related to the formal designation of authority in Figure 12.1. Only a few ministries excel in integrating tasks and other ministries. The relatively higher centrality of these actors (MFA, PO, MEco, Ministry of Finance [MF]) is conspicuous. They are the stars of this system connecting tasks and other officials. On the other hand, the parliamentary committees (EU-C) were not perceived as influential.

The aggregated subjectively perceived influence of actors with regard to tasks reflects one of the most important measures of administrative self-organization: who was perceived to be successful in the views of the relevant participants of the system? Actually, this constitutes the "variable commonness of conjecture" about the informal authority system. Given the notorious uncertainty of power in organizations, I consider this line of investigation a valuable empirical tool for identifying task-specific core executives and the "critical value-adding" processes in ministerial bureaucracies or other public and private administrations.

Based on our ex-post tracking of administrative work flows we are now able to select a team of functional specialists that reduces the number of participants while maintaining the coherence of the system and level of information extraction. Accordingly, betweenness centralities and closeness centralities were calculated for all the informal networks in each member state (Everett and Borgatti 2005, 63 ff).[12]

Figure 12.3 provides a clearer picture of the betweenness centralities of the involved ministries in Germany, with larger node size indicating a higher degree of centrality. As expected, the central role of the ministries of foreign affairs and the premiers' offices in the formal system is also reflected in the informal system. In addition, the ministries for economics comprised an important subdepartment for EU affairs at the time of the negotiations, which is reflected in their systemwide reputation of being influential.

As there are no discrepancies in the ordering of betweenness-central and closeness-central actors, the choice for a three-member team in the above example is clear. However, if all nations were required to provide four-person negotiation teams as was the case for the IGC, additional criteria would be necessary to break the tie for the fourth place between the German Ministry of Finance and the Ministry of Interior. In this case, we use the transgovernmental betweenness centrality of an actor as a relevant tie breaker.[13] The resulting team for Germany is illustrated in Figure 12.4.

---

[12] I dichotomized the network by assigning a value of 1 if the frequency of perceived influence was above the mean value.

[13] The item for reconstructing transgovernmental ties was, "Sometimes, it proves to be useful for a ministry – before taking the final national official position – to come to an agreement with an equivalent ministry of another Member State. (Interviewer: Please show list F [List F showed the EU-15 member states in an alphabetical order]). Could you indicate the Member States where you have practiced such an agreement building?" Naturally, there are manifold possibilities to fill up the team. The general function of a team composition would be tc $= \alpha_b + \beta_c + \gamma_D$ where the weights α, β, γ_r of the centrality measures, and the sequence of filling up the team have to be specified.

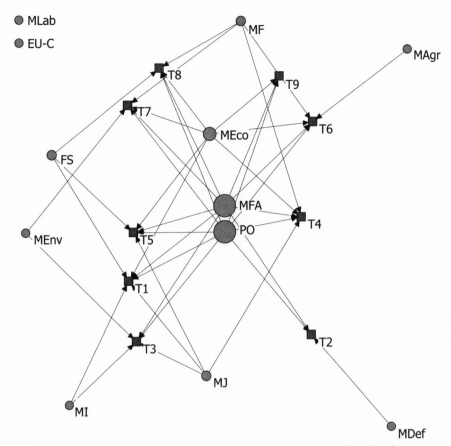

FIGURE 12.3. Within-Governmental Betweenness Centralities of Involved Ministries (Germany). *Notes*: T: Tasks 1-9; Premiers' Offices = PO; Ministries of Agriculture = MAgr; Ministries of Defense = MDef; Ministries of Foreign Affairs = MFA; Ministries of the Interior = MI; Ministries of Justice = MJ; Ministries of Finance = MF; Ministries of Economy = MEco; Ministries of Labor = MLab; Ministries of the Environment = MEnv; EU-Committee of the Parliament = EU-C; Chamber of the Federal States = FS.

The darkness of the nodes in this figure represents increasing transgovernmental centrality of a ministry in its intergovernmental networks. In Germany, the Ministry of the Interior exhibits the comparatively highest centrality in transgovernmental relations, and therefore it fills the fourth position of the delegation, as indicated by the curved line circling the four selected team members. Of course, intercultural competencies and other potentially desirable characteristics could also be included in

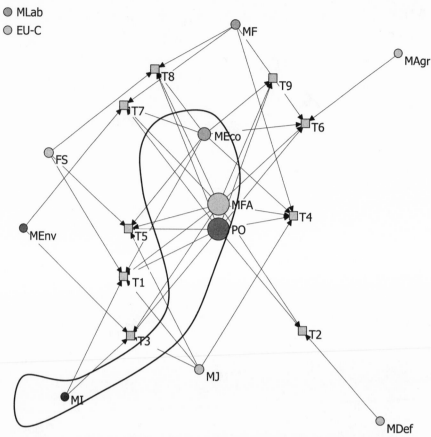

FIGURE 12.4. National Process Team of Functional Specialists, N = 4 (Germany). *Notes*: T: Tasks 1-9; Premiers' Offices = PO; Ministries of Agriculture = MAgr; Ministries of Defense = MDef; Ministries of Foreign Affairs = MFA; Ministries of the Interior = MI; Ministries of Justice = MJ; Ministries of Finance = MF; Ministries of Economy = MEco; Ministries of Labor = MLab; Ministries of the Environment = MEnv; EU-Committee of the Parliament = EU-C; Chamber of the Federal States = FS.

the choice algorithm. My purpose with this simple example is to illustrate the workings of the algorithm and to show that this counterfactual thought experiment suggests the inefficiencies that resulted from considering only formal authority in selecting the actual delegations.

Table 12.1 indicates the team members selected by our criteria for all 15 member states. The numbers in the matrix are the rank orders of the ministries as a result of applying the composite algorithm. Note that the result does not infringe on the established authority system: the role

TABLE 12.1. *Team Composition (N = 4): Efficiency, Effectiveness, and Transgovernmental Mediation*

	PO	MFA	MI	MJ	MF	Meco	MLab	Msoc	MEnv	Other
Belgium	1	1	o	4	o	o	o	o	o	FS (3)
Germany	1	1	4	o	o	3	o	o	o	
Denmark	1	2	o	o	o	o	4	o	o	EU-C (3)
France	2	2	o	o	o	4	o	o	o	Pres-O (1)
Finland	1	1	o	o	o	o	o	4	o	EU-C (3)
UK	o	1	4	o	3	o	o	o	o	EU-Sec (1)
Greece	3	1	4	o	o	2	o	o	o	
Italy	2	1	4	o	3	o	o	o	o	
Ireland	2	1	o	4	3	o	o	o	o	
Luxembourg	1	1	o	3	o	o	4	o	o	
Netherlands	2	1	o	o	3	4	o	o	o	
Austria	1	1	o	o	o	o	o	o	o	FS (3), EU-C (4)
Portugal	o	1	o	o	o	o	o	o	o	
Spain	2	1	3	4	o	o	o	o	o	
Sweden	1	1	o	4	3	o	o	o	o	

Note: Premiers' Offices = PO; Ministries of Foreign Affairs = MFA; Ministries of the Interior = MI; Ministries of Justice = MJ; Ministries of Finance = MF; Ministries of Economy = MEco; Ministries of Labor = MLab; Ministries of Social Affairs = MSoc; Ministries of the Environment = MEnv; EU-Committee of the Parliament: EU-C; Chamber of the Federal States = FS; President's Office = PresO; EU-Secretariat of the Cabinet = EU-Sec.

of the MFAs as a central coordinator remains unchanged. And states keep their within-governmental "administrative autonomy." However, the flows of information, the degree of accountability, and the sustainability of negotiation outcomes should have been enhanced by the inclusion of ministries that play central roles in the informal system. At the same time, uncontrolled foreign policy making of special ministries would have been avoided. Due to the additional consideration of transgovernmental relations, the management of interfaces between states should be facilitated.

INSTITUTIONALIZING TRANSGOVERNMENTAL LEGITIMACY AND FACILITATING EU EXTERNAL ACTION

This method of selecting teams to represent a member state externally can also be applied to the transgovernmental problem of establishing teams to

institutionalize international cooperation. With regard to interorganizational relations, it is of the essence to optimize the management of interfaces between states. The large number of participating states in the EU
makes it difficult to consult on all issues, particularly on those requiring
rapid responses to changing situations such as challenges from terrorism or
responses to disasters or international crises. Hence, it is often necessary to
deviate from the principle of unanimity and consent and instead recognize
the need for a potential reduction of participation at the executive level.
This leads to the problem of selecting a limited team that can effectively
decide for the EU while maintaining transgovernmental legitimacy.

Besides the challenge of integrating different administrative cultures,
manifold incentive problems like hold ups and putting at risk ex-ante
investments arise in developing a limited team. Short-term and mid-term
forms of flexible cooperation – so-called dynamic networks (cf. Miles and
Snow 1995) – provide one approach for dealing with these problems.
Loosely connected associations of organizations remain autonomous
while cooperating on specific tasks. For each new project the composition
of and contribution by partner organizations are determined anew. In an
early stage of interorganizational cooperation, one organization may step
in as a commissioner and lead the virtual enterprise – using a joint institutional architecture. This flexible form of collaboration may gradually
become institutionalized and bring about a new accepted authority system; transgovernmental relations of the ministries and the state officials
potentially develop informal authority systems directed and supported by
an administrative process management of the political executives.

In the following example I extrapolate from the tasks of the previous
application case to design a supranational process team to be mandated
with an external mission. Table 12.2 presents all page rank prestige centralities of the ministries, with the four top-ranking ministries in each
country indicated in gray shading and the potential four-person transgovernmental team indicated in dark shading. For a team composition
of $N = 4$ with an external mission, we demand, first, that the ministries
are part of the domestic core executive – that they meet the requirement of
holding an efficient and effective position at the domestic level. This is the
reason, for example, that the ministries of the environment of Germany,
France, the Netherlands, and Sweden are not considered. Second, there
should be only one ministry from a state in order to guarantee national
heterogeneity. The resulting team then consists of the foreign ministries
of Germany and France and the premiers' offices of Belgium and
Luxembourg.

TABLE 12.2. *Team Composition for External Missions Based on Transgovernmental Prestige (Page Rank)*

	PO	MFA	MI	MJ	MF	MEco	MLab	MSoc	MEnv	Other
Belgium	0,13	0,04	0,02	0,04	0,06	0,07	0,12	0,09	0,02	FS
Germany	0,20	0,34	0,34	0,24	0,16	0,19	0,09	–	0,17	
Denmark	0,02	0,02	0,02	0,02	0,06	0,09	0,10	0,11	0,14	EU-C
France	0,13	0,34	0,11	0,24	–	0,09	–	–	–	Pres-O
Finland	0,02	0,02	0,03	0,03	0,03	–	0,09	0,10	0,11	EU-C
UK	0,09	0,03	0,14	0,14	0,12	–	0,09	0,08	0,10	EU-Sec
Greece	0,02	0,01	0,02	0,01	0,02	0,03	0,02	–	0,02	
Italy	–	0,03	0,07	0,02	0,02	–	–	–	–	
Ireland	0,03	0,02	–	0,13	0,04	–	0,02	0,02	0,02	
Luxembourg	0,13	0,03	–	0,03	0,04	–	0,11	–	0,02	
Netherlands	0,08	0,05	0,15	0,04	0,15	0,15	0,15	–	0,14	
Austria	0,04	0,02	0,02	0,01	0,05	0,07	–	0,15	0,09	FS, EU-C
Portugal	–	0,01	–	–	–	–	–	–	–	
Spain	0,07	0,02	0,07	0,02	–	0,04	0,02	0,02	–	
Sweden	0,02	0,04	–	0,03	0,11	–	0,12	0,14	0,17	

Note: Premiers' Offices = PO; Ministries of Foreign Affairs = MFA; Ministries of the Interior = MI; Ministries of Justice = MJ; Ministries of Finance = MF; Ministries of Economy = MEco; Ministries of Labour = MLab; Ministries of Social Affairs = MSoc; Ministries of the Environment = MEnv; EU-Committee of the Parliament = EU-C; Chamber of the Federal States = FS; President's Office = PresO; EU-Secretariat of the Cabinet = EU-Sec.

A variety of scenarios and application cases for an active organization of vertical and horizontal boundaries can be imagined. For example, the European presidency may wish to implement a business management design by appointing national functional specialists who belong to task-specific core executives but who also share high intercultural reputations.

Another application may be enhanced cooperation in the field of Common Foreign and Security Policy (CFSP) of the EU as made possible in Title V, Art. 27a-e and, more generally in Title VII, Art. 43 of the Treaty on the European Union (TEU):

Member States which intend to establish enhanced cooperation between themselves may make use of the institutions, procedures and mechanisms laid down by this Treaty and by the Treaty establishing the European Community provided that the proposed cooperation . . .

Changing combinations of participating states and levels may be included in process teams for different mission – just as postulated by the governance form of "dynamic networks." Such forms of selective enhanced cooperation based on joint institutional platforms involve difficult and highly demanding contract logistics. However, as long as process managers have clear process and outcome responsibilities to ensure their accountability, these notorious problems of legitimacy and performance would be minimized.

SUMMARY

How can federalist governments deal with the multitude of problems involving overlapping authorities and decision externalities? The main thrust of transaction cost theory suggests that the solution lies in developing appropriate horizontal and vertical boundaries of authority that minimize the adverse impacts of such decision externalities. However, reformulating boundaries imposes political conflicts, particularly in the case of attempts to integrate independent nations into a common EU framework.

I have argued that to facilitate institutional collective action and to avoid the second-order free-rider problem, governance forms must be incentive compatible and exhibit low transaction costs for self-organizing leadership networks. Existing knowledge stocks as well as reliable and experienced interaction structures must be taken into account – that is, the human capital of individuals and the social capital of organizations should be brought into play in a clever way.

I propose a method of developing coordinating devices that meet these criteria and also minimize political conflicts associated with reorganizations. Process management with functional specialists involves a specific combination of business management and functional divisionalization, based on the characteristics of self-organizing activities that develop to overcome fragmentation in the formal system of authority.

The procedure described in this chapter provides a natural extension to the suggestions of *Feiock and Scholz* in Chapter 1 that informal policy networks be encouraged and nurtured to develop informal mechanisms to resolve everyday fragmentation problems: by analyzing the emergent informal mechanisms for particularly difficult coordination tasks, governments can utilize this knowledge to harness the power of self-organizing systems. The underlying assumption is that self-organizing networks reveal the kind of expertise and skills sought by officials in their informal attempts to cope with externality problems and fragmented authority. By vesting formal authority in the central actors that emerge in the informal networks of influence, authorities can take advantage of expertise and legitimacy already enjoyed by central actors and at the same time increase their accountability for the specific tasks delegated to formal team members.

The EU context has provided an extreme test for illustrating the procedure in a context fraught with all the problems described in *Jones*. The main objective of this article was to suggest a method to restructure negotiations of the EU at the occasion of a constitution-building conference. How should national negotiation teams for international negotiations be composed? The simple illustrative examples presented in this article should not conceal the fact that, in reality, algorithms for the design of dynamic processes are much more complicated. Planning, implementing, and controlling such processes require the application of sophisticated information and communication techniques. Only computer-integrated designs make it possible to integrate processes horizontally, vertically, and sequentially. A crucial prerequisite is the integration of data required for different parts and sequences of the process and for a simulation-based planning of process designs (cf. Lomi and Larsen 2001)! For such processes to be implemented, political and administrative scientists and experts must be able to communicate political goals to computer scientists in ways that are adequately translated into usable algorithms, so that the results can be presented in achievable outcomes. Much remains to be done in improving this translation process.

PART FOUR

SELF-ORGANIZING GOVERNANCE AND INSTITUTIONAL COLLECTIVE ACTION

13

Self-Organizing Mechanisms for Mitigating Institutional Collective Action Dilemmas: An Assessment and Research Agenda

Richard C. Feiock and John T. Scholz

Policies and services in communities and regions increasingly confront externalities in which one authority's decisions have major unanticipated impacts on other authorities and their constituencies. A multitude of innovative institutions have evolved within our decentralized federalist system to coordinate policies and mitigate the resultant collective action dilemmas, many of which are self-organizing institutions developed by those affected by such dilemmas. This volume is premised on two beliefs: first, an integrated approach to analyze the multitude of self-organizing institutions is necessary to understand the potential benefits and limitations of these institutions in enhancing the efficiency of federalist governance; second, a better understanding will accelerate the evolution of self-organizing institutions as an integral part of our federalist system, thereby expanding the system's ability to mitigate a broader range of institutional collective action (ICA) dilemmas without threatening the safeguards of a robust federalism.

Our first chapter outlined an ICA framework for addressing three critical questions about these mitigating mechanisms:

- How does the mechanism reduce transaction costs in obtaining the benefits of coordinated decisions?
- What incentives do potential members have to create the mechanism?
- How do the incentives induced by the mechanism affect its sustainability, its adaptability to other ICAs, and its overall impact on the system of formal authority?

In this final chapter we summarize the basic findings from the remaining chapters about the circumstances under which alternatives to formal centralized structures will emerge and be successful. Taken together they offer a rigorous examination of the conditions that motivate and shape the development and design of self-organizing mitigating mechanisms. We should reemphasize that the intellectual purpose of this volume is not (alas!) to fully understand the array of mitigating mechanisms, but rather to lay out the critical questions posed by the ICA framework for understanding these mechanisms and to demonstrate fruitful methods for answering these questions.

SELF-ORGANIZING VERSUS IMPOSED SOLUTIONS TO ICA DILEMMAS: THEORETICAL CONSIDERATIONS

The first four chapters elaborate the basic framework proposed in Chapter 1. *Whitford* sets the stage by considering the limits of centrally imposed consolidation and elaborating alternative incentive-compatible solutions that can preserve some of the advantages of self-organizing solutions even when greater centralization of authority proves necessary. *Steinacker* then lays out a framework that links categories of ICA dilemmas to appropriate incentive-compatible solutions, and *Jones* considers critical factors that limit the possibilities of self-organizing solutions.

Whitford: Local Autonomy and Incentive-Compatible Consolidation

Consolidation of authority in the hands of a central coordinator is generally considered a primary solution when governmental subunits face the ICA dilemmas we consider in this volume. *Whitford* elaborates one of the primary assumptions of the self-governing approach to ICA mitigation: consolidation is only one of many mechanisms for mitigating ICAs, and well-intended central policy planners can often achieve better resolution through intermediate forms of centralized intervention that preserve some degree of autonomy for local authorities.

He argues that consolidation can internalize the externality problems facing independent local governments or specialized agencies, but that the problems do not disappear – they are simply transformed into an internal principal-agency problem between the central coordinator and the now-internal subunits of the new organization. Maintaining control over subunit performance generally comes at the expense of reducing the motivation and ability of the subunit to optimize performance (from the central authority's perspective) in its specific functional or geographic situation. For example, local governments are responding to different underlying preferences of citizens, and specialized agencies are responding to local conditions that require different trade-offs between values – in both cases, central decisions need to provide both flexibility and incentives for subunits to develop and utilize their local knowledge to make the best decisions. Thus, centralization converts the externality problem facing independent units adapting to their localized environment into a principal-agent problem in which the ability of the center to monitor and evaluate subunit decisions becomes critical.

The novelty of *Whitford*'s approach to this standard argument comes from his application of franchise contracting theory, a subfield of the organizational design literature in economics that is concerned with the relationship between quasi-independent subunits (franchisees) and central authority (franchisor). The franchise contract provides a governance structure that combines some of the advantages of geographically dispersed market-based production (e.g., local knowledge, adaptability, strong incentives to optimize) with those of fully integrated producers (economies of scale, mechanisms to mitigate externalities among subunits). They also closely parallel features of the American federalist system relating to the delegation of authority to lower levels of government.

Franchisees face a horizontal dilemma similar to that of local governments that have been delegated implementation authority by a central coordinator – they can gain many advantages (particularly related to economies of scale) by joining a franchise rather than creating their own product, but each franchisee faces temptations to cut costs and free ride on the investments of others. The franchisor is expected to mitigate this moral hazard problem among franchisees; sufficient punishment relative to the probability that misbehavior can be detected will resolve the horizontal dilemma by deterring free riding. If the central authority acts as an optimizing franchisor, then, agencies or local governments would have a strong incentive to give up some of their independence and seek a franchisor for specific service or policy arenas where ICAs were most harmful.

Whitford's most novel contribution in applying this particular principal-agent model to understanding self-governance, however, is his equal focus on the moral hazard issue facing the central authority or franchisor. A franchisor with sufficient ability to punish misbehaving franchisees could misuse this ability to extract all the advantages obtained by mitigating the moral hazard problem, leaving the franchisees no better off than they would have been as independent agents. In our context, for example, a creative local government that found a better way to reduce pollution without strictly implementing costly federal regulations might still be required to follow the regulations. The federal agency could thus claim even more credit for additional pollution reduction while the local government pays the cost of innovation without saving the normal implementation costs.

Providing credible assurances against moral hazard on the part of the franchisor imposes the second critical challenge to franchise contract design. *Whitford* discusses several mechanisms from the franchise contract literature that address the joint moral hazard problems and shows how they may be relevant for our consideration of self-governing solutions to ICAs.

Most important, the structure of the federalist system itself constrains the problem of opportunism in ICAs. The threat of central intervention and consolidation, even with all its potential problems, provides a constraint on the opportunism of local authorities even when no intervention occurs. Absent this potential for intervention, opportunism would exacerbate existing ICA dilemmas – a counterfactual claim that is both plausible and probably difficult to verify empirically. The threat also provides an important incentive for the self-organizing institutions to keep ICA dilemmas out of the range that might trigger higher level intervention. For example, the Tampa Bay water war was not resolved until an impending threat of state legislation convinced recalcitrant local governments to consolidate their independent water authorities (Dedekorkut 2005). Thus the federalist structure itself stimulates self-organizing activities in an important way even without direct intervention by higher authorities, although this stimulation is probably less effective on issues with lower political salience for higher level authorities.

In addition, *Whitford* introduces several novel mechanisms not mentioned in Chapter 1 for resolving ICAs that have been developed in the franchise contracting literature. These mechanisms are already an established aspect of federalist relationships in America but are not currently recognized for the function they perform in mitigating ICAs. Two mechanisms in particular are highlighted. First, the role of dual distribution in franchise contracts suggests a mechanism to enhance the role of higher authorities in mitigating ICAs. In dual distribution, the franchisor distributes a product both through centrally owned shops and through franchisees. The information, experience, and operating capacities obtained from internal operations can reduce the problems of monitoring and punishing franchisees. Similarly, higher authorities can achieve comparable advantages by delegating implementation and enforcement to many local governments but by directly providing these processes in some areas where it is more efficient to do so directly. For example, central authorities could provide a standardized product for the most common conditions but allow subunits facing different problems to develop alternatives more suited to their conditions – as the Clean Air Act allows California to set alternative standards that other states facing similar problems can also adopt.

The second mechanism is analogous to bonding by franchisees and helps mitigate the moral hazard problem facing the franchisee or local government equivalent. Local governments are seldom required to post actual performance bonds, but they generally must meet predetermined standards that require considerable "asset-specific" investments – for example, providing project-specific capital investments or narrowly focused training to enforcers. These prerequisites can function like bonds in enhancing the ability of the central authority to minimize misbehavior once authority has been delegated.

Elsewhere, Whitford (2007) notes the relationship between moral hazard and adverse selection issues and argues that governance institutions frequently reduce the moral hazard problem discussed in *Whitford* by utilizing selection mechanisms whenever possible to eliminate potentially troublesome agents. Indeed, this is one of the major potential advantages of self-organizing over mandatory membership in regional decision-making bodies – by including only members interested in the particular goals of the organization, less effort needs to be expended for monitoring and punishment.

In sum, *Whitford* links the horizontal dilemmas between local governments or agencies with the vertical dilemmas that are added when central authorities step in to resolve the horizontal dilemmas. He discusses conditions under which the central coordinating authority can do better by franchising autonomous local agents rather than relying solely on hierarchical controls over a consolidated structure, and discusses some of the relatively little-appreciated mechanisms for resolving the dual dilemmas while maintaining some level of autonomy of local agents. His chapter challenges future researchers both to recognize the role of "franchising" mechanisms already a part of the American federalist system and to extend the analysis to other mechanisms that could attack the moral hazard and adverse selection problems within the federalist context.

Steinacker: **Linking ICA Dilemmas with Self-Organizing Mechanisms**

A common classification of the underlying ICA dilemmas provides the foundation for *Steinacker* to analyze the motivational issues affecting the possibility of self-organizing mitigation for each type of dilemma. She applies the transaction cost perspective by systematically analyzing how four common barriers to agreements (information costs, agency costs, negotiation and division costs, and monitoring and enforcement costs) affect three primary types of ICA dilemmas (economies of scale, negative externalities, and common-pool resources).

Steinacker argues first that economies of scale in service provision can provide positive benefits for all affected stakeholders, whichmakes these ICA dilemmas most amenable to the simplest types of self-organizing mechanisms. The horizontal service provision problem among local governments in a metropolitan area is a typical setting for this type of problem, and *Andrew* and *Shrestha* offer further details about the types of risks and resultant motivations associated with agreements and contractual arrangements frequently utilized to mitigate such dilemmas. All three chapters emphasize the different risks and incentives that arise because of the difference in asset specificity and measurability for different services and the need to carefully analyze the resultant incentives to understand both the potential advantages and constraints of these bilateral or multi-party local agreements. All three chapters note that the remaining well-known risks of contractual arrangements can themselves be mitigated if they are embedded in broader informal relationships, as discussed later in the chapter. This is a major subtheme of our volume: mitigating mechanisms (networks and contracts in this case) frequently interact with each other and can only be understood by considering the broader context of mitigating institutions and overlapping sets of ICA dilemmas.

Steinacker next argues that negative externalities impose more difficult problems and are therefore more likely to require external intervention associated with the mechanisms further toward the right side of the scale in Figure 1.1 of Chapter 1. In particular, a status quo that favors the perpetrators of a negative externality provides a difficult setting for negotiating agreements unless the sufferers can engage higher levels of government to challenge the de facto right of those producing the harms. The types of vertically linked policy networks and consensual regional organizations studied by *Weible* and by *Lubell, Henry, and McCoy* can alter these incentives by expanding the issues involved in the negotiating arena and increasing the threat of external intervention discussed by *Whitford*.

The specific types of negative externalities associated with common pool resources are somewhat less problematic, on the other hand, in part because there is less asymmetry between producers and sufferers when everyone's actions affect the same common resource. In general, the broader set of stakeholders involved in these problems would require broader organizations or multiparty agreements than those involved in more decomposable service delivery issues.

We believe that *Steinacker's* categorization of problems and pairing with incentive-compatible mechanisms provides an important foundation for integrating the many separate policy studies that frequently fail to realize that they are dealing with the same categories of underlying problems. Future research will test the extent to which these categories and the transaction cost framework they reflect will provide an adequate foundation to understand the full range of governance mechanisms and ICA dilemmas. This book reflects a simple division into positive externality horizontal dilemmas and negative externality vertical dilemmas represented in the two empirical sections of this volume, but we hope that this division will quickly be replaced by a theoretically nuanced set of critical dimensions that are less wed to the historically generated different research traditions.

Jones: The Limits to Self-Organizing Solutions of Metropolitan Conflicts

In the final theoretical exploration *Jones* argues that the ICA model of metropolitan organization will overstate the likelihood of self-organizing solutions unless it incorporates three additional factors:

- a conflict theory perspective in which zero-sum games can outweigh positive sum games (e.g., dilemmas);
- boundedly rational actors engaging in incomplete, localized search for solutions that they subsequently become emotionally attached to; and
- negative spillovers from positive sum gains in one policy subsystem that adversely affect other subsystems in the metropolitan area connected through overlapping policy networks.

These thoughtful criticisms have important implications for the ICA framework. Taken together with the attention to these issues in other chapters in this volume, they suggest how these issues can be addressed in research based within an ICA framework. We consider each in the order presented.

Conflict Theory and State Intervention. Jones focuses attention on the coercive authority of higher level governments and the associated potential for high decision costs. He emphasizes the distinction between transaction costs that are barriers to voluntary exchange and external decision costs that arise when decisions can be imposed involuntarily on losers in a policy contest – that is, when majorities are able to coerce minorities into taking action (or failing to take action) that they do not want to take. The decision costs concept extends the transaction cost logic of negotiation over dividing the gains (developed primarily to explain voluntary exchange) to authoritative situations where losses can also be imposed. In such authoritative settings, ICA analyses will be misleading if they ignore conflict theories such as those commonly used in urban studies. This idea supports our categorization of mitigating mechanism in Chapter 1 based on the relative loss of autonomy; the greater the loss, the higher the decision costs. *Jones* emphasizes the trade-off noted in Chapter 1 between capacity to resolve dilemmas and the reluctance to give up local autonomy; mechanisms most capable of reducing transaction costs generally impose greater decision costs, thereby limiting the kinds of conflicts that self-organizing institutions are capable of resolving when coercive authority is involved – a point also noted in *Steinacker*. The most appropriate mechanism for a given dilemma presumably minimizes the sum of transaction and decision costs.

In addition, *Jones* emphasizes the potentially coercive role of state governments, pointing out that actual intervention by powerful state officials in pursuit of their specific policy preferences can restructure incentives in a manner that can severely limit the range of self-organizing activities, as occurred in the Seattle case. His perspective suggests that the parochial interests of the state place important limitations on the potentially positive role of higher authorities reflected in most of the chapters in this volume. For example, *Whitford* argues that the threat of state intervention can provide a strong positive incentive for the development of self-organizing mechanisms, although his primary analysis also emphasizes the dual problems of moral hazard by both local and state officials. *Steinacker's* analysis distinguished between situations requiring benevolent, centrally imposed solutions and those in which self-organized solutions may emerge. Other chapters have reiterated that states determine the configuration and powers of local units and the institutional options available to them; the existing set of statutes and case law – the externally imposed rules – shape both the nature of the underlying ICA dilemmas and the motivations to resolve them. State statutes and rules determine the specific authority of many actors in the arena and help shape the strategies available to each of the actors in their individual efforts to avoid negative externalities and capitalize on positive externalities. These externally imposed rules combine with the underlying collective problem to determine the specific incentives facing each actor.

On the issue of city-county consolidation imposed by state authority, for example, informal policy networks still played important roles in the state's creation of the consolidated Indianapolis metropolitan government, or "Unigov" (Blomquist and Parks 1995). State-imposed consolidated governments and special districts more often emerge from self-organizing activities that reach out to external authorities primarily to legitimize the unification desired by those being consolidated (Carr and Feiock 2004). Understanding the informal policy networks and other relationships involved in the consolidation process is likely to provide a clearer understanding of the prerequisites of successful consolidation efforts.

Jones reminds us that state involvement in major political battles (zero-sum games) in the local domain can overwhelm these other factors favoring self-organizing solutions, at least until the "attention vortex" dies down. He focuses specifically on the consequences of state interventions that create an attention vortex that consolidates multiple ICA dimensions into a single zero-sum game and suggests ways to understand such situations in terms of bounded rationality and spillovers among multiple policy games.

Bounded Rationality. Jones outlines some aspects of bounded rationality that help clarify the limited ability to resolve policy disputes when conflicts over authority create an attention vortex: the limited attention of key policy makers and the related tendency to limit a search for new solutions, the cognitive and emotional attachment to policy means that severely restrict the space for negotiation on how to reach policy goals, the tendency to block progress in any arena that benefits opponents. These destructive, noncollaborative tendencies may indeed be rational in the sense that they reflect viable strategies for creating the "winning coalition" needed to prevail in a zero-sum, winner-take-all authoritative policy arena (e.g, Sabatier 2005).

The discussion of policy learning and the processes that define perceptions of problem-spaces are important for the ICA perspective even beyond *Jones*'s concern with the destructive impact of attention vortices. Learning involves not just finding out how a policy works but also learning about the context within which policy is delivered. Self-organizing mechanisms incorporate both the desire and the information-processing capacity to shape and redefine problems and solutions. For example, a policy network that reduces barriers to a policy agreement also may aid in reducing decision costs by stimulating policy learning in which participants' preferences tend to converge through joint experiences over time. *Weible* and *Lubell et al.* describe instances in which self-governing institutions in regional policy arenas provide benefits to participants that facilitate additional exchanges. Over time, these relationships accumulate into a regional network that builds the participants' reputations for being competent, trustworthy, and reliable. This endogenous process then enhances future cooperation and collective action (Gulati and Gargiulo 1999). As *Jones* notes, the ICA perspective can benefit by incorporating the advocacy coalition perspective on learning process in authoritative, zero-sum decision arenas (Sabatier 2005) as well as the conflict resolution perspective on alternative decision process designs that foster positive policy learning processes (Susskind 2005).

Spillovers among Multiple Games. In studies of regional governance, relationships among actors in one arena are typically analyzed with little regard for their relationships in other arenas. *Jones* references Liu's (2006) spatial supergame model to argue that the ICA approach needs to capture the complexity involved when institutional actors simultaneously play multiple games with overlapping sets of actors in multiple policy arenas. The idea of simultaneous multiple games captures the complexity of self-organizing across policy arenas better than conventional approaches that focus on a single policy and assume policy arenas operate independently of each other.

ICA dilemmas can readily be represented by a set of games similar to the illustration in *Jones* in which a separate game represents each independent authority in the metropolitan area. Each major ICA dilemma is represented as one "dimension" in Figure 4.1 defined by the impact of outcomes in one game on payoffs in the other games affected directly by the ICA or indirectly by the common participants in both games. This formulation is particularly useful for visualizing our primary question about the impact of a given mechanism in one policy arena on other ICA dilemmas in the region, just as simultaneous game structures have proven useful for understanding complex organizational and hierarchical structures (Scharpf 1997; Tsebelis 2002). Whether formal models capturing the complexity that *Jones* believes necessary can produce testable equilibrium results remains to be seen. In the meantime, however, *Lubell et al.* demonstrate how some implications of an analogous informal approach, Norton Long's (1958) conception of policy as an ecology of games, can be tested empirically. Similarly, *Weible* develops and tests alternative hypotheses about the impact of participation in multiple policy arenas on policy learning. We will discuss their findings later.

In summary, *Jones* discusses the impact of conflict within an attention vortex on one transportation-induced ICA but does not address questions about the relative frequency and long-term impacts of such conflicts. Are these disruptions sufficiently frequent to completely discourage more fragile self-organizing attempts in most metropolitan areas? Does this perspective suggest that self-organizing mechanisms must be relegated to more isolated and obscure ICA dilemmas less likely to attract state intervention? Or do the disruptions actually redefine policy arenas in a way that integrates previously disparate ICA dimensions, thereby creating new opportunities for broader mitigation efforts once the attention vortex moves on – a hopeful hint raised by *Jones* in the conclusion. In terms of the equity issue raised by *Jones,* how often is collaboration really collusion to subsidize solutions preferred by a small but influential group with revenues from unrepresented taxpayers?

Whether or not the attention vortex and related concepts prove to be a primary limiting factor for the role of self-organizing mechanisms in federalist systems, *Jones* adds several important issues to the research agenda for the ICA perspective that focus on the critical role of the state, the processes of policy learning under different conditions, the interrelationship among different ICA dimensions and other conflicts in the same region, and the potential problem of collusion masquerading as cooperation.

INTEGRATING METROPOLITAN SERVICE DELIVERY: THEORETICAL ISSUES AND EMPIRICAL FINDINGS

The collective action problems facing service delivery in metropolitan areas provide the empirical context for chapters in the second section of this volume. We focus here on ICA dilemmas of service delivery relating primarily to economies of scale and the resultant positive externalities, and on contracting and flexible agreement mechanisms that allow local governments to gain efficiencies with a minimum loss of autonomy. *Andrew*'s investigation of interlocal agreements for public safety services and *Shrestha*'s investigation of interlocal contracts for nine types of local service provision both analyze the mitigating mechanism of intergovernmental agreements that establish specific roles and responsibilities for coordinating two or more jurisdictions providing a common service. *Mullen*'s analysis focuses on the impact that consolidated districts – an alternative coordinating device – have on the use of interlocal contracts for water supply. And *Bickers et al.*'s investigation considers the role of electoral incentives among local government officials in encouraging or limiting the use of contracts as well as broader collaborative activities among local governments.

Before summarizing the contributions of these studies, we emphasize that the collaborative partnerships studied in the next section are just as relevant to metropolitan issues as to the regional resource management issues that provide the empirical focus in that section (e.g., Feiock 2007; Park and Feiock 2007). Similarly, the bilateral contracts and flexible agreements studied here are as relevant to regional policy integration studies as to metropolitan areas, where memos of agreement frequently play critical roles in both *Berardo*'s joint projects and *Lubell et al.*'s broader collaborative partnerships. In both sections, the overlapping empirical studies focus on a relatively narrow set of mechanisms to explore more thoroughly the broader range of questions for these mechanisms.

The contract and agreement mechanisms studied in this section reflect the relatively well-understood ability of exchange-based mechanisms to resolve decision externalities as long as transaction costs are relatively low (*Steinacker*). Contracts and agreements can promote self-organizing resolution of relevant ICAs in several ways. They allow each participant to determine whether to accept the constraints imposed by the agreement, so they raise little opposition. Higher levels of government are not required except to provide a legal framework supportive of such agreements. Federal and state statutes can enhance the scope of agreements by ensuring that the legal framework minimizes transaction costs by, for example, clarifying the nature of access to existing judicial institutions to enforce agreements. Agreements can readily be employed simultaneously for multiple ICA dilemmas, limited only by the capacity of individual local governments to develop and maintain agreements in multiple policy arenas. For example, *Shrestha* finds that several of the same 25 local governments in the Tampa Bay are contractual partners in all nine different service areas he studied, although he does not systematically investigate the multiplexity of relationships in his chapter.

The unique contribution of *Andrew* and *Shrestha* is to address the issue of transaction costs not just in terms of the specific agreement, but rather to analyze the bilateral agreements within the broader regional pattern of agreements and contractual relationships in which individual agreements are embedded. In doing so, they expand the argument that risks and transaction costs associated with contractual exchanges can be reduced when these exchanges are embedded in other relationships (Granovetter 1985). They identify and analyze specific network characteristics associated with the capacity to reduce different kinds of risk, a key task for the theoretical development of the self-governance approach to ICA.

Andrew: Transitive Contractual Patterns Reduce Risk for Adaptive and Restrictive Agreements Alike

Andrew focuses on the difference between *adaptive* and *restrictive* agreements. Adaptive arrangements are similar to incomplete contracts; they provide local governments with the flexibility to adapt to unforeseen circumstances but increase the potential risk of opportunistic behaviors. Restrictive arrangements, on the other hand, refer to well-specified contracts; the greater specificity of contracts reduces risks of opportunism but increases transaction costs of writing and implementing the contract and minimizes flexibility when unspecified circumstances and unanticipated outcomes are confronted. *Andrew* argues that local governments are particularly likely to utilize adaptive agreements to deal with issues involving many unforeseen circumstances, such as emergency management agreements. Restrictive agreements, on the other hand, are more likely for better-understood service agreements and leasing arrangements.

Andrew then considers two alternative network structures that have different capabilities to reduce the risks of contracting. *Interdependent* risks posed by the opportunism of contracting partners can best be controlled by mutually reciprocating, overlapping relationships within closed subgroups, as associated with the development of trust and social capital (Coleman 1988). If mutual interdependencies in the pattern of contracts can constrain opportunism, then local governments can reduce risks of contracting by selecting contract partners who already have contracts with other partners. In network analysis terms, they prefer transitive relationships among their contracting partners and thus are more likely to select new partners who already have contractual relationships to existing partners.

Andrew notes that transitive relationships may actually increase risks when the interrelated partners all need the same resources at the same time, as when some common disaster strikes the full cluster of cities with mutual aid contracts. To protect against such situations, nonoverlapping relationships may decrease the likelihood that all contractual partners are under the same stress. To enhance the *independence* of risks, local governments can select contract partners that do not have contracts with each other. *Andrew* represents this pattern with the network analysis concept of betweenness – a preference to contract with individuals who are not connected by other contractual arrangements.

Although *Andrew* hypothesizes that the greater risk of opportunism in adaptive agreements favors transitivity more than in restrictive agreements, he actually finds very similar patterns for both. Both transitivity and betweenness are significant factors in the choices of contract partners, since they occur significantly more frequently than would be the case if contract partners were selected without any consideration for these broader relationships. In terms of magnitude of preference, however, transitivity appears to be the dominant concern for both types of agreements, suggesting that contract partner selection does indeed use the embeddedness of networks to help reduce the threat of opportunism even with restrictive agreements. In terms of self-organizing governance, local governments appear to reduce the transaction costs of contracting by paying attention not just to a potential partner's individual characteristics that were also described by *Andrew*, but also by considering the relational characteristics of the partner within the broader network of contractual relationships.

Shrestha: Different Risks Produce Different Contractual Patterns

Shrestha also considers structural characteristics that can mitigate contractual risks but focuses on the characteristics of different services as the determinant of the types of risks facing the buyers of each service. Most of the nine services studied require very specific investments by the sellers in order to provide the service, leading to the problem of opportunism because of asset specificity, measurement, and holdup problems (Williamson 1981). Some of the services, particularly fire and emergency management, also impose problems of interdependent risk arising when a common disaster strikes multiple contract partners.

Shrestha finds evidence in all but one service area that local governments seek specific patterns of contractual relationships to mitigate contractual risks. Buyers preferred contracts with popular sellers in four service areas, presumably because reputational effects provide an alternative means of controlling the seller's opportunism while also allowing maximum benefit from economies of scale. In three of these four services and in two additional cases, buyers tend to create extended network patterns that provide alternative sources of supply in case one supplier suffers a breakdown in services, which also provides a different safeguard against seller opportunism. Finally, for the two services with greatest environmental uncertainty, *Shrestha* finds a tendency to seek multiple independent contracts as the primary means of spreading risks.

One surprising difference between the two studies is that *Shrestha* finds little evidence that transitivity is used to control opportunism in any service delivery area, while *Andrew* finds it to be prevalent in both adaptive and restrictive contracting. Both study service agreements at the county level in Florida, with *Shrestha* analyzing services individually in one county and *Andrew* pooling data over several counties and service areas. *Shrestha* obtained data directly from the towns involved and found considerable stability in contractual agreements – new contracts were signed all the time, particularly in the past decade, but contracts were almost always renewed and seldom discarded. The strong continuity in these agreements suggests that contracting partners may constrain opportunism through repeated play rather than through transitive contractual patterns in this county. *Andrew*'s data, on the other hand, shows considerable change over four time periods in the contractual data provided by the state, possibly suggesting that transitivity becomes more important as the length of the typical contract becomes shorter.

By providing empirical evidence about contractual patterns for several distinct service-provision arenas, these chapters establish the potential utility of theories linking the specific kind of risk associated with the characteristics of a service area and the expected patterns of contracts that can reduce those risks. In ongoing studies both authors intend to explore remaining questions important for understanding the potential role of contractual networks in enhancing the use of agreements. Do bilateral contracts in one service area provide credibility for contracts between the same local governments in other areas as well? Do multilateral agreements encourage or dampen additional bilateral agreements in other areas – *Andrew* finds, for example, that local governments involved in multilateral agreements tend to be less involved in bilateral agreements, suggesting a substitution effect similar to what *Mullin* finds for special districts. Can the critical risk and the associated contractual pattern be measured directly for some contracting arena rather than relying on indirect measures of the asset specificity of different services, so the analysis of structure actually tests the prediction under? Perhaps more important, can empirical evidence show directly the extent to which the structure found in these studies actually decreases the risks of contracting? Extending these questions to other arenas of intergovernmental agreements is also critical for establishing their generality, since they presumably should apply to patterns of memos of understanding, memos of agreement, and contractual arrangements among government agencies as well as between agencies and other stakeholders.

The structure of interlocal service agreements described by *Shrestha* and *Andrew* illustrates how self-organizing mechanisms can resolve many horizontal ICA dilemmas with minimal external intervention as long as the transaction costs are not too high. When asset specificity and other sources of risk reach a very high level, transaction costs may preclude the use of contractual arrangements even when embedded in the most supportive pattern of relationships. As *Jones* notes, mutual adaptation may be very costly in terms of delays in reaching consensus because opportunism combined with bounded rationality makes it difficult to foresee a partner's moves. Hence, the parties may prefer to adopt some unified management such as an independent authority or specialized district. Although a unified structure suffers from bureaucratic delays and internal agency costs, it can also reduce extreme coordination (adaptation) costs and behavioral opportunism associated with very high asset specificity. At the same time, consolidation poses principal-agent problems as discussed by *Whitford,* and different rules of consolidation may either complement or supplement the mitigating effects of intergovernmental agreements.

Mullin: Rules for Consolidation Can Suppress Self-Organizing Alternatives

The relationship of consolidated districts to other local government units described by *Mullin* provides an illustration of the trade-offs between consolidation and contracting solutions. *Mullin* first compares the potential advantages of the centralized institution of consolidated special districts with the more self-organizing mechanism of interlocal government contracts. Her analysis examines water supply districts in 17 states and explores the compatibility of mandated and self-organizing governance mechanisms in mitigating ICA dilemmas in water supply. *Mullin* focuses on the role of state-level rules in shaping the motivation of local actors in addressing collective problems. She finds that by allowing special districts with slack resources to expand into new territory, state rules that promote boundary flexibility reduce the likelihood that districts will develop contracting relationships to share their surplus capacity with neighboring governments. Thus, districts with flexible boundary rules appear to compete with intergovernmental contracting as a solution to ICA dilemmas, not complement them.

Mullin does not argue that this outcome of flexible boundaries is necessarily inefficient, which would require a broader research design that could compare the relative efficiency of contracting versus special district mechanisms for supplying water. Her results demonstrate instead the importance of considering the impact of any mitigating mechanism in the context of the entire range of mitigating institutions. In particular, they show how alternative sets of operating rules (flexible versus fixed boundaries of special districts) can change the relationship of an otherwise compatible mechanism imposed from above into one that competes with other self-organizing mitigating mechanisms; whether this spillover effect reduces self-organizing solutions in policy areas not directly related to the special district remains an important issue to be investigated.

Bickers, Post, and Stein: Electoral Incentives Support Self-Organizing Mechanisms

Finally, *Bickers et al.* focus specifically on electoral incentives to adapt mitigating mechanisms in the context of horizontal problems. They analyze two main hypotheses. The ambitious politician hypothesis argues that the need to develop a broader electoral constituency provides a critical incentive for ambitious local elected officials to cooperate with other local governments. The career path from local government to increasingly higher offices with broader geographic constituencies requires electoral support beyond the official's currently limited constituency. The potential gains that could be claimed from resolving ICA dilemmas provide one means of building support. Involvement with groups from the next higher level constituency during intergovernmental collaboration provides such an opportunity, so ambitious politicians have strong motivations to develop new collaborative activities that can deliver outputs desired by groups beyond the official's current constituency. If ambitious politicians are a driving force behind collaboration, then areas with greater levels of intergovernmental collaboration should also have a greater proportion of local officials running for higher office.

In contrast, the incumbency protection hypothesis argues that incumbents in higher positions are motivated to encourage collaboration among local governments within their jurisdiction specifically to protect their positions. Collaboration provides a means of providing benefits that can attract a broader support base for the incumbent, so incumbents are motivated to invest heavily in the informal collaborative networks necessary for successful collaboration. To the extent that constituencies that gain from collaboration depend on incumbents' networks to supply desired collaborative policy outcomes, the involved constituencies are likely to defend political incumbents who play critical roles in the network. Thus collaborative networks help suppress challenges from ambitious politicians that might disrupt the networks. If incumbency efforts to develop supportive local networks are the driving force behind collaboration, then incumbents most successful at developing local networks of collaboration are also likely to be most effective in suppressing ambitious politicians. We would thus expect fewer local officials to run for office in areas with higher levels of collaboration.

The very imaginative empirical analysis presented by *Bickers et al.* links intergovernmental aid agreements (IGAs, representing collaboration) to electoral trajectories of local elected officials (representing political ambition) in a sample of 108 cities in eight Metropolitan Statistical Areas. Unfortunately, they find no significant relationship between the number of IGAs in which a city collaborates and the proportion of the city's elected officials who run for higher office. If anything, the insignificant but negative coefficient would support the suppression of ambition associated with the incumbent protection hypothesis.

Given this inconclusive finding, they next analyze the relative success of challenges. Here they find a significant positive relationship between the proportion of a city's services that involve collaboration and the proportion of the city's elected officials that successfully seek higher office. The significant relationship is limited to collaboration with governing units having overlapping jurisdictions (e.g., city and county or special districts), and is not significant for collaboration with governing units with shared borders. Nonetheless, the result initially seems more supportive of the ambitious politician hypothesis.

Bickers et al. provide a particularly intriguing perspective on self-organizing governance to explain the combined result; collaboration appears to both protect incumbents by suppressing the ambition of local officers to run for higher office and also to enhance the success of the ambitious officers when they do run for office. Higher level officials assiduously cultivate collaborative networks to protect their incumbency. This in turn forces ambitious lower level officials to play an active role in the collaboration to build support for their anticipated eventual run for higher office. Although the collaboration network initially impedes the career progress of an ambitious local official, the apprenticeship years invested in extending this network can pay off in terms of support when the higher level incumbent vacates the position.

In short, electoral incentives at both upper and lower levels of the federalist system strongly support the development of collaborative networks that play such a critical role in the development and maintenance of successful collaborations among local governments. Collaborative agreements provide incumbents with a means to suppress challenges from ambitious politicians seeking higher offices while also providing a means for the same ambitious politicians to enhance the likelihood of their eventual success.

This chapter makes an important contribution to understanding the role of electoral incentives in the formal system in the development and maintenance of both formal and informal self-organizing institutions. Although the empirical study is more suggestive than conclusive, it provides an important foundation for future studies. For example, the *Andrew* and *Shrestha* types of studies could be combined with this approach to test the extent to which geographic boundaries of higher office provide an independent influence on the patterns of interlocal agreements. Similarly, the surveys of network participants in *Weible* or *Berardo* could add questions of support for political incumbency to provide a direct test of the interaction between the political system and collaborative institutions.

INTEGRATING REGIONAL POLICY THROUGH NETWORKS AND PARTNERSHIPS

The next section focuses primarily on the interaction between two common forms of self-organizing activities: informal policy networks and collaborative institutions. *Weible* considers factors that shape informal policy networks within the context of a very large and multifaceted regional policy arena. Two other chapters explore these interactions in the context of multipartner projects (*Berardo*) and multiple partnerships (*Lubell et al.*), two types of collaborative institutions that have become the most common forms of self-organizing institutions for integrating environmental and resource management policies of multiple agencies over geographic regions. Finally, *Thurner* studies European Union negotiations designed to create a consolidated governance structure. All chapters analyze different aspects of policy networks and how they interact with other mechanisms intended to voluntarily coordinate policies. We will discuss their contributions beginning with the least intrusive informal network mechanism for resolving ICAs.

Weible: Beliefs and Common Policy Participation Shape Alliance Networks

Weible analyzes factors affecting the process of policy network formation among allies and opponents for water policies in the North California Delta area, a highly fragmented and contentious regional policy arena. *Weible* argues that fragmentation in the policy arena has led to the development of policy networks of allies and opponents to coordinate policy activities across symbiotic functional arenas. These alliance networks include government agencies, their constituencies, and other stakeholders involved in water policy issues that affect most of the state, since much of the water heading for San Francisco Bay and for Southern California flows through the Delta. Networks provide a self-organized, informal means for participants to gain some control over how the policy decisions of multiple authorities in different functional areas affect their particular interests.

Weible's analysis is based on questionnaire data from all active participant organizations recognized by others as being active in the policy arena in 1997. Respondents representing each organization were asked to identify their three primary allies and opponents from a list of participant types ranging from agencies (e.g., Environmental Protection Agency or federal and state fish and wildlife agencies) and experts (consultants, scientists) to interest groups (e.g., agriculture, Bay water suppliers, shoreline developers). Respondents reported that collaborative activities like sharing information and developing joint strategies were common with the reported allies, confirming that networks identified by the allies question captured the kind of self-organizing coordination mechanism of interest in this volume. To explain the observed pattern of alliances, respondents were also asked about the extent of their participation in different functional arenas as well as their policy beliefs about the severity of water-related problems and their policy preferences for protecting natural systems and for building a peripheral canal.

Weible's first two hypotheses address one of this volume's critical questions about how informal policy networks are formed. The first hypothesis predicts that informal policy networks will form among actors who are active in the same functional areas. Joint participation in the same set of functional issues enhances the likelihood of contacts and discoveries of mutual concerns. In addition, actors themselves involved in multiple functional arenas can receive greater rewards from allies that can coordinate activities in these same arenas and hence will seek allies involved in similar functional arenas.

The second hypothesis emphasizes the role of common beliefs in forming and maintaining alliances. Common beliefs minimize both transaction costs of agreement on joint activities between allies and the decision costs of creating and maintaining networks, since common beliefs increase the likelihood of shared goals and efficient communication. *Weible* notes that the network structure appears relatively stable over time, since a 1992 and 1997 survey produce similar alliance patterns. This should increase the level of shared beliefs among allies, since the learning process over time should lead to convergence beliefs among allies and contrasting beliefs among their opponents. Note that the shared function hypothesis can also be congruent with the belief hypothesis, particularly if stable patterns of interactions across functional arenas lead to stable alliances and hence long-term learning patterns.

The hypotheses are tested first by identifying sets of actors who participate in the same functional areas and sets who have similar beliefs about the seriousness of policy problems and the advantage of proposed canal and wetland protection policies. A more aggregated approach using multidimensional scaling and cluster analysis first identifies the specific clusters that share functional arenas and that have common beliefs, and then compares these clusters with the clusters that emerge from those with common allies and those with common enemies. The four different mappings are finally compared systematically using quadratic assignment procedure regression to statistically test the strength of correlation between beliefs and functional mappings on the one hand and ally and opponent networks on the other.

The regression results demonstrate most clearly that both beliefs and functional arenas are significantly related to the structure of alliance networks, while only beliefs have significant influence on opponent networks. The results support *Weible*'s expectations that the search for allies to coordinate policies is influenced equally by the regular interactions undertaken to influence functional arenas and by the attraction of those sharing similar beliefs and policy preferences. Common beliefs are important in shaping policy networks, but even after controlling for the effect of beliefs, common functional area participation provides an additional boost to the likelihood of a network link between actors sharing the same functional areas.

Clarifying the means by which participation and beliefs shape networks remains an important question for the study of self-organizing mechanisms, since *Weible*'s empirical study cannot establish the direction of causality. In particular, do beliefs shape networks, in which case networks would tend to reinforce existing divisions in political culture? Or do participation and overlapping activities lead to discovery of joint tactical opportunities that over time encourage consistent beliefs? Both of the first two hypotheses are undoubtedly at play in different circumstances, but each leads to different expectations for the potential role of networks in resolving ICAs – particularly the most difficult ICAs discussed in *Jones*. As *Weible* found, the first two hypotheses are likely to have important explanatory power, so the critical question is to determine which influence is more prevalent under what particular circumstances.

In his third hypothesis, *Weible* investigates the role of institutional brokers in encouraging collaboration. He argues that collaborative institutions characterized by open rules of participation, consensus-based rules of decision making, and joint fact finding are most likely to play the role of institutional brokers. In the empirical study, he identifies CALFED as a collaborative institution established to resolve long-standing policy disputes. He finds some evidence that CALFED is in a position to reduce transaction costs based on its diverse involvement in different functional areas, mostly moderate beliefs, and low number of opponents. One implication *Weible* draws is that collaborative institutions probably have a stronger capacity to mitigate collective action problems when competitive functional areas intersect and transaction costs are high, whereas informal policy networks are probably better suited for mitigating situations when symbiotic functional areas intersect and transaction costs are low. *Weible*'s findings suggest that one of the next steps in the application of the ICA framework is to investigate the relative and overall contribution of different mitigating mechanisms in reducing transaction costs.

Berardo: Networks among Partners Enhance Future Collaboration

Berardo studies the implementation of joint water resource projects involving multiple agencies in Florida. As mitigating mechanisms, joint projects lie a bit to the right of informal networks in Figure 1.1 of *Feiock and Scholz*, somewhere between bilateral contracts and larger collaborative partnerships. Like intergovernmental agreements among local governments, joint projects allow specialized agencies to gain mutual advantages by coordinating on specific projects. Elsewhere, Berardo (2008) analyzes the impact of a project's embeddedness within the combined external network of joint projects (a task similar to that of *Andrew* and *Berardo*), but in this chapter he focuses on the internal network relationships between partners.

In particular, he directly addresses our question of how the incentives induced by participation in a collaborative institution affect the adaptability and sustainability of future joint projects. Once agencies experience mutual gains in one project, what aspects of informal relationships within the project enhance the likelihood of involvement in future joint projects to meet new ICA challenges that are constantly evolving? He considers two theoretical perspectives that emphasize different aspects of the internal networks; the first emphasizes resource exchange and dependency, while the second emphasizes the strength of relationships.

The empirical analysis finds that a partner's ability to provide political support for the joint project enhances the likelihood of future collaboration, but contrary to expectations, support in the form of financial resources, technical expertise, and regulatory assistance do not have a significant effect. The willingness to provide political support appears to play a more critical role than the other resources, perhaps because it is the most difficult to secure and guarantee through the formal, contractual aspects of the joint project.

In addition, *Berardo* finds that the frequency of contacts and the intensity of the relationships between project partners both significantly increase the likelihood of future collaboration, suggesting that the quality of the informal relationship rather than the exchanged resources plays the stronger role in enhancing future collaboration. Extending this research to other types of collaborative institutions is particularly important for understanding how the ability of the collaborative to respond to future problems is likely to depend on the quality of informal networks developed within the formal structure of the institution. If the impacts are as significant in other collaborative institutions as *Berardo* finds for joint projects, the impact of formal designs of collaborative institutions on the informal network structure (e.g., Schneider et al. 2003) will become an important question for future research.

The importance of informal networks within the formal institution underscores the importance of understanding the dynamic interactions between the initial policy networks and the underlying ICA in shaping the emergence of a mitigating mechanism. If political support, frequency of contacts, and intensity of network relationships enhance the likelihood of future joint projects for those already participating in water projects, presumably they would also be important in predicting the emergence of joint projects in new policy arenas. If networks do play a critical role in the evolution of collaborative institutions, does the presence of simpler mechanisms like joint projects enhance or diminish network support for broader partnerships? The next chapter by *Lubell et al.* provides some preliminary findings for this research agenda.

Although *Berardo* is most concerned with resource exchange and network relationships, the study finds that expectations and problem perceptions also have significant impacts on future collaboration. Respondents reporting that the project is likely to meet the organization's initial expectations are more likely to favor future collaboration with all partners in the project. *Berardo* thus cautions about the adverse impact that the failure of poorly designed projects might have on future self-organizing efforts – a conclusion likely to apply across the entire spectrum of self-organizing mechanisms. He also notes that respondents who perceive water-related problems to be most serious are also more likely to support future collaboration on water-related projects. Recognition of the underlying ICA dilemmas in itself appears to enhance the incentives to collaborate in resolving them (Lubell et al. 2002).

Lubell, Henry, and Mccoy: Multiple Coordinating Mechanisms Impose Diminishing Returns on Collaborative Activities

Lubell et al. consider many of the issues from the previous two chapters in the context of multiple coordinating institutions operating in the same policy arena. They analyze the impact of participation in multiple institutions on the extent of participation in joint projects and other forms of collaboration as well as on general policy perceptions (fairness, satisfaction, and consensus) that reflect cooperative attitudes.

The authors emphasize that self-organizing mechanisms must be studied within the "ecology of games" that includes all related mechanisms in all common policy arenas within a given geographic territory – a point similar to the connected-game metaphor in *Jones*. The description of the evolution of multiple coordination mechanisms to resolve ICA dilemmas common to transportation, environmental, and land-use policies provides one of their unique contributions to this volume.

Their major contribution compares the impact of participation in two types of mechanisms. The "traditional" mechanisms include local land-use planning and transportation planning venues that are vested with different degrees of state authority to impose their decisions on recalcitrant participants. They correspond to more authoritative mechanisms more to the right in Figure 1.1 that impose a greater loss of autonomy because decisions can be made without their consent, at least in comparison to the "collaborative" mechanisms.

The "collaborative" mechanism, on the other hand, provides a venue for building agreement on issues, developing social capital among stakeholders, and improving the scientific/information basis of decision making. We refer to the collaborative mechanism here as "partnership" to distinguish it from the range of collaborative activities that the partnership is hypothesized to influence. Since partnership decisions are generally advisory and dependent for implementation on the authoritative decisions of its members, the process is of necessity consensus based and inclusive (Scholz and Stiftel 2005), requiring participation and agreement from the authorities and constituencies involved in the ICA dilemma being addressed. Thus, partnerships are more self-organizing than traditional mechanisms in the sense that they have little authority to impose externality costs and restrict the autonomy of members. At the same time, the emphasis on consensus and unanimity imposes higher participation costs. Critics argue that participation costs outweigh the potential advantages to be gained, and that policy outputs are largely symbolic acts that do little to mitigate the actual ICA dilemma.

To test the differences in collaborative activities associated with participation in the two types of mechanisms, *Lubell et al.* survey all identifiable actors involved in land-use and transportation planning issues in two California regions that have developed partnerships to coordinate these issues. The survey asks the frequency of participation in five related policy arenas, including "traditional" venues of environmental review permitting, city/county planning, transportation planning, and natural resource planning in addition to the partnership. To measure network relationships they asked respondents to identify on a list of 53 prominent agencies and actor types those with whom they collaborate, those they trust, and those they believe to have the most influence on policy outcomes.

The most striking finding in their study is that participation in both the traditional and collaborative mechanisms enhances collaborative activities and cooperative attitudes (except for perceived consensus). However, the positive effect of participating in the partnership diminishes with greater participation in the other arenas and actually becomes negative in the rare case of actors participating in all arenas. So participation in partnerships does enhance collaboration, but so does participation in the more traditional mechanisms that do not share the partnership's collaborative nature. Combined with *Weible*'s finding, it suggests that participation in multiple arenas stimulates the development of informal networks and that these networks in turn enhance collaborative activities. Understanding the role of networks in enhancing participation in related venues is a high priority goal for understanding self-organizing solutions to ICA dilemmas.

What is less clear from our perspective is the extent to which *Lubell et al.*'s traditional venues (particularly natural resource planning) and *Weible*'s functional areas correspond to specific authoritative decision-making arenas that simply reflect formal authority structure or whether they actually represent ongoing self-organizing activities. For example, each of *Weible*'s functional areas include multiple authorities whose decisions have externality effects on some commonly perceived "policy arena." Indeed, the concept of "policy arena" (as defined by participants, not by analysts) may itself be conceived as an important self-organizing mechanism to be studied along with more formal joint projects and partnerships, since the development of common perceptions among those affected by externalities is one means of reducing the transaction costs, and most likely one preliminary step in the development of partnerships. This would expand the study of informal coordinating mechanisms to include concepts like policy communities, communities of shared knowledge and beliefs, and epistemic communities. Haas (1992: 3) provides one of the more influential definitions:

An epistemic community is a network of professionals with recognized expertise and competence in a particular domain and an authoritative claim to policy-relevant knowledge within that domain or issue-area . . . from a variety of disciplines and backgrounds, they have (1) a shared set of normative and principled beliefs, which provide a value-based rationale for the social action of community members; (2) shared causal beliefs, which are derived from their analysis of practices leading or contributing to a central set of problems in their domain and which then serve as the basis for elucidating the multiple linkages between possible policy actions and desired outcomes; (3) shared notions of validity – that is, inter-subjective, internally defined criteria for weighing and validating knowledge in the domain of their expertise; and (4) a common policy enterprise – that is a set of common practices associated with a set of problems to which their professional competence is directed, presumably out of the conviction that human welfare will be enhanced as a consequence.

As concepts, epistemic communities have much in common with advocacy coalitions (Sabatier and Jenkins-Smith 1993), except that advocacy coalitions coordinate activities among subgroups and opponents in divided policy arenas (*Weible*). We need to understand the conditions under which self-organizing activities create unified communities and when it creates opposing coalitions, and the role played by network relationships in this evolutionary process. To what extent can such communities serve to coordinate fragmented authorities, and with what policy consequences? For example, the highly fragmented water supply system in Florida appeared to function well as an epistemic community until growth outstripped readily available water supplies, at which point the isolated technical community became an obstacle to the development and coordination of policies requiring trade-offs among growth and conservation issues (Berardo 2005; Dedekorkut 2005). As *Jones* warns, collaboration per se does not necessarily enhance overall efficiency.

In any case, the *Lubell et al.* and *Weible* studies, like the *Mullin* study, emphasize the importance of understanding the context of all mitigating mechanisms active in a given territory and the interactions among these mechanisms. We recognize the analysis of multiple games as an important tool for advancing the study of self-organizing responses to ICA dilemmas, particularly since actors intentionally select the arenas in which to participate based on their overall perceived interests. As noted in our earlier discussion of *Jones*, however, we prefer to define each game in terms of the independent formal authority involved in the ICA. As in *Lubell et al.*, the system of games then describes the formal allocation of authority, and the externalities of concern for a given ICA dilemma are reflected in the impact of the decision by one authority on payoffs in the game of a different authority. A "policy arena" in this context may be interpreted in *Jones*'s sense of independent games that become consolidated in ways that restrict the choices in the independent games and the strategies of those attempting to influence the games. From this perspective, *Lubell et al.*'s finding that participation in more traditional mechanisms enhances collaboration is not surprising, since these mechanisms themselves evolved to mitigate newly perceived externalities among existing games. *Lubell et al.* focuses attention on the critical question of what specific characteristics of the consolidated game in each arena and of the mechanisms available to coordinate the consolidated games lead to enhanced collaboration. They also demonstrate a powerful research design and analytic techniques that can be used to answer the question.

Thurner: Using Self-Organizing Networks to Design Formal Coordinating Mechanisms

The chapters discussed to this point have compared the effectiveness or considered the relationships between different mechanisms, with a particular emphasis on informal networks. *Thurner* takes the further step of considering the relationship between a formal allocation of decision-making rights in regional negotiations between nation-states and the informal transgovernmental networks that enabled the formal structure to operate. In doing so, he raises the classic issues about the relationship between formal and informal authority. He analyzes the 1996 Intergovernmental Conference of the European Union (EU) in which 15 national delegations negotiated the contents of a new constitutional treaty intended to create a stronger EU central government. Although the geographical scale and policy scope of these negotiations are dramatically different from the regional, specialized ICA dilemmas of the other empirical cases, the generic problems and motivations for achieving a coordinated solution are similar.

Thurner begins with a discussion of the continuous failure of the EU since the mid-1990s to produce an accepted constitutional treaty, and he argues that the design of the formally constituted negotiating process was the cause of failure. The design followed the existing hierarchical allocation of authority within each country that gave primary negotiating authority to the foreign affairs ministries, under the supervision of the prime minister. The specialized ministries that actually formulated the proposals for their domain were relegated to advisory roles, reflecting the implicit assumption that a central coordinator could best determine the optimal position for the country as a whole; specialized ministries were not to be given a chance to cut their own deals with their counterparts in other countries.

Thurner traces the problem of the 1996 conference to the limited expertise each country's central coordinators could have about the 46 major issues to be negotiated and about the externalities when positions on one issue affected other issues in complex ways. Despite formal restrictions, many ministries involved in the preparatory process consulted informally with other ministries within their country as well as with their counterpart ministries in other countries, creating a self-organized policy network to aid in dealing with the broad range of alternatives and the complexity of issues.

Thurner analyzes the structure of these self-organizing policy networks, based on survey data from 140 top officials representing the major participating ministries from each country – a truly remarkable dataset! The survey asks which issues the ministry was involved in, who they consulted during the negotiations, and who was perceived as most influential on the relevant issues.

To compare formal authority and informal networks, the analysis first categorizes the 46 issues into nine tasks, and uses a sociogram to illustrate which ministries in Germany had formal authority over which tasks. The resultant Figure 12.1 illustrates that more than one authority has jurisdiction over each issue, as portrayed by the multiple ministries connected to each task. *Thurner*'s Figure 12.2 presents a sociogram with the same ministries and tasks, but now the links reveal the most influential ministries for each task area as identified by eliciting the mutual assessment of all involved actors of this system. Potential differences between these sociograms illustrate the differences between formal authority and informal influence for the German negotiating team. In the case of Germany, the perceived influence of the Ministry of Economy in particular is far greater than would be expected from the formal authority it has. *Thurner*'s example demonstrates how formal and informal relationships can be studied for regional integration issues of any scope.

Given the failure of this combined formal and informal process in achieving the self-imposed negotiation goals, *Thurner*'s main question is how to design a better mechanism to advise the EU when coordinated decisions need to be made – particularly on crisis issues when a consensus needs to be created in very short time periods. The problem is particularly complex because it involves multiple jurisdictions (nation-states) as well as expertise in multiple policy domains and distributed decision-making rights (specialized ministries). Any formal reorganization of authority among ministries and countries to improve coordination would impose the dual moral hazard problem discussed in greater detail by *Whitford*. Instead of reallocating authority in formal structures, the managerial literature cited by *Thurner* suggests developing teams composed of participants from the existing formal structures with the specific task of the team in mind. Teams develop plans that must still be approved by those with relevant authority – an approach very similar to those advocating collaborative institutions to coordinate policies of authorities who subsequently must act on decisions made in the collaborative before the collaborative's decisions have any impact.

Thurner's main contribution to this design literature is to illustrate how network analysis can help in designing task-oriented teams to coordinate EU decisions based on existing authority structures – a more plausible solution than a wholesale reorganization that would consolidate authority in completely new units at the domestic as well as at the EU level. He provides two examples that identify critical ministries to include on a given team: one for teams to represent each country, and another for a unified team representing the EU as a whole. In both cases, the analysis of each ministry's "influence centrality" in the informal network determines the choice. Most country teams would still include the prime minister and ministry of foreign affairs, although the other influential ministries vary considerably from country to country because of cross-national differences in the relative centrality of ministries. The unified team for the EU would select the most central ministries for the EU as a whole, although only the highest ranking ministry would be taken for each country to prevent dominance by one country. The resultant team would include the foreign ministries of Germany and France, not surprisingly, but also the premiers' offices in Belgium and Luxembourg as well as the ministry of interior or of finances from the Netherlands. The latter selections apparently reflect the greater activities and recognized prominence of Benelux officials in EU negotiations.

The argument *Thurner* makes is that participants identified as having the most influence are most likely to be able to craft an agreement that they subsequently can persuade others to accept. Given the need to restrict participants to reduce the costs of negotiation, selecting actors perceived as most central at least increases the likelihood of success. Note that no changes are made in the formal allocation of competencies, but only in the designation of the negotiating team. *Thurner*'s approach stands on its head the common concern of intervening in the informal system to make it congruent with the formal system of authority and instead uses characteristics identified from the self-organizing informal system to design a more efficient formally recognized coordination device! If the network characteristics *Thurner* or others propose can be tested and indeed prove an efficient method for designing coordinating mechanisms, they could be used to custom-design efficient mechanisms to coordinate authorities without requiring extensive reorganization of the authorities.

Of course, the equity issues noted in *Jones* remain to be addressed even if such mechanisms can be shown to be efficient. Proponents of collaborative processes tend to favor expanded participation of all stakeholders, even inactive stakeholders who may not even realize that they will be impacted in the future (Susskind 2005). These proponents are partly concerned with the potential that those excluded from the process will challenge agreements and disrupt policies when the unanticipated effects become known – an efficiency argument based on a longer time horizon than the case considered by *Thurner*. The equity issue is more concerned with who is and is not represented in the custom-designed coordination mechanism (Scholz and Stiftel 2005). As *Jones* notes, successful cooperation among a small group can also be called collusion to the extent that taxpayer money is being spent without representation.

Thurner argues that decisions within the small group do not alter representation as long as all authorities whose decisions are being coordinated still need to approve any decision. But if the choice for nonparticipating ministries is between a biased outcome from the small group and the previous uncoordinated and presumably unsatisfactory condition, their approval does not necessarily signal that their interests have been adequately represented. At minimum, those who are represented can potentially claim the lion's share of the gains from cooperation, leaving others no worse off than they were in the previously unsatisfactory condition, but also no better off under the newer policy. As Moe (2005) has noted, some who voluntarily agree to a given institution do so primarily because they do not have the power to prevent it from developing. They may actually be worse off under the new institution than they would have been without it, but they would be even worse off if they do not join the new institution at all. Designing more efficient formal coordination mechanisms by utilizing those who have become most influential in the self-organizing responses to the problem may indeed enhance effectiveness, but lack of representation may pose considerably difficulties in maintaining and justifying collaboration. Scholz and Stiftel (2005) argue that developing representation standards for formally recognized mitigation mechanisms will be a critical need if they are to become legitimized as common institutions within the government.

SELF-ORGANIZING FEDERALISM: THE RESEARCH AGENDA

The primary argument presented in this volume is that collaborative self-organizing institutions provide an essential aspect of federalist systems of governance, and that their dramatic growth in recent decades signals both the increasing complexity of policy interactions in the global system and the adaptive ability of federalist systems.

We have based our argument on the long-standing notion of federalist systems most recently described by Bednar (2008): federalist systems are designed for their gains in efficiency, which in turn depends on developing a robust, finely balanced distribution of authority across different institutions and levels of government. A robust system must be at once "strong, flexible, and resilient" so Bednar focuses her attention on redundant safeguards capable of guarding the careful balance of authority against the "temptation for constituent governments to exploit the union for their own gain" (Bednar 2008, 11).

We argue that this delicate balance of powers will inevitably create externalities as decisions by one authority affect multiple other authorities. The safeguards analyzed by Bednar provide some flexibility in reassigning authority when disputes occur, but such resolution must consider potential threats to the system as much as efficiency in resolving such disputes. The self-organizing mechanisms we have explored provide an alternative means of mitigating the inefficiencies of fragmented authority without requiring a major reallocation of authority, a means that until recently has taken place below the radar of scholars and practitioners concerned with intergovernmental relations. Just as Bednar argues that redundant safeguards are essential to provide a robust federalist system, we argue that redundant self-organizing mechanisms to resolve externality problems are equally critical for an adaptive system capable of maintaining the gains of efficiency associated with federalist systems.

With this in mind, we briefly consider the research agenda implicit in our approach and the studies in this volume. What remains to be learned about the three questions we raised initially? How can studies create this knowledge?

How Do Self-Organizing Mechanisms Reduce Transaction Costs?

This central question is the primary focus for the discussions in the first section of this volume and is discussed briefly for each of the mechanisms considered in the empirical studies. The empirical chapters report variation in the types of mechanisms and also design variation within specific categories of mechanisms employed to mitigate ICA dilemmas. Several chapters expand the preliminary list of mechanisms provided in Chapter 1 by including franchise contracting methods of delegation (*Whitford*), formalization of informal networks (*Thurner*), and by at least suggesting the inclusion of advocacy coalitions, epistemic communities, and in general the process of policy definition. There are, of course, many variations and subcategories within the primary categories we have discussed, and we need to explore which factors are the most critical and which would make little difference in the performance of each mechanism.

Unfortunately, the relatively rich theoretical understanding of how these mechanisms can reduce transaction costs and hence mitigate ICAs is not matched by a strong empirical base about the actual ability of the mechanism to reduce externalities. This problem is well known in the study of collaborative partnerships because measuring the difference in outcomes specifically attributable to the partnership is extremely difficult and costly. Evaluations therefore tend to rely on indirect and self-reported measures (Leach, Pelkey, and Sabatier 2002). The empirical work suggests that transaction costs can be reduced by external resources such as the provision of resources to support collaboration or provision of institutions for enforcement and dispute resolution. Transaction costs can also be reduced by internal resources such as social capital or embedded relationships. In short, careful empirical evaluation of the actual impacts of mechanisms remains a major impediment to our study, one that our volume does little to resolve.

What Incentives Do Potential Members Have to Create the Mechanism?

The empirical studies have devoted the greatest effort to exploring the incentives to create mechanisms in both metropolitan and in regional policy integration settings. Local actors seek to maintain autonomy for important issues, especially where they will be held accountable by important political constituencies. Where the ICA dilemma poses risks for participants, effective mitigating mechanisms require them to sacrifice autonomy to some extent. When interdependencies and payoffs among actors in an ICA are asymmetric, conflict over rules and the availability of external resources play a decisive role in shaping the outcome. Several regression and sophisticated network analysis techniques demonstrated in this volume show promise for exploring factors affecting the development and structure of networks, joint projects, and collaborative efforts. One of the biggest remaining tasks required to address this question, however, is the development of a more comprehensive theoretical framework or more generic model for understanding motivations applicable to the multiple-game, multiple-mechanism settings that commonly affect ICA dilemmas.

How Do the Incentives Induced by the Mechanism Affect its Sustainability and Impact on Other ICAs?

The introduction of new mechanisms shapes incentives in ways that create their own problems and possibilities. The empirical chapters have provided several innovative examples for studying the impact of one mechanism on another. Because the altered incentives provided by an institution developed to resolve one ICA may have positive or negative impacts on other ICAs and other mitigating mechanisms, multiplexity of relationships or multiple games may introduce externalities and trade-offs. This is most evident in the negative interaction found by *Lubell et al.* that suggest that collaborative processes might actually increase transaction costs and reduce cooperation in other games.

Participation in multiple policy arenas and the ability of consolidated districts to alter boundaries have had negative impacts on the effectiveness of collaborative partnerships (*Lubell et al.*) and intergovernmental contractual relationships (*Mullin*), although participation enhances other forms of collaboration, and network relationships play an important role in enhancing the likelihood of future collaboration. As with the second question, the biggest remaining task here is the development of appropriate theoretical models capable of systematically explaining these different results.

In sum, we have attempted in this volume to provide both a unifying framework and examples of research capable of integrating the relatively unorganized research on self-organizing mechanisms to resolve ICA dilemmas. In some ways, our slow progress illustrates how little is known about this critical component of federalist systems, and we believe that considerable theoretical and empirical work will be necessary before the role of self-organizing governance will be understood. On the other hand, the rapid spread of collaborative mechanisms poses a challenge to consider these mechanisms not just as one more possible policy tool of potential use to improve policy design but rather as a fundamental aspect of our governance structure that enhances the capacity for adaptive policy responses while minimizing impacts on the critical balance of authority required for a stable federalist system.

References

Advisory Commission on Intergovernmental Relations. 1985. Intergovernmental Service Agreements for Delivering Local Public Services: Update 1983. (A-103) Washington, D.C.: Government Printing Office.

Advisory Commission on Intergovernmental Relations (ACIR). 1992. *Local Boundary Commissions: Status and Roles in Forming, Adjusting, and Dissolving Local Government Boundaries*. Washington, D.C.: ACIR.

Agranoff, Robert, and Michael McGuire. 1998. "Multinetwork Management: Collaboration and the Hollow State in Local Economic Policy." *Journal of Public Administration Research and Theory* 8:67–91.

———. 2003.*Collaborative Public Management*. Washington, D.C.: Georgetown University Press.

Alchian, A., and H. Demsetz. 1972. "Production, Information Costs, and Economic Organization." *American Economic Review* 62:777–95.

Aldrich, Howard E., and Jeffrey Pfeffer. 1976. "Environments of Organizations." *Annual Review of Sociology* 2:79–105.

Altshuler, Alan, William Morrill, Harold Wolman, and Faith Mitchell (eds.). 1999. *Governance and Opportunity in Metropolitan America*. Washington, D.C.: National Academy Press.

Andreae, Lisette, and Karl Kaiser. 2001. "The 'Foreign Policies' of Specialized Ministries." In *Germany's New Foreign Policy*, edited by Wolf-Dieter Eberwein and Karl Kaiser. New York: Palgrave.

Atkins, Patricia S. 1997. Local Intergovernmental Agreements: Strategies for Cooperation. *International City/County Management Association Management Information System Report* 29(7):1–10.

Austin, D. Andrew. 1998. "A Positive Model of Special District Formation." *Regional Science and Urban Economics* 28:103–22.

———. 1999. "Politics vs. Economics: Evidence from Municipal Annexation." *Journal of Urban Economics* 45:501–32.

Axelrod, Robert. 1984. *Evolution of Cooperation*. New York: Basic Books.

Baird, Douglas G. 1990. "Self-Interest and Cooperation in Long-Term Contracts." *Journal of Legal Studies* 19:583–96.

Banks, Jeffrey, and Barry Weingast. 1992. "The Political Control of Bureaucracies under Asymmetric Information." *American Journal of Political Science* 36:509–24.

Bardach, E. 1998. *Getting Agencies to Work Together.* Washington: Brookings Institution Press.

Barnes, William R., and Larry C. Ledebur. 1998. *The New Regional Economies: The U.S. Common Market and the Global Economy.* Thousand Oaks, Calif.: Sage.

Bates, Robert H. 1998a. "The International Coffee Organization: An International Institution." In *Analytic Narratives,* edited by Robert Bates, Avner Greif, Margaret Levi, Jean-Laurent Rosenthal, and Barry R Weingast. Princeton, N.J.: Princeton University Press.

———. 1998b. "Contra Contractarianism: Some Reflections on the New Institutionalism." *Politics and Society* 6:387–401.

Baumgartner, Frank R., and Bryan D. Jones. 1991. "Agenda Dynamics and Policy Subsystems." *Journal of Politics* 53:1044–74.

Bay Conservation and Development Commission (BCDC). 2007. "About the Bay and BCDC." San Francisco, Calif.: BCDC.

Bea, Keith. 2004. *Emergency Management Preparedness Standards: Overview and Options for Congress.* Washington, D.C.: Congressional Research Service.

Becker, Jörg (ed.). 2003. *Process Management: A Guide for the Design of Business Processes.* Berlin: Springer.

Bednar, Jenna. 2004. "Authority Migration in Federations: A Framework for Analysis." *PS-Political Science and Politics* 37:403–8.

Bednar, Jenna, John Ferejohn, and Geoff Garrett. 1996. "The Politics of European Federalism." *International Review of Law and Economics* 16:279–95.

———. 2008. *The Robust Federation.* Cambridge, U.K.: Cambridge University Press.

Bender, Jonathan, and Piotr Swistak. 1997. "The Evolutionary Stability of Cooperation." *American Political Science Review* 91:290–307.

Benson, J. Kenneth. 1975. "The Inter-organizational Network as a Political Economy." *Administrative Science Quarterly* 20:229–49.

Berardo, Alfredo Ramiro. 2005. "The East Central Florida Regional Water Supply Planning Initiative: Creating Collaboration." In *Adaptive Governance and Water Conflict. New Institutions for Collaborative Planning,* edited by John T. Scholz and Bruce Stiftel. Washington, D.C.: Resources for the Future Press.

———. 2008. *Resource Exchange and Collaboration in Fragmented Policy Arenas: A Study of Water Projects in Southwest Florida.* Ph.D. Dissertation, Department of Political Science, Florida State University.

Berardo, Ramiro, and John T. Scholz. 2009. "Self-Organizing Policy Networks: Risk, Partner Selection and Cooperation in Estuaries." *American Journal of Political Science* (forthcoming).

Bickers, Kenneth N., and Robert M. Stein. 2004. "Interlocal Cooperation and the Distribution of Federal Grant Awards." *Journal of Politics* 66:800–22.

Bingham, Richard, Mary LeBlanc, and John Frendries. 1981. *Professional Associations and Municipal Innovation.* Madison: University of Wisconsin Press.

Bish, Robert L. 1971. *The Public Economy of Metropolitan Areas*. Chicago: Markham.

Bish, Robert L., and Vincent Ostrom. 1973. *Understanding Urban Government: Metropolitan Reform Reconsidered*. Washington, D.C: American Enterprise Institute.

Blair, Roger D., and Francine Lafontaine. 2005. *The Economics of Franchising*. Cambridge, U.K.: Cambridge University Press.

Blau, Peter M. 1964. *Exchange and Power in Social Life*. New York: Wiley.

Bledsoe, Timothy. 1993. *Careers in City Politics: The Case for Urban Democracy*. Pittsburgh: University of Pittsburgh Press.

Blomquist, William, and Roger B. Parks. 1995. "Fiscal, Service, and Political Impacts of Indianapolis-Marion County's Unigov." *Publius: The Journal of Federalism* 25:37–54.

Blomquist, William, and Edella Schlager. 2005. "Political Pitfalls of Integrated Watershed Management." *Society and Natural Resources* 18:101–17.

Boer, Peter, Mark Huisman, Tom Snijders, Lotte Wichers and. Evelien Zeggelink. 2006. *Stocnet: An Open Software System for the Advanced Analysis of Social Networks: User's Manual*, Version 1.6 Groningen, Netherlands: ICS/Science Plus.

Bollens, Scott A. 1986. "Examining the Link between State Policy and the Creation of Local Special Districts." *State and Local Government Review* 18:117–24.

Borgatti, Stephen, and Martin Everett. 1997. "Network Analysis of 2-mode Data." *Social Networks* 19:243–69.

Borgatti, S. P., Everett, M. G., and Freeman, L. C. 2002. *Ucinet 6 for Windows*. Harvard, Mass.: Analytic Technologies.

Borgatti, Stephen, and P. Foster. 2003. "The Network Paradigm in Organizational Research. A Review and Typology." *Journal of Management* 29:991–1013.

Brant, Rollin. 1990. "Assessing Proportionality in the Proportional Odds Model for Ordinal Logistic Regression." *Biometrics* 46:1171–78.

Breton, Albert. 1998. "Bureaucracy." In *The New Palgrave Dictionary of Economics and the Law*, edited by Peter Newman. London: Macmillan.

Breton, Albert, and Ronald Wintrobe. 1982. *The Logic of Bureaucratic Conduct: An Economic Analysis of Competition, Exchange, and Efficiency in Private and Public Organizations*. Cambridge, U.K.: Cambridge: University Press.

Brickley, J. A., and F. H. Dark. 1987. "The Choice of Organizational Form: The Case of Franchising." *Journal of Financial Economics* 18:401–20.

Brierly, A. B. 2004. "Issues of Scale and Transaction Costs in City-County Consolidation." In *City-County Consolidation and Its Alternatives: Reshaping the Local Government Landscape*, edited by J. B. Carr and R. C. Feiock. Armonk, N.Y.: M. E. Sharpe.

Brown, Trevor L., and Matthew Potoski. 2003. "Transaction Costs and Institutional Explanations for Government Service Production Decisions." *Journal of Public Administration Research and Theory* 13:441–68.

Buchanan, James. 1967. *Public Finance and the Democratic Process*. Chapel Hill: University of North Carolina Press.

Buchanan, James M., and Gordon Tullock. 1962. *The Calculus of Consent*. Ann Arbor: University of Michigan Press.

Burns, Nancy. 1994. *The Formation of American Local Governments: Private Values in Public Institutions.* New York, N.Y.: Oxford University Press.

Burt, Ronald S. 1992. *Structural Holes: The Social Structure of Competition.* Cambridge, Mass.: Harvard University Press.

——. 2005. *Brokerage and Closure: An Introduction to Social Capital.* New York: Oxford University Press.

Carpenter, Daniel, Kevin Esterling, and David Lazer. 2003. "The Strength of Strong Ties: A Model of Contact-Making in Policy Networks with Evidence from U.S. Health Policy." *Rationality and Society* 15:411–40.

——. 2004. "Friends, Brokers, and Transitivity: Who Informs Whom in Washington Politics?" *Journal of Politics* 66:224–46.

Carr, Jered B. 2004. "Whose Game Do We Play? Local Government Boundary Change and Metropolitan Governance." In *Metropolitan Governance: Conflict, Competition, and Cooperation,* edited by Richard C. Feiock. Washington, D.C.: Georgetown University Press.

——. 2006. "Local Government Autonomy and State Reliance on Special District Governments: A Reassessment." *Political Research Quarterly* 59: 481–92.

Carr, Jered B., and Richard C. Feiock. 2001. "State Annexation 'Constraints' and the Frequency of Municipal Annexation." *Political Research Quarterly* 54: 459–70.

——. 2004. *Reshaping the Local Landscape: Perspective on City County Consolidation and Its Alternatives.* Armonk, N.Y.: M.E. Sharpe.

Carrington, Peter J., John Scott, and Stanley Wasserman. 2005. *Models and Methods in Social Network Analysis.* New York: Cambridge University Press.

Caves, R. E. and W. F. Murphy. 1976. "Franchising: Firms, Markets, and Intangible Assets." *Southern Economic Journal* 42:572–86.

Chisholm, Donald. 1989. *Coordination without Hierarchy.* Berkeley: University of California Press.

Chubb, J. E. 1985. "The Political-Economy of Federalism." *American Political Science Review* 79:994–1015.

Clingermayer, James, and Richard Feiock. 2001. *Institutional Constraints and Policy Choice: An Exploration of Local Governance.* New York: State University of New York Press.

Coase, Ronald H. 1937. "The Nature of the Firm." *Economica* 4:386–405.

——. 1960. "The Problem of Social Cost." *Journal of Law and Economics* 3:1–44.

——. 1988. *The Firm, the Market and the Law.* Chicago: University of Chicago Press.

Coleman, James S. 1988. "Social Capital in the Creation of Human Capital." *American Journal of Sociology* 94:95–120.

——. 1990. *Foundations of Social Theory.* Cambridge, Mass.: Belknap Press.

Combs, James G., Steven C. Michael, and Gary J. Castrogiovanni. 2004. "Franchising: A Review and Avenues to Greater Theoretical Diversity." *Journal of Management* 30:907–31.

Connelly, Rachel, and Jean Kimmel. 2003. "The Effect of Child Care Costs on the Employment and Welfare Recipiency of Single Mothers." *Southern Economic Journal* 69:498–519.

Cook, Karen S. 1977. "Exchange and Power in Networks of Interorganizational Relations." *Sociological Quarterly* 18:62–82.

Cook, Karen S., Richard M. Emerson, Mary R. Gillmore, and Toshio Yamagishi. 1983. "The Distribution of Power in Exchange Networks: Theory and Experimental Results." *American Journal of Sociology* 89:275–305.

Cook, Karen S., and Toshio Yamagishi. 1992. "Power in Exchange Networks: A Power-Dependence Formulation." *Social Networks* 14:245–65.

Crémer, Jacques, and Thomas R. Palfrey. 2000. "Federal Mandates by Popular Demand." *Journal of Political Economy* 108:905–27.

Crockett, Sean, Vernon L. Smith, and Bart J. Wilson. 2006. "Exchange and Specialization as a Discovery Process." Unpublished manuscript. George Mason University.

Crotty, Patricia McGee. 1987. "The New Federalism Game: Primacy Implementation of Environmental Policy." *Publius: The Journal of Federalism* 17: 53–67.

Cumberland, John H. 1979. "Interregional Pollution Spillovers and Consistency of Environmental Policy." In *Regional Environmental Policy: The Economic Issue*, edited by H. Siebert et al. New York: New York University Press.

———. 1981. "Efficiency and Equity in Interregional Environmental Management." *Review of Regional Science* 10:1–19.

Dahlman, Carl J. 1979. "The Problem of Externality." *Journal of Law and Economics* 22:141–62.

Danielson, Michael N. 1972. *The Politics of Exclusion*. New York: Columbia University Press.

Dann, Philipp. 2007. "The Political Institutions." In *Principles of European Constitutional Law*, edited by Armin von Bogdandy and Jürgen Bast. Oxford: Hart.

Dant, R. P. and N. I. Nasr. 1998. "Control Techniques and Upward Flow of Information in Franchising in Distant Markets: Conceptualization and Preliminary Evidence." *Journal of Business Venturing* 13:3–28.

Davis, Charles. 1992. "State Environmental Regulation and Economic Development: Are They Compatible?" *Review of Policy Research* 11:149–57.

Dedekorkut, Aysin. 2005. "Tampa Bay Water Wars: From Conflict to Collaboration?" In *Adaptive Governance and Water Conflict. New Institutions for Collaborative Planning*, edited by John T. Scholz and Bruce Stiftel. Washington, D.C: Resources for the Future Press.

Dekker, David, David Krackhardt, and Tom Snijders. 2003. "Multicollinearity Robust QAP for Multiple Regression." In *NAACSOS Conference June, 2003*. Pittsburgh, Penn.: Omni William Penn.

Derthick, Martha. 1974. *Between State and Nation: Regional Organizations of the United States*. Washington, D.C.: Brookings Institution Press.

DiMaggio, P., and W. Powell. 1983. "The Iron Cage Revisited: Institutionalized Isomorphism and Collective Rationality in Organizational Fields." *American Sociological Review* 48:147–60.

Dixit, Avinash K. 1996. *The Making of Economic Policy*. Cambridge, Mass.: MIT Press.

Dnes, Anthony. 1996. "The Economic Analysis of Franchise Contracts." *Journal of Institutional and Theoretical Economics* 152:297–324.

Donahue, John. 2006. "On Collaborative Governance." Working Paper. John F. Kennedy School of Government, Harvard University.

Douma, Sytse, and Hein Schreuder. 2002. *Economic Approaches to Organizations*, 3rd ed. New York: Prentice Hall.

Dowding, Kenneth. 1995. "Model or Metaphor? A Critical Review of the Policy Network Approach." *Political Studies* 43:136–58.

Downs, Anthony. 1972. "Up and Down with Ecology – The 'Issue-Attention Cycle.' " *The Public Interest* 28:8–50.

———. 1994. *New Visions for Metropolitan America*. Washington, D.C.: Brookings Institution Press.

Drier, Peter, John Mollenkopf, and Todd Swanstrom. 2001. *Place Matters: Metropolitics for the Twenty-first Century*. Kansas: University of Kansas Press.

Dunlap, R. E., K. D. Van Liere, A. G. Mertig, and R. E. Jones. 2000. "Measuring Endorsement of the New Ecological Paradigm: A Revised Nep Scale." *Journal of Social Issues* 56:425–42.

Dutton, William H. 1995. "The Ecology of Games. The Ecology of Games and Its Enemies." *Communication Theory* 5:379–92.

Dye, Thomas R. 1964. "Urban Political Integration: Conditions Associated with Annexation in American Cities." *Midwest Journal of Political Science* 8:430–66.

Dye, Thomas R., Charles S. Leibman, Oliver P. Williams, and Harold Herman. 1963. "Differentiation and Cooperation in a Metropolitan Area." *Midwest Journal of Political Science* 7:145–55.

Edelman, Murray. 1971. *Politics as Symbolic Action: Mass Arousal and Quiescence*. New York: Academic Press.

Emerson, Richard M. 1962. "Power-Dependence Relations." *American Sociological Review* 27:31–41.

———. 1976. "Social Exchange Theory." *Annual Review of Sociology* 2:335–62.

———. 1999. *Delegating Powers: A Transaction Cost Politics Approach to Policy Making under Separate Powers*. New York: Cambridge University Press.

Erk, Jan. 2006. "Review Article: Does Federalism Really Matter?" *Comparative Politics* 39:103–20.

Everett, Martin, and Stephen P. Borgatti. 2005. "Extending Centrality." In *Models and Methods in Social Network Analysis*, edited by Peter Carrington, John Scott, and Stanley Wasserman. Cambridge, U.K.: Cambridge University Press.

Feiock, Richard C. 2002. "A Quasi-market Framework for Local Economic Development Competition." *Journal of Urban Affairs* 24:123–42.

———. (ed.). 2004. *Metropolitan Governance: Conflict, Competition, and Cooperation*. Washington D.C.: Georgetown University Press.

———. 2007. "Rational Choice and Regional Governance." *Journal of Urban Affairs* 29:49–65.

Feiock, Richard C., and Simon A. Andrew. 2006. "Non-Profit Organizations and the Delivery of Public Services." *International Journal of Public Administration* 29:759–69.

Feiock, Richard C., and Jered B. Carr. 2001. "Incentives, Entrepreneurs, and Boundary Change: A Collective Action Framework." *Urban Affairs Review* 36:382–405.

Feiock, Richard C., Annette Steinacker, and Hyung Jun Park. 2009. "Institutional Collective Action and Economic Development Joint Ventures." *Public Administration Review* 69:256–70.

Fenger, Menno, and Pieter-Jan Klok. 2001. "Interdependency, Beliefs, and Coalition Behavior: A Contribution to the Advocacy Coalition Framework." *Policy Sciences* 34:157–70.

Fernald, Edward A., and Elizabeth D. Purdum. 1998. *The Water Atlas of Florida.* Tallahassee: Institute of Science and Public Affairs, Florida State University.

Ferris, J. M., and Elizabeth Graddy. 1986. "Contracting Out: For What, with Whom?" *Public Administration Review* 46:332–44.

Fesler, James W. 1949. *Area and Administration.* Tuscaloosa: University of Alabama Press.

Filippov, Mikhail, Olga Shvetsova, and Peter C. Ordeshook. 2004. *Designing Federalism: A Theory of Self-Sustainable Federal Institutions.* Cambridge, U.K.: Cambridge University Press.

Foster, Kathryn A. 1997. *The Political Economy of Special Purpose Government.* Washington, D.C.: Georgetown University Press.

———. 1998. "Municipal Cooperative Agreements in Western New York: Survey Findings."

Friedkin, Noah. 1982. "Information Flow through Strong and Weak Ties in Intraorganizational Social Networks." *Social Networks* 3:273–85.

Friesema, H. Paul. 1971. *Metropolitan Political Structure: Intergovernmental Relations and Political Integration in the Quad-Cities.* Iowa City: University of Iowa Press.

Furubotn, Eirik G., & Rudolf Richter. 2005. *Institutions and Economic Theory: The Contribution of the New Institutional Economics.* Ann Arbor: University of Michigan Press.

Galaskiewicz, Joseph. 1979. *Exchange Networks and Community Politics.* London: Sage.

Gallini, N. T., and N. A. Lutz. 1992. "Dual Distribution and Royalty Fees in Franchising." *Journal of Law, Economics, and Organization* 8:471–501.

Galloway, Thomas D., and John Landis. 1986. "How Cities Expand: Does State Law Make a Difference?" *Growth and Change* 17:25–45.

Gerber, Elisabeth R., and Clark C. Gibson. 2005. "Balancing Competing Interests in American Regional Government." In *Program in American Democracy Speaker Series*, Notre Dame University, February 1, 2005.

Gillette, Clayton P. 2001. "Regionalization and Interlocal Bargains." *New York University Law Review* 76:190–271.

Goldsmith, Stephen, and William D. Eggers. 2004. *Governing by Network: The New Shape of the Public Sector.* Washington, D.C.: Brookings Institution Press.

Granovetter, Mark. 1973. "The Strength of Weak Ties." *American Journal of Sociology* 78:1360–80.

———. 1985. "Economic Action and Social Structure." *American Journal of Sociology* 91:481–510.

Gulati, R. 1998. "Alliances and Networks." *Strategic Management Journal* 19:293–317.

Gulati, Ranjan, and Martin Gargiulo. 1999. "Where Do Interorganizational Networks Come From?" *American Journal of Sociology.* 104:1439–93.

Guo, David. 2007. "Municipal Authority to Sell Water to Neighboring Zelienople." *Pittsburgh Post-Gazette*, W4.

Haas, Peter M. 1992. "Introduction: Epistemic Communities and International Policy Coordination." *International Organization* 46:1–35.

Hackett, Steven C. 1992. "Heterogeneity and the Provision of Governance for Common Pool Resources." *Journal of Theoretical Politics* 4:325–42.

Hamann, Richard. 2005. "Florida's Water Management Framework." In *Adaptive Governance and Water Conflict: New Institutions for Collaborative Planning*, edited by John Scholz and Bruce Stiftel. Washington, D.C.: Resources for the Future Press.

Hamilton, David K. 1999. *Governing Metropolitan Areas: Response to Growth and Change.* New York: Garland.

Hammer, Michael, and James Champy. 1993. *Reengineering the Corporation: A Manifesto for Business Revolution.* New York: HarperBusiness.

Hanak, Ellen. 2005. *Water for Growth: California's New Frontier.* San Francisco: Public Policy Institute of California.

Hanf, Kenneth, and Laurence O' Toole Jr. 1992. "Revisiting Old Friends: Networks, Implementation Structures and the Management of Interorganizational Relations." *European Journal of Political Research* 21:163–80.

Hanneman, Robert and Mark Riddle. 2001. "Introduction to Social Network Methods." Available at http://faculty.ucr.edu/~hanneman/nettext/index.html (last accessed April 15, 2009).

Hansen, Morten. 1999. "The Search-Transfer Problem: The Role of Weak Ties in Sharing Knowledge across Organization Subunits." *Administrative Science Quarterly* 44:82–111.

Hawkins, Robert B., Jr. 1976. *Self Government by District: Myth and Reality.* Stanford, Calif.: Hoover Institution Press.

Hayek, F. 1945. "The Use of Knowledge in Society." *American Economic Review* 35:519–30.

Hayes-Renshaw, Fiona, and Helen Wallace. 2006. *The Council of Ministers*, 2nd ed., comprehensively revised and updated. Basingstoke: Palgrave Macmillan.

Heckathorn, Douglas D. H. 1989. "Collective Action and the Second-Order Free-rider Problem." *Rationality and Society* 1:78–100.

———. 1987a. "Bargaining and the Sources of Transaction Costs: The Case of Government Regulation." *Journal of Law, Economics, and Organization* 3:69–98.

Heckathorn, Douglas, and Steven Maser. 1987b. "Bargaining and Constitutional Contracts." *American Journal of Political Science* 31:142–168.

Heclo, Hugh. 1978. "Issue Networks and the Executive Establishment." In *The New American Political System*, edited by Anthony King. Washington, D.C.: American Enterprise Institute.

Heikkila, Tanya, and Andrea Gerlak. 2005. "The Formation of Large-scale Collaborative Resource Management Institutions: Clarifying the Roles of Stakeholders, Science, and Institutions." *Policy Studies Journal* 33:583–612.

Hix, Simon. 2005. *The Political System of the European Union*. Houndsmill: Macmillan.

Hojman, Daniel and Adam Szeidl. 2006. "Core and Periphery in Endogenous Networks." Faculty Research Working Paper Series RWP06-022. JFK School of Government, Harvard University.

Holden, Matthew. 1964. "The Governance of a Metropolis as a Problem in Diplomacy." *Journal of Politics* 26:627–47.

Holmstrom, Bengt. 1982. "Moral Hazard in Teams." *Bell Journal of Economics* 13:324–40.

Holmstrom, Bengt, and Robert Milgrom. 1991. "Multitask Principal-Agent Analyses: Incentive Contracts, Asset Ownership, and Job Design." *Journal of Law, Economics and Organization* 7:24–52.

Honaker, James, Gary King, and Matthew Blackwell. 2006. "Amelia II: A Program for Missing Data." Available at http://gking.harvard.edu/amelia.

Hooghe, Liesbet, and Gary Marks. 2003. "Unraveling the Central State, but How? Types of Multi-Level Governance." *American Political Science Review* 97:233–43.

Hundley, Norris, Jr. 2001. *The Great Thirst*. Rev. ed. Berkeley: University of California Press.

Hurwitz, Jon, and Mark Peffley. 1987. "How Are Foreign Policy Attitudes Structured? A Hierarchical Model." *American Political Science Review* 81:1099–120.

International City/County Management Association (ICMA). 1997. "Local Intergovernmental Agreements: Strategies for Cooperation." *Management Information Service* 29:1–11.

Jacobs, Katharine, L. Samuel, N. Luoma, and Kim A. Taylor. 2003. "CALFED: An Experiment in Science and Decision Making." *Environment* January/February: 30–41.

Jones, Bryan D., and Lynn Bachelor. 1986. *The Sustaining Hand*. Lawrence: University of Kansas Press.

Jones, Bryan D., and Frank R. Baumgartner. 2005. *The Politics of Attention*. Chicago: University of Chicago Press.

Jones, Candace, William S. Hesterly, and Stephen P. Borgatti. 1997. "A General Theory of Network Governance: Exchange Conditions and Social Mechanisms." *Academy of Management Review* 22:911–45.

Katz, Bruce. 2000. *Reflections on Regionalism*. Washington, D.C.: Brookings Institution Press.

Kaufman, Herbert. 1960. *The Forest Ranger*. Baltimore: Johns Hopkins University Press.

Kearney, Richard C., and John J. Stucker. 1985. "Interstate Compacts and the Management of Low Level Radioactive Wastes." *Public Administration Review* 45:210–20.

Keleman, Daniel. 2003. "The Structure and Dynamics of EU Federalism." *Comparative Political Studies* 36(1-2):184–208.

Kenneth Prewitt, and William Nowlin. 1993. *Cities without Suburbs*. Washington, D.C.: Woodrow Wilson Center Press.

Kettl, Donald. 2002. *The Transformation of Governance*. Baltimore: John Hopkins University Press.

King, Gary, Michael Tomz, and Jason Wittenberg. 2000. "Making the Most of Statistical Analyses: Improving Interpretation and Presentation." *American Journal of Political Science* 44:347–61.

Klein, Benjamin. 1991. "Vertical Integration as Organizational Ownership: The Fisher Body-General Motors Relationship Revisited." In *The Nature of the Firm: Origins, Evolution, and Development*, edited by Oliver E. Williamson and Sidney G. Winter. New York: Oxford University Press.

———. 1995. "The Economics of Franchise Contracts." *Journal of Corporate Finance* 2:9–37.

Knight, Jack. 1992. *Institutions and Social Conflict*. Cambridge, U.K.: Cambridge University Press.

Knoke, David, Franz Urban Pappi, Jeffrey Broadbent, and Yutaka Tsujinaka. 1996. *Comparing Policy Networks: Labor Politics in the U.S., Germany, and Japan*. Cambridge, U.K.: Cambridge University Press.

Knoke, David, and David L. Rogers. 1979. "A Blockmodel Analysis of Interorganizational Networks." *Sociology and Social Research* 64:28–52.

Knoke, David, and Song Yang. 2008. *Social Network Analysis*. 2nd ed. Thousand Oaks, Calif.: Sage.

Koontz, Tomas M., Toddi A. Steelman, JoAnn Carmin, Katrina Smith Korfmacher, Cassandra Moseley, and Craig W. Thomas. 2004. *Collaborative Environmental Management: What Role for Governments?* Washington, D.C.: Resources for the Future Press.

Koontz, Tomas M., and Craig W. Thomas. 2006. "What Do We Know and Need to Know about the Environmental Outcomes of Collaborative Management?" *Public Administration Review* 66:111–21.

Koremenos, Barbara. 2002. "Can Cooperation Survive Changes in Bargaining Power? The Case of Coffee." *Journal of Legal Studies* 31:259–83.

Krackhardt, D. 1988. "Predicting with Networks: Nonparametric Multiple Regression of Dyadic Data." *Social Networks* 10:359–81.

Krackhardt, David. 1990. "Assessing the Political Landscape: Structure, Cognition, and Power in Organizations." *Administrative Science Quarterly* 35: 342–69.

Laffont, Jean-Jacques, and David Martimort. 2002. *The Theory of Incentives: The Principal-Agent Model*. Princeton, N.J.: Princeton University Press.

LaFontaine, Francine. 1992. "Agency Theory and Franchising: Some Empirical Results." *Rand Journal of Economics* 23:263–89.

———. 1993. "Contractual Arrangements as Signaling Devices: Evidence from Franchising." *Journal of Law, Economics, and Organization* 23: 263–83.

Landau, Martin. 1973. "Federalism, Redundancy and System Reliability." *Publius: The Journal of Federalism* 3:173–96.

Landsberg, Brian K. 1997. *Enforcing Civil Rights: Race Discrimination and the Department of Justice*. Lawrence: University Press of Kansas.

Langlois, Catherine, and Jean-Pierre Langlois. 2001. "Engineering Cooperation: A Game Theoretic Analysis of Phased International Agreements." *American Journal of Political Science* 45:599–619.

Laver, Michael, and Shepsle, Kenneth A. 1996. *Making and Breaking Governments: Cabinets and Legislatures in Parliamentary Democracies.* Cambridge, U.K.: Cambridge University Press.

Lazega, Emanuel. 2000. "Rule Enforcement among Peers: A Lateral Control Regime." *Organization Studies* 21:193–214.

Leach, W. D., N. W. Pelkey, and P. A. Sabatier. 2002. "Stakeholder Partnerships as Collaborative Policymaking: Evaluation Applied to Watershed Management in California and Washington." *Journal of Policy Analysis and Management* 21:645–70.

Ledyard, J. O. 1991. "Coordination in Shared Facilities. A New Methodology." *Journal of Organizational Computing* 1:41–59.

LeRoux, Kelly, and Jered B. Carr. 2007. "Explaining Local Government Cooperation on Public Works: Evidence from Michigan." *Public Works Management Policy* 12:344–58.

Levin, Jonathan. 2003. "Relational Incentive Contracts." *American Economic Review* 93:835–57.

Levine, Sol, and Paul E. White. 1961. "Exchange as a Conceptual Framework for the Study of Interorganizational Relationships." *Administrative Science Quarterly* 5:583–601.

Libecap, G. 1989. *Contracting for Property Rights.* New York: Cambridge University Press.

Libecap, G. D. 1994. "The Conditions for Successful Collective Action." *Journal of Theoretical Politics* 6:563–92.

Lin, Nan, Walter M. Ensel, and John C. Vaughn. 1981. "Social Resources and Strength of Ties: Structural Factors in Occupational Status Attainment." *American Sociological Review* 46:393–405.

Linden, R. 2002. *Working across Boundaries: Making Collaboration Work in Government and Nonprofit Organizations.* San Francisco: Jossey-Bass.

Liner, Gaines H. 1990. "Annexation Rates and Institutional Constraints." *Growth and Change* 21:80–94.

Liner, Gaines H., and Rob Roy McGregor. 1996. "Institutions and the Market for Annexable Land." *Growth and Change* 27:55–74.

Liu, Xinsheng. 2006. *Modeling Bilateral International Relations.* New York: Palgrave.

Liu, Xinsheng, and Bryan D. Jones. 2005. "How Do Nations Choose What Games to Play? A Spatial Supergame Model of Bilateral Interactions." Paper presented at the annual meeting of the International Studies Association, Honolulu, Hawaii March 5, 2005.

Lomi, Alessandro, and Erik Larsen (eds.). 2001. *Dynamics of Organizations: Computational Modelling and Organization Theories.* Cambridge, Mass.: MIT Press.

Long, Norton E. 1958. "The Local Community as an Ecology of Games." *American Journal of Sociology* 64:251–61.

Lowery, David. 1998. "Consumer Sovereignty and Quasi-Market Failure." *Journal of Public Administration Research and Theory* 8:137–72.

———. 2001. "Metropolitan Governance Structures from a Neoprogressive Perspective." *Swiss Political Science Review* 7:130–36.

Lubell, Mark. 2000. "Cognitive Conflict and Consensus Building in the National Estuary Program." *American Behavioral Scientist* 44:628–47.

———. 2003. "Collaborative Institutions, Belief-Systems, and Perceived Policy Effectiveness." *Political Research Quarterly* 56:309–23.

———. 2004a. "Collaborative Environmental Institutions: All Talk and No Action?" *Journal of Policy Analysis and Management* 23:549–73.

———. 2004b. "Resolving Conflict and Building Cooperation in the National Estuary Program." *Environmental Management* 33:677–91.

———. 2006. "Familiarity Breeds Trust: Collective Action in a Policy Domain." *Journal of Politics* 69:237–50.

Lubell, Mark, Mark Schneider, John Scholz, and Mihriye Mete. 2002. "Watershed Partnerships and the Emergence of Collective Action Institutions." *American Journal of Political Science.* 46:148–63.

Lynn, Phil. 2005. "Mutual Aid: Multijurisdictional Partnerships for Meeting Regional Threats, New Realities: Law Enforcement in the Post 9/11 Era." U.S Department of Justice, Office of Justice Program, Bureau of Justice Assistance.

Maccaulay, S. 1963. "Non-contractual Relations in Business." *American Sociological Review* 28:55–70.

Macey, Jonathan R. 1990. "Federal Deference to Local Regulators and the Economic Theory of Regulation: Toward a Public-Choice Explanation of Federalism." *Virginia Law Review* 76:265–91.

MacManus, Susan A. 1981. "Special District Governments: A Note on Their Use as Property Tax Relief Mechanisms in the 1970s." *Journal of Politics* 43: 1206–14.

MacManus, Susan, and Robert Thomas. 1979. "Expanding the Tax Base: Does Annexation Make A Difference?" *Urban Interest* 1: 15–28.

March, James G. and Johan P. Olsen. 1983. "Organizing Political Life: What Administrative Reorganization Tells Us about Government." *American Political Science Review* 77:281–296.

———. 1984. "The New institutionalism: Organizational Factors in Political Life." *American Political Science Review* 78:734–49.

Marella, Richard L. 2004. "Water Withdrawals, Use, Discharge, and Trend in Florida, 2000." Scientific Investigations Report 2004-5151. U.S. Geological Survey.

Markovsky, B., D. Willer, and T. Patton. 1988. "Power Relations in Exchange Networks." *American Sociological Review* 53:220–36.

Marsden, Peter V., and Karen E. Campell. 1984. "Measuring Tie Strength." *Social Forces* 2:482–501.

Marsden, Peter V., and Jeanne S. Hurlbert. 1988. "Social Resources and Mobility Outcomes." *Social Forces* 66:1038–59.

Marsh, David, and Rhodes R. A. W. (eds.). 1992. *Policy Networks in British Government.* Oxford: Clarendon Press.

Maser, Steven M. 1998. "Constitutions as Relational Contracts: Explaining Procedural Safeguards in Municipal Charters." *Journal of Public Administration Research and Theory* 8:527–64.

Mathewson, G. F. and R. Winter. 1985. "The Economics of Franchise Contracts." *Journal of Law and Economics* 28:503–26.

Mayhew, David. 1970. *The Electoral Connection*. New Haven, Conn.: Yale University Press.

McCabe, Barbara C. 2000. "Special District Formation among the States." *State and Local Government Review* 32:121–31.

McCabe, Barbara Coyle, and Richard C. Feiock. 2005. "Nested Levels of Institutions: State Rules and City Property Taxes." *Urban Affairs Review* 40:634–54.

McCoy, Mike, and Candice Steelman. 2005. "Integrating Community Values and Fostering Interagency Collaboration." In *Proceedings of the 2005 International Conference on Ecology and Transportation*, edited by C. L. Irwin, P. Garrett and K. P. McDermott. Center for Transportation and the Environment, North Carolina State University, Raleigh, pp. 80–5.

McGann, Chris. 2006, November 30."Speaker Chopp Fights Viaduct Tunnel Plan." *Seattle Post Intelligencer.*

McGinnis, Michael D. (ed.). 1999. *Polycentricity and Local Public Economies: Readings from the Workshop in Political Theory and Policy Analysis*. Ann Arbor: University of Michigan Press.

McGrath, Cathleen, and David Krackhardt. 2003. "Network Conditions for Organizational Change." *Journal of Applied Behavioral Science* 38:324–36.

Michael, S. C. 1999. "Do Franchised Chains Advertise Enough?" *Journal of Retailing* 75:461–78.

———. 2000a. "The Effect of Organizational Form on Quality: The Case of Franchising." *Journal of Economic Behavior and Organization* 43:295–318.

———. 2000b. "Investments to Create Bargaining Power: The Case of Franchising." *Strategic Management Journal* 21:497–514.

Miles, R. E., and C. C. Snow. 1995. "The New Network Firm: A Spherical Structure Built on a Human Investment Philosophy." *Organizational Dynamics* 23:5–18.

Milgrom, Paul, and John Roberts. 1992. *Economics, Organizations, and Management*. Upper Saddle River, N.J.: Prentice Hall.

Milward, H.Brinton, and Keith G. Provan. 2000. "Governing the Hollow State." *Journal of Public Administration Research and Theory* 20(2):359–79.

Minkler, Alanson P. 1992. "Why Firms Franchise: A Search Cost Theory." *Journal of Institutional and Theoretical Economics* 148:240–59.

Moe, Terry. 1991. "Politics and the Theory of Organization." *Journal of Law, Economics and Organization* 7:106–29.

Moe, Terry M. 2005. "Power and Political Institutions." *Perspectives on Politics* 3:215–53.

Morgan, David R., and Michael W. Hirlinger. 1991. "Intergovernmental Service Contracts: A Multivariate Explanation." *Urban Affairs Quarterly* 27:128–44.

Mullin, Megan. 2009. *Governing the Tap: Special District Governance and the New Local Politics of Water*. Cambridge, Mass.: MIT Press.

Munro, John F. 1993. "California Water Politics: Explaining Policy Change in a Cognitively Polarized Subsystem." In *Policy Change and Learning: An Advocacy Coalition Approach*, edited by Paul Sabatier and Hank Jenkins-Smith. Boulder, Colo.: Westview Press.

Nice, David C. 1987. *Federalism: The Politics of Intergovernmental Relations*. New York: Saint Martin's Press.

North, Douglass C. 1981. *Structure and Change in Economic History*. New York: Norton.

North, Douglass C. 1990. *Institutions, Institutional Change, and Economic Performance*. Cambridge, U.K.: Cambridge University Press.

Norton, S. W. 1988. "An Empirical Look at Franchising as an Organizational Form." *Journal of Business* 61:187–218.

O'Leary, Rosemary, Catherine Gerard, and Lisa Blomgren Bingham. 2006. "Introduction to the Symposium on Collaborative Public Management." *Public Administration Review* 66:6–9.

Olson, Mancur. 1965. *The Logic of Collective Action*. Cambridge, Mass.: Harvard University Press.

Orfield, Myron. 1997. *Metropolitics: A Regional Agenda for Community and Stability*. Washington D.C.: Brookings Institution Press.

Osborne, David, and Ted Gaebler. 1992. *Reinventing Government: How the Entrepreneurial Spirit Is Transforming the Public Sector*. Reading, Mass.: Addison-Wesley.

Ostrom, Elinor. 1990. *Governing the Commons: The Evolution of Institutions for Collective Action*. New York: Cambridge University Press.

———. 2005. *Understanding Institutional Diversity*. Princeton: Princeton University Press.

Ostrom, Elinor, Roy Gardner, and James Walker. 1994. *Rules, Games, and Common-Pool Resources*. Ann Arbor: University of Michigan Press.

Ostrom, Vincent. 1973. "Can Federalism Make a Difference?" *Publius* 3:197–237.

———. 1991. *The Meaning of American Federalism: Constituting a Self-Governing Society*. San Francisco: Institute for Contemporary Studies.

Ostrom, Vincent, Robert Bish, and Elinor Ostrom. 1988. *Local Government in the United States*. San Francisco: Institute for Contemporary Studies Press.

Ostrom, Vincent, and Elinor Ostrom. 1999. "A Behavioral Approach to the Study of Intergovernmental Relations." In *Polycentricity and Local Public Economies: Readings from the Workshop in Political Theory and Policy Analysis*, edited by Michael McGinnis. Ann Arbor: University of Michigan Press.

Ostrom, Vincent, Charles M. Tiebout, and Robert Warren. 1961. "The Organization of Government in Metropolitan Areas: A Theoretical Inquiry." *American Political Science Review* 55:831–42.

O'Toole, Lawrence J. 1997a. "Treating Networks Seriously: Practical and Research-Based Agendas in Public Administration." *Public Administration Review* 57:45–52.

———. 1997b. "Implementing Public Innovations in Network Settings." *Administration and Society* 29:115–38.

Ouchi, W. G. 1980. "Markets, Bureaucracies and Clans." *Administrative Science Quarterly* 25:129–41.

Oxenfeldt, A. R., and A. O. Kelly. 1969. "Will Successful Franchise Systems Ultimately Become Wholly-owned Chains?" *Journal of Retailing* 44:69–83.

Pagano, Michael A. 1999. "Metropolitan Limits: Intrametropolian Disparities and Governance in U.S. Laboratories of Democracy." In *Governance and Opportunity in Metropolitan America*, edited by William Morrill, Alan

Altshuler, Harold Wolman, and Faith Mitchell. Washington, D.C.: National Academy Press.

Panchanathan, K., and R. Boyd. 2004. "Indirect Reciprocity Can Stabilize Cooperation without the Second-Order Free Rider Problem." *Nature* 432: 499–502.

Park, Hyung Jun, and Richard C. Feiock. 2007. "Institutional Collective Action, Social Capital and Regional Development Partnerships." *International Review of Public Administration* 11:57–69.

Parks, Roger B., and Ronald J. Oakerson. 1989. "Metropolitan Organization and Governance: A Local Public Economy Approach." *Urban Affairs Quarterly* 25:18–29.

Parsa, H. G. 1999. "Interaction of Strategy Implementation and Power Perceptions in Franchise Systems: An Empirical Investigation." *Journal of Business Research* 45:173–85.

Pfeffer, Jeffrey, and Gerald R. Salancik. 2003. *The External Control of Organizations. A Resource Dependence Perspective*. Stanford, Calif.: Stanford University Press.

Picot, Arnold, Helmut Dietl, and Egon Franck. 2005. *Organisation: eine ökonomische Perspektive. 4. überarbeitet und erweiterte Auflage*. Stuttgart: Schäffer-Poeschel.

Poppo, Laura, and Todd Zenger. 2002. "Do Formal Contracts and Relational Governance Function as Substitutes or Complements?" *Strategic Management Journal* 23:707–25.

Posner, Paul L. 1998. *The Politics of Unfunded Mandates: Whither Federalism?* Washington, D.C.: Georgetown University Press.

Post, Stephanie Shirley. 2002. "Local Government Cooperation: The Relationship between Metropolitan Area Government Geography and Service Provision." Paper presented at the Annual Meeting of the American Political Science Association, August 29–September 1, Boston, Mass.

Post, Stephanie S. 2004. "Metropolitan Area Governance and Institutional Collective Action." In *Metropolitan Governance: Conflict, Competition, and Cooperation*, edited by Richard C. Feiock. Washington, D.C.: Georgetown University Press.

Prewitt, Kenneth, and William Nowlin. 1969. "Political Ambition and the Behavior of Incumbent Politicians." *Western Political Quarterly* 22:298–308.

Provan, Keith G., and H. Brenton Milward. 1995a. "Do Networks Really Work? A Framework for Evaluating Public-Sector Organizational Networks." *Public Administration Review* 61:414–23.

———. 1995b. "A Preliminary Theory of Interorganizational Network Effectiveness: A Comparative Study of Four Community Mental Health Systems." *Administrative Science Quarterly* 40:1–33.

Putnam, Robert D. 1976. *The Comparative Study of Political Elites*. Englewood Cliffs, N.J: Prentice Hall.

———. 1993. *Making Democracy Work. Civic Traditions in Modern Italy*. Princeton, N.J.: Princeton University Press.

Raab, Jörg. 2002. "Where Do Policy Networks Come From?" *Journal of Public Administration Research and Theory* 12:581–622.

Rabe, Barry G. 1986. *Fragmentation and Integration in State Environmental Management*. Washington D.C.: Conservation Foundation.

Rhodes, R. A. W. 1981. *Control and Power in Central-Local Government Relationships*. Farnborough: Gower.

———. 1986. "Power-Dependence Theories of Central-Local Relations: A Critical Reassessment." In *New Research in Central-Local Relations*, edited by Michael J. Goldsmith. Aldershot: Gower.

———. 1997. *Understanding Governance: Policy Networks, Governance, Reflexivity, and Accountability*. Buckingham: Open University Press.

———. 2007. "Understanding Governance: The Years On." *Organizational Studies* 28:1243–64.

Riker, William H. 1964. *Federalism, Origin, Operation, Significance*. Boston: Little, Brown.

Robins, Gary. L., and Pattison, Pip. E. 2005. "Interdependencies and Social Processes: Generalized Dependence Structures." In *Models and Methods in Social Network Analysis*, edited by P. Carrington, J. Scott, and S. Wasserman. New York: Cambridge University Press.

Robins, Gary, Tom Snijders, Peng Wang, Mark Handcock, and Philippa Pattison. 2007. "Recent Developments in Exponential Random Graph (p*) Models for Social Network." *Social Networks* 29:192–215.

Roch, Christine, John T. Scholz, and Kathleen McGraw. 2000. "Social Networks and Citizen Response to Legal Change." *American Journal of Political Science* 44:777–91.

Ross, Joseph V. H. 1984. "Managing the Public Rangelands: 50 Years since the Taylor Grazing Act." *Rangelands* 6:147–51.

Rubin, Claire B., and Daniel G. Barbee. 1985. "Disaster Recovery and Hazard Mitigation: Bridging the Intergovernmental Gap." *Public Administration Review* 45:57–63.

Rubin, P. H. 1978. "The Theory of the Firm and the Structure of the Franchise." *Journal of Law and Economics* 21:223–33.

Rusk, David. 1993. *Cities without Suburbs*. Washington, D.C.: Woodrow Wilson Center.

Rydin, Yvonne, and Eve Falleth. 2006. *Networks and Institutions in Natural Resource Management*. Cheltenham, UK: Edward Elgar Publishing.

Sabatier, Paul (ed.). 1999. *An Advocacy Coalition Lens on Environmental Policy*. Cambridge, Mass.: MIT Press.

———. 2005. "Linking Science and Public Learning: An Advocacy Coalition Perspective." In *Adaptive Governance and Water Conflict. New Institutions for Collaborative Planning*, edited by John T. Scholz and Bruce Stiftel. Washington, D.C.: Resources for the Future Press.

Sabatier, Paul A., Will Focht, Mark N. Lubell, Zev Trachtenberg, Arnold Vedlitz, and Marty Matlock (eds.). 2005. *Swimming Upstream: Collaborative Approaches to Watershed Management*. Cambridge, Mass.: MIT Press.

Sabatier, Paul, and Hank Jenkins-Smith (eds.). 1993. *Policy Change and Learning: An Advocacy Coalition Approach*. Boulder, Colo.: Westview Press.

Sabatier, P., and M. Zafonte. "Are Bureaucrats and Scientists Members of Advocacy Coalitions? Evidence from an Intergovernmental Water Policy

Subsystem." In *An Advocacy Coalition Lens on Environmental Policy*, edited by P. Sabatier (forthcoming).

Salamon, Lester M. (ed.). 2002. *The Tools of Government: A Guide to the New Governance*. New York: Oxford University Press.

Salisbury, Robert H., John P. Heinz, Edward O. Laumann, and Robert L. Nelson. 1987. "Who Works with Whom? Interest Group Alliances and Opposition." *American Political Science Review* 81:1217–34.

Sandler, Todd. 1992. *Collective Action: Theory and Applications*. Ann Arbor: University of Michigan Press.

Sapotichne, Joshua, Bryan D. Jones, and Michelle Wolfe. 2007. "Is Urban Politics a 'Black Hole'? Analyzing the Boundary between Political Science and Urban Politics." *Urban Affairs Review* 43:76–106.

Savitch, Hank, Ronald K. Vogel. 1996. *"Regional Politics: America in a Post-City Age."* Thousand Oaks, Calif.: Sage.

Scharpf, Fritz W. 1977. "Does Organization Matter? Task Structure and Interaction in the Ministerial Bureaucracy." *Organization and Administrative Sciences* 8:149–67.

———. 1978. "Interorganizational Policy Studies: Issues, Concepts and Perspectives." In *Interorganizational Policy Making. Limits to Coordination and Central Control*, edited by Kenneth Hanf and Fritz W. Scharpf. London: Sage.

Scharpf, F. W. 1997. *Games Real Actors Play: Actor-Centered Institutionalism in Policy Research*. Boulder, Colo.: Westview Press.

Schlesinger, Joseph. 1966. *Political Ambition*. Chicago: Rand McNally.

Schneider, Mark, John Scholz, Mark Lubell, Denisa Mindruta, and Matthew Edwardsen. 2003. "Building Consensual Institutions: Networks and the National Estuary Program." *American Journal of Political Science*. 47:143–58.

Scholz, John T., Ramiro Berardo, and Bradley Kile. 2008. "Do Networks Solve Collective Action Problems? Credibility, Search, and Collaboration." *Journal of Politics* 70:393–406.

Scholz, John T., and Bruce Stiftel (eds.). 2005. *Adaptive Governance and Water Conflict. New Institutions for Collaborative Planning*. Washington, D.C.: Resources for the Future Press.

Scholz, John T., and Chueng-Lung Wang. 2006. "Cooptation or Transformation? Local Policy Networks and Federal Regulatory Enforcement." *American Journal of Political Science* 50:81–97.

Scott, Frank A. 1995. "Franchising vs. Company Ownership as a Decision Variable of the Firm." *Review of Industrial Organization* 10:69–81.

Scott, John. 2000. *Social Network Analysis: A Handbook*. 2nd ed. Thousands Oaks, Calif.: Sage.

Scott, Richard W. 1995. *Institutions and Organizations*. Thousand Oaks, Calif.: Sage.

Selznick, Philip. 1949. *TVA and the Grass Roots: A Study in the Sociology of Formal Organization*. Berkeley: University of California Press.

Shapiro, Debra L., Blair H. Sheppard, and Liza Cheraski. 1992. "Business on a Handshake." *Negotiation Journal* 8:365–77.

Shrestha, Manoj K. 2008. *Decentralized Governments, Networks and Interlocal Cooperation in Public Goods Supply*. Ph.D. Dissertation, School of Public Administration and Policy, Florida State University.

Simon, Herbert. 1962. "The Architecture of Complexity." *Proceedings of the American Philosophical Society* 106:467–82.

Slaughter, Anne-Marie. 2004. *A New World Order.* Princeton, N.J.: Princeton University Press.

Snijders, Tom A. B. 2001. "The Statistical Evaluation of Social Network Dynamics." In *Sociological Methodology,* edited by M. E. Sobel and M. P. Becker. Boston: Basil Blackwell.

Snijders, T. A. B. 2005. "Models for Longitudinal Network Data." In *Models and Methods in Social Network Analysis,* edited by J. Scott, P. J. Carrington, and S. Wasserman. Cambridge, U.K.: Cambridge University Press.

Snijders, Tom A. B., et al. 2005. *Manual for SIENA Version 2.1.* The Netherlands: University of Groningen ICS, Department of Sociology.

Snijders, T. A. B., P. Pattison, G. L. Robins, and M. Handcock. 2006. "New Specifications for Exponential Random Graph Models." *Sociological Methodology* 36:99–153.

Snijders, Tom A. B., Christian E. G. Steglich, and Michael Schweinberger. 2005. "Modeling the Co-Evolution of Networks and Behavior." Working paper. University of Groningen, ICS/Department of Sociology.

Snijders, Tom A. B., Christian E. G. Steglich, Michael Schweinberger, and Mark Huisman. 2007. *Manual for SIENA version 3.1:* University of Groningen: ICS/Department of Sociology; University of Oxford: Department of Statistics.

Spinelli, S., and S. Birley. 1996. "Toward a Theory of Conflict in the Franchise System." *Journal of Business Venturing* 11:329–42.

Spriggs, M., and J. Nevin. 1995. "The Relational Contracting Model and Franchising Research: Empirical Issues." *Journal of Marketing Channels* 4:161–76.

Steglich, Christian. 2006. "Actor-Driven Alternatives to Exponential Random Graph Models." Paper delivered at Sunbelt Conference XXVI. Vancouver, April 24–30.

Steglich, C. E. G., Tom A. B. Snijders, and P. West. 2006. "Applying SIENA: An Illustrative Analysis of the Coevolution of Adolescents' Friendship Networks, Taste in Music, and Alcohol Consumption." *Methodology* 2:48–56.

Stein, R. M. 1990. *Urban Alternatives: Public and Private Markets in the Provision of Local Services.* Pittsburgh: University of Pittsburgh Press.

Steinacker, Annette. 2004. "Models of Metropolitan Cooperation." In *Decentralized Governance: Local Government Organization in Metropolitan Areas,* edited by Richard Feiock. Washington, D.C.: Georgetown University Press.

Stephens, G. Ross, and Nelson Wikstrom. 2000. *Metropolitan Government and Governance: Theoretical Perspectives, Empirical Analysis, and the Future.* New York: Oxford University Press.

Stinchcombe, Arthur. 2001. *When Formality Works. Authority and Abstraction in Law and Organizations.* Chicago: Chicago University Press.

Stone Sweet, Alec, Wayne Sandholtz, and Neil Fligstein (eds.). 2001. *The Institutionalization of Europe.* Oxford, U.K.: Oxford University Press.

Stoney, Louise, and Mark H. Greenberg. 1996. "The Financing of Child Care: Current and Emerging Trends." *The Future of Children* 6:83–102.

Storholm, G., and E. E. Scheuing. 1994. "Ethical Implications of Business Format Franchising." *Journal of Business Ethics* 13:181–88.

Stubb, Alexander. 2002. *Negotiating Flexibility in the European Union. Amsterdam, Nice and Beyond.* Basingstoke: Palgrave.

Susskind, Lawrence. 2005. "Resource Planning, Dispute Resolution and Adaptive Governance." In *Adaptive Governance and Water Conflict. New Institutions for Collaborative Planning*, edited by John T. Scholz and Bruce Stiftel. Washington, D.C.: Resources for the Future Press.

Taveras, Antonio. 2003. "State and Local Institutions and Environmental Policy: A Transaction Cost Analysis." Ph.D. Dissertation, Florida State University.

Tetlock, Philip E., and Aaron Belkin. 1996. "Counterfactual Thought Experiments in World Politics: Logical, Methodological, and Psychological Perspectives." In *Counterfactual Thought Experiments in World Politics. Logical, Methodological, and Psychological Perspectives*, edited by Philip E. Tetlock and Aaron Belkin. Princeton, N.J.: Princeton University Press.

Thompson, Grahame, Jennifer Frances, Rosalind Levacic, and Jeremy C. Mitchell. 1991. *Markets, Hierarchies and Networks: The Coordination of Social Life.* London: Sage.

Thompson, James D. 1967. *Organizations in Action.* New York: McGraw-Hill.

Thompson, R. S. 1992. "Company Ownership vs. Franchising: Issues and Evidence." *Journal of Economic Studies* 19:31–42.

———. 1994. "The Franchise Life Cycle: A Contractual Solution to the Penrose Effect." *Journal of Economic Behavior and Organization* 24:207–18.

Thurmaier, Kurt, and Curtis Wood. 2002. "Interlocal Agreements as Overlapping Social Networks: Picket-Fence Regionalism in Metropolitan Kansas City." *Public Administration Review* 62:585–98.

Thurner, Paul W. 2006. *Die graduelle Konstitutionalisierung der Europäischen Union. Eine quantitative Fallstudie am Beispiel der Regierungskonferenz 1996.* Mohr Siebeck: Tübingen (Die Einheit der Gesellschaftswissenschaften, Band 136).

Thurner, Paul W., and Martin Binder. 2008. "EU Transgovernmental Networks: The Emergence of a New Political Space beyond the Nation State?" *European Journal of Political Research.* 48:80–106.

Thurner, Paul W., and Franz Urban Pappi. 2009. *European Union Intergovernmental Conferences: Domestic Preference Formation, Transgovernmental Networks, and the Dynamics of Compromise.* New York: Routledge.

Thurner, P. W., F. U. Pappi, and Stoiber M. 2002. "EU Intergovernmental Conferences." In Mannheimer Zentrum für Europäische Sozialforschung: Arbeitspapiere – Working Papers Nr. 60, IINS Research Paper No. 15.

Tocqueville, Alexis de. [1840] 2003. *Democracy in America.* Reprinted in *Foundations of Social Capital*, edited by Elinor Ostrom and T. K. Ahn. Cheltenham, UK: Edward Elgar Publishing.

Tomz, Michael, Jason Wittenberg, and Gary King. 2001. *CLARIFY: Software for Interpreting and Presenting Statistical Results. Version 2.0.* Cambridge, Mass.: Harvard University.

Truman, David. 1951. *The Governmental Process.* New York: Knopf.

Tsebelis, G. 2002. *Veto Players: How Political Institutions Work.* Princeton, N.J.: Princeton University Press.

United States Advisory Council on Intergovernmental Relations. 1985. *Intergov-ernmental Service Arrangements for Delivering Local Public Services: Update 1983*. Washington, D.C.: Government Printing Office.

United States Census Bureau. 2002. *Census of Governments*. Washington, D.C.: Department of Commerce.

United States Census Bureau. 2005. *Census of Governments*. Volume 1, Number 2, Individual State Descriptions. Washington, D.C.: Department of Commerce.

United States Environmental Protection Agency, Office of Water. 1997. *Community Water System Survey*. Volume I: Overview. Washington, D.C.: Office of Water, Environmental Protection Agency.

United States Government Accountability Office. 2004. *Federal-Aid Highways: Trends, Effect on State Spending, and Options for Future Program Design*. GAO-04-802.

Uzzi, Brian. 1996. "The Source and Consequences of Embeddedness for the Economic Performance of Organizations: The Network Effects." *American Sociological Review* 61:674–98.

Warner, Mildred, and Amir Hefetz. 2001. "Privatization and the Market Restructuring Role of Local Government." In Economic Policy Institute Briefing Paper, available at http://www.epi.org/publications/entry/briefingpapers_bp112/(accessed 04/09/2009).

Wasserman, Stanley, and Katherine Faust. 1994. *Social Network Analysis: Methods and Applications*. Cambridge: Cambridge University Press.

Wasserman, Stanley, and Garry Robins. 2005. "An Introduction to Random Graphs, Dependence Graphs, and p*." In *Models and Methods in Social Network Analysis*, edited by John Scott, Stanley Wasserman, and Peter J. Carrington. Cambridge, U.K.: Cambridge University Press.

Waste, Robert J. 1998. *Independent Cities: Rethinking U.S. Urban Policy*. New York: Oxford University Press.

Watts, Duncan J. 2003. *Six Degrees: The Science of Connected Age*. New York: W.W. Norton.

Waugh, William L. 1994. "Regionalizing Emergency Management: Counties as State and Local Government." *Public Administration Review* 54:253–58.

Waugh, William L., and Gregory Streib. 2006. "Collaboration and Leadership for Effective Emergency Management." *Public Administration Review* (Special Issue on Collaborative Public Management):131–40.

Weible, Christopher M. 2006. "An Advocacy Coalition Framework Approach to Stakeholder Analysis: Understanding the Political Context of California Marine Protected Area Policy." *Journal of Public Administration Research and Theory* 17:95–117.

Weible, Christopher M., and Paul A. Sabatier. 2005. "Comparing Policy Networks: Marine Protected Areas in California." *Policy Studies Journal* 33:181–204.

Weimer, David, and Adian Vining. 2004. *Policy Analysis: Concepts and Practice*. Upper Saddle River, N.J.: Prentice Hall.

Weingast, Barry R. 1995. "The Economic Role of Political Institutions: Market-Preserving Federalism and Economic Development." *Journal of Law, Economics, and Organization* 11:1–31.

Whitford, Andrew B. 2007. "Decentralized Policy Implementation." *Political Research Quarterly* 60:17–30.

Williamson, Oliver E. 1975. *Markets and Hierarchies: Analysis and Antitrust Implications*. New York: Free Press.

———. 1981. "The Economics of Organization." *American Journal of Sociology* 87:548–77.

———. 1983. "Credible Commitments: Using Hostages to Support Exchange." *American Economic Review* 73:519–40.

———. 1985. *The Economic Institutions of Capitalism*. New York: Free Press.

———. 1991. "Comparative Economic Organization: The Analysis of Discrete Structural Alternatives." *Administrative Science Quarterly* 36:269–96.

———. 1996. *The Mechanisms of Governance*. New York: Oxford University Press.

Wintrobe, Ronald. 1997. "Modern Bureaucratic Theory." In *Perspectives on Public Choice: A Handbook*, edited by Dennis C. (Hg.) Mueller. Cambridge, U.K.: Cambridge University Press.

Wise, Charles R. 1990. "Public Service Configuration and Public Organizations: Public Organization Design in the Post-Privatization Era." *Public Administration Review* 50:141–55.

Wondolleck, Julia M., and Steven L. Yaffee. *Making Collaboration Work*. Washington, D.C.: Island Press, 2000.

Wood, Curtis H. 2004. "Metropolitan Governance in Urban America: A Study of the Kansas City Region." Ph.D. dissertation, University of Kansas.

Woods, Neal D. 2006. "Primacy Implementation of Environmental Policy in the U.S. States." *Publius: The Journal of Federalism* 36:259–76.

Zafonte, Matthew, and Paul Sabatier. 1998. "Shared Beliefs and Imposed Interdependencies as Determinants of Ally Networks in Overlapping Subsystems." *Journal of Theoretical Politics* 10:473–505.

Zeller, R., D. Achabal, and L. Brown. 1980. "Market Penetration and Locational Conflict in Franchise Systems." *Decision Sciences* 11:58–80.

Zhang, Yahong. 2007. *Local Official's Incentives and Policy-Making: Through the Lens of the Politics-Administration Relationship*. Ph.D. Dissertation, School of Public Administration and Policy, Florida State University.

Index